Bernard S

A GENERATION OF U.S. SECRET SERVICE ADVENTURES

IN CRIME'S WAY

CARMINE J. MOTTO

CRC Press
Boca Raton London New York Washington, D.C.

Library of Congress Cataloging-in-Publication Data

Catalog record is available from the Library of Congress

International Standard Book Number 0-8493-2259-6
Printed in the United States of America 1 2 3 4 5 6 7 8 9 0
Printed on acid-free paper

Table of Contents

Preface

With a real flair for storytelling, Mr. Carmine Motto has provided us with a volume of true stories from his long and colorful career in the field of law enforcement. While these stories were written by Mr. Motto, he is not necessarily the central character in them. He presents the stories like the narrator in the drama "Cabaret." He observes and participates in the action, but the people he encountered form the basis of the stories. The characters are presented in their own environment and in situations of their own making as a result of their pursuit of "an easy dollar." Mr. Motto brings life to the characters, many of whom could be described as "Runyonesque." It is a book with a historical perspective about the life and times of one person who made a difference.

This book resembles Mr. Motto's other books, *Undercover* and *Undercover, Second Edition* in that it brings real dialogue of people and situations that only an experienced and sensitive participant could hope to achieve. There is a lesson in every story, whether it is in personal relationships while dealing with the criminal element or in the historical value of preserving the memory of a fading lifestyle.

This book contains authentic and fascinating accounts of bringing counterfeiters, conspirators, and scoundrels to justice. Some of his stories are gritty, some are humorous, some evoke emotions of pity, even a tear or two. His powerful account of witnessing a triple execution in New York's notorious Sing-Sing prison will emotionally involve a reader.

Mr. Motto made a conscientious effort to not use the real names, places, and dates of the people in his stories unless he had their permission or they have publicly told their stories elsewhere. His reasoning is that he did not want to embarrass anyone who had "paid his debt to society." He is proud, and rightly so, of the fact that if he ever happened to encounter anyone he had ever arrested, he would be able to sit down with him and over a cup of coffee and enjoy some cordial conversation. That is the kind of man Mr. Carmine J. Motto is. Law enforcement needs more individuals of his caliber.

When I was asked by the publisher, and Mr. Motto, to help in preparing this book for publication and to write this foreword, I was more than pleased — it was an honor for me. This enjoyable task has been like traveling through a time tunnel, sharing moments as an unseen observer, in the lives of people as they matched wits with a legend of the U. S. Secret Service.

As a young U.S. Secret Service agent I always kept Mr. Motto's first book, *Undercover*, at arm's reach on my desk for reference. I never had the pleasure of working directly with Mr. Motto, but I did have occasion to work cases with some of his hand-picked team members. I learned from them as they had learned from him. If there were such a thing as a Law Enforcement Hall of Fame, Mr. Carmine J. Motto would undoubtedly be enshrined there with the best of them.

Dale L. June, M.A.
Los Angeles, California 1999

About the Author

Mr. Carmine J. Motto is a retired Special Agent-in-Charge of the U. S. Secret Service's special anti-counterfeiting detail in New York — a position he held for many years. Mr. Motto began his career in law enforcement as a New York State Police Trooper in 1936. At his retirement from his last position as Commissioner of Police for the City of Harrison, New York in 1996, Mr. Motto had served over sixty years in the field. The years in between were filled with ever-increasing responsibility, adventure, and devotion to duty in one of the most elite law enforcement agencies in the world.

After serving as a New York State Trooper for five years, Mr. Motto joined the U. S. Secret Service, serving with distinction from 1941 to 1970. Putting his law enforcement career on hold during the war years, Mr. Motto enlisted in the U. S. Marine Corps in 1942. He was promoted through the ranks from private to captain, the rank he held until he left the Corps in

1946. Upon his discharge, he resumed his U.S. Secret Service career.

Retiring from the U.S. Secret Service, he served in the U. S. Treasury Department as Deputy Director of Law Enforcement until his second retirement. However, retirement was not yet in the cards for Mr. Motto as he was asked to serve on the special commission investigating the original Attica Prison riot inquiry. Completing his service on that commission, he was subsequently asked to serve as the Deputy Commissioner of Public Safety for the City of White Plains, New York, where he had settled after retiring from the federal government. He then went on to serve three more years as the Commissioner of Police in Harrison, New York.

In 1996, due to the fragile health of his beloved wife, Flora, Mr. Motto finally accepted retirement, but has remained active in a variety of endeavors. He is still called upon to address the new agents in training at the U.S. Secret Service Academy and occasionally works as a consultant for various police departments.

As the Special Agent in Charge of the U.S. Secret Service special counterfeiting detail in New York, Mr. Motto literally wrote the book on undercover operations. His first book, *Undercover,* became a classic and was required reading for a generation of U.S. Secret Service agents while in training. *Undercover, Second Edition* was published earlier this year.

About the Author

Acknowledgments

Who to acknowledge after a career in law enforcement spanning more than sixty years is an extremely difficult task. Is it the man who gave you your first break; the informant who helped give you a reputation; the teachers in the training academies; the men you worked with; the men who worked for you; your family who had to put up with your continual and extended absences and the telephone calls that took you away in the middle of the night; the district attorneys who successfully prosecuted your cases; all your brother officers and fellow agents, city, state, and federal, who cooperated with you even though they knew the case was not theirs; the unsung witnesses who gave testimony in spite of the fact they might later be in some danger? It is to all these people, and many others, that I give the credit, because without them, one cannot be a truly successful police officer nor can there be a successful fight against crime.

I would, however, like to single out the late Director of the U.S. Secret Service, James J. Rowley. I am proud to call him a friend and a contemporary. He served as the inspiration and role model for a whole generation of U. S. Secret Service agents. He had the foresight to realize the need for increased training in the art of undercover work for the men and women of the Service who endeavor to keep a stranglehold on the modern-day counterfeiter. The U.S. Secret Service Training Center near Washington, D.C. has rightfully been named in his honor.

Execution at Sing-Sing

It was already hot that July morning as the milkman made his morning rounds. It sure was going to be a scorcher today, he thought to himself as he walked up the to the Jansky house. When he got to the porch, he saw that the previous day's milk delivery was still outside. No one had picked it up and taken it inside. That was definitely strange and he was more than a little concerned. The Janskys were an elderly retired couple who rarely left the house. It wasn't like them to leave the milk to sour on the doorstep. The milkman asked the nearest neighbors if they had seen the Janskys, but no one could recall having seen either of them during the past three days. The house was a small bungalow in a small rural town where everyone knew each other. Mr. Jansky was a retired railroad worker and had lived with his wife in the same house for nearly 40 years. They were poor, honest people, well-liked in the community.

The milkman sensed something was wrong and called the State Police Barracks. The sergeant-on-duty promised to send a trooper immediately. I had just returned from patrol as he was hanging up the phone. He instructed me to go directly to the Jansky residence and find out if anything was wrong. When I arrived at the house some 20 minutes later, the milkman was still there. He was certain something was wrong because the Janskys never left home and they would never leave the milk outside to sour. No one had answered his repeated knocking at the front door. I tried the door, but it was locked. The back door was also locked. I peered through a window, but was unable to see into the dark interior. I decided to enter the house through a small side window. When I cracked the window to squeeze through, the stench from inside almost knocked me off my feet. It was the unmistakable smell of death. Not only was the smell overpowering, the heat in the closed-up house was stifling. The living room was a shambles. It appeared as though a terrible fight had taken place — furniture was knocked over, the drapes were torn down, and books from the overturned bookcase were scattered about the floor. And the blood — it was spattered everywhere. It was a very gruesome scene.

I found Mr. Jansky's body crumpled in a corner next to the couch. His head had been horribly crushed. A necktie was tightly twisted and knotted around his neck. His bloated face had an otherworldly look. His unseeing eyes were still open, piercing the dried blood that covering his face. I turned away and headed for the kitchen. Pots and pans were scattered all over the floor. Mrs. Jansky had been in the middle of preparing a meal, and the food and utensils still sat on the kitchen table. The kitchen was also spattered with blood. Mrs. Jansky was lying in a heap in the center of the room. Her skull had also been crushed and a leather thong was tightly bound around her neck.

I notified Headquarters about the horrific scene and, within a matter of minutes, more troopers arrived. The area was cordoned-off and photographed from every angle. Technicians dusted the crime scene for fingerprints and plainclothes troopers questioned neighbors for any information that might assist the investigation. A search was made of the entire neighborhood for any evidence that might have been thrown away. The news media quickly converged on the house, taking photos, and interviewing the neighbors. The coroner arrived and made an examination of the bodies. He estimated that the couple had been dead for three, possibly four, days.

Since the house had been ransacked, it appeared that robbery had been the motive, although it was hard to imagine that there would have been anything of real value in the house.

A few hours later, a police briefing and a review of the findings was held at Headquarters. The District Attorney's office, the sheriff's office, and the local police were represented. The lieutenant in charge of the investigation of the case reviewed all the known details. He read the coroner's report and the results of the various interviews. He advised everyone that the principal suspect was the Jansky's 29-year-old son, Emil. He had been observed four days earlier entering the house and leaving several hours later carrying a suitcase. The lieutenant then read the available history and description of Emil: he was six feet three inches tall, weighed 260 pounds, and had a shock of black hair; he had lived at home until he was 26 years old; he was an introvert who never socialized much with anyone in the neighborhood; he didn't have any friends; and he had dropped out of school after the ninth grade. At one time he had held a job as a guard in a state hospital, but had been fired for cruelty to the patients. As an only child, both of his parents had pampered him during his childhood. Later, police records indicated that the Janskys had called the troopers more than once when Emil came home drunk and disorderly. Each time he had been let off with a warning. The records also listed two other arrests: one for assault and the other for burglary. Each arrest resulted in probation.

The probation officer had insisted that Emil get a job. He was granted permission to move to New York City where he found odd jobs in restaurants. After his probation, Emil stayed in New York City, visiting his parents whenever he needed some money from them.

The lieutenant put his papers down and said, "Gentlemen, right now everything points to Emil. There are several troopers in the city trying to locate him. There are no other suspects, and I doubt if there will be any until we talk with Emil."

But finding Emil wasn't going to be an easy task. He had left his last-known residence in New York City without a forwarding address. After five days of running down slim leads that led nowhere, the troopers returned empty handed. Emil was nowhere to be found. One long shot was yet to be played. In searching the Jansky home, two postal money order receipts had been found. They were payments for insurance policies, which each parent had taken out. The policies were for $1,000 each and Emil was listed as the beneficiary. The actual policies were not found in the house. The insurance company was instructed not to pay on the policies without first getting clearance from the District Attorney or the state police.

Three weeks later, the main office of the insurance company called the state police. They had received a letter from Emil Jansky requesting a check for the $2,000 life insurance policies. He stated in the letter that his mother and father were both dead, and that he was the sole beneficiary. He had enclosed the policies and requested the check be sent to him, in care of General Delivery, at a small upstate post office. Troopers were immediately dispatched to the area and the post office was put under tight surveillance. The community was a resort area and there were many hotels catering to the summer vacation crowd. While the post office was staked out, discrete inquiries were made at the local hotels and employment agencies to see whether Emil was employed locally.

Finally, on the morning of the fifth day of surveillance, a large man got off a bus in front of the post office. He had been drinking and was unsteady on his feet. He staggered into the post office to inquire if any general delivery mail had arrived for Emil Jansky. The troopers on duty at the post office recognized Emil and immediately took him into custody. He was transported to the nearest state police headquarters for questioning. These were the days prior to the Supreme Court decisions regarding suspects' rights, so Emil was vigorously questioned — at length. It soon became obvious that he wasn't a very good liar. He claimed he hadn't been home in over six months and said he didn't even know his folks were dead. He claimed not to know who had killed them and that he wasn't on the lam from anything.

It was established that he had obtained a job at a local hotel under an assumed name. He had been given lodgings in a rooming house for the hotel staff. The only personal belonging he had at the hotel was a cheap suitcase containing all the evidence needed to convict him: the pawn tickets from his mother's rings, some bloodstained clothing, and $13 in cash, which was in an envelope postmarked a day before the murder. The envelope was addressed to his father. There were also some newspaper clippings giving an account of the murders and the fact that he was being sought for questioning. Later, the rings were retrieved from the pawn shop, and Emil was positively identified as the person who had pawned them. The bloodstained clothing was analyzed and the blood type matched his mother's.

During questioning, Emil sobered up pretty quickly and even made a feeble attempt at denying he was involved in any way. However, confronted with the evidence, he finally acquiesed. The State Police had a full confession from him within three hours. It was short and to the point: he was unemployed; his rent was due; he needed money for some liquor; and he didn't have any friends to borrow from. So he decided to visit his folks and borrow some money from them. When he got there, Emil's father told him there wasn't any more money for him — the well had run dry. He dared suggest that Emil get a job. An argument ensued, and for the first time in his life, Emil was ordered out of his father's home. He flew into a rage and struck his father. His mother, who had been in the kitchen preparing dinner, came to her husband's assistance. At this point, Emil's temper was out of control. He struck his mother with a bottle and then grabbed his father and repeatedly struck him with the same bottle. His mother got up from the floor and tried to get to the phone. Emil went after her, knocking her down again, and strangling her with a rawhide shoelace.

After he finishing off with his mother, he returned to the living room and strangled his father who was bleeding from the head and face and was lying nearly unconscious on the floor. He then ransacked the house for money. He found very little, but he did stumble upon his mother's rings and the insurance policies. He grabbed them and left the house.

Emil was charged with murder in the first degree. The trial was swift and the outcome was a foregone conclusion. The jury found Emil Jansky guilty as charged and the judge set the date for execution. Emil Jansky's appeal was automatic and was turned down. The execution was rescheduled.

The state mandates that there be official witnesses at all executions. Invitations to executions are generally extended to the press and members of the criminal justice system. I had given much thought to witnessing an execution. I felt that an officer should have first-hand knowledge of what transpires at an execution, so that he could never be vindictive; especially in cases involving capital punishment. Inasmuch as I had played a part in the Jansky case, I felt that if I had to view an execution, this might as well be the one. I asked a friend to get me an official invitation to Emil's execution.

Some weeks later, the letter arrived: "You are cordially invited to attend the execution by electricity of Emil Jansky to take place at Sing-Sing State Prison in Ossining, New York ...." I steeled myself to attend the execution, and to be at there exactly as I had been ordered, or rather "invited." I had a great deal of apprehension and many second thoughts, but I needed only to recall the horrible fate of the elderly Janskys at the time their son was to be executed. I felt I had to build up an immunity to any undesirable effects of viewing an execution. Surely, no one could have compassion for Emil Jansky, the son who murdered his own mother and father.

Finally, the night of the execution arrived. The night was as dark as my mood as I reluctantly changed into civilian clothing and headed for the state prison.

Half an hour before the execution, all the witnesses had to be registered in the office of the principal keeper. We were searched to ensure that no one would enter the death house with a camera. That had happened some years earlier during the execution of Ruth Snyder and it was determined that nobody would ever get a chance to get another exclusive or surreptitious photograph of an execution. Each of us signed the witness book, because a minimum number of people were required to witness the fact that the State was exacting the last drop of legal vengeance before the case could be closed.

Once all the witnesses had arrived and had all been signed in, we were addressed by the principal keeper. We were told that there were to be three executions that night. Three executions! That was two more than I had expected or had any desire to see. Suddenly, I had misgivings about being a part of the proceedings, but by now it was too late to be excused.

It was twelve minutes before the hour of nine o'clock. We were ushered out of the principal keeper's officer and into the warden's office. He addressed us, laying down the ground rules: absolutely no photographs and no conversation with the condemned. I believe there was also some reference about not repeating what transpired at the execution. This seemed ridiculous, as the majority of the witnesses were newspaper reporters who would rush to file their stories just as soon as the executions were over. The warden had presided over many executions, but it was said that he had never actually witnessed one.

It was now eight minutes before the hour. The executions were scheduled to commence precisely on the hour. We were led out of the warden's office, down a flight of stairs, into a waiting bus, across a dark courtyard, and into a small isolated building known as the "Death House."We were frisked once again and then ushered to our seats in a very small, cold room. I found myself in the front row of the darkened room, only a few feet from the infamous electric chair. There wasn't a wall with a plate glass window or even a railing between the chair and the gallery. The reinforced wooden chair stood in the center of a slightly raised, brightly illuminated platform. The thick leather straps of the chair dangled at the sides for now, but they would soon wrap around the condemned one in a final death embrace To the left of the chair was another small room, no bigger than a broom closet. This was the domain

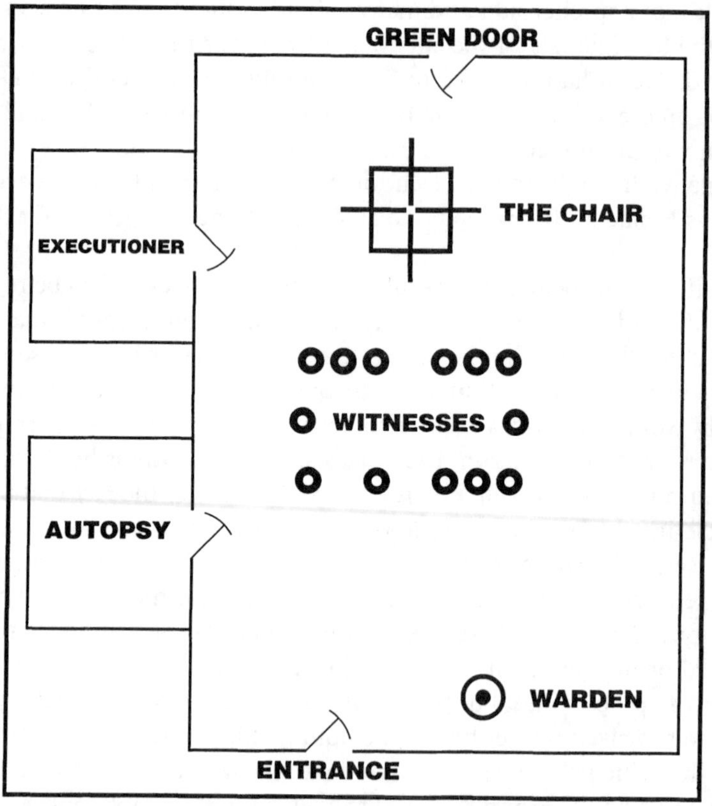

Layout of the execution room at Sing-Sing as best I can recall.

of a gnome-like little man who was busy readying the chair — the bucket of brine, the soaking sponges, the electrodes, the headpiece, a maze of wires and electrodes — all the props were ready for the drama that was about to unfold.

One minute before the hour. All eyes turned to the little green door to the rear and slightly to the right of the chair. It was quite literally the proverbial death's door. It was only ten or twenty yards from the death row cells, but to the condemned, it was the end of the road — the long and bitter end. His last entrance to the final act of the macabre death play was through that little green door.

Precisely on the hour, the door opened. First to walk through the door was a chanting priest carrying a large crucifix. Behind him was Emil Jansky, the hulk of a man, who only months earlier had savagely slain his mother and father in a fit of rage. He had to be supported by two guards.

"My God," I thought, "was this really the same man, the big, powerful man who had mercilessly killed his parents for a few lousy dollars? Was this pitiful, slobbering wretch the man the State called an unconscionable, vicious killer?" He now seemed helpless enough. The guards were practically carrying him along. "How could the few months in prison have reduced him to this pitiful state? What had been the worst part: the last weeks, days, perhaps the last hours? Did time drag interminably? Or did the days rush by? What could his dreams in the past month have been like? Is it true the coward dies a thousand times? How many times did Emil Jansky die?"

I kept trying to conjure up the images of his slain parents to justify what was about to transpire, but I couldn't concentrate. All I could see was this pitiful wretch of a man. He was terrified, and justifiably so. The months of waiting had taken their toll. Bleary-eyed and pale, he glanced about the room. Then his gaze turned to the chair. His eyes glazed over in sheer terror. He turned to look at his audience sitting in darkened silence, his glassy eyes pleading to his God to "let this chalice pass." He couldn't say anything. Shaking his head as if saying, "No, no, no," to banish this nightmare from becoming reality, he was gently, but firmly, pushed down into the seat as though the guards were afraid of hurting him and to overcome what little resistance his weight offered. The straps were buckled around him, holding him in a cataclysmic embrace. Each guard did his work with expert, practiced precision. The mask was lowered over his face, the straps tightly secured over his arms and legs, the electrodes placed on his shaved head, and the bare flesh of his legs. The sponges were soaked in the brine to better conduct the electricity. When the experts were finished with their preparations, the little gnome, the maestro of the scenario, double-checked their work. Satisfied, he returned to his broom-closet control room and stood ready for the signal. The warden took his place behind the last row of spectators. The signal was a nod of his head. Gnome-man spun the wheel and threw the switch, sending thousands of volts of crackling electricity surging into the body of the man held fast in the chair. The whirring sound of the motors filled the room with a strange cacophony of sounds. The weight of the victim was thrown forward with such force that the thick leather straps squeaked and strained to hold him. It appeared that he would be splashed across the room into the spectators' laps. But the straps held, and the chair did not fail to hold him — it performed its duty well. Suddenly, the room was filled with the odor of burning flesh. The man's chest turned from pink to gray to black. Only his jaw was visible under the mask — it drooled a thick bile-colored liquid. His pants were wet and filled with excrement. The vile odor of death permeated the small room.

I suddenly became aware that people to the left and right of me were retching. Then a short fat man with a stethoscope entered the stage from the autopsy room, which was next to the maestro's place of business. He placed the stethoscope on the dying man's chest. Detecting a sign of life, he shook his head, and returned to his position off stage. The gnome took the signal and worked his wheels and switches again. Once more, the motors whirred and did their ghastly deed. The doctor again approached the victim and made his examination. This time he was satisfied with the result and the man was pronounced dead. At his signal, the guards stepped forward and released the man from the chair's embrace. Emil Jansky's remains slumped down, were placed on a stretcher and wheeled to the autopsy room where the doctor would slit him open and to make an official report on the cause of death. Could there be any doubt?

Four minutes past the hour — incredible! An entire drama had been played out in those minutes. It seemed like days, perhaps weeks, had elapsed. And there wasn't anywhere we could go to reflect on what had just transpired. The back door was locked. No one could leave — there was no escape! This was a three-act play with no intermissions.

At five minutes past the hour, the little gnome was ready for the next performance. The electrodes, the bucket of brine, the sponges, the examination of the chair, the hasty clean up — everything was ready for the next actor.

Again, the little green door opened and the chanting priest heralded the entrance of the next condemned man. He was a small, gaunt, dark-skinned man, who looked like he could have been a preacher himself. Who was this small seemingly insignificant man, who was next to step into the spotlight before the hushed (and decidedly squeamish) audience?

Arthur Brown had been the product of a large family and a broken home. In his adolescent years, he had spent several years in reform school, but they hadn't brought about any change in the man who had served nine of his last sixteen years in jail. He had run the gamut of every crime in the book, but his total haul from all of them all didn't amount to a year's honest salary. His parole agreement demanded that he be gainfully employed. A job with a cleaning service had satisfied his parole officer. The jobs he was sent out on were in an affluent community. Cleaning the apartments of the well-to-do put him in temptation's way. The residents often were not at home when Arthur Brown came to clean. And clean up he did. At first it was some small item, just to see what he could get away with. Later, emboldened by his successes, he took more valuable items. One day as he was about to enter an apartment to do the cleaning, he noticed that the door to the adjacent apartment was slightly ajar. He peered through the opening and saw a woman, dressed only in her underwear, standing before a large mirror combing her hair. Suddenly, his body responded to the sight. Before he knew what was happening and before he had time to consider the consequences of his actions, he slipped into the apartment and stealthily approached the woman. By the time she saw him in the mirror, he was on her. She didn't even get a chance to scream for help. His hand was clamped over her mouth and he pressed his arm tightly across her throat. Within seconds, she was limp and lifeless. Yet even her lifeless body aroused him. When he was satisfied, he picked her up, and carried her to the bed in the adjoining room. He then ransacked the apartment and took whatever items he thought he could pawn. He never did go to his cleaning job. He called his boss and told him he had suddenly become sick and was going home.

The rape and murder was discovered several hours later. The police went on a manhunt and ended up at Arthur's door. The murdered woman, a divorcee named Mrs. Phillips, had been asked by her neighbor to monitor the cleaning man's comings and goings, so she had left her door ajar so she could hear when he arrived at the neighbor's apartment. When the neighbor returned home several hours later and her apartment had obviously not been cleaned, she went to Mrs. Phillips' apartment. She knocked, and when there wasn't any answer, she tried the door. It was unlocked. She entered and discovered Mrs. Phillips' body on the bed. The police were notified and the cleaning man, Arthur Brown, became the prime suspect. He was questioned and his apartment was searched. Some of Mrs. Phillips' belongings were found. The evidence, together with the discovery of Brown's fingerprints in the apartment, clinched the case against him. It also secured him a lead role in "Act II" at the Death House.

All eyes were on the small frame of Arthur Brown as he entered through the green door. For a split second, he felt that he had, at last, reached a point where he was the most important person in the room. But one look at the sturdy chair made him realize that the spotlight was on him for only the briefest of minutes and then, for never more. It wasn't the kind of attention he wanted. He was given an opportunity to say some last words, upon which he began to babble incoherently. When it became obvious that he had nothing substantial to say, he was escorted to the waiting chair. Each man knew exactly which strap to fasten, and momentarily, Arthur Brown was poised to become a statistic. The warden solemnly gave the nod, and then closed his eyes, and lowered his head. The law made his presence compulsory, but could not dictate his emotions. He kept the record straight with his presence, and was still able to say he never witnessed an execution.

The gnome in his small kingdom responded to the signal and immediately sent the motors whirring on their mission of death. Arthur Brown was still babbling when the first volts hit him. His voice rose to an inhuman pitch. Ungodly sounds and stenches again filled the room. The wait for the doctor seemed eternal this time. When the noise of the motors had died down, the doctor stepped up to the lifeless body, placed his stethoscope on the man's chest, and indicated that he was satisfied that Arthur Brown — apartment cleaner, rapist, and murderer — had paid his debt to society in full.

At the doctor's proclamation, the guards stepped up as though on cue. They picked up the limp body, placed it on the waiting stretcher, and gave him up to the autopsy room.

It was only twelve minutes past the hour. My sigh of relief was interrupted by the activities of the little stage manager as he busied himself with making the chair ready to receive the next victim. Would this night ever end! No time to think…no time to react…no way to stop it. It was all legal and it was justified.

Slowly the green door opened a third time. This time the priest was desperately trying to console the man who would conclude "Act III." But the redheaded man in his mid-forties would have none of it. He didn't want to be consoled. His hate-filled face wore a look of contempt. His crime was murder.

Many years earlier, a group of men had gathered in a downtown hotel room to gamble. A great deal of money was involved and the man who had Lady Luck with him at that session would walk out with a small fortune. In the midst of the game, someone surreptitiously entered the room and announced a holdup. The lone bandit then relieved each participant in the game of his money and valuables. The last man attempted to put up a fight, but was stopped by two bullets from the bandit's gun. As soon as the robber left, the police were notified. The wounded man died within the hour. Four of the victims were able to identify "Red" Pearce as the killer. The case was presented to a grand jury and Red was indicted for murder in the first degree. A warrant was issued for his arrest.

Red had been quick to make his getaway. He had planned it in advance. He flew to South America, bought a ranch, and eventually became a respected citizen in the local community. He worked hard and parlayed the stolen money into a sizable fortune. Some years later, he decided he needed a gun to protect his holdings and applied for a gun permit. He was photographed and fingerprinted in accordance with the law. Because he wasn't a citizen of his adopted country, his fingerprints were routinely sent to Washington for verification. It was determined that Red was a fugitive from justice and arrangements were made to have him extradited. The process was a long and drawn-out affair, but successful in the end. In a few months, Red found himself back in New York State to stand trial for murder. The court system eventually brought Red before a sentencing judge. The usual amenities were quickly disposed of, and Red was sentenced to die in the electric chair. It all seemed unreal to Red. His one crazy act was a million years and a lifetime ago. How could anyone demand retribution for something that no one should have remembered? Red argued that he had paid his debt to society by his voluntary absence from his native land, his hard work, and good conduct in his adopted country. His ill-founded logic fell on deaf ears. He had committed a murder and would have to pay the price. The appeals judge upheld the conviction. The execution date was rescheduled and now, here he was about to be strapped into the electric chair and die. And for what? A senseless act committed those many years ago.

He wondered didn't anyone forgive or forget any more? It took some time to shave his head so the electrodes would make good contact. The pants legs of his new special prison uniform were slit so more electrodes could be placed to the skin of his legs. The priest was allowed into his waiting cell to give him some spiritual help. The clergyman told him to ask the Lord for forgiveness. 'The Lord' was the wrong word! Red exploded. "I not only want the Lord to forgive; I want the judge and jury to forgive! I want the appeals court to forgive! I want the warden, the guards, the executioner to forgive!" He shouted and threw the priest from his cell. The priest continued his waiting in the corridor to walk the "last mile" with Red. In the last twelve minutes, the lights had dimmed once, twice, three times as the normal flow of electricity was drained by the surge of power to the chair.

When the guards arrived to escort Red to his seat in center stage, the priest quietly took his place at the head of the procession. As they reached the slowly opening green door he made one last attempt to have Red make his peace with God, but Red defiantly pushed the priest aside, taking his place front and center. He eyed each and every witness. He then turned on his heels and uttered, "I hope I can come back and haunt every one of you bloodthirsty bastards!" He stepped unflinchingly to the waiting chair, made himself comfortable, and even assisted the guards in adjusting the straps. He was ready, and so was the little man at the controls. He glanced at the warden to catch his nod and the final act of the surreal drama commenced. The little man was sweating both from his exertions and the stifling heat in the unventilated room. He turned the motors and switches into action. The straps holding Red's body creaked under the strain. Red seemed to disintegrate. His color changed. The stench from his burning flesh and excretion filled the room. A man in the back of the room became hysterical and begged the guards to let him leave. He put his head against the wall and sobbed uncontrollably. Nothing could be done — not for Red, not for any one in the audience — until the final curtain came down. Red Pearce helped the only way he could — by dying quickly. The doctor pronounced him dead after the first shock. He was unstrapped, placed on the stretcher, and carried away just as quickly as he had entered.

At last it was over. The doors were thrown open and a welcome blast of cold air rushed into the room. The guard told everyone to step lively onto the bus and we were whisked away to the main gate — and freedom. I took a few steps to the side of the gate, to join three other people to puke up our last meal. Could it really be only nine thirty? It was. A cloud slowly passed overhead and uncovered the moon. I had the rest of the night — and a lifetime ahead of me.

The Beginnings

My entry into police work wasn't by accident. I was a product of the Great Depression, and along with hundreds of thousands of other city kids, I dreamed about the security of a Civil Service career. The most sought-after civil service positions were in the police and fire departments. My choice was the police department and I could hardly wait until I was old enough to take the exam. I can still recall the encouraging and eloquent speech given by the Principal to the 1932 graduating class of New York City's DeWitt Clinton High School. I listened intently with my classmates as he told us we were the brightest and best graduating class ever. So armed with our diplomas, we set out to conquer the world. The fact that the streets were lined with apple-peddlers and panhandlers didn't intimidate us in the least. After all, we were the "best graduating class ever" and those words were all we needed to make us feel we could "make it."

However, after several months of searching for employment, I was beginning to get a little discouraged. A friend came to my rescue, however, with information about a job. That tip resulted in a job in the receiving department at Macy's Department Store. The hours were long and the work was monotonous, but it was a job and that was important. I'm sure that I must have affixed a million gummed price labels on everything from women's shoes to liquor bottles, and, after taking several night classes in marketing and salesmanship, I was promoted to checker and then to squad leader. By this time I was old enough to take the police exam, but it wasn't scheduled for a few more years. The depression was still on and jobs were hard to come by. I was doing very well at Macy's, making $27 a week as a junior executive supervising the receiving department. I should have been satisfied, but I still had the desire to become a policeman.

One summer, I vacationed with some friends in upstate New York. I stayed at the Florence Inn, allegedly owned by the notorious gangster "Legs" Diamond. The hotel was under constant surveillance by the State Police. It was my first exposure to New York State's "finest"—"the Men in Gray." Each officer was resplendent in a gray uniform, riding breeches, boots, and a .45-caliber revolver complete with a Sam Browne belt and a lanyard. That was it! I decided then and there that it was the State Police for me.

When I got back to the city, I read everything I could find out about the organization. I learned that prior to 1917, the rural areas of New York State were virtually without police protection. Major crimes often went uninvestigated and unsolved because many local sheriffs were merely political appointees who did not possess even the basic fundamentals of police work. Interesting enough, the organization of the New York State Police was established as a result of the unfailing efforts of two women who were sufficiently incensed over a murder to do something about it.

The year was 1913. Sam Howell was the construction foreman on a home being built in Westchester County for Miss M. Moyca Newell. One Saturday morning, Sam was enroute to deliver the payroll to the construction site, when he was waylaid: shot and robbed by four men. He was mortally wounded, but before dying, he managed to identify two of his assailants as men he had previously hired to work for him.

Complete apathy on the part of the sheriff and local law enforcement officers made it possible for the murderers to go free. Miss Newell, and her friend, the writer Katherine Mayo, were dismayed to see how little the local constable and sheriff did to pursue the murderers who were still known to be in the area. Even with positive identifications by the dying man, the murderers were never arrested. Misses Newell and Mayo decided to take action against this travesty of justice. They undertook a campaign to establish a state constabulary providing police protection for the rural areas of the state.

Miss Mayo, who was a writer of some repute, journeyed to Pennsylvania to study the organization and workings of the Pennsylvania State Constabulary. At the time, only Pennsylvania had a State Police force. Upon her return, Miss Mayo wrote a book called *Justice for All.* She and Miss Newell formed the "Committee for a State Police" and were successful in getting the bill passed in the state Senate in 1916. However, the bill failed to get through the Assembly and was "dead in the water" for the time being.

At the next legislative session, the committee enlisted the aid of Governor Charles S. Whitman. This time, with the the backing of the State Agricultural Society and other rural organizations, the bill passed. Organized labor, however, was solidly against the formation of a State Police force for fear the organization would be used as strike breakers. To satisfy the labor interests, the bill was amended to limit the use of the state police to suppress disorders in cities, except upon the invitation of the mayor of the city or on orders of the governor. Even with this limitation, the bill barely passed both houses. Finally, on April 11, 1917, Governor Whitman signed the bill and the New York State Police force was officially created.

The new organization was comprised of four semi-military troops, each with about 55 men and officers, for a total of 250 men to police all the rural areas of the state. Troopers were appointed by the superintendent for a two-year enlistment and it was a misdemeanor to leave without his consent. The original appropriation of $500,000 gave the superintendent the funds to buy horses, uniforms, barracks, vehicles, arms, and all the other accoutrements needed to get the outfit up and running.

The man selected to head the State Police was George F. Chandler, a close friend of the Governor. Superintendent Chandler was a doctor and a surgeon and his friendship with the Governor went back many years. Chandler accepted the position, fully believing that the organization would be inducted into the army under the State Military Act; however, the induction never came to pass. The war department refused to accept the organization as a unit. Chandler threw all his efforts into organizing the new outfit, and in a short time, it was ready to be launched.

Chandler conferred with any and all police agencies that could help make a success of his organization, getting ideas from sources as near as the Pennsylvania State Police and as far-off as the Royal Canadian Mounted Police. He purchased 250 horses and in the next few years raised 36 colts. A training camp was aquired in Manluis, New York and it was nicknamed "Newayo" for the two women responsible for getting the state police started in the first place. With equipment borrowed from the army, he was able to get recruits at the school within seven weeks after his appointment.

The troopers did their jobs well and the public accepted them with open arms. Horses gave way to the automobile in the late 1930s. Patrolling in cars gave the troopers far more exposure to the public. Over the years, the organization grew in manpower and equipment. A new training facility in Albany, the Scientific Criminal Laboratory, and the latest in sophisticated technology have made it one of the finest organizations of its type in the world today.

My own interest in police work led me to offer suggestions to the security department at Macy's on how to cut down on theft by employees and customers. I was about to seek a transfer to the security department, when, one day, I noticed an item in the newspaper. The caption read: "The State Police announces test for Troopers. Applicants must be 21 years of age, possess a high-school diploma, have 20/20 vision, and be 5 feet 10 inches tall. Applicants must appear in person for the examination in Albany."

I sent for the application immediately and on the given day appeared in Albany as directed. The test wasn't difficult and in due time I was notified that I had passed. A date was set for an interview and the physical examination. The interview went well and I passed the physical, but was disqualified for being an eighth of an inch too short.

That might have been the end of a career before it had even begun, but I refused to accept that the decision was final. I haunted Headquarters until

I was given an appeal and was finally accepted. It just happened that they were in need of a teletype operator, and since I was admitted through the "back door" I was assigned to the position. First, however, I had to receive regular trooper training. All new recruits were required to be thoroughly trained as troopers with specialty assignments coming later.

Leaving a job paying $27 per week for one paying $15 per week seemed foolhardy to many of my friends, but my mind was made up. I was going to be a New York State Trooper!

The State Police organization was styled after the military. Discipline was strict and the troopers were required to live in barracks. In those early days the hazing was merciless — much was done to see whether the recruit could "stand the gaff." I didn't much appreciate the hazing and was ready to call it quits on more than one occasion, but my determination carried me through the "necessary evil." Otherwise, the probationary period passed uneventfully. I didn't have any difficulty with the training school, which was a month-long course held at the Hotel Troy, in Troy, New York. By today's standards, the training would be considered woefully inadequate. However, it did prepare the trooper of the day to face the duties required of a state police law enforcement officer.

Often when my day shift in the teletype bureau was over, I would double-up with the trooper working night patrol. I developed a lot of experience in a hurry and worked on some interesting cases as well. But after a few years, I decided that chasing speeders and being a rural police officer really wasn't what I wanted to do for the rest of my life. I enjoyed the investigating end of it, but the men assigned to the Bureau of Criminal Investigations (BCI) were old-timers, hand-picked by the brass. I knew I was pegged as a guy who could do a good job in the teletype bureau and was destined to spend many years there. For a young man with a yen to match wits with criminals and do some meaningful police work, operating the teletype was not exactly the adventure I had in mind.

One of the special details of our troop was to do guard duty at Hyde Park, the New York home of President Roosevelt when he came up from Washington. This was quite often and, like everyone else, I pulled my share of the duty. The U. S. Secret Service accompanied the President, having the responsibility of protecting him and his family. The State Police patrolled the grounds and manned the security posts at the entry to the estate. I was always eager to get away from Headquarters and break up the monotony.

One day while completing an assignment at Hyde Park, I went to dinner with one of the agents, named Charlie, with whom I was rather friendly. I told him about my desire to change jobs and to get into something more challenging. He suggested that I put in an application for the U. S. Secret Service. He explained that because of the emminent onset of war, there were plans to enlarge the Service and if I got by the interview, I might be considered when the exam came up. I liked the idea and decided to put in my application. The following day I talked about my plans to Dennis, a trooper friend who had about as much time on the job as I did. He agreed to apply for the Secret Service with me. We carefully composed a letter, citing our experience and background, and forwarded it to Jim Maloney, the Special Agent in Charge in New York; who by coincidence, was also a former New York State Trooper.

A week later we were asked to return for an interview. The interview went well. We were motivated, clean-cut, and had sufficient police experience in lieu of the required college degree. All that remained was a full-field background investigation and the physical. In due course, the investigation was completed and we found ourselves back in New York to be sworn in. We were advised that the appointment was provisional and that we would be required to take and pass the next Federal Civil Service examination. Dennis and I bid farewell to our buddies at trooper headquarters. As it turned out, our farewells weren't for long. With the gathering war clouds presaging World War II, the Secret Service began increasing its personnel, just as Charlie had predicted and at least a dozen troopers from our old organization were hired to boost the ranks.

In 1941, the Secret Service was one of five enforcement agencies of the U. S. Treasury Department. Its sister organizations were the Federal Bureau of Narcotics, the Internal Revenue Bureau, the Customs Service, the Alcohol, Tobacco, and Tax Unit, and in peacetime, the United States Coast Guard. Treasury enforcement was a formidable foe of the underworld and I knew that I would enjoy working toward suppressing crime on a national level.

The U. S. Secret Service has two principal duties. The first is the protection of the president, his immediate family, and all other officials and dignitaries as mandated by Congress or presidential decree. The second function could be called "the watchdog" of the Treasury. The Service has the responsibility of suppressing counterfeiting and forgery of all Federal obligations, including those of all friendly countries. The obligations are in the forms of currency, coins, stamps, bonds, checks, and almost anything else that the Government has an obligation to pay or perform a service for.

The U. S. Secret Service was created out of necessity during the 1860s, when the monetary situation was a mess. At the time, money was made by banks that operated with permission from each State. They were allowed to print money with the name of the bank on it. This, of course, led to many abuses. "Fly-by-night" banks seemed to spring-up overnight to print their own bank notes and the public began to lose confidence in paper money. Because of hoarding, coins were becoming scarce, so it became necessary to do something about the situation.

Right after the start of the Civil War, the United States Government began issuing its own currency, redeemable for gold and silver. Counterfeiting flourished at this time and about one of every three notes in circulation was bogus. This was an intolerable situation, requiring immediate intervention by the government to restore confidence in the currency. Rewards were offered for the arrest of violators and the Government even hired private investigators (from the Pinkerton Detective Agency) and bounty hunters to track down counterfeiters. This system didn't meet with much success and eventually the Secretary of the Treasury approached President Lincoln with a plan to establish a force of government investigators. The President agreed; the U. S. Secret Service was formed and placed under the jurisdiction of the Treasury Department.

William P. Wood, a flamboyant, progressive lawman, who had previously been warden of the Capitol Prison in Washington D.C., was sworn in as the first Chief of the U. S. Secret Service on July 5, 1865. His mandate as Chief of this new service was to suppress counterfeiting and to restore the public's trust and confidence in their currency. To do this he hired about forty like-minded men who fanned out across the country to the areas where counterfeiting was flourishing. The group was very successful and, before long, several hundred counterfeiters were behind bars. Within the next several years, counterfeiting was down to controllable limits. The U. S. Secret Service had established a reputation as an efficient, incorruptible, dedicated agency. There wasn't a similar federal investigative agency in the government at the time, so it became very popular to borrow Secret Service agents to investigate other crimes; for example, agents of the Secret Service investigated the famous oil deposit and land fraud scandal known as "Teapot Dome."

Police academies have come a long way since the Treasury instructor obtained a suite of rooms in a Brooklyn hotel and guided his students through a maze of Treasury Regulations, Laws of Arrest, and Rules of Evidence. The Captain and his instructors traveled to all the principal cities and held classes in whatever quarters were available. The training covered all the necessary basics, providing the agents with what was considered adequate instruction in administrative and legal duties, procedures, and responsibilities. The gaps would have to filled by on-the-job training.

Working with a partner in those days was a luxury no agency could afford. After a short breaking-in period, an agent was assigned a number of cases and was expected to go out and work them. It was how the agent handled these cases, whether alone or with a team, that determined if he would make the grade or eventually fall by the wayside. The agency produced some of the most outstanding lawmen in law enforcement.

Presidential protection was not an original function of the Secret Service. It came about after President William McKinley was shot and killed in Buffalo, New York by Leon Czolgosz, an avowed anarchist who was obsessed with the idea that all rulers should be eliminated. This happened in September of 1901. Czolgosz was electrocuted in the electric chair at the State Prison in Attica, New York. These events occurred only twenty years after President James A. Garfield was shot and killed at the Washington, D.C. railroad station by Charles Guiteau, a religious fanatic and mentally deranged pauper who aspired to governmental office.

The first U. S. president to be assassinated was Abraham Lincoln, shot on April 14, 1865, at Ford's Theater in Washington, D.C., by John Wilkes Booth. Coincidentally, this was the same day the President signed the law establishing the U. S. Secret Service. President Lincoln died the following day.

Following the assassination of President McKinley, the U. S. Secret Service was assigned to protect President Theodore Roosevelt, although the appropriate legislation did not pass until 1906. Further legislation in 1913 extended protection by the Service to include the president-elect. In 1917, the Service was given authority to protect the members of the president's family and in 1951 the vice-president was given protection if he requested it. This was later changed in 1962 to make it mandatory for the vice-president and then later the vice-president elect to receive protection. In 1965, the law was further extended to protect a former president and his wife or widow and minor children. A change in the law in 1968 provided protection for certain presidential candidates during an election campaign year.

The White House Police Force (formerly officers of the Metropolitan Washington D.C. Police Department) was originally used to protect the Executive Mansion and grounds. The law was amended in 1971 to change the name to the Executive Protective Service, and to extend the jurisdiction to include protection of certain embassies and consulates in the District of Columbia and anywhere else the president might direct. Now, the uniformed officers assigned to protect the grounds of the White House and the embassies are known as the U. S. Secret Service, Uniform Division. The uniformed guard force protecting the main Treasury building in Washington D.C. is also under the supervision of the U. S. Secret Service.

After the assassination of President John F. Kennedy on November 22, 1963 in Dallas, the agency was enlarged and given additional funds to purchase much-needed equipment and personnel. From the original 40 operatives, the Service now has a roster of over 2,000 agents and an equal number of administrative staff, uniformed personnel, and highly trained technical specialists. The Chief is now the Director and all agents are called Special Agents. Agents attend an eight-week training course in Glenco, Georgia before attending the specialized U. S. Secret Service school — the James J. Rowley Training Center in Beltsville, Maryland. The school is named for its late Director who had the foresight to anticipate the increased responsibility and role of the U. S. Secret Service in protecting world leaders and the investigation of financially related crime. The investigative responsibilities of the Secret Service still include counterfeiting and forgery of government checks and bonds, but have been expanded to include sophisticated financial and computer fraud. The hand-engraved counterfeit notes of the past have given way to modern technological advances, creating new investigative challenges for the modern agent, who must be as proficient in computer skills as he or she is in people skills.

The world of the modern Secret Service agent is similar to, but also very different from, the world and people of my generation. The rules are still the same even if the investigative techniques are more sophisticated, but the elements have remained and the results are constant. The main changes are in the people and the equipment. In this book I reflect on the people and tell their stories along with my own. After all, if not for the people and their stories, I might as well have remained at Macy's.

I chased the check thief, the forger, the would-be assassin, and the counterfeiter in all corners of the country and in many parts of the world. I started working in a special undercover detail to ferret out the counterfeiters and arrest them. At one time, I was the only agent working undercover, so I was assigned to work in many parts of this land. I knew many of the violators and many knew me, either by sight or reputation. I eventually formed my own undercover unit, pursuing the counterfeiter in every state in the union and in many foreign countries.

Occasionally, I run into a criminal I had arrested years earlier and will sit back and have a cup of coffee and discuss the old cases. That is how I am able to relate what they were thinking at the time, their conversations, and their feelings.

I don't think I can ever totally retire. I remain interested in modern policing techniques, as that "cop bug" that bit me in 1932 is still under my skin. This book is an attempt to recount some of the past 60 plus years of being "in crime's way" and the stories that were a little different, and to describe the actions, sometimes the thoughts, of those responsible for the crimes that came to our attention. We don't always have the answer as to why the crimes were committed, but we can relate how they were accomplished and the means that were used to bring some of the "coniacker" criminals to justice.

I first heard the word "coniacker" from the real old-timers in the Service who referred to makers and passers of counterfeit money as "coniackers." That word is now an antiquated relic found only in dictionaries of the 1930s and 1940s, having passed into an era like the old-time investigators themselves. This book is about them all — the coniacker, the counterfeiter, the conspirator, and the scoundrel.

The Men from Mars

Chuck, a senior trooper, and I were on patrol in a 1937 Ford Phaeton. It was a beautiful autumn day and the top was down, giving us an excellent view of all our surroundings and also alerting motorists that the "Dolly Sisters" were out. The late Sunday afternoon flow of traffic was mostly toward the city, since most people wanted to get home before the real crush was on. The majority of the troop's strength was on the road, keeping the heavy weekend traffic moving and handling accidents and other mishaps.

After patrolling for several hours, we stopped in at Headquarters to check in with the duty corporal. At the time, we didn't have radios in the cars and checking in was done either in person or by telephone. After checking in, we went up to the teletype room to see if Rusty, the trooper-on-duty, had any alarms, "look-outs," or "wants" for us. He gave us a list of cars that were reported stolen and mentioned that he had just heard over the radio that there was some kind of lunar disturbance in South Jersey. He mentioned that the regular programs were being periodically interrupted to inform listeners about the disturbance. He said he hoped it wasn't an earthquake because he came from South Jersey and his folks, who were quite old, still lived there, and he was concerned about their safety. We took note of the alarms and went out again. Rusty returned to his teletype duties, keeping one ear to the radio so as not to miss any of the updates.

He sat back in his chair and puffed on the old corncob pipe he never seemed to be without. He jumped up when the radio music was interrupted by an announcer who excitedly reported that the disturbances were being reported more frequently. There were reports that a large vehicle from outer space was attempting to make a landing in a wooded area in South Jersey. The announcer stated that a mobile radio unit was being dispatched to the scene and several scientists were enroute from Princeton University to investigate. Rusty thought it was important enough to notify the duty corporal who was at the duty desk two floors below.

The corporal went to the day room and turned on the radio to the station Rusty suggested. All he heard was an orchestra playing some popular music. The corporal called Rusty on the phone and accused him of fooling around. Rusty insisted he was giving the corporal the straight dope and urged him to stay tuned to the station. Against his better judgment, the corporal sat and listened, thinking of what he would do to Rusty if this turned out to be a practical joke. The corporal didn't have to wait very long. The music was soon interrupted again. This time there was a sense of urgency in the announcer's voice. He reported that terrible things were happening. A large vehicle from outer space had indeed landed and horrible creatures were exiting it, spewing fire and smoke. He switched the broadcast to the mobile units who were close to the scene. The on-the-scene announcer reported that his partner tried to get too close to the vehicle, was sprayed by the creatures, and was instantaneouly vaporized. The crackling of the fire was audible over the mobile unit. Within seconds, the hapless announcer was also consumed by fire. The broadcast went dead momentarily, and then was picked up again by the local station.

The corporal, now satisfied that an invasion from outer space was, indeed, in progress, rushed to the phone to notify the lieutenant who lived nearby. The lieutenant, nicknamed "Flannel Mouth," wasn't very popular with the men (his nickname was whispered only in select company). The lieutenant listened to the corporal, tuned in to the station, and within minutes, was barking out orders.

In the meantime, another trooper joined Rusty to listen to the radio. Rusty puffed furiously on his pipe as it was announced that the creatures were emitting a poisonous gas that was killing anyone who came into contact with it. The smoke from Rusty's pipe floated out one window and into another window where the other trooper was listening. When the smoke reached his nose, he clutched his throat and shouted, choking, "Rusty, its here…its here!" Rusty jumped to his aid, puffing even more furiously.

The radio announcer gave details of local villages that were being destroyed. He said the creatures were spreading out over the area destroying everything in their path. He gave specific instructions on which highways were safe to use and which ones to avoid. Calls were placed for fire equipment and ambulances. The endless announcements spoke of nothing but destruction and chaos.

Chuck and I were blissfully unaware of what was happening and continued patrolling the highway. Then we began to notice that the traffic heading north was picking up substantially and most were driving at unusually high rates of speed. The whole traffic pattern was erratic. We decided to turn around and start handing out summonses for speeding and reckless driving. We singled out one car, which was speeding and gave chase. It was obvious we were after him, but that didn't slow him down. We were doing 80 miles per hour, but were barely gaining on him. Finally, we drew alongside him and motioned for him to pull over. The driver rolled his window down and shouted, "No way," or some other words to that effect, and continued to race along the highway. The man had his wife and several children in the car and refused to pull over. We didn'tt want to force him off the road for fear of causing injury to the children. While we continued to blast the siren and motion for him to pull over, we suddenly realized that motorists behind us were honking their horns and were most anxious to pass by us, in spite of the fact we were already doing 80 miles an hour! This was definitely unusual. We decided that discretion was the better part of valor. It was obvious that law and order on the highway had totally broken down. Something was seriously wrong. We pulled off the road for a minute and watched the motorists drive wildly along the highway. The only way to find out what was wrong was to call headquarters. We got to a phone as quickly as possible. It was difficult to get through, since the switchboard was besieged with calls. The corporal and a few men had all they could do to keep up with the frantic calls from people who wanted the latest information on the creatures who were invading South Jersey. It took ten minutes for to get the operator who managed to get me headquarters on an emergency basis. Finally, the corporal was on the phone. I tried to explain to him about the traffic. He interrupted and told me that there was an invasion from Mars, that the countryside was afire, that people were being consumed by monsters from outer space. He insisted that he had no time for details. He ordered us to drop everything and return to headquarters for further instructions.

I went to the car and tried to explain to Chuck about the invasion from Mars and the horrible creatures. I told Chuck that I was only repeating what the corporal had told me. Chuck shook his head, shoved the car into gear, lurched forward, and started for headquarters at the best speed he could manage. The highway was still full of crazy people driving north like their very lives depended on their getting away as fast and as far as possible.

Things weren't better at headquarters. Everyone was trying to obey the corporal's orders. The quartermaster sergeant had arrived on the scene and was issuing rifles, machine guns, and ammunition to the troopers. When the lieutenant arrived on the scene, he took command. He came in his personal car with his wife and many household possessions. His wife was nearly hysterical. She clutched a large crucifix in one hand and a bottle of rye in the other. She alternately kissed the crucifix and took a swig from the bottle. The lieutenant was barking orders when Trooper Kurtz, who nursed a long-time grudge against him, approached. Kurtz looked the lieutenant in the eye and said, "Lieutenant, I know we're all going to die. I've been waiting seven years to tell you that you are nothing but a flannel-mouthed son of a bitch, a no-good, rotten bastard. I've got a mind to grab you by your miserable neck and squeeze it until your tongue turns black. I'd be doing everyone a favor if I shoved this .45 up your tail and pulled the trigger, but I just hate the thought of wasting a good bullet on your miserable carcass."

Having finished his tirade he spat on the ground and turned away. The lieutenant's face turned red and said, "Men, this is no time to pull old chestnuts out of the fire…let bygones be bygones…forgive and forget, that's what I've always said…let us pool our energies and fight the common enemy that threatens us. We will make our last stand on the hill. Go to your posts. You men with the machine guns will concentrate your fire on the approaches to Headquarters, and you men with rifles will make the last-ditch defense from high ground."

While the men were busy setting up the defenses, the lieutenant got into the car with his wife and took off with a screech, heading north.

We still didn't know what in the hell was going on, when a trooper shouted from a second-floor window, "Come on in you guys, the whole thing is a phony. It was only a radio show by some guy named Orson Welles." Sheepishly we all returned to Headquarters, put the firearms away, and returned to our business with a minimum of conversation. In a few hours things were back to normal.

The next morning, the lieutenant stormed into his office, red-faced and full of fight. He opened the door and barked at the sergeant, "Send in Trooper Kurtz — immediately!"

They Called Him "Lucky"

The man who was called "Lucky" by his friends had no way of knowing what a misnomer that name would become, or that a series of seemingly unrelated events and coincidences would make years of his life a hellish nightmare. I ran into Lucky on two separate occasions: once as a State Trooper and once again as a U. S. Secret Service Agent.

The best eatery in town was a small tavern and I always tried to stop by whenever I was in the neighborhood. The owner knew what I liked and always had some set aside for me. One evening, before I arrived, a customer paid for his drink with a counterfeit $20 bill. The bartender was suspicious of the bill and examined it. While he was scrutinizing it, the man tried to snatch it from him, and run out with it. There was a brief scuffle and the bill was dropped, and the man got away. He jumped into his car and sped away on the road out of town. The bartender managed to get his licence plate number.

Half an hour later, when I arrived, the man was long gone. It turned out, however, that he was stopped the same night for speeding, was given a summons and released. After an investigation, the man was picked up and then identified by the bartender. The man's nickname was "Lucky." He had several prior arrests, but no convictions. He was held on federal charges of attempting to pass counterfeit money.

Lucky was born and raised on New York's Lower East Side. He began his depredations at an early age. He learned how to survive on the street and became adept at shoplifting, picking pockets, selling narcotics, and passing counterfeit money. He was different from many of the other kids because he had never been caught in the act of committing a crime. Everyone who knew him called him "Lucky." The name stuck. All the local police knew him and many would have given a day's pay to "get him right." Lucky lived quite well for a man who never did an honest day's work and it appeared that he would have a niche carved for himself in the neighborhood underworld.

Then came the all-important day of Lucky's trial for attempting to pass counterfeit money. It seemed that everything had suddenly gone wrong.

Someone forgot to properly mark and initial the bill for evidence, the bartender couldn't be positive about the identification, the person who got the license number wasn't positive if he got it right. Any one of the above circumstances was enough to lose the case and so it was. Lucky was found "not guilty." He swaggered out of the courtroom, certain that his luck would last forever. I met him outside the courtroom and cautioned him not to stretch his luck too far. He looked at me and kind of sneered and said, "They don't call me 'Lucky' for nothing!"

Lucky continued on his merry way until one day he fell in love with Millie. He had known Millie all his life. For some unknown reason, Millie started to look good to Lucky and he began seeing her more frequently. Millie, knowing Lucky's reputation in the neighborhood, refused to get serious about him until he got himself a legitimate job. They had many long talks about his future and finally, one day, Lucky announced to Millie that he was going to join the Merchant Marines and go to sea. World War II was about to begin and Lucky thought that if he went to sea he could earn enough money to marry Millie and start a new life.

Lucky didn't have any trouble getting seaman's papers, since he had never been convicted of a crime. He signed on a freighter as an ordinary seaman. Before setting out on his first voyage, Lucky made the rounds of his friends and relatives, reserving the last few hours for Millie. They spent a long time planning what they would do when he returned from the voyage. She accompanied him to the dock and they said their good-byes and parted.

The work was routine and Lucky didn't have any trouble getting along with the other seamen.They were then getting extra pay because German submarines were plying the Atlantic. Lucky learned that after stops in France and Italy, the last stop before returning home would be Greece. After work, the tables were cleared for nightly card games. Lucky just watched for the first two weeks. When he discovered that many players were not expert gamblers, he began to join them in the games after supper.

Two days before landing in Greece, Lucky lived up to his name and won several thousand dollars in some pretty wild poker games. He decided to stash his money aboard ship and take it all back home. It would give him a good start in setting up his apartment with Millie. Although Lucky had allowed himself very few luxuries while on the voyage, he thought he would buy some presents for Millie in Greece. He left the ship alone and did some sight-seeing around town. Passing a jewelry store, he noticed a gold locket in the window and he thought he would like to get it for Millie. After bargaining with the shop owner for several minutes, he purchased the locket for $175 in American currency. Lucky took the locket and began to return to his ship. There was not much to do around town and, besides, Lucky wanted to be on his best behavior.

When Lucky approached the dock area, a small automobile containing two men pulled alongside of him. One man got out of the car and showed him something that resembled a badge. Lucky was searched and put in the back seat of the car. The two men were talking, but Lucky couldn't understand a word they were saying. The car eventually pulled up before a stone building in the center of town. It reminded Lucky of a police station. He was taken inside where the three men were joined by two men in police uniforms. One man spoke broken English and Lucky understood that he was arrested for the possession and passing of counterfeit American money.

It appeared that the money he had given the shopkeeper contained five counterfeit $20 bills. Lucky was carefully searched and on his person they found $82 in American money. Four of the twenties were counterfeit. Lucky then realized that all the money he had won in the card game was probably counterfeit, and put into the game by one of the crew. Since the money had continually changed hands, he couldn't remember who put the money into the game. The police tried to question Lucky, but the language barrier was too great. Lucky, true to the code of the underworld, decided not to volunteer any information. Later he was taken to a cell in the basement of the same building. He was sure that a representative of the U.S. Government or a member of his ship would visit him shortly.

After spending two days in the cell, Lucky became apprehensive and asked the jailer for a lawyer or to speak with someone who could understand him. Two more days later, a Greek officer who spoke fairly good English finally visited him. Lucky learned that he would be charged in criminal court with possessing and passing counterfeit money. When he appeared in court he would enter a plea; he then would be assigned an English-speaking lawyer. The case would be called to trial sometime in the future. He was told that his ship had sailed, that someone in the American Consul's office was advised of his arrest and that, in all probability, he would be interviewed by someone from that office. Although Lucky objected strenuously to his being held incommunicado, he still wasn't allowed to make a call or write a letter. The answer he received was always the same. In due time he would be allowed to see a lawyer and make telephone calls. Lucky did not understand what they meant by "in due time," as the days stretched into weeks and each week seemed like a month. He soon lost all track of time.

Time passed very slowly for Lucky. He was never let out of his cell. He had to fight the rats for the meager food he was given. He tried to play games to keep his mental equilibrium. He drew a circle on the dirt floor, captured cockroaches and tried to race them around the track. He knew the guards could be bribed for some favors; unfortunately, he had nothing to offer as a bribe. Everything he had was taken from him except his clothes, which were rotting on his back.

As the weeks passed, Lucky noticed unusual excitement around the prison. He sensed something was happening, but he didn't know what. One day, finally, everything made sense. He heard rumblings and explosions. The city was being bombarded. Most of the people at the jail were disturbed and uneasy. Some guards and a few officials were abandoning their posts. A man, who spoke some English, was thrown into a cell next to Lucky. The man told Lucky that the Axis powers were invading Greece; that some fierce battles were raging and that Greece might fall to the Axis at any time.

The battles raged but nothing changed for Lucky and time continued to drag. No one ever gave him any information. Political prisoners that he could not communicate with were being thrown into the overcrowded jail. There were many executions in the courtyard. But no one had time for Lucky. He could not get his case heard. All efforts to communicate with the American Consul were fruitless. Lucky's luck had run out. He was a forgotten man.

Weeks, months passed in endless, monotonous succession. Lucky lost all sense of time. He had one miserable meal a day. He had no contact with anyone, although other prisoners were occasionally put into the cell with him, they were all Greek nationals who disappeared as suddenly and mysteriously as they came. Lucky still wasn't given permission to write letters, nor did he receive any. Lucky spent his time thinking of Millie and the plans they had made.

After much bombardment and fighting around the city, one day, the jail was stormed and taken by the Germans. He didn't know whether this new situation would be good or bad for him. Lucky didn't know what to think. Would he be summarily executed by the invaders, or would he be able to tell his story and be released? As far as he knew, the United States wasn't at war with anyone.

After the occupation of the city was complete, the Gestapo set up headquarters in the prison. Eventually Lucky was taken out of his cell and questioned by a Gestapo officer who spoke perfect English. Lucky tried to explain to the officer that the Greek authorities had wrongly arrested him when he innocently came into the possession of counterfeit money and had unknowingly used it to make a purchase in a local jewelry store. The officer laughed. He accused Lucky of being an American agent who had been planted in the Greek jail. He accused Lucky of being a naval officer attached to the Merchant Marine for espionage purposes. Lucky pleaded with the officer to believe him, but the officer only laughed and told him that one day Lucky would tell the truth. Until then, he was returned to his miserable cell.

Lucky's only respite from his loneliness during the next several months were the many times that he was brought before the Gestapo for further interrogation. Lucky sometimes thought he should confess that he was a spy and be put out of his misery.

Lucky received some very little sketchy information. He knew the United States was in the war, but he didn't know how it was going. He heard about places like Pearl Harbor, Iwo Jima, and landings in France. As the years went by, it appeared to Lucky that the war was going badly for the Germans. His sessions with the Gestapo were becoming infrequent; new faces were seen around the prison; there was an increase in executions in the prison yard. Lucky didn't care if he was next.

Late in 1945, when he learned that the Germans might capitulate and the war could come to an end, he hoped and prayed that he would be released. One day after a terrific amount of shooting, explosions, and street fighting the prison was taken over by Greek and English troops. Lucky was elated. He believed that at long last he would be free. He was wrong. He fared no better with the victors. Advised that the counterfeiting charges against him were still pending and that he would have to face trial, Lucky managed to see the American Consul and obtain legal representation and an interpreter.

After many more months, his case came to trial in the local first District Criminal Court. The jewelry storekeeper testified that Lucky was the man who gave him the counterfeit notes; an expert testified that the notes were counterfeit; Lucky was found guilty and later appeared before the judge for sentencing. He was sentenced to two years of hard labor. The judge said he took into consideration the time that Lucky had spent in jail awaiting trial. He stated he would have imposed at least a ten-year sentence under normal conditions. Lucky was dazed by the sentence. He was transferred to a prison outside Salonika. He received better treatment than in the local jail, worked in the fields every day and wrote one letter a week. The news from home was not encouraging. His mother and father had died, his two younger brothers had been killed in the service and his letters to Millie were returned, stamped as "Not known at the address given."

Lucky lived through the two years at the prison and on the day he was released, a representative of the U. S. Consul's office met him at the prison gates. The government official told Lucky that the U. S. government would finance his trip home, but that he would be escorted home by a member of the military police and when he landed in New York he would be taken into custody by a U. S. Marshal. There were pending counterfeiting charges against him in the United States.

Lucky was beyond surprise and accepted the bad news as routine. He couldn't imagine why there were any charges pending against him. He later learned that when his ship returned to the United States after his arrest in Greece, his ship bunk had been searched and a quantity of counterfeit money had been found. The case had been presented to a grand jury. Lucky was indicted and a bench warrant had been issued for his arrest. Since he had been in jail in Greece, nothing could be done. Now that he was back home, the case was reactivated.

Lucky was assigned a legal-aid counsel who made sure that the court was told of what had happened to him in Greece. A sympathetic court decided to dismiss the indictment against him and let him pick up the broken pieces of his life. The necessary paperwork was completed in record time. Lucky was released. He had lost everything — his liberty, his family, his ambitions and his beloved Millie. He heard rumors that she was happily married and had two children. Lucky knew that nothing was to be gained by trying to contact her.

I met Lucky shortly after his release. He was surprised that I had changed from the State Police to the U. S. Secret Service. He managed some humor by saying: "I hope you didn't make the change just to keep track of me." We stopped to have a cup of coffee and Lucky told me the story of his arrest and confinement. When we finished, I also made a feeble attempt at some humor. I said: "Well, you did it again — you beat me twice in just under ten years." He turned and said, with a rueful attempt at a smile, "They don't call me 'Lucky' for nothing!"

The Bat Man

During World War II, Washington, D.C., like most other cities, was quite a dreary place to be, especially at night. The windows of all homes and businesses had to be blacked out. Included in the blackout were automobile headlights. The windows in the White House were covered with heavy blinds and life after dark was pretty monotonous. On this particular weekend, the President had decided to spend a quiet sojourn at his home in Hyde Park, New York. Mrs. Roosevelt elected not to go with the President, but invited some lady friends to the White House for dinner.

At the time I was assigned on temporary duty to the Washington Field Office and was told to report to the White House until dinner was over and the guests had departed. After everyone arrived and dinner was underway, my post was in the Usher's Office, just inside the main entrance. I found a nice comfortable chair and hoped the ladies would enjoy their evening in relaxed peace and quiet.

I leaned back in the chair, put my feet up on a low desk, and laced my hands behind my head. From this relaxed position, my gaze lazily and naturally was drawn to the upper wall near a corner spot at the ceiling. There, hanging upside down, clinging to a molding, was a bat! I immediately jumped up and decided it was my duty to kill this wretched mammal. Somewhere I had learned that bats suck your blood, build nests in your hair, and spread all kinds of dreadful pestilence. None of which was going to happen on my shift!

I looked around the room and saw a long window pole. I grabbed it and started poking at the bat. He became disconcerted with my attempts to dislodge him and he immediately began to fly around the usher's office. I was right behind him with my pole and the determination that he was not going to disturb the ladies. The bat had other ideas!

After flying around the room and the main hall area he decided to fly directly into the dinning room. His presence caused quite a disturbance. Some of the ladies dove under the table, others threw bread rolls at it, and there was plenty of screaming all around. Mrs. Roosevelt in her controlled manner kept explaining, "Oh, my goodness," as she kept patting the back of her hair. All the while, I was trying to down the beast with the pole. In the midst of all the mayhem, one of the ushers calmly pulled back the blinds and opened the window. The dazed bat made a beeline for the open window and flew out.

I returned to my post, feeling very proud of myself. It isn't every day that you prevent a bat attack on the First Lady. I knew Mrs. Roosevelt had suffered some embarrassment, but I felt I had seen my duty and attended to it.

The following day, I received a telephone call from the Chief's office and was told to report to the Chief — immediately. I straightened my tie, combed my hair, and ran upstairs to meet the Chief. I was fully prepared to accept the accolades I felt certain were forthcoming. I had less than a year on the job and it would be a thrill to receive an award from the head man in the Service.

When he started off by roaring, "What in the hell were you trying to do last night?" I knew better than to expect any praise for my actions. I started to reply, but he continued, "Do you know you caused quite a commotion in the White House last night? You caused the First Lady and her friends a lot of embarrassment with your stupid antics. Why couldn't you leave the bat well enough alone? He probably would still be hanging there, or at least you could have waited until everyone went home, and then you could have done your wild circus act. I don't need animal trainers on this job. What I need are agents that have common sense!" He kept up the tirade for several more minutes. I was waiting to tell him about how these particular wild creatures can suck your blood and build nests in your hair. Then on second thought I decided to keep my mouth shut and not make matters any worse.

After he had finished berating me, he said, "Motto, I wanted to fire you on the spot when I heard about your antics, but I didn't know what to charge you with." He then sent me on my way saying, "There have always been bats in the White House!" I left his office and slowly walked down the stairs. No medal, no congratulations, just one dejected U. S. Secret Service agent who just had all the air taken out of his wings.

I don't remember who first said it, perhaps it was Shakespeare, but it was very appropriate, "No good deed goes unpunished." The bat? Well, I heard when it left the Executive Branch it flew to Congress where it lived quite happily in the Capitol Rotunda.

I Learn to Pray

In 1941, a letter signed "Lonesome" was written to the President. The letter contained a direct threat against the President's life. The envelope bore a return address of a rundown, midtown New York location.

Shortly thereafter, I went to the address on Lonesome's letter. Although the vestibule inside the building had mailboxes, the names on them had long since disappeared. I knocked on the door of a ground floor apartment. The door opened and before I could make any inquiries, a gun was placed over my left ear; I was then invited inside the apartment. He could have handled me very easily without the gun. The man holding the gun was in his early thirties, about 6 feet 1 inches, and 200 pounds. His face was pockmarked and his eyes were wild. The room was plastered with holy pictures and religious statues; each one with a candle flickering before it. Rotogravure photos of the last two Popes, the Cardinal and other religious leaders also adorned the walls.

He pulled me across the room and unceremoniously threw me onto the top of the bed. With the gun still pointing at my head he said: "The D.A. sent you, didn't he?" I said, "No! and I don't know any D.A.!" I was about to say I had knocked at the wrong door when he shouted, "Well, who sent you?" I said, without thinking, "The Cardinal sent me!" Looking at me in astonishment he said, "You mean he wants to see me?" I said, "Yes, that's why I came to your apartment." He was so happy he couldn't contain himself. Then he said: "I'll get dressed and be right with you." A moment later he added, "Let's pray." Lonesome sank to his knees. I did too. He then recited the first part of the Lord's Prayer and I said the remainder. We continued on through the rosary. I was praying just as fervently as he was, grateful for the time I had spent in a parochial school. After the praying session, careful to have his gun nearby, he got dressed.

While Lonesome took his time getting dressed , he told me why he hated the D.A. According to him, he had been a private investigator several years before. There had been a scandal in one of the state mental institutions, concerning the use of inmates in medical experiments that resulted in many deaths. Lonesome said the D.A. asked him if he would get himself committed to the institution to report about conditions there. He agreed to take the assignment and was successful in getting himself committed. He carefully monitored all the conditions at the hospital and shortly had enough information to prove there were a lot of illegal activities occurring there. Carefully noting everything down on paper, he tried to smuggle the information to the D.A. He was unsuccessful and was found out. When the hospital authorities discovered he was an undercover agent for the D.A., they put him in a kind of solitary confinement. All his efforts to reach the D.A. were unsuccessful.

While telling this story, Lonesome's mood fluctuated. By the end he was raving, wielding the gun menacingly at me as though I were the D.A. He continued, saying that about three months ago he escaped from the hospital. He had stolen some money and rented this furnished two-room apartment. All during his confinement his only solace was praying, he said. He was sure the Lord heard his prayers and gave him the opportunity to escape. He was very anxious to see the Cardinal and get his help. If that didn't work, he had also written letters to the Governor and the President, threatening them if they didn't help him. I remembered that nowhere in his letters did he identify himself as anything but "Lonesome" nor did he ever explain what kind of help he needed.

I asked him to hurry since the Cardinal had many appointments and we had to be on time. Although I convinced him to leave his gun at home, he insisted on carrying a large butcher knife in his belt. We finally left his apartment and got to the street. I told him I had to call the Cardinal's residence to let him know we were en route. He wasn't happy about the delay, but agreed. Although there were several opportunities for me to draw my own gun and try to take him, it was clear I'd be no match for him in physical combat. Gunfire was something that could be put off till the very end if there were no other alternatives.

I made a hurried call to the office and quickly explained my predicament to the squad leader. He suggested that we go to the local hospital's psychiatric ward. He would have several agents meet me outside to help with Lonesome. As we neared the hospital, I recognized a Secret Service car with two agents behind me. They signaled they would help when I pulled up to the entrance of the psychiatric division. Upon recognizing the institution, Lonesome reached over and grabbed me. I stopped the car and began struggling with him. In a few seconds, the two agents who had been following us jumped into the fray. The issue was in doubt until we were joined by two uniformed patrolmen who were near the hospital entrance. Lonesome was relieved of his knife, but not before he managed to do some minor damage with it. With the help of a hospital restraining jacket, Lonesome was subdued and admitted to the hospital.

Lonesome, we learned, had spent most of his adult life in various mental institutions and was considered a homicidal maniac. He had escaped from a maximum security institution, after killing two people and stabbing several others. He was a good one to get off the street. I prayed again. I gave a prayer of thanks for the outcome.

Reliving *Les Miserables*

Two men, Joe Bianco and Lou Caldor, were believed to be responsible for the manufacture and distribution of a very deceptive counterfeit $10 note. Neither man appeared to have the technical ability to manufacture the notes, but information from informants placed them squarely in the middle of the operation. This particular note would appear, get good distribution, then suddenly disappear from the streets. Every lead, however minute, was followed. Many people were arrested for passing these notes, but no distributors of any consequence were found. No one would talk. When the note appeared, Bianco and Caldor would disappear. When the note disappeared, Caldor and Bianco would return to the scene. Surveillance was unsuccessful because both men were extremely "tail conscious." Following them never produced any productive leads.

Caldor was a tall, thin man with a sallow complexion who emigrated to America in the mid-1920s. Bianco, a short, fat, ruddy complexion man, came to the United States with his parents when he was four years old. He had been raised in a ghetto on the lower east side.

Surprisingly, neither man had a criminal record. Caldor was once questioned by the police after he tried to pass a counterfeit quarter to a storekeeper. He convinced the authorities that he was an innocent victim and was released. Later information made him a prime suspect in the manufacturing of counterfeit coins. In spite of the investigations that followed, Caldor was never arrested. No one seemed to know how or when Caldor and Bianco met.

On one occasion, when I was watching Bianco's home, I saw Bianco drive out of his garage. I watched him go the wrong way on a one-way street, circle the neighborhood twice, then drive two blocks from the subway where he parked his car. I made no attempt to follow him and accidentally met him when he left his car and walked toward the subway. I let him get a good distance away from me. I casually walked to the subway and proceeded to the opposite end of the station. The train pulled in, Bianco got on, and so did I. But just before the door closed, Bianco jumped off the train and stood on the platform, grinning from ear to ear and waving as I passed by him in the train. There was no problem explaining it to the boss. He had heard this story before.

Five years later, after World War II, I was assigned to the case again. Very little work had been done on the case during the war years, and although the counterfeit note was no longer of any particular concern, the Secret Service wanted the investigation continued and the file brought up to date. The only interesting information a prior investigation disclosed was that Caldor had purchased an old house with several acres of land about 150 miles from New York City. The old house, which was on top of a mountain, could have been the place where the notes were printed. The files indicated that exhaustive investigations had been made in the area. Surveillance had been maintained around the clock. Agents had obtained rooms in a nearby town and had posed as migrant workers, surveyors, and state highway employees. One agent spent three days at Caldor's farmhouse helping him with some painting and odd jobs. The agent saw enough of the house to convince him that the printing plant was not there. When information was received that the counterfeit plates were sealed in the wall of a well on the property, an agent lowered himself into the well when Caldor was away, and carefully inspected it. He found no indication that anything was hidden in the well. The house was surreptitiously entered but still there was no evidence that Caldor was making notes at the farm.

Both men had lost their wives in the meantime. Their children married and left the area. Few new leads were developed. After many months, I interviewed one of Bianco's distant relatives and learned that Bianco had once worked in the "needle trade." He supposedly had been employed as a finisher on clothing and had worked somewhere in the Midwest for a time. He had allegedly returned to New York, although his address was unknown. Although the unions couldn't have been expected to be very cooperative in aiding an investigation, they were approached. A canvas of the various unions was proving unsuccessful. Once, at a union, the only person around was the union's president. He and I had a nice chat. He said he understood my problem, but he was loyal to his members. I explained how much time and effort had been invested in finding this man who was responsible for flooding the city with bogus bills. He said: "Isn't that what you're getting paid for?" I said, "Yes, but what would your reaction be if you found your treasury loaded with counterfeit bills, or if some of your members found counterfeit bills in their pay envelopes?"

He asked to be excused and returned several minutes later with a card in his hand. He said he had to leave again and requested that I not look at the card. After he left the room, I picked up the card. It was Bianco's membership card. It had a Brooklyn address on it.

Caldor still had to be found. The last information on him, when he became a restaurant worker, was several years old. The trail was cold. The only possibility was to locate an old paramour, Sonja Biald, who had lived for several years with Caldor after his wife had died. Finally, a woman with the same name who was receiving welfare at a downtown address in New York City, was found. The only information on her was that she was ill, didn't have any relatives, and lived alone. Her address was verified. Sonja had become a recluse who made nocturnal raids on the neighborhood garbage cans. The neighbors had all agreed she should have been placed n a mental institution. The owner of the tenement said a man had paid Sonja's rent years ago. From the description, that man had to be Caldor.

Caldor still owned the upstate farmhouse, although his appearances there were infrequent. The house was in disrepair but the property was valuable and very much sought after; however, no one could locate the owner. The taxes were scrupulously paid by a bank money order drawn in midtown, New York. An investigation at the bank showed that Caldor had deposited several thousand dollars several years before, authorizing the bank to pay the taxes. He no longer used the address he gave the bank.

The nearest neighbors to the farmhouse said Caldor generally came up by train and was brought to the farm by taxi. One taxi driver remembered Caldor. He said it had been several years since he had driven Caldor, but he remembered him as a quiet, inoffensive man who said little on the journey from the railroad station to his farm. I pressed the cab driver for any information he could recall. He remembered that Caldor said he was living in New York City with his "wife" who was too sick to make the trip with him. The taxi driver said that Caldor had mentioned that he was a "salad man" in a large hotel in New York City.

The long, tedious job of checking all the hotels in New York City began. Finally, after checking over thirty hotels, the management said that Caldor was, indeed, working there, and was considered to be one of the better "salad men" in the business. He had been employed there for several years and was well thought of there. He kept to himself and rarely socialized with anyone.

It was then fourteen years since I had first become involved in the case. It was time to bring this long, drawn-out investigation to a conclusion by interviewing the two men and closing the case. That was all that could be done. They beat us at our own game. They had gambled and had won, and we had to own up to the fact that, for the present, we were losers. There was no way we could change it. The statute of limitations erased any violations that either man might have committed. It had been several years since any of the notes had appeared. There was no indication that either man had been in contact with the other.

I knocked at the door at Bianco's rooming house several times. All I could hear were moans coming from the other side of the door. Finally, pushing my way through the flimsy door, I found a man more dead than alive in a miserable room. Bianco was obviously in much pain. He was apparently in an advanced stage of arthritis or rheumatism. No one else was in the apartment, so I stayed with Bianco, called for an ambulance, and waited until it arrived. When he was being carried out, he finally looked at me and asked, "What's your name?" I said, "Just remember Carmine." He made a feeble effort of thanking me. I told him I would see him after he got out of the hospital.

Several weeks later I called again at his rooming house. This time he was able to answer the door. When he saw me, his face lit up and he said, "Carmine?" I said, "Yes," went in and sat down. He looked at me quizzically and finally asked, "But who are you and why are you here?"

I said, "Joe, my name is Carmine Motto and I'm a U. S. Secret Service agent. I'm going to level with you and maybe you'll do the same for me." He poured a glass of wine and said, "Go ahead; I still don't know why you want me." I then told him that a long time ago he had been suspected of being a counterfeiter, that the files on him were voluminous, that I had spent many months investigating him, that I was not in a position to make a case against him, and that the statute of limitations prevented me from taking any action on whatever he might tell me. I then spent the next fifteen minutes bringing him up to date on all the things we had learned over the years. During my monologue he kept shaking his head in disbelief. I pressed on and on, trying to convince him that we knew all about the counterfeiting operation and that we wanted to finally close the case. The pursuit of this investigation was getting ridiculous, I said, especially since it could be easily closed by the surrender of the printing plates. Warning him of the futility of passing or distributing any more counterfeit notes, I told him he and Caldor were my special problems and I would watch them for as long as they lived.

Bianco remembered being followed by government agents for many years. He said that although he had moved with a fast crowd in his younger days, he did not remember Caldor, that if he had known him they were only casual acquaintances. He agreed he had been no angel and had done many wrong things in his life; however, he had never been arrested and he said he had never knowingly done any work with counterfeit money. After he managed to answer most of the specific questions I asked, he wanted to know if I was sure he was a counterfeiter. I lied and said "Yes." Actually, after talking with him, I was not sure. As I left I told him I would be back again. He smiled and said he would be happy to see me anytime.

In the following weeks, my visits were more to the point. It was clear that I wanted the plates if they still existed. Bianco smiled a bit, shook his head and said, "Carmine, my friend, if I could, I would make you a set of these plates so you could be happy. But, I am a tailor and I know nothing about plates. Can't you believe that? You have my permission to search and ask any questions. Please forget about ancient history and go after the people that rob and steal."

After making another trip upstate and talking with some of Caldor's neighbors, I learned that he had been making more visits to the farm. The indications were that he was going to fix up the place and live there permanently. I walked over to the house, walked around it, and decided to jimmy a window and go in. There was very little furniture in the old house. After twenty minutes, I had poked my nose into everything and found nothing.

Caldor had a set pattern. He would arrive on a Friday and stay until Sunday. The best place to interview him would be at the farmhouse, where he would be alone and, perhaps, more at ease.

The following Friday, a hot, sunny afternoon, I pulled up to the house. Caldor was sitting on the front steps. I walked up and greeted him by his full name. He invited me to have a glass of ice water and sit with him on the steps. He didn't ask me what I wanted. I asked him if he knew me. He smiled and said, "No." I said, "Remember, years ago, when you were a bad guy?" He said, "Who, me, a bad guy? Naw, what did I do?" I told him about the counterfeit money and what a problem he had been, telling as much as I knew about him. In the middle of my speech he burst out laughing and when he was through he said, "What's your name again?" I said, "Carmine." "Carmine," he said, "let's go inside and get something to eat." He told me when he arrived in this country, his first job had been in the coal mines. From there he moved to New York where he lived in a rooming house with a group of men who were gangsters, many of whom had done time in prison for various crimes. His association with them lasted a number of years. He then commented, "Carmine, if you had only came to me then, maybe I could have made your life easier." He then denied every allegation I had accused him of. He told me how ridiculous it was to think a coal miner could print counterfeit money and was evasive on pertinent questions. He spent the early evening relating the misadventures of his youth. Then he told me of his relationship with Sonja and of her recent demise. He was absolutely alone in the world, he said, and that while he was well off financially, he was a very lonesome man. As the day ended, he knew what I was after and I knew it was going to be a tough, if not impossible, mission. We parted on a very friendly note. He told me to come visit him again and I replied that he could be certain that I would be a frequent visitor. I suggested that he read *Les Miserables* in his spare time. He waved good-bye and, as I turned my back, he laughed and shouted, "Be careful, Carmine, don't fall into the well."

In the intervening months, I called on Bianco and Caldor from time to time. Caldor did his homework well. Whenever I met him, he would refer to me as "Javert" and I naturally would call him "Jean." The relationship continued for several more years, although my visits became less and less frequent since none of the counterfeit notes had shown up for years.

Due to a heavy case load and a lot of out-of-town work, I neglected this case for six months. While I had been away, a package had arrived at the office for me. Since the address on it was incorrect, delivery had been delayed. Inside the package were the plates. There was a midtown New York postmark, a date, and little else to indicate where they came from or who sent them. I checked back with the two old men.

Bianco was a hopeless cripple in an upstate hospital. He had been completely bedridden for several months. Caldor had died at his upstate farmhouse about ten days after the package had been sent. No one knew where he had been on the date the package had been mailed. He had left a considerable amount of money; however, there was no will. Ironically, his estate was eventually forfeited to the State.

Ken and His Fortune

During the time I worked in Washington, D.C. for the U. S. Secret Service, my partner George and I received word that the Bureau of Engraving and Printing was missing some money. We spoke with the agent in charge of security at the Bureau. He told us that a large amount of incomplete bills were missing. The missing money lacked serial numbers and the treasury seal, which were to have been the last items to be printed. Some of the bills were turning up in the Washington area; as yet, there were no leads.

George and I decided to examine the personnel folders of all the individuals involved in the printing process, up to the printing of the serial numbers and seal. We went through all the folders and there was nothing particularly revealing about any of them. We pondered for several hours and agreed that we would concentrate on the newest male employees. We chose two men who had been working for the Bureau less than a month in the suspected areas.

Tom, the first subject, was married with two children and lived in nearby Virginia. We followed him during selected hours. His life pattern was simple. He worked in the Bureau, went home, had supper, then drove a cab for several hours each night. Although any man who worked that hard wouldn't be likely to have a small fortune in stolen money, we followed him when he wasn't working and tried to pinpoint all the stores in which he shopped. Whenever possible, we examined the money he spent right after he left the store. The money was always genuine. Tom was rapidly becoming a poor suspect. The notes were still coming in, a few at a time, and we had all but eliminated Tom as the passer.

We then turned our attention to Ken. He was a young kid of 22 and came from a good family. Ken was a newlywed, living with his wife in small apartment in Maryland. Ken's life was typical for a young man his age. He worked, went home for supper. Then, he and his wife would go to a movie, play bingo, or occasionally, go out to a bar. On every occasion we checked the money he spent. We had hoped to pick up a bill that didn't have a serial number or seal. We had no such luck.

One morning George suggested we run Ken's name through the Identification Bureau to see if he had a record. I thought that it would be a waste of time since Ken was a government employee and must have been checked for a record and references. But, as George continued to insist, we ran Ken's name through and, sure enough, he had a criminal record. He had been arrested twice for theft and was then on probation.

The security agent at the Bureau looked at Ken's file and told us that Ken had been hired on his own word that he did not have a record. He added that getting help was a problem and the agency was way behind in its investigations of new employees. Sooner or later, he assured us, Ken's record would have come to light.

In light of this latest information, we redoubled our efforts to cover Ken. We were on his tail every night after he left work and checked the bills he spent in our presence. We did everything possible to try to solve the case. Several uneventful weeks passed and we still had no evidence. The bills continued to show up and we continued to get nowhere. Finally, George and I agreed that we should detain Ken for questioning.

The next day, as Ken left the building after work, we stopped him, searched him and his locker, and took him to the security office for questioning. Ken was clean and he vehemently denied any knowledge of the stolen bills. These were the days before all the Supreme Court decisions regarding how and when a person could be questioned; Ken was questioned for several hours, without luck. It was decided to release him, but to separate him from his job since he had lied on his job application when he said he had never been arrested.

We had worked on Ken long and hard and it was time to let him go. I decided to walk him from the office to the main entrance of the building. After a few feet he asked, "Where are we going?" For want of anything better to say, I said, half in jest, "To jail." He stopped dead in his tracks and said, "You fellows have been pretty decent to me. I'm going to level with you. Let's go back and talk some more."

George was delighted to hear that Ken wanted to talk. Our suspect said that his job at the Bureau was to take skids of money from one location to another. In the course of his work, he noticed that the guards were lax in their surveillance. One day, he took a package of money from the skid and hid it under his shirt until he had the opportunity to put it into his locker. From there, he took a little home every night. He said he didn't tell his wife what he had done, but always gave her one or two of the bills whenever she needed money. He said he never passed any of them himself.

He took us out to a wooded area near where he lived, and then stopped in his tracks and refused to go any further. He said he just realized the deep trouble he was in and that he would undoubtedly have to go to jail for a long time. The situation was disheartening. It would have been impossible, naturally, to search the woods.

We weren't far from Ken's home, so we decided to to go to his house and speak with his wife. We asked him to follow us. He said, "Where to?" "To your house," we replied, "We're going to search the premises and speak to your wife." This didn't appeal to Ken in the least. He couldn't understand why we were involving his wife. We told Ken that since he had admitted that his wife, knowingly or unknowingly, had passed the bills, she was involved. He asked us to wait for a minute while he thought it over again. He paced back and forth for several minutes and then, pointing to a tree about ten feet away, said: "Okay, just go over to that tree and you'll find the money inside it."

We walked over to the tree and saw a big hole in the bottom. I reached in and took out a bag containing over $9,000 in unfinished bills. We initialed the bills for evidence and then returned to the security room at the Bureau. We notified a number of pleased superiors that Ken had confessed and that the bulk of the stolen money had been retrieved.

We were told to take Ken over to U. S. Secret Service Headquarters immediately since some high-level people wanted to question him about how the security system inside the nation's currency print shop could be improved. We rushed Ken over to Headquarters and into a big conference room full of top managers, supervisors, and senior agents where he became the center of attraction. Ken seemed to enjoy every minute of the questioning, and contributed his own ideas about how security could be tightened up to prevent similar "walk-aways."

Just before the conference broke up, I decided to ask Ken just one more question. I asked him if, at any time during the investigation, he knew he was being followed. He smiled and said, "Sure, I knew I was being followed and I knew you guys must be U. S. Secret Service agents." I asked him how he knew (and I should have bitten my tongue for asking him). He replied, "The first time you whistled at my wife I knew you were agents." Of all the silly, stupid answers to get from a defendant, this one was totally unexpected. We had never whistled at his wife. If he was looking for an opportunity to get even with us, he sure picked the right time and the right audience. And, I walked directly into it. Every supervisor from Headquarters was there! I was speechless and George looked like he was in shock. Disapproving looks were visible on every face around the table.

Subsequently, every time George or I entered the squad room, we were greeted with whistles. As the lawyers say, "Don't ask a question, if you don't know the answer!"

Redeeming Mutilated Bills

One day the office received the remnants of about $150 in torn and mutilated bills. Accompanying the bills was an affidavit from the owner swearing that the missing parts of the bills had been destroyed and were no longer available. He requested full value on the bills. Several days later, another letter was received with approximately $150 in mutilated currency accompanied with an affidavit indicating that the missing parts of the bills had been destroyed and were no longer available. Both communications came from the same town. These letters wouldn't have raised any eyebrows except that the remnants in each envelope were the missing portions of the money from the other envelope. Someone was lying and trying to collect twice for the same bills.

I was given the case for investigation. The first letter was from a Mr. White, an affable bachelor, who owned a bar and grill in a city not far from Washington D.C.. The second letter was from a bank in the same city. I proceeded to Mr. White's business establishment. He was a good-natured man, who appeared quite anxious to answer any questions. I told him I was from the Secret Service and was looking into the matter of his mutilated currency. I asked him to explain how the money became so mutilated.

He said that he generally closed his bar at about two o'clock in the morning; after making a night deposit around midnight. Any money he took in after midnight, he would take home with him. He said he usually put the money in his back pocket. That particular morning, he came home quite tired and rested on the sofa in his living room. He played with his dog for awhile and then went upstairs to bed. The next morning he came downstairs and found pieces of money all over the living room. His roll of bills had fallen out of his back pocket onto the sofa and apparently his dog had jumped on the sofa and tore up the money. Mr. White retrieved as many pieces as were around and forwarded them all to the Treasury with the necessary affidavit.

I said, "Then there is no doubt in your mind that what you say is true, and the missing pieces are destroyed and not available?" He said, "Absolutely correct. There is no chance that the missing pieces would turn up anywhere." I then told him that there was something wrong because a local bank had sent in the missing pieces with an affidavit swearing that the remainder of their notes no longer existed. Mr. White's face turned colors. There was no doubt that he was an honest gentleman, but there appeared to be no resolution to the dilemma. He seemed genuinely interested in finding out what happened. I invited him to join me at the bank where we could find out who returned the matching portions of the money. He was happy to come along.

At the bank, we learned that the bank was merely acting as a depositor's agent in sending the portions of money to the Treasury. The bank gave me the name and address of the depositor, a Mrs. Folsom.

When I told Mr. White that a Mrs. Folsom was the person who gave the bank the mutilated currency, he turned pale and said that the whole thing was crazy. He knew this woman very well; she was his next-door neighbor, a widow, and his pretty steady date. He kept shaking his head, saying that he couldn't understand what had happened. I suggested that he come with me to his friend's home and perhaps we would get the answers. He asked if we couldn't just forget the whole matter and make believe it never happened. I told him that the mystery had to be resolved since one of the affidavits was false. Somewhere there was an answer.

We drove to Mrs. Folsom's home, which was next door to Mr. White's. Mrs. Folsom was quite surprised to see us; especially when I introduced myself as a U. S. Secret Service agent. I told her that I was investigating the bills she had given the bank for redemption and I was anxious to learn where she got the mutilated currency. This upset Mrs. Folsom. She became embarrassed, hid her face in her hands and ran upstairs. Mr. White and I looked at each other and he asked, "Where do we go from here?" I said, "She's your girlfriend; see if you can make her come downstairs. She is obviously very upset." He was successful, finally, in getting her to come speak with me.

She said that one morning Mr. White's dog was playing in her front lawn. He defecated on the grass so Mrs. Folsom got a shovel and picked up the waste. She noticed that there was something that looked like money in the dog's excretion. Mrs. Folsom got a pair of tweezers and carefully extracted the pieces of money. The same thing happened the next day. Again, she extracted the pieces and washed them off. She mentioned the incident to the man at the bank and he told her that it was possible to redeem the pieces through the U. S. Treasury. He offered to have the pieces redeemed for her. Mrs. Folsom said that she hadn't told Mr. White about it because she had wanted to surprise him when the new bills arrived. Along with the money, she was going to suggest that the dog be put in a museum as a wonder dog that could make his owner rich. Before she had finished the story, Mr. White roared with laughter, rolling all over the floor until he almost made himself sick. By this time, Mrs. Folsom and I were also laughing heartily.

Mr. White then asked if I would join him and Mrs. Folsom for supper. He told me confidently that he intended to propose to her soon. He said, "You shouldn't let a woman who is that careful about money, get away." I agreed with him, but didn't take him up on the meal. Thereafter, whenever I was in town, I'd stop by for a visit. Needless to say, the conversation always turned to dogs, especially Mr. White's golden retriever.

Betty and the Torn Bills

Flores Medina worked as a cargo handler on the docks in New York. He worked long and hard to support his family. He "shaped-up" every morning and after several years became a regular and worked quite often. On payday he usually joined some of the boys at a waterfront bar where he would have a few drinks before going home to his wife and five children.

On one particular night, Flores had more than his usual two or three drinks. One of his friends was getting married and the boys decided to have a bachelor party for him. It was after 10 o'clock when Flores left the bar. He had to walk about seven dark blocks to get to the subway. He had gone about three blocks when he heard footsteps behind him. He turned to get a look at who was following him, but it was too late. The mugger's arm was already around Flores' throat and an ice pick was pressed against his temple. Someone else was going through his pockets. Flores wasn't about to let anyone take the money that he worked so hard for without a fight. He fought hard but was no match for the ice pick that was repeatedly jabbed into his arms, chest, and back. His attackers then ran off leaving him bleeding in the street. A by-passer found him sprawled out in the dark street in a pool of blood. An ambulance raced to the scene. Flores was examined by a young intern, was found to be still alive, and was rushed to the emergency ward of the city hospital.

It was unknown whether he would recover from the severe beating and multiple stab wounds that he had received. He was stitched up, given several pints of blood, and admitted to the hospital for further treatment. All during the emergency treatment he had kept his right fist tightly closed. No one tried to open his hand until he was out of the emergency room and placed in a regular hospital bed. When he regained consciousness he was asked what he was clutching in his hand. He opened his fingers and showed the torn remnants of his money. He had held onto his money.

Police Detective Curran was assigned to the case. He called me to ask how Flores could redeem the remaining portions of the money. I advised him to send the bills and an affidavit to the currency redemption division of the Treasury Department. That would serve two purposes: first, it would get him his money back, and second, in the event the other halves showed up, it would give the police a lead on the muggers. Flores got his money and within a month was discharged from the hospital.

The stolen remaining portions of Flores' money were received at the Redemption Division three months after the crime was committed. The money was sent by a woman named Betty who gave a fashionable mid-town New York address as her home. I was assigned to the investigation and decided to interview Betty. After making myself known to the doorman, I entered the building. Betty wasn't in, so I slipped a note under her door asking her to call me.

The following day she called and wanted to know the reason for my visit. I told her that I was required to interview her regarding the request she made to have some mutilated currency redeemed. She asked me if there was a problem. I said there wasn't, but it was still necessary. She seemed annoyed at the red tape, but agreed to be interviewed on the following afternoon.

When I arrived at the building the next day, the doorman accompanied me to a young girl who was waiting in the lobby. She introduced herself as Betty and demanded to see my credentials. I showed them to her, she examined them carefully, and then took me to her apartment. The apartment was exquisitely furnished and while I was surveying it she said, "I might just as well answer all your questions now. I am 19 years old and the apartment belongs to me. I'm a music student and a musician." She motioned to a guitar in a gesture to prove she was telling the truth. She continued, "The rent for the apartment is $400 a month. Now, is there anything else you want to know?" "Yes," I said, "How can you afford this setup?" Without blinking one of her false eyelashes, she said, "I entertain men." This, at least, explained why she was careful about who she let into her apartment. It also answered a lot of other questions.

I asked her about the bills she sent to the Treasury for redemption. She said a "client" had brought them to her. He told her he won them gambling and gave them to her in payment for the evening's entertainment. I asked her for the man's name. She claimed she didn't know. She said that the person who gave her the bills was a first-time customer who gave her the torn bills as a sort of tip. She refused to say who recommended this customer or how she came to know him. She insisted that she couldn't give me any more information. At that point, I didn't feel compelled to tell her why I was so interested in the man since I knew she was lying. I didn't want to give her any information. She hadn't submitted an affidavit with the money so as far as I was concerned, she hadn't committed any crime. I told her I thought she was lying and that it might have serious repercussions. She acted as though she didn't care, but appeared quite relieved when I got up and left.

When I returned to the office, I called Detective Curran and informed him about what had happened. He asked that I retain the bills in the event they were needed as evidence. He said he was going to look into the matter some more and give Betty a hard time. And that he did, because a month later, Betty called me and said she wanted to talk. I invited her down to the office for another interview. She showed up the following day and she was very angry. She started off by saying she had been interviewed by Detective Curran and had told him the same story she had told me. He hadn't believed her and had promised to end to her idyllic existence. She said her house had been raided several times since the interview. Her "clients" had been questioned coming and going. The management had ordered her to move. She complained that she was being treated as a common prostitute; she admitted she entertained men, but she wasn't running a whorehouse. I told her that I didn't understand and, frankly, it didn't make any difference to me. I knew she had some vital information. She chose not to give it to the authorities. Someone had to pay and she hadelected herself, She said, "Okay, I am going to give you the whole story right from the beginning, so you'll understand how I got into this business."

I said, "Betty, if you are going to tell it to me, tell it straight and don't give me the routine." She asked, "What kind of routine?" I said, "Try this one. 'I was born in a small mining town in Pennsylvania. I was one of twelve children. Dad worked in the mines. There was never enough food to keep us all going. I can't remember when I wasn't hungry. One day there was a horrible explosion at the mine. We all ran down hoping and praying that it wasn't in Pop's shaft. It wasn't until two days later that they recovered his body. I was fifteen at the time and I realized it would be my responsibility to help raise the family. Then, one day a man came, he . . .'" Betty smiled and said, "Okay, wise guy, I heard that one too. I won't use that one. I'll save it for the soap operas."

"Well, here goes. . . I was born in the Bronx. Mom and Pop were your average middle-class couple. They had two children — me and my brother. I didn't even realize it was happening, but there came a time when my parents realized that they no longer loved each other and decided to split up. By that time I was 17 years old and saw it as my opportunity to quit school and get out on my own, which I did. I got a job as a receptionist in a large textile factory. The owner was about sixty, married, with grandchildren. He wasn't living with his wife and spent a lot of time around the office. We became friendly and he told me that he was anxious to set me up in an apartment; that he would pay all the bills. He said I wouldn't have to work; that all I had to do was be available for him whenever he wanted to be with me. I agreed and he kept his part of the bargain. He supplied me with money to keep the apartment going and to take care of food and clothes. He gave me enough notice when he intended to visit me or take me on vacation. This, of course, gave me a lot of time for myself. After all, I am not a sixty-year-old. I learned how to meet other businessmen and entertain them. This gave me a lot of extra spending money and allowed me to take music lessons. Now, can you tell me what Curran thinks he's going to accomplish by pulling cheap raids on my apartment? Does he think I'm running a common whorehouse? Does he expect to find hookers and pimps in my apartment? He keeps all my clients away by harassing me every time I get company. Is there any way to stop him?"

I suggested that she probably could make her peace with Curran by telling him the truth about the origin of the torn bills. She indicated that she would have liked to tell the truth, but she was afraid. Furthermore, she said, that she never would give Curran, "that no-good flatfoot," any information that would help him. I asked her why she had come down to the office since she could have told me all this over the phone. After some thought, she said she would tell me the truth and that I could give the information to "that no-good flatfoot fuzz" Curran on his promise that he wouldn't interfere with her "arrangements."

I excused myself and called Detective Curran on the phone. He said he'd be happy to get the information and if Betty leveled with us he wouldn't bother her anymore. I went back and told Betty that Curran agreed. She then tried to make me promise that she would never be called to testify. I told her that I wasn't in a position to make any promises. I was merely going to give the information she gave me to Curran.

She sighed, took a deep breath, and said, "About three months ago, my brother came to my apartment with two of his friends from the old neighborhood. I hadn't seen him for months, so I sent out for some food and tried to treat them as well as I could. My brother's friends, Harry and Frankie, were really impressed with my setup. They looked like rough characters and I told my brother later that I didn't want him to bring either one to the apartment again. He promised he wouldn't. Harry asked me all kinds of questions on how I paid for the apartment and who comes to visit me. I told him a bunch of lies and I was happy when they all left. I thought they were all some kind of junkies and they could only bring trouble. One evening, not long afterward, I had a couple of girlfriends at the apartment and we were later joined by some businessmen who I had known for some time. We were having a good time when there was a knock at the door. I opened it and there was Harry and Frankie. They both had guns and pushed their way in and ordered the men to take off their clothes. Then they took our money, wallets, and jewelry. When they got everything, they pushed us all into the bathroom and said they'd shoot anyone who came out. We waited for about ten minutes, then came out. I never told anyone that I knew the two men because I was scared to death. We all decided that the police would have to be notified, so we went to the nearest police station and reported the robbery to the detectives. Again, I never mentioned to anyone that I knew the men.

Nothing happened until three weeks ago, when Frankie and Harry again came to the apartment. This time I was alone. I asked them what they wanted and they said they had a business deal for me. They showed me this torn money and said it was worth a couple of hundred dollars if I took it to the bank. They said they'd give it to me for $50 because they needed some cash right away. So I gave them the $50 and they left. I later took the money to the bank and was told to mail it to the Treasury Department in Washington. So that's the whole story and it's the truth. I can't see what the big deal is, over a couple of torn bills."

I asked her if her friends that were robbed gave their true names and addresses when they reported the robbery. Betty was indignant and said, "Of course. These friends of mine aren't creeps. They're decent people." I said, "Okay, that's fine. I'm only trying to get you off the hook. If witnesses are needed against these bums, your friends can identify them and no one need know that you supplied the information; however, it will be necessary for you to get the full names and addresses of Frankie and Harry so the investigation can be completed." Betty gave it some thought and said she would call me when she got the information.

After she left, I called Curran and told him about my interview with Betty. He said he wouldn't bother her at the apartment and promised to do all he could to keep her name out of the investigation.

Three days later, Betty called. She gave me the full names of Harry and Frankie and their addresses. She found out that both had criminal records and were junkies. I thanked her and told her to be sure to file for the next police examination. She said something like "drop dead," and hung up.

Detective Curran was delighted to be supplied with the full information on his suspects. He obtained photos from headquarters and, together with the detective who had dealt with the original complaint about the apartment robbery, interviewed the victims. Five of the victims positively identified the photos of Harry and Frankie as the men who stuck them up. Curran was not successful in getting an identification from Flores Medina because Medina never did see his assailants.

Based on the identifications, Curran and his co-workers were able to get arrest and search warrants on Harry and Frankie. They hit the apartment early in the morning and struck pay dirt. The apartment was a veritable department store of stolen merchaandise. There were stolen televisions, radios, appliances, fourteen shot guns, five hand guns, assorted jewelry, clothing, and loot taken from at least ten midtown burglaries. Faced with the pile of evidence against them, Frankie and Harry pleaded guilty to a number of charges and were both sentenced to long prison terms.

There never was any need to use Betty as a witness and I didn't hear from her for a long time until one day I received a theatrical handbill in the mail. It was for an opening of a new Broadway show and Betty was listed as one of the lead actresses. Written in the corner was, "I would have made a lousy cop. Good luck, Betty."

Larry and the Spies

One rewarding aspect of police work is the element of uncertainty of each new case. You never know what twists and turns lie ahead — a case can start out as very routine, and then turn into a thriller. Or the exact opposite may occur — the case that you thought would be excting, just fizzles.

Such a case was one involving Larry. Larry was a big, strong, two-fisted man who had grown up in New York's "Hell's Kitchen" where he had been a teenaged gang leader. His first arrest had been on a robbery charge. He had followed a drunk from a local bar, mugged him, and made off with the man's wallet. Larry was caught trying to cash one of the man's checks. When his case came up in court, he was declared a juvenile delinquent and sentenced to two years in a state reformatory. During his stay in the reformatory, Larry learned how to pick pockets, break into stores, and shoplift, among other crimes. He also rekindled friendships with some of his old neighborhood buddies. While they reminisced, they made big plans for their future on the street.

Upon release, Larry returned to the old neighborhood and became involved in some store burglaries. The proceeds kept him going for awhile and, again, his successes were short-lived. In burglarizing a radio shop, Larry and his friends set off a silent alarm. They were arrested while taking radios out of the store.

Larry again stood before a judge. He pleaded guilty to burglary and was sentenced to serve four to seven years in a state prison. He made up his mind to be a model prisoner so would be paroled quickly. He came up before the parole board after five years in prison. Since he knew he couldn't be paroled without assuring the board he had employment, Larry made sure to secure work through a relative. His job consisted of driving a delivery truck for a small company whose business was transporting automotive supplies.

Larry was granted parole. He made a fairly good living and saved up enough money to marry a neighborhood girl. For awhile he led a relatively normal life. He abided by the regulations of his parole supervisor. Eventually, however, he finished his parole and could again do what he wanted. He chose to revive his friendship with the old gang. Before long, he was again involved in petty thefts.

Larry made good use of the delivery truck after working hours. He transported his friends to the thefts and then used the truck to move the merchandise. Finally, he was invited by his group to participate in a good-sized warehouse burglary. The group thought it could make an enormous amount of money if the job were successful, since the warehouse contained imported liquor. One of the men employed there was going to leave a door unlocked. Larry agreed to transport the booty to a garage that had been rented to stash the stolen liquor. The gang met near the warehouse at three in the morning and entered through the door that was left unlocked. Within an hour, they had loaded the truck and were preparing to leave. Suddenly sirens shrieked, the lights went on and the police surrounded the truck and placed everyone under arrest. Larry faced serious charges. Since he had been caught red-handed and the group had probably been infiltrated by an informant, Larry decided not to fight the case. He made the best deal he could and went back to prison.

By now, Larry was an older and more bitter prisoner. He decided to do anything he could to secure an early release from prison. He volunteered for programs and served as a human guinea pig for every medical experiment conducted at the prison. Even that didn't guarantee him an early release; but he kept trying anyway.

Larry met a fellow inmate named Max who had been transferred from another state prison. Max had seemed to be a loner. He was of German extraction and spoke with a hint of an accent. Something about him intrigued Larry. He figured Max would be someone to cultivate as a friend. Max didn't get any visitors nor did he receive any mail. All this added to the mystery that surrounded him. Both men were assigned to the same shop and the same call block. They had many opportunities to talk and Larry felt that somehow he was not wasting his time. Finally, Larry decided to ask Max some direct questions. Little by little, Max unraveled a story. He told Larry that he was in the United States illegally and was serving a term for forgery. Undoubtedly, he would be deported to Germany after his release. Each day Max told Larry a little bit more about himself. One Sunday afternoon, Max swore Larry to secrecy and then told the story of his life.

He told Larry that he had been born in a small town outside of Munich. His father had been a bank official, wealthy enough to send Max to private schools. Max had always been a restless youth, ripe for Hitler's youth movement, which he eventually joined, much to his parent's chagrin. At that time, they weren't Nazi sympathizers. They sent Max to the United States to live with relatives in Pennsylvania. Max didn't make many friends in his new country. His accent had made him the butt of many jokes in school, and he came home on many nights nursing a black eye or some bruise or another.

He desired to return to Germany. When Hitler marched into the Sudetenland, Max had just finished high school. His afterschool jobs earned him enough money to return to Germany. Upon his return, he discovered that his parents had become ardent Nazis. Shortly after his return, the Gestapo visited Max and took him to local headquarters and to question him about everything he could remember regarding his stay in America. The Gestapo told Max that everything he said would be checked and double-checked until they were certain that he could be trusted.

Max volunteered for military service, but was told to sit tight and wait for orders. Eventually he was contacted and told to prepare to return to America. Before leaving, he was sent to a special school outside of Berlin to recieve special training at an "espionage school."

At that point, Larry could hardly contain himself. He excused himself and, as soon as possible, began making notes of Max's stories. Larry was convinced that some agency would be interested in Max's story. He would use Max to his own advantage.

At subsequent meetings, Max continued his story. He told Larry that at the school he learned how to set up a short-wave radio station, how to handle explosives, pick locks, blow up factories, and make contact with other Nazi sympathizers in various cities in the United States. At times, Max instructed the class in idiomatic English to help the fledgling spies pass as Americans. Max performed his work well and was soon sent to a more advanced school. That school had been part of a submarine base in Germany and Max learned to handle a rubber boat, seamanship, survival on tropical islands, and the handling of more sophisticated explosives.

In December of 1941, after Pearl Harbor, activity at the base intensified. With the training accelerated, students felt that an important assignment was imminent. Finally the students were split into two groups and put aboard two submarines. They received orders at sea. A Gestapo agent, who told them that the voyage would be a dry run, briefed Max's group. The group would be taken to a landing spot where the submarine would anchor. The group would be put into rubber boats and would make their way to the shore. There they would hide the boats, go to a nearby town, and follow instructions. The town had a factory which manufactured airplane parts. The group was to blow up the factory, separate, follow instructions, and make contact with sympathizers who would shelter them until they received further instructions.

Max recalled that when the appointed time arrived, the group landed somewhere off the coast of France, hid their boats and carried their explosives in satchels. They followed their instructions and arrived near the factory. There, the Gestapo, who had evidently watched their every move , contacted the students. They were told it wouldn't be necessary to blow up the building. They returned to the beach, retrieved their rubber boats and boarded the waiting submarine. When they arrived in Germany, Max's class was elated to hear that since they had passed the test, they would have a short rest, after which they would be given an assignment, the success of which was important to the fatherland.

When this session ended, Larry was convinced he had something to sell. He could trade an important item like Max. Careful to mask his excitement so as not to not arouse Max's suspicions, Larry made copious notes of what Max had told him and used every opportunity to bring them up to date.

At the next meeting, Max wasn't very talkative. Larry became alarmed. Max said he was depressed because no one cared for him. When he finished doing his time, he would be deported to Germany to face an uncertain future. Larry turned on all his charm and promised Max his friendship and help. Larry shared his cigarettes with Max and performed other favors for him. Before long, Max continued his story.

Two groups had been ordered to America to engage in sabotage. One group had to land off the coast of Florida and the other off the coast of Long Island. The Long Island group carried two extra men who had to be dropped off near a Coast Guard station on Staten Island. They had to make their way to an old abandoned building near the beach, proceed to the building's cellar, dig a hole and hide a box in the foundation. Another group, who would be leaving Germany later, would eventually retrieve the box. Max said the journey to America was long and uneventful. He was in the submarine headed for Long Island and was one of the two men that would be dropped off near the Coast Guard station.

Max and his partner, Ernst, received final instructions. They were supplied with a detailed map showing the abandoned building on Staten Island. The box they carried contained a large amount of American currency, a large quantity of narcotics, a number of sophisticated explosives and incendiary devices and a quantity of master plates for counterfeiting American currency. He was told that these plates had been made by an expert engraver who, at one time, had worked for the American Bureau of Printing and Engraving and who had returned to Germany, offering his services to the Fatherland. The plan was to return the plates to the United States, get them into the hands of printers who had Nazi ties, counterfeit millions of dollars in American money, use the money for causes sympathetic to the Fatherland, and ruin the American economy. Max's orders were to bury the box and go to an upstate New York city where his contact, a trusted printer, awaited. He was told to alert the printer that the plates had arrived. Under no conditions was the printer to be told where the plates were hidden. Eventually, the plates would be taken to the printer by the later arriving group. After his chores were finished, Max would be advised where and when to make contact with the submarine for his return to Germany.

Max said that the Long Island landings went off smoothly. After the rubber boat had departed and the submarine proceeded to the vicinity of Staten Island, he and Ernst were given final instructions and set off alone in their boat.

Larry sensed, as that session had ended, that the conclusion would come soon. He knew he would have to make his move shortly. His problem then became methodological: how could he get the story to the proper authorities without being labeled an informer? Larry used each waking moment to concoct a plan to exploit Max.

At their next meeting, Max said he wanted to make sure Larry would never repeat his story. There would be a good deal for them both if Larry would cast his lot with him. Larry was ready to sign an agreement, anything, just as long as Max finished his story. Larry remembered reading about the landings from the Nazi submarines back in 1941 or 1942. He recalled that there had been some arrests, a trial, and that some, maybe all, of the spies had been executed. Nevertheless, Larry needed to hear the whole story, which Max then continued.

There was no moon the night Max and Ernst got onto their rubber boat, and the water was choppy. The box, which weighed heavily, had been placed in the center of the boat. Max and Ernst rowed toward shore. The sub slid under the water and disappeared. The choppy water made the boat so uncontrollable, it almost capsized. The movement was so violent that Ernst had been thrown from the boat into the black waters. Max called softly to Ernst, but received no answer. Straining his eyes, he saw no sign of Ernst. So Max rowed toward shore, hoping that Ernst would make it on his own. When he got near the beach, Max let the air out of the boat and disposed of it as he had been directed. He hid the box, took out his map and went looking for the abandoned building. The map was accurate. Max approached the unused building and entered with great caution. There were no doors or windows; they had been disposed of long ago. Max found his way into the cellar and felt the floor's soft, sandy dirt. Digging would be easy. He went back to the beach, retrieved the box and opened it. His eyes bulged when he saw that it contained very large amounts of American money... possibly $50,000. The box also included the explosives, narcotics, incendiary devices and plates for making counterfeit money, about which he had been previously told. He carefully buried the box as he had been instructed. He couldn't remember exactly when he had the idea, but shortly after he actually saw the money he began to think about defecting. Max thought about it for ten or fifteen minutes and then decided to steal the money. He dug up the box, took the money out, replaced the box, carefully wrapped the money and cautiously made his way to the vicinity of the Staten Island Ferry.

Several hours later, he was submerged in the commuter rush hour. He got a room in New York, a city that he knew well. He decided that before anything else, he was going to enjoy the better things in life. He purchased fine clothes, dined in the best restaurants, had innumerable dates, bought a second-hand car, and, in general, had a wonderful time.

Max never contacted the people to whom he had been ordered to report. He read about the capture of his fellow spies. He was convinced that he would never go back to Germany, nor continue his spy activities. Certain that he could find his way into the mainstream of American life, he picked up the broken pieces of his life and never admitted to anyone that he had ever left America.

Max continued that on one occasion he returned to the abandoned building, dug up the box, and buried it anew in another location close to the building. He felt certain that the box would be secure in its hiding place and he could retrieve it any time. In answer to Larry's specific questions, Max admitted that he lost most of the money gambling. After the war he had become a check forger and he was serving his second term for forgery. No one, he said, had ever learned of his spy activities for the Fatherland.

Larry asked Max to make a map showing exactly where the box had been buried. Max refused. Larry insisted and threatened to call off the whole deal unless Max drew the map. Larry then agreed to help Max retrieve the box and find a printer to produce the counterfeit money. After much bickering, Max drew a map showing where the box was buried.

With the map safely stowed away, Larry made his move. He decided that, on his brother's next visit, he would ask him to contact a distant relative who had a government job. Larry knew Al, his relative, would have no trouble in coming to the prison to talk with him. Al would contact the proper federal agency and then Larry would lay down the ground rules for a deal.

Al was a friend of mine and an investigator for another federal agency. He came to me with Larry's proposition. The first part of the deal was that I would interview Larry at the prison under a suitable pretext, possibly for income tax evasion. Al stressed that Larry didn't want me to confide in any of the prison officials or ask any questions of them until he spoke with me and a deal was made. I agreed and, within a short time, Al and I were at the prison talking with Larry. Larry carefully recited his rules. If the information proved reliable, Larry would get an immediate parole, a new truck so he could start a business, and $5,000 in cash. Unless this was agreed upon, Larry wouldn't give any information. I told Larry that I was not in a position to agree to his terms. First of all, I could not speak for the parole board and I couldn't imagine paying him $5,000 for any information. I suggested that he tell me the story and that I would evaluate it, investigate it and do the best I could for him regarding the parole and the reward. Larry was visibly upset. He believed that this was his opportunity to get released from prison and have enough money to start a new life. He refused to budge. Al then spoke to him privately, telling Larry that I could be trusted to give him better than an even shake.

After some misgivings, Larry produced his carefully prepared notes and spent the next half-hour reciting Max's life story. When he finished, he looked for signs of belief in my face. I told him I had understood the story and that Al and I could check it out in a very short time. Larry insisted that for his own protection, the prison officials not be contacted. If any information leaked out prematurely he was sure he would be a marked man in the prison.

As Al and I left and on the long ride back to the city, he filled me in on Larry's background. He assured me that Larry could be trusted to repeat only what he had heard. Larry was not a con man and had nothing to gain by fabricating a story. I mentioned that I'd like to spend about ten minutes with Max. There were many flaws in the story that only an interview with Max could straighten out. We discussed all the possibilities and finally decided we would go to the Coast Guard station, follow the map and see if the building and the box really existed.

We arrived at the station the following day and were admitted to the office of the Commandant. We were secretive about our mission and just asked for permission to obtain two shovels and to walk around the area. The Commandant walked to a closet several feet away, took out two brand new shovels and said, "Here are your shovels, now go on your way. When you finish, come back." Al and I thanked him. We were sure he was annoyed with us, perhaps because we hadn't discussed our work with him. We followed the map and, sure enough, the building was right where it was supposed to be. We entered the building and went to the cellar. The floor was just as it had been described: soft, sandy dirt. We dug exactly where we had been told to dig. No luck. We tried another spot; still no luck. We tried for several hours but found nothing. At that point the Commandant arrived, accompanied by two Coast Guard men in dungarees. The Commandant told the men to take our shovels and then proceeded to laugh uncontrollably. When he stopped laughing, he asked us to join him back at his office. Back at his office, he looked me straight in the eye and said, "Motto, you're a fool. Like so many of your kind, you're so obsessed with your job that you won't take even the simplest precautions to find out whether you're engaged on a nebulous mission." He went on to say if we hadn't been so secretive about our purpose, he could have saved us hours of labor and supplied us with the information we needed.

He repeated Max's story in greater detail than Larry. He was obviously enjoying the role he was playing. He went on and on, right up to Max's confinement on the second forgery charge. When he finished he said, "That's only half of the story and now, out of the goodness of my heart, I'll fill you in on the rest of it. Your friend, Max, was born in Brooklyn, his parents were of German extraction. He had a fairly normal boyhood; however, he was an introvert and never got along with his friends. When World War II started, he enlisted in the Coast Guard. He was stationed on Staten Island, assigned to the quartermaster shack. He stole a lot of supplies, was caught, received a court's martial, and received a bad-conduct discharge."

"After leaving the Coast Guard, he got into one scrape after another. Max got one job and stayed at it long enough to steal a couple of blank checks from the office. For awhile, he was a fairly successful forger until one day he was arrested. He did a short stint in the penitentiary. He found serving time very difficult — being sort of an introvert didn't endear him to the other prisoners. No one bothered with him and he remained a loner."

"Max was released, stayed out for several years and got himself a job in an import–export house. He did fairly well at this job and his knowledge of German was helpful as he worked for a German firm. But, when the business failed; Max was jobless again. On the last day at work he stole a book of checks that the company had intended to destroy. His knowledge of the company and its workings made it easy for Max to pass several of these checks. Several weeks after the firm closed, Max went into a check-cashing agency and attempted to cash one of the company checks. Unknown to Max, that agency belonged to a group of agencies that had banded together to exchange information about bad checks. Max's company check had already been discussed at the agency's meetings and had been placed on a "watch list" available to each agency. The man behind the cage stalled Max and notified the police. Max was arrested on the spot and again faced a judge. That time he received five to seven years."

"Max went back to prison and this time tried to mix with the prisoners. It just didn't work. Several months after arriving at the prison, Max read a story about the German spies who had landed in America from a submarine. He noticed how closely he resembled one of the spies who hadn't been executed and who had been returned to Germany after serving a sentence."

"Max decided to assume the identity of that man. He concocted the story about his landing on Staten Island. Max would tell the story to another inmate and invariably the inmate would report the matter to the authorities with a view to helping himself with the parole board."

"The investigators always ended up at this Coast Guard station. Those who were upfront with us, saved themselves a lot of work and embarrassment — those who didn't, fared no better than you gentlemen." A knock on the door interrupted the Commandant. The two Coast Guard men returned with the shiny shovels and placed them carefully in the closet. The Commandant smiled for the first time and said, "Got to have them ready for the next round of brilliant investigators that come knocking."

We left the base mentally and physically exhausted. I preferred to let Al break the news to Larry. Al later reported that Larry nearly went out of his mind when he was informed about the hoax. He attempted to attack Max in the prison yard; Max had to be transferred to another prison. It was his third transfer for the same reason.

A Day to Remember

Ernie Eastman was a paraplegic. He was one of the veterans who had come home from the war with far less than what he had when he went. He was only eighteen when he enlisted in the infantry. He had just graduated from high school and was anxious to do his part for his country. He planned to go to college after he returned and he hoped to marry Clara, his girlfriend since grammar school.

Ernie enjoyed being in the army, especially after "basic training" had finished. He enjoyed the travel, the new buddies and his newfound manliness. He liked being on his own and making his own decisions. Eventually he was shipped overseas and was one of several million soldiers fighting in Europe. Ernie was the ideal soldier. He was intelligent, eager, and obedient. He soon became a corporal, in charge of a small squad.

His service in Europe had been almost without incident. His outfit was part of the Normandy invasion. He landed about six days after D-Day and was fortunate to be in a spot where the combat action was minimal. His division moved all over the European checkerboard, and people were thinking about an end to the conflict. Then, one day, all hell broke loose. The newspapers called it the "Battle of the Bulge."

Ernie and his squad were victims of the first day's surprise: a mortar shell landed right in the area where Ernie and his men stood. Ernie was out of the war. Days passed before he knew how badly he really had been hurt. He had awakened in a makeshift hospital, his body numb. A quick look around the room convinced him that many more were worse off than he was. A doctor came. Ernie could recall having heard the word "paraplegic" before, but he wasn't quite sure knew what it meant. It took the young doctor five minutes to explain to Ernie that he had lost both legs and had become a paraplegic.

At the first opportunity, he was flown home for further treatment and rehabilitation. He stayed at the hospital for six months. After he was discharged, he completed the endless paperwork necessary for receiving veteran's benefits.

Finally, Ernie came home in his wheelchair. He had been away for over two years. He was a bit apprehensive about returning because he knew people would feel sorry for him and he just didn't need that. The brightest part of his return was the reunion with his family and, of course, with Clara. It soon became evident that Clara's affections had remained true and she was anxious to marry him.

A few months later, Clara and Ernie were married. He had set up a small, but comfortable home and tried to find his place in the world. Ernie found a part-time job in a local factory and, together with his disability pension, they managed to get by. The pension check arrived around the third of each month and Clara was usually at home to receive it. One day, the mailman made his rounds, dropped the check in their mailbox, and rang the bell so Clara or Ernie would know the check had arrived.

Clara had dropped Ernie off at the factory and did some shopping before returning home just after noon. She went to the mailbox straight away. When she saw that the box had been pried open and the precious check was gone, she immediately went to the post office to report the loss. The mailman distinctly remembered both putting the check in the box and ringing the bell.

The Postal Inspector investigating the case was aware of a thief operating in the neighborhood, since other boxes had been broken and their contents stolen. The theft of a government check from a mailbox is within the postal inspector's jurisdiction. When the check is forged and passed, it becomes a matter for the U. S. Secret Service.

Both agencies made an investigation and discovered that the check had been cashed at a bar and grill just outside the city. The owner of the bar recalled that he cashed the check for a man who had been drinking heavily. After he cashed the check, he had some misgivings. When the man left, he had followed him outside and copied the license number of his car onto the back of the check. A call to the license bureau revealed that the car belonged to a man named Greg Lyles.

Lyles lived on the other end of town. He had a criminal record that dated back to his adolescence. An alcoholic, he always reverted to petty thefts to keep himself in liquor. An investigation at his rooming house revealed that he had hurriedly left about a week before. Some letters found in his room indicated that he had planned to marry a girl in a small city in upstate New York. A Father Kelly was going to perform the ceremony in a local parish church.

The agent obtained a photo of Lyles and the owner of the bar identified him as the check passer. Based on the identification, the agent got a U. S. Commissioner's warrant charging Lyles with the check forgery and passing. Since the priest who was to marry Lyles was in my area, I received the warrant for execution.

It was a beautiful spring morning and I was pleased the investigation wouldn't be far from where I lived. I stopped first at the nearest Catholic church. There I learned that there were four Father Kelly's in various Catholic churches in the vicinity. Within two hours, I had eliminated the Father Kellys assigned to three of the churches. While enroute to see the fourth Father Kelly, I noticed a priest walking a dog down the street. I stopped the car and called out, "Would you be Father Kelly?" He turned to look at me and answered, "Yes. Would you be Carmine Motto?" I was completely surprised. I got out of the car and finally recognized Father Kelly, an old grammar school chum that I hadn't seen since graduation day in 1932. He insisted that I return to the Rectory and join him and the Monsignor for lunch.

We went to the church, where I met the Monsignor. As we settled down to a pleasant lunch, another priest was about to leave the Rectory. Father Kelly called to him and asked to come over and meet an old friend. The priest appeared to be a little annoyed, but after we were introduced he said, "Don't tell me you're Joe Motto's son." I then recognized his name as being the same as that of an old friend of my father's. His father and my father had worked on the same U. S. mail truck for thirty years. They had both retired and each thought the other had died. We exchanged phone numbers and promised our fathers would contact one another.

Father Kelly and I then attempted to squeeze thirty passing years into a brief lunch hour. In the midst of the conversation, Father Kelly interrupted me and said, "Before we go any further, Carmine, there must have been some reason why you stopped me on the street. Can it wait?" I confessed that I had been completely carried away by the day's events. I told Father Kelly why I came to see him and explained that I had a warrant for the arrest of Greg Lyles. Father Kelly looked at Lyles photo and said, "That fellow was here some time ago with a young woman. They wanted to get married. I told them it would be necessary to have banns published. They said they couldn't wait and would go to some other church. They came back yesterday and I told them I still could not marry them until they filled all the requirements of the church. They decided to try to get married by the city judge."

He suggested that I go to City Hall, since they would probably be getting married any day. I bid Father Kelly a hasty farewell and promised to come see him again soon.

As I approached the Judge's Chambers at City Hall, I saw Lyles and his girlfriend waiting outside. I told Lyles that I was a U. S. Secret Service agent and I had a warrant for his arrest. He told me that he was getting married. and his bride-to-be, Marta, begged me to let them go through with the marriage first. I explained that the warrant required that he be brought immediately before a U. S. Commissioner where bail would be set pending a hearing. Marta wouldn't accept that and begged me to let them go into the Judge's Chambers. I tried to reason with them, but nothing changed their minds. Finally I said to Marta, "Do you really want to get married?" She said, "Yes, I do." I said, "Okay, go ahead, I won't stop you. You know that your husband is going to be arrested as soon as you come out of the chambers." She said she understood, but still wanted to get married. They entered the judge's chambers. I shook my head, not comprehending why the woman wanted to marry this guy. About two minutes later, Marta left the Judge's Chambers, walked over to me and sheepishly asked for one more favor. She asked, "Will you stand up for us? We don't have a witness." The situation was deteriorating rapidly and I had reached the point of no return, so I agreed. The ceremony went without incident and as soon as we left the judge's chambers, I kissed the bride and put the handcuffs on the groom. I had visions of being tarred and feathered, maybe even transferred to an office far out west, if anyone at the office found out what I had done.

I took the couple to our office and processed the groom. Then, to further aid the cause of love, I called the office of the U. S. Attorney and told an assistant that I would be arriving with a man arrested on a forgery charge. I explained that since the man had been married that day, it would be a nice gesture if he could be released on his own recognizance. The assistant agreed, I took the prisoner over to the courthouse where he was arraigned and then released to return on another day for a hearing. When we stepped outside the courthouse, the couple was thrilled to be able to continue on their honeymoon.

They asked me to join them for a drink after driving them to their hotel, but I refused. I gave them my name and telephone number in the event they needed to reach me. They were appreciative and thanked me profusely. Driving back to the office, I couldn't remember when I felt any better. It had been a good Christian day — what with the priests, the church, the wedding and the prisoner's release.

A little later, while completing the paperwork at the office, a city detective called and asked me if I knew a Greg Lyles. I said I did and he told me there had been some trouble and asked me to come to the hotel. Just as I entered the lobby, the bride was being carried out on a stretcher. As she passed, she looked up at me and said something through her bloody, swollen lips. I leaned over and asked what had happened. She spat right in my face. I left her and walked over to the detective standing in the lobby. He told me that shortly after arriving at the hotel, Lyles went out to purchase a bottle of liquor. He promptly got drunk and started an arguement with his new bride. After beating her up, he had tried to throw her out the window. Lyles had then gone to the lobby and tried to rob the desk clerk. A detective who was in the lobby hit him on the head with a blackjack to subdue him. The police had found my name and number in his pocket.

The detective asked me to give him any background I could on the young couple since Lyles would be held on several felony charges. I told him what I knew about Lyles, but couldn't tell him anything about Marta, nor did I want to talk with her any further. Lyles was then led to a waiting police car. When he saw me he said, "You bastard, if it wasn't for you, I'd only be facing a simple check charge."

I left the hotel feeling bewildered. I couldn't help but think that I had made more than my share of mistakes for one day. Any one of my decisions could be misinterpreted and be the cause for disciplinary action. I wondered, but I felt that there was still a place for the old cliché about tempering justice with mercy.

Subways are for Riding

Not long after World War II most people were receiving one kind of government check or another in the mail. Many of these checks were stolen from depressed areas. Since most of the people receiving these checks did not have bank accounts, they had a great deal of trouble in getting their checks cashed. Consequently, check-cashing agencies, charging 25 cents for cashing the average check, sprang up all over the city. The agencies became very popular and soon expanded their services. They paid light and phone bills, sold stamps and money orders, prepared tax forms and the like.

In the early days, the agencies cashed checks for their customers indiscriminately. They were easy victims for the forgers and many were wiped out because they cashed checks for thieves who operated in groups. The forgers brought all their business to agencies which were lenient in cashing checks. When the checks bounced, the cashing services were in serious financial trouble.

It didn't take very long for these agencies to begin demanding proper identification. They asked pertinent questions and even made phone calls to verify the validity of a questionable check. Investigators involved in check forgeries went to these agencies on "check days" and waited for the thieves.

On days when checks were sent through the mail, the agencies' back rooms were filled with representatives of the local police, postal inspectors, welfare investigators and Secret Service agents. If a suspicious person offered a check for cashing, someone in the back room would be notified. The suspect would then be interviewed and the officer would try to determine if the check had been stolen. On some days ten or twelve arrests were made in just one agency. Contact between the check cashing stores and the investigators was always maintained.

One day, I arrived at an uptown check-cashing agency a little earlier than usual. I parked my car outside the agency and walked in. The man behind the counter was waiting on a customer. When he saw me, the cashier pointed to the customer and said, "Get him!"

The customer spun around and ran out the door to the main street. I dropped my briefcase and ran after him. He darted in and out among parked cars and I followed him. A crowd gathered and cheered the suspect. They intervened enough to permit the man to get to the subway entrance. He looked over his shoulder, saw me pursuing him, then ran headlong down the steps. When I reached the steps, I tripped and fell down the whole flight. I picked myself up and continued the chase with torn pants and a bleeding knee. The suspect vaulted over the turnstile, knocked some people over and headed toward the north end of the station platform. Thinking I now had the man cornered, I relaxed a bit. Once he reached the end of the platform, there would be no place to go. He again looked over his shoulder and when he saw me still following him, he jumped off the platform, onto the tracks going north in the darkened tunnel. The next local station was ten blocks away.

The commotion on the street had caught a uniformed police officer's attention. He caught up with me on the platform. In a few seconds, I told him what had happened. I requested that he call someone at the next station and tell them about the man running on the tracks. Then I jumped down onto the tracks hoping to catch the suspect somewhere along the way. It suddenly occurred to me that I was on subway tracks and didn't know a damn thing about them. What about the electrically charged third rail? The express trains that roar by? Was there enough room along the wall to stand while a train passed? What other unforeseen dangers were there in the tunnel? I decided that if my suspect could do it, maybe I could too. The man was running along the tracks, perfectly silhouetted against the lights of the next station. I drew my revolver and aimed. He was a perfect target. One shot would have brought him down easily.

Taking a long breath to steady my aim made me realize that I had drawn the gun in anger. I was angry because my knee hurt, because my suit was torn, because he was getting away, because my pride was hurt. The Secret Service school lesson about judgmental shooting passed quickly through my mind. "Don't shoot at a fleeing prisoner or suspect. Only shoot if your life or someone else's is in danger. Was this crime worth a life?" What crime? I didn't even know why I was chasing that man. The cashier in the agency said, "Get him," and I responded. That the man had tried to cash a stolen check was only an assumption. I really didn't know. Pulling the trigger became unthinkable. Suppose some innocent person was hit by the bullet?

The earsplitting shriek of an oncoming train shocked me. I carefully stepped over the tracks and pushed my back hard against the grimy tunnel walls. The train sped by, its whistle still screaming, only inches away from my body. I just held my breath, closed my eyes, and prayed while holding my suit coat tightly, preventing it from snagging on an outcropping of the train. Lord knows what the engineer thought when he saw me on the tracks. After the train passed, I had lost sight of my quarry so I inspected every niche and exit door that lined the subway tunnel. I was aware that, at any moment, the suspect might jump out of the darkness and we could be engaged in a struggle on the tracks. After some anxious moments, I managed to get to the next station. The police were waiting there. They said no one had come out of the tunnel. Trains were coming and going, but there was no sign of a fleeing man.

Since the station was well covered, I decided to head south, using the tracks on the opposite side. No one wanted to accompany me, so I went alone. I investigated the walls along the tunnel and heard the shrieking whistles set off by engineers who noticed someone on the tracks. I was a little more sure of myself the second time and moved a little faster. I reached the station with no sign of the suspect. I spoke with another police officer who was waiting at the station and he said no one came out of the tunnel. While we were trying to figure out what had happened, a call was received at the change booth. An engineer reported he had stopped his train between the two stations because he saw a man flagging him down on the tracks. The conductor told the engineer that a man had boarded the train between two cars and had gotten off at the next station. The description given by the conductor was general enough to portray many people; however, there was one element we both remembered: A fairly noticeable lump on the back of the suspect's neck.

My gray suit was covered with black soot, my pants were torn, my leg was bleeding, and I limping. I went back to the check-cashing agency. The cashier told me that the man had attempted to cash a $62 check. When the check was offered, the clerk asked if this was the customer's veteran's check. When the man replied in the affirmative, the clerk knew he had a forger at the counter. The check was an income tax refund. The clerk figured the man had stolen the check and hadn't even taken the time to see what the check was for. The cashier gave me the original check and I returned to the office to report to the agent in charge.

I must have been quite a sight. The agent in charge's, first remark was, "What in hell happened to you?" I told him the story of the stolen check and the chase through the subway. He interrupted with, "That was a pretty damn foolish thing to do." That made me mad enough, but then he looked at my disheveled appearance and added, "It's a good thing it wasn't a new suit." I stormed out of the office and went home. The next morning, when I returned to the office, the only thing on my mind was to try to find the man I had been chasing.

I went to the check address and examined the payee's mail box. Someone had tampered with it. I then went to the payee's apartment. He could not give me any information other than that he had expected the check and it had never reached him. I took handwriting samples from him and all members of his family. None of their handwriting bore any resemblance to the forged endorsement on the check. No one could give me any leads. I visited several apartments in the building inquiring about the mail service and how often checks were known to be stolen. The building superintendent was not in, so I went to the local post office and spoke to the mailman who delivered mail to the building. He recalled putting a check in the payee's mailbox. He said when he put the envelope in the box it was in good shape. He stated, however, that there were many complaints about missing mail in the neighborhood and that the postal inspectors were working on it. I had already talked with the inspectors and they were also working on the case.

Returning to the address on the check, I interviewed the building superintendent. He also talked about people complaining about their mail. He said that although he was continually fixing broken mailboxes, some days there were just too many to fix. I took his handwriting sample with the same negative results.

I didn't want to talk to too many people about the man with the lump on the back of his neck, but I described the man to the superintendent and asked if he knew him. He said that he did recall seeing a man matching the description come into the building to visit a girl in one of the apartments, but he wasn't sure which one of the three apartments. At the first one, no one was at home. At the second one, a young woman answered. I interviewed her under a suitable pretext (I told her we were double-checking the census takers.) She said that there were three people living in the apartment: she, her sister and her mother. She said her mother was a widow. She herself had been married and was divorced. Her younger sister was single and worked in a local cleaning establishment.

I kept the conversation geared toward the younger sister and learned that she had been going with a man named Al Handy, until several months before. The third apartment housed an old couple who claimed they were the only occupants.

Al Handy was not too common a name, so I checked the records. The local police had a file on an Al Handy who had been arrested several times on bad check charges. His description fit the suspect except that there was no mention of any lump on the neck. I found a picture of Handy, but couldn't identify him as the man I wanted. I had only gotten a quick glimpse of his face in the check-cashing agency; after that, all I saw was his back. I took the picture to the cashier at the agency. He said he couldn't positively identify the picture because he had been quite nervous at the time.

From prison records I located Al Handy's handwriting samples. There was a strong similarity between his writing and the forged endorsement on the government check. I spent quite a bit of time trying to find Al's friends and relatives, but the records were old and he was not the type to keep in touch with his family. There appeared to be one last lead to follow: the ex-girlfriend. If she was still going with him, she could have tipped him off about my visit. If she was not seeing him, perhaps she could give me a few leads as to his whereabouts.

I found out where she was employed and met her after work. She was affable and quite anxious to help. She said she met Al Handy at a neighborhood bar about six months before. She started going out with him and noticed that he had plenty of money but never worked. After several dates she began to suspect that he was a thief. He always had checks in his pocket and he looked curiously at mailboxes whenever they went into a building. She said she had gotten fed up with Al, and after several dates, she began making excuses to him. Eventually she had broken off with him. He made several more attempts to see her again. Al was still seen frequently in the neighborhood. She suspected that he was up to no good and asked why I was interested in him.

I told her he was a suspect in a case. She promised she would call me if she ever found out where he was staying. I gave her my number and thanked her for her cooperation. After our conversation, I still wasn't sure whether the girl had been leveling with me. However, I had learned many years ago that if you don't talk with people, you never learn. There were calculated risks that had to be taken all the time.

Several months passed without any more leads into the Al Handy case. One day all the agents in our office were on duty. New York City was the site of a Presidential visit that took precedence over any other work. When the President visits, there is no time to even think about check forgery or attempted check forgery cases. On these visits there are a million details to handle: liaison with police, covering the arrival at the airport, the motorcade into the city, the arrival at the function, the security at the hotel, the check of employees who will be in the vicinity of the President, security check points at the function, security for the motorcade, screening of guests at the function, and arrangements for the departure. If it's a fast visit, the day usually ends at an ungodly hour at the airport, waiting for the presidential plane to become airborne.

In the midst of this particular day's activities, I received a phone call from Al's ex-girlfriend. She said she had just learned that Al was living with a girl in the Bronx and told me the address. She suggested that I get there as soon as possible because she did not know how long he would be there. I thanked her and couldn't go. The President's visit came first, it was impossible to leave.

The following day, another agent and I went to the Bronx address. No one was at home at the apartment number. We made inquiries in the building and made no progress. Everyone was reluctant to talk. It was obvious that the people were going out of their way to avoid being interviewed. Across the street from the house a shoemaker worked at the store window. He would be aware of everything going on around him since his window gave him a good view of the whole street.

At first, his replies were typical. He said, "Man, I don't know nothing. I mind my own business. I don't want nothing to do with cops or the law." I said, "Something happened around here. Everyone's avoiding us like the plague." He interrupted, "if you guys are cops, you people ain't doing much talking either. You gotta know what happened last night." I explained that we were federal officers and didn't know what happened. He said, "You'd better go ask the cops. They'll tell you quicker than the people here will." We headed for the nearest precinct.

The lieutenant in charge of the detective squad told us of the preceding night's events. He said, "Friday night is a big night around this neighborhood. The bars are jumping all over. It's also a big shopping night. The stores stay open late and most of them have quite a bit of cash on hand. The Friday night stickups were getting quite numerous so we had special teams secreted in stores that might be targets. At about half past eight last night at the big supermarket, this clown comes in and announces a stickup. The manager gives a signal to the cops in the back of the store. The place is crowded and no one wants to shoot. The stickup guy sees the cops coming. He fires a shot and runs from the store. He makes it to the street, runs a couple of blocks with our guys close behind. He gets to a building, fires, turns around, fires at the cops and then continues up the stoop. One of the cops takes a good aim, lets one go, and the bastard crumbles right in his tracks. The ambulance comes, but he's DOA at the hospital. We check on the bum and find that he's shacking up at the same house with some broad. He's got a fairly long sheet, mostly for checks. His name is Al Handy."

That was it. The lieutenant practically closed the case for us. There was one more stop: the city morgue. Although the attendant was a little annoyed at being disturbed on a Saturday afternoon, he dutifully took me to the storage area, pulled out a drawer, rolled back the sheet and let me have a look at Al. His face meant nothing to me. I asked the attendant to turn the body over so I could see if he had the lump on the neck. He turned the body over. The police bullet had struck Al in the back of the neck right where the tumor should have been. In order to retrieve the bullet, it had been necessary to make several incisions in the back of Al's neck which was then stitched back up. A positive identification was impossible.

I returned to the office, got out the case folder, and stamped it"closed." My pride may have been salvaged, but I still had 121 more checks to go.

"Mr. 880"

The name "Mr. 880" sounds like it should be the title of a science fiction novel or a Hollywood movie. Actually the subject and name really did become a movie that portrayed the U. S. Secret Service in a less than favorable light. But again, it was a case of Hollywood taking creative license with art imitating life. In real life, "Mr. 880" was the name the Secret Service gave to a notorious counterfeit passer who managed to elude detection for nearly two decades.

The note in question was a very poorly made dollar bill, a U. S. silver certificate. The passer of the note was so successful only because it was a note of low denomination. People who accept dollar bills usually don't give them a second glance as to whether they are genuine or counterfeit. It wouldn't have taken an expert to determine that the bill was bogus. It was only one step above play money. The counterfeiter generally passed about five or ten notes a week and the area that was victimized was the upper West Side area of New York City.

Every new counterfeit note that appears is given a file number by the Secret Service. The number of this note happened to be 880, thus the name "Mr. 880" that was given to the manufacturer and passer of this counterfeit. The passing of these notes did not pose any particular threat to our economy. However, it was more than a nuisance to the Secret Service. The note was actively passed from 1932 to 1948, the longest of any counterfeit in the history of the service. Finally in 1948 a man was arrested for manufacturing and passing these phony bills.

He was over seventy years old and he made a living scavenging the city streets and trash bins for other people's junk. He fixed them up if they needed it and sold the castoffs for what he could get for them. It usually wasn't very much. There came a time when his scrounging activities could not sufficiently cover even his meager needs, so he decided to find another way to augment his income.

Mr. 880 had been an inventor and a printer in his youth so he knew what he had to do to supplement his earnings. He was able to get a small hand-press and the chemicals needed to etch copper plates. He did some experimenting and before long, the 880 note was made. His story impressed a lot of people and before long Hollywood decided to make a movie based on his escapades.

After the arrest of Mr. 880, I was interviewed by several screen writers and I told them what little I knew about him:

I first heard about Mr. 880 shortly after my appointment to the U. S. Secret Service in 1941. The Special Agent in Charge told me that whenever I was investigating an 880 note I shouldn't take the matter lightly even if it was a poor reproduction of a genuine note. He instructed me that the note made its first appearance in New York City in the early 1930s. It wasn't affiliated with any other known counterfeits. The note was very crude and appeared to be made by a photoetching process. The word "Washington" on the face of the note was misspelled "Wahsington." The printing was done on regular white unlined tablet paper. The department thought that this case would be closed in a hurry; however, ten years later, it was still going strong.The Agent in Charge stated again that I wasn't to take this case lightly, even if the note was amateurish and lacked any great distribution. He felt it was a one-man effort and so we shouldn't expect any help or information from informers. He told me to personally interview anyone who was victimized by this note with a view to getting some sort of description of the passer. Up to that time no one had been able to get any information or description of Mr. 880.

Dutifully, I interviewed every person who was victimized by the counterfeits. The answer was always the same, "Who looks at a dollar bill?" or "I was busy and don't remember the transaction." One man said, "After I learned that the bill was counterfeit, I framed it, and I always show it to the customers; it always gets a laugh."

In all the time I worked on the investigation, I was never able to get any kind of a description of the passer. There even came a time, when out of some desperation, we offered two dollars for every 880 note that was brought into our office, providing there was a description of the passer — there were no takers. I wasn't any more successful than any of my precedessors had been in solving the 880 note case. After a year on the case, I enlisted in the Marine Corps and didn't return to our New York City office until four and one half years later.

When I returned, the same Agent in Charge brought me up to date on the 880 note and told me that during the war years, no counterfeit 880 notes had been circulated. He thought that the maker had either died or was in the service serving away from New York or, as silly as it seemed, perhaps the passer was patriotic and didn't want to interfere with the war effort. Just as soon as the war was over, the 880 notes started to be passed again in the same part of the city. The investigation continued — still no results.

"Mr. 880 "

One day a young boy came into the office with several 880 notes. He immediately gained our attention and we could feel the excitement rising. To the obvious question, he replied, "I found them in the back yard of a tenement house."

The boy showed us where he had found the notes. A search of the yard produced an old handpress and some plates of the 880 note. We learned that there had been a fire in one of the apartments and in an effort to extinguish the blaze, the firefighters threw most of the furnishings out of the window. An evening snowstorm had blanketed the yard and most of the furnishings had been buried under ten inches of snow. It wasn't long after the snow had melted that the boy had discovered the notes. We proceeded to the apartment where the fire had ocurred. A slightly built, old gentleman in his seventies opened the door. We had found Mr. 880! He was interviewed in his apartment.

He readily admitted that he had manufactured and passed the counterfeit notes. A search of his apartment revealed additional counterfeiting paraphernalia. Mr. 880 was a kindly old gentleman and he insisted he was actually doing the government a favor by passing these notes. He remarked that he had no way of earning a livelihood and that he could have gone on welfare and been entitled to far more money than that he received by passing the bogus bills. He said that he continued to search for castaway junk and didn't didn't pass any counterfeits during the war years so that he wouldn't tie up the federal investigators.

I don't believe the screen writers were impressed with the true story I had told them. They wrote their own version of the story and it became a movie known as "Mr. 880" starring Edmund Gwen (as Mr. 880), Dorothy McGuire, and Burt Lancaster. The movie version was a delightful story and was very successful: it eventually found a second life on late-night television.

The movie story begins when the agent in charge of the New York field office sends for one of his top investigators to handle the problem of the appearance of the 880 notes. He explains the whole background of the story and tells the investigator (Burt Lancaster) that the case is his and he has to solve it and close down the counterfeiter. The Burt Lancaster character takes all the necessary investigative steps but is getting nothing to resolve the case. The scene moves to a decrepit apartment in the upper west side. Here we see an old man (Edmund Gwen) printing counterfeit notes and then hanging them to dry in a closet. Living in the building is a young beautiful girl (Dorothy McGuire) who is employed by the United Nations. She is friendly with the old man and he is constantly selling her some of the junk that he picks up from the city streets. On one occasion, he inadvertently gives her an 880 note while making change. She eventually passes the note which brings Burt Lancaster into her life. After a lengthy interview, he realizes she is only a second passer. She convinces him that she has no idea where the note came from.

Burt is smitten in love with her and before long they are an item. (Boy meets girl and they fall in love). One day two boys find a printing press on the sidewalk, some counterfeit plates and several counterfeit bills. The boys are taken into custody and agree to show officials where they found the contraband. Burt finally arrests Mr. 880 and vows that he will send him away for life. Dorothy, who has grown quite fond of the old man, pleads with Burt to show him some mercy. But Burt refuses, (boy loses girl). Finally Mr. 880 comes before the sentencing judge and pleads for mercy. At the last minute, Burt steps up and explains the whole case to the judge. The judge sentences Mr. 880 to nine months in the Federal House of Detention. Dorothy is thrilled and she and Burt leave the courthouse hand-in-hand, (boy regains girl) and they live happily ever after…fade out. The End.

In the real-life case, I was in court on the day of the sentencing and my recollection is that Mr. 880 had a court-appointed public defender representing him. The judge sentenced Mr. 880 to a year and a day in jail. The lawyer continued his pleas, "But your Honor, a year and a day is like sentencing this poor old man to death." The judge thought for a minute and said, "O.K., I'll change the sentence to nine months." The lawyer thanked the judge and was about to leave the court when he turned on his heels and said, "Wait, your Honor. I made a mistake!" The judge replied, "I wondered how long it would take you to realize that you were better off with a year and a day rather than a sentence of nine months. A year and a day can be done in four months, a nine month sentence requires serving the full time."

I think I prefer the Hollywood version of the Mr. 880 story.

They Weren't Wild About Harry

Blair House is owned by the government and is used as a guest house for visiting heads of state during their stay in the United States. Located on Pennsylvania Avenue across from the White House, Blair House is exquisitely furnished and conveniently located. However, from a security point of view, everything is not quite so perfect.

At 2:15 in the afternoon of November 1, 1950, two Puerto Rican nationals, bent on a mission of assassination, quietly went their separate ways after leaving their hotel room. Moments later, each man, armed with German-made, semiautomatic pistols, approached Blair House from opposite directions. Their mission was to assassinate Harry S. Truman, the President of the United States, who was living in Blair House while the White House was being renovated. They couldn't have known that the President had just awakened from his afternoon nap or that he had made plans to attend a memorial service at Arlington National Cemetery later that day. If the men had known this, perhaps they would have waited for a more advantageous opportunity.

A police command post had been constructed outside Blair House as the first line of defense against any unauthorized entry. Three officers from the White House Police had been assigned to this post. The two Puerto Ricans were 37-year-old Oscar Collazo, a resident of the Bronx, New York, employed as a metal polisher, and Greselio L. Torresola, 30, also of the Bronx. Both men were members of the militant Puerto Rican Nationalist Party, headed by Pedro Albizu Campos, a fiery militant who advocated complete independence for Puerto Rico. The group had been responsible for staging a bloody uprising in Puerto Rico earlier that week. Collazo and Torresola calmly approached Blair House to avoid arousing suspicion. Without warning, they opened fire on the policemen outside the police command post. The police immediately returned the fire. Secret Service agents assigned to Blair House joined in and, within moments, the exchange of gunfire died out.

Inside Blair House, President Truman heard the shooting, and was about to look out the window when an agent ordered him to a safer spot. Agents armed with automatic weapons took up their assigned posts, ready for any eventuality.

But nothing else happened. Torresola lay dead on the sidewalk and Collazo had been badly wounded. Patrolman Leslie Coffelt died of his wounds; several other officers had been wounded, but would recover.

Several hours after the shooting, I was called to Headquarters in New York City. The Agent in Charge ordered me to take as many agents as needed and make an investigation of Collazo's residence. We rushed to the address on Brook Avenue in the Bronx. The chaos outside the building was unbelievable. Large crowds had gathered in the street; the press had set up cameras and were interviewing friends and neighbors. The police were in the process of sending extra squads to handle the crowd. We had to make a flying wedge and fight for every inch until we reached the apartment. It was far worse in the apartment. A police inspector and six detectives were already inside. They found the press having a field day swarming over every corner of the apartment, taking pictures, interviewing Mrs. Collazo and her teenaged children. The arrival of the police had not reduced the bedlam.

When I arrived, the police inspector cried out, "For Christ's sake, Motto, where in hell have you guys been? We came over to give you some assistance. Let's go!" I told the inspector that we had been delayed, but were ready to work.

It was my first opportunity to run an operation and I was ready. I said, "Okay, here's what I want. Clear the apartment of everyone who isn't family. Post a guard at the door to interview anyone who wants to enter. I'll team an agent with one of your men and they'll make a detailed search of the apartment. Send for the emergency squad to search the basement, yard, air shafts, any place where weapons could be hidden. You and I will question Mrs. Collazo and the children." It took the Inspector about two minutes to get everything organized. In no time, order was restored in the apartment.

Mrs. Collazo was as militant as her husband. She professed to know nothing about his trip to Washington, but supported whatever he did. While we were still questioning her, the agents and detectives reported that they had found nothing in their search. That was too incredible to believe! We conducted another search. There were several photographs on the parlor wall; some were of known party members at a restaurant for an annual dance. That was too much! I shouted, "What the hell are you guys looking for — machine guns? Cannons? Dynamite? I could care less about that stuff! I want to find out everything you can about this Party and its members. Dammit, take everything that isn't nailed down — letters, pictures, notebooks, old Christmas cards, anything that can give us a lead on why this attempt took place and who else is involved. Tomorrow might be too late. There'll be all kinds of legal sanctions, but right now, search!"

The men found hundreds of leads that aided the investigation. One agent found a mimeograph machine under the bed and papers that showed the name and address of every party member. That was pure gold.

There was a knock at the door. A detective opened it to find a man wh demanded to see Mrs. Collazo. He said he was a friend. Under furthe questioning, he became belligerent and started scuffling with the officer. H was quickly subdued and searched. He was carrying a loaded revolver. I and the Collazo family were taken to U. S. Secret Service headquarters f further questioning.

The fruits of the search were also taken for further scrutiny. The nig was long and arduous. Teams were sent out to locate and interview party members. By 10 o'clock the next morning, we had located, interviewed, photographed, and fingerprinted every Puerto Rican Nationalist Party member in the New York area. It was 7 o'clock that night, before I was finally relieved from duty. I was told to go home, get some sleep, and prepare to continue the investigation early the next morning.

As I left the office, I picked up a newspaper with banner headlines about the attempted assassination. One reporter quoted the President as saying, "If they would have gotten into the House, I would have taken their guns and shoved them up their gullets." That remark said a lot about the kind of man President Truman was.

When the trials and all the appeals had been exhausted, Oscar Collazo was found to be guilty and sentenced to death However, before the sentence could be carried out, the President commuted it to life imprisonment. That act said a lot about President Truman's character.

Divert Attention

Some time later, another presidential incident occurred, rooted in mystery half-a-world away, keeping us busy in New York. A man taking a midnight walk on the darkened deck of a tramp steamer heading for a Mediterranean port, overheard a conversation between two men on the overhead deck. The night was dark, as it can only be on the open sea. The only light was from the ship's running lights and the glow from the bridge. The two men met and spoke quietly and briefly in a foreign language. After the short exchange of conversation they parted. The man whose walk had been interrupted remained hidden in the darkness until he was certain the other men were gone. He never saw the men again during the rest of the voyage.

The man who overheard the conversation reported it to the U.S. Consulate in the next port-of-call. He told the Consul that someone was headed to the United States ostensibly to work for the United Nations, but he was really a trained assassin whose mission was to kill the President. The source had no other information except that he thought he heard the assassin referred to as what sounded like "Deevart."

The Consul immediately reported the conversation to Washington. The Secret Service launched an extensive investigation. After several weeks of exhaustive searching, a man with a similar sounding name was located working at the United Nations. He had the ethnic background and nationality as described by the informant.

A group of us were briefed in the office of the Special Agent-in-Charge. We were relieved from all other duties and told to establish round-the-clock surveillance on Mr. Divart. Our orders were simple: "Don't lose him, don't burn him, and don't let him accomplish his mission!"

Within a few days we had a good line on Divart. He was a tall, good-looking young man in his early thirties. He had a dark complexion, and carried himself with a military bearing. His position at the United Nations was innocuous; he was little more than a glorified clerk. Divart rented rooms in midtown New York on the West Side. Fortunately, his room faced the street so we could observe when he was home.

In those days, the U. N. Headquarters was located at Hunter College in the Bronx, so Divart used the subway to get to work. He was always neat, but seemed to own only a gray suit and a pair of rust-colored trousers. He always wore sunglasses when he was outdoors.

He always left work precisely at 4 o'clock in the afternoon. If he turned left, it generally meant he was on his way to meet a fellow countryman, walk through the park and go to a cafeteria at Mosholu Parkway. The men would order two orders of rolls each and drink several glasses of water. They would chat for a few minutes then take the subway to Divart's home, arriving there at about 5:45. Divart and his friend, apparently a fellow employee, would reappear at 6:30, go to a cheap restaurant and have a bowl of soup with several extra orders of bread.

If he turned right after leaving work, it usually meant that he was headed for the Kingsbridge Park Station and home. Most evenings he had a social function to attend. His habits were well-established and he had a penny-pinching nature. We noted that he ate well when the food was free, but stinted when he had to pay. The weekends were especially long for Divart. He generally went sightseeing or window-shopping alone.

Week after week, he faithfully attended to his duties and just as faithfully, we attended to ours. He never gave us any reason to be overly suspicious.

After several months of surveillance,we could almost anticipate Divart's every move. Tailing him was becoming monotonous. The man never deviated from his routine; he appeared to be living a Spartan, womanless existence. Finally, one Saturday afternoon he walked to a midtown address, entered a brownstone building, and exited a half hour later with an attractive young lady. They got into her automobile and drove off. Our spirits rose. At last we had all the elements of a spy thriller! The couple headed out of the city.

After trailing them for a hundred miles or so, we were in rural, upstate New York. When they finally stopped, it was at a small motel on the outskirts of a small town. Just as soon as they had checked in, we got the room next-door. Divart and his lady friend didn't leave the room the entire weekend. They ordered room service and didn't make any phone calls from the room It was pretty obvious by now that they hadn't driven to this faraway location to meet up with someone nor was it to take in the beauty of the local scenery.

We did a quick background check on the girl. She was a college senior from a good family and didn't have a subversive background. That was all we learned from the weekend.

So after the weekend outing, it was back to the same old boring case for us. The monotony was wearing on me, so I asked the boss if we couldn't bring it to a head in some way. He became became very agitated and threatened to have me fired if I did anything other than to follow the suspect. Several days later, I followed Divart to Fifth Avenue. He appeared to be shopping for a new suit. Suddenly, a patrolman stepped up behind him, drew his gun, and ordered Divart to put up his hands. I couldn't believe what I was seeing! As I had been following Divart all day, I was sure he hadn't done anything wrong. The patrolman took Divart into a lobby of one of the buildings to search him. I got close enough to the officer to get his badge number and then called my boss. He thought that somehow I was involved in trying to force Divart's hand, and he repeated his threat to fire me if he learned that I had anything to do with the situation. I assured him of my innocence. He sent for the patrolman later on that day, and was told that Divart had been stopped because he closely resembled a suspect who had been burglarizing stores in the area. The patrolman had decided to question anyone who resembled the burglar.

Shortly afterward we tailed Divart to a pier. He met a girl arriving on a trans-Atlantic ship. He lived with the girl several months and then one day they were married.

Unexpectedly one day, both of them were observed leaving the apartment carrying suitcases. They proceeded to the bus terminal and got on a tour bus that was traveling coast to coast. We managed to plant an agent on the bus in the midwest. He continued on the month-long trip. While our agent had an enjoyable "vacation," we learned nothing more about our quarry. The couple eventually returned to New York and we resumed our routine surveillance.

The White House announced that the President would address the United Nations at its second home at Lake Success, New York. If Divart was going to make a move, we were certain that it would be at this time. Surveillance was tripled. The New York City Police gave an enormous amount of assistance. When the day arrived, all teams were at their assigned posts early and they were ready for anything. About 9 o'clock that morning, Divart and his wife left the apartment carrying several suitcases. I thought, "This bastard is already planning his getaway." I decided it wasn't going to work.... that come what may, I would stop Divart!

They got into a cab and we followed it over the Queensboro Bridge to Long Island City. Sure enough, it appeared he was on his way to Lake Success! All units were put on alert. Various plans were put into effect depending on Divart's movements at the United Nations. Then something happened. Instead of driving to Lake Success, the cab turned at the exit leading to the airport. Divart and his wife proceeded to the Air France counter, checked their baggage, and boarded a plane bound for Paris. Their plane took off precisely as the President arrived in New York. The President gave his speech without incident and returned to Washington D. C. several hours later. Divart never returned to the United States. While the 13 months we had spent on the case appeared to have been a wasted effort, we still felt that the whole matter was a valuable learning experience. You never never know what it takes to protect the President.

We later learned that the patrolman who had stopped Divart on Fifth Avenue, had continued stopping people who resembled the burglar, and one day he really did catch him. He had better luck than we did. But then, we were lucky too. There was no attack against the President by the mysterious man who received his orders on a dark night aboard a ship at sea.

Dom — A Born Loser

Dom was a born a loser. His father was serving a prison sentence when he was born, and his mother died in childbirth. His grandmother took him in and he lived with her in a Lower East Side tenement. She died when Dom was six years old and he was sent to live in an orphanage. Dom ran away from the orphanage for the first time when he was twelve. At fourteen, he was arrested for theft and sent to a "reform school." He escaped several times, but was always caught and returned to the institution. Just after his sixteenth birthday, he was released and he returned to the streets of New York City.

His first legitimate employment was in a neighborhood drugstore. He delivered orders and did odd jobs, like putting away merchandise and cleaning up after the store had closed. Dom was diligent about his duties for a while, but he gave in to the temptations of pocket watches, perfumes, and cigarettes. He helped himself to anything that wasn't nailed down and soon was selling as much merchandise after the store had closed as the pharmacist did during regular store hours. He expected that the boss would miss the merchandise, but after several weeks, the boss still hadn't said anything.

Dom noticed that many of the customers got their medicine in dark brown bottles. The medicine cost one dollar per pint and the boss had a closet full of the stuff. Dom figured out that the boss was really making his money bootlegging and after some snooping around, found the money from the liquor sales was kept locked in a cabinet in the back of the store. He suspected that there must be a small fortune in the cabinet, and he decided to take it.

After a particularly busy day, Dom made sure that the back door was left unlocked at closing time. Dom returned to the store about two oclock in the morning. He went to the back door, pushed it open and went to the cabinet where the money was kept. He made no attempt to open the lock. He kicked savagely at the door until it crumbled. He wasn't disappointed. The canvas money bag was sitting on the lower shelf. He grabbed it, opened it, and was satisfied that there was a fortune in it. He put the bag under his coat and quietly slipped out the back door.

He returned to his fourth floor walkup where he had a room off the back hall of the tenement building. He locked the door, lit the gaslight, opened the bag, and poured the contents onto the cot. When he finished counting the money, he had $640 in cash. He carefully rolled the money in a blanket and placed it under the cot. He went to bed and dreamed about all the things he could do with the money. He had only been asleep for a few hours when he was awakened by a loud pounding on the door. He jumped up and sleepily opened the door. A large man with a handlebar mustache and a derby hat grabbed him by the scruff of the neck. Another man, his boss, kept shouting, "That's him, that's him." The big man was obviously a detective. He back-handed Dom soundly across the face and said, "Okay, where it?" Dom yelped in pain, "I don't know what you're talking about." Another slap sent him reeling across the floor. When he tried to get up, he got another wallop just under the right eye. That did it, it was over — he slumped to the floor. The detective pulled the cot aside, grabbed the blanket roll, shook it out, and the canvas bag fell to the floor. The boss snatched it and shouted, "It's mine, it's mine." Dom recalled getting hit again and then riding in the paddywagon to Police Headquarters.

At Headquarters, there were questions by the police, then by the District Attorney. He couldn't see any use in denying anything. He had taken the money, and he had been caught. He recalled pleading guilty. Not long afterward, someone said a lot of bad things about him. At least he didn't remember anyone saying anything good. He held his breath as the judge looked down his nose, and droned in a disinterested monotone, "Five years in a state penitentiary. Next case."

The institution was the same as the others he had been in. He was assigned to work in the ice house and the kitchen. His job was to take the ice off the delivery trucks, store it in the ice house, then take it to the kitchen when it was needed. For the next three years, the job didn't change much, but Dom did. He became smarter. He knew he was in a position to do favors and he did them with great regularity. That made him friends who taught him all the short cuts that were a necessary part of prison life.

When Dom was released, he joined a gang delivering bootleg whiskey to speakeasies in and around town. Dom was one of several helpers assigned to a truck that picked up the liquor at various out-of-town places. His job was to get the cases to pickup and delivery points, give envelopes to certain officers who were always at the right spot at the right time, and to be alert for hijackers from rival gangs. The job paid well and Dom felt like he was becoming a success.

Another part of the job, he learned later, was to be the subject of "accommodation arrests." He had to be periodically "caught" delivering several gallons of alcohol at pre-arranged spots. The arrest would consist of being taken to the police station, being carried off to night court, pleading guilty to a minor charge, paying a fine and being released.

As time went on, the group he worked for became more sophisticated. They had made a connection to pick up Canadian whiskey at the border and transport it to New York City. Later the group was given an assignment to unload imported whiskey at a rendezvous point on Long Island Sound. Dom and his group were to board a small launch, go out to a larger boat, unload the liquor and place it on trucks that would be waiting nearby. That particular night, everything was just right for the transfer. The moon and tides were perfect, all connections were made, and the launch left on schedule. Six men were aboard, armed with assorted weapons. The launch met the larger boat and the unloading proceeded smoothly. Just as the last case was put aboard the launch, a siren wailed, a spot light flashed on them, and a megaphone voice advised them that the Coast Guard was approaching to board them. The larger boat took off immediately. Dom's launch was weighed down heavily and could not move rapidly. Dom shot out the spotlight and the cutter opened up with machine gun fire. Dom was shot in the leg and attempting to escape, jumped into the water. He swam furiously for a few seconds and went only a few yards from the boat before he lapsed into unconsciousness. A Coast Guardsman fished him out of the water and he was taken to a nearby hospital. After his leg wound was treated, he was remanded to a federal detention house to await trial. Dom pleaded guilty to the liquor violation and was sentenced to three years in a federal penitentiary.

Two years later he was released and was back on the street. Many friends of his had made it big in the bootlegging business and were investing much of their money in legal enterprises. Dom visited many of those friends, but no one wanted to bother with him or give him a job. He was on parole and had to be careful of the type of work he would do. He finally found a job as a helper on a moving van. It was hard work, but Dom had one more year of parole to finish. Before the year was up, he was laid off because business was slow. Prohibition had been repealed and many old bootlegging combinations had been broken up. Jobs of any kind were hard to find. The depression had begun. Dom broke into stores and lived off the burglary proceeds. He was arrested after his fourth job. The arresting officer was a foot patrol officer who had been checking the back doors of businesses. The store Dom was in opened when the officer tried the door knob. The policeman entered the store and found Dom crouched behind a counter, his pockets full of loot.

The officer arrested Dom, handcuffed him and then called the precinct from inside the store. Dom was taken to a police squad room and was questioned by several detectives. The young arresting officer, Fred Short, was there but didn't participate in the questioning. He had been on the job for only four months. Dom was his first arrest. When anyone attempted to get rough with Dom during the questioning, Officer Short interceded and reminded the group that Dom was his prisoner and he was responsible for him. Fred gave Dom a couple of cigarettes and made sure he got a sandwich and cup of coffee before being confined for the night. Although Dom was familiar with the "good cop/bad cop" routine, he still felt that Fred was a decent straightforward officer. Fred never asked Dom any questions and always treated him like a human being. Dom deeply appreciated Fred's treatment.

The next day when Dom was taken to court, he wanted to thank Fred for taking care of him. Fred brushed it off by saying he'd do it for anyone. During the course of the conversation, they discovered that both of them were orphans, both were raised in orphanages, and neither had ever been adopted. From that moment, both men took a liking to each other. Fred was all cop; he would do his job, but in a way that made him a likable person. Dom was all trouble. He would also work at what he could do, but would henceforth try to be a little more sophisticated. No one objected to Dom "copping a plea." The sentence was a minimal three to five years. To Dom, it was another stretch that would undoubtedly be followed by others.

This time Dom did some serious thinking in prison. He was getting older and couldn't continue being a small-time hood or burglar. One more arrest and he would be a three-time loser. Under the old Baumes Habitual Criminal Act, there was a possibility of getting life. Being a hood hadn't kept him living in luxury. A lot of his old cronies were living in high style. They had been successful during prohibition and had then made plenty of money from good investments. Some of them began to look down on the likes of Dom.

Dom shared a cell with a man serving a sentence for embezzlement and grand larceny. Dom understood that his cell mate had been some kind of stockbroker who ran off with a lot of stock. Dom nicknamed him "Doc" and the two of them became good friends. Doc was basically an honest man who had yielded to temptation when times got rough. His job as treasurer in a brokerage house had paid him very well. He was a model citizen until he began stretching the afternoon martinis into evening "pick-me-ups" before train time. The bars he frequented were well stocked. Then the inevitable happened.

Doc met an attractive blond, a regular patron of the bar. Doc started seeing her regularly. The friendship developed into an affair and Doc began supporting a second "family." For the first few months he could make ends meet, but each month the bills began to get heavier. Doc understood that he had to supplement his income. With the suburban home and the love nest and his job, he didn't have time for legitimate work. He knew enough about his firm to be able to embezzle funds from various accounts. He could juggle the books, draw checks and fix things. He was sure he'd never get caught.

After working out the details in his mind dozens of times, Doc tried his scheme. The auditors had recently checked the books and they weren't due again for several months. The first time he took $2,500. Everything went well, but the money didn't last for long.

His girlfriend wanted new furniture in the apartment, a fur coat, and some jewelry. The next embezzlement was for $5,000. Again Doc was certain that there wasn't much chance of being caught. The ease with which he swindled money amazed even him. He soon lost track of the stolen amounts and became less sophisticated about covering his tracks. Doc started to drink a good deal. He spent four or five nights a week in the city. Even his paramour was getting fed up with his drunkenness.

His wife had become suspicious. She started her own investigation and found the love nest. A confrontation degenerated into a hair-pulling contest. The blonde sex-pot came out second best and, when faced with the loss of hearth and home , she decided to go to the District Attorney. In his drunkenness, Doc had bragged about his scheme. Blondie had a lot to tell. The District Attorney was eager to listen.

The auditors poured over the books and found that Doc had embezzled in excess of $100,000! There wasn't any way he could make restitution. He had to pay another way. He was represented by a public defender, but there was no defense. He pleaded guilty and received a five-year sentence.

The relationship between Doc and Dom was perfect. They complemented each other. Dom was big and strong, ill-bred and uneducated, but streetwise. He was a hood — small-time and unsuccessful. All his life he had supported himself by stealing and knew nothing but street life. Doc, on the other hand, was tall, handsome, and well-educated, with a home in the suburbs and a place in the city. He was accustomed to the finer things in life. He had never even been in the "other side of town." His life had been exemplary. If he wanted, he could learn a lot from Dom. Doc decided to learn all he could.

The days and months passed. Dom learned about Wall Street businesses and Doc learned about life's seamy side. Together they formed an alliance to circumvent the law. For the first time in his life, Dom believed he was going to make it big.

Dom was released first. He knew exactly what to do. Doc had told him to locate a personable young man with a clean record, someone Dom could control and trust. The young man should then get a job in a Wall Street brokerage house, preferably a job in the cage, since that is where the actual stock certificates are handled, stored, and exchanged. Then the young man would find opportunities to steal some of the certificates and turn them over to Dom. When Doc was released, he would handle the negotiations of the certificates.

Dom searched around and finally found Sonny, a neighborhood kid with a high school education. He was a whiz with figures and the local lottery operators had given him a job working with the comptroller, handling the tapes and keeping up with the payoffs. Sonny still had a clean record so Dom propositioned Sonny, who was receptive. They agreed that Sonny would share in the proceeds of any stock certificates, once they were negotiated.

Three weeks later a brokerage house hired Sonny. After the first day, Sonny reported that the place was wide open for a rip-off. He was absolutely amazed at how easy it would be to steal certificates from the cage. Dom cautioned Sonny not to be in a hurry, to make sure he was not being watched and to be selective about the certificates he was going to steal. After a couple of weeks Sonny could not stand the temptation any longer. He selected a package of blue chip stocks, quickly stuffed them under his shirt and went to lunch. He left the building, went to a public locker and stashed the certificates until closing time. After work, he retrieved the stolen items and later that night gave them to Dom.

Dom had a few other things going for himself and advanced Sonny several hundred dollars. He advised Sonny to keep a low profile, keep his ears open, and not to take any more securities until he was told to. Dom himself was successful in his personal life as well. He had found Goldie, a much younger woman, who was a prostitute. She worked out of a midtown hotel. Goldie and Dom got along well and she liked his company. Besides being one of the more successful prostitutes, Goldie was trusted by some syndicate boys who used her to get rid of a lot of swag. Stolen jewelry, perfume, watches, liquor, just about anything that had been hijacked the day before, was offered to Goldie to buy. Dom handled all the fencing for Goldie and for the first time in many years had ample funds.

Dom was outside the prison when Doc was released. They greeted each other warmly, got into Dom's car and drove to the city. Dom briefed Doc about Sonny and the securities. Doc estimated it would be a few weeks before he could turn the certificates into cash.

Meanwhile, unknown to Sonny and his two mentors, the president of the brokerage house, in a secret meeting behind closed doors, advised the other company officers that several hundred thousand dollars in stock certificates had been stolen, possibly from the cage. He reported that he had hired a private investigator to work for the company. Some time later, the investigator declared that he had narrowed the suspects down to two people. One was a long- time employee whose heavy indebtedness made him a suspect; the other was a new employee who had had no previous employment but who dressed well, had a late model car and frequented the better bars and restaurants. The investigator reported he distrusted the young man, and decided he was the best suspect. The president asked his colleagues not to discuss the theft until it became public knowledge.

The undercover investigator busied himself around the office but his eyes were always on Sonny. He watched him for over a week. He was positive Sonny was the thief. The investigator arranged to have Sonny followed home several nights. Sonny's friendship with a lot of well-known neighborhood hoods was observed. One particular day, Sonny was acting strangely. He appeared to be handling the securities carelessly when suddenly, he slipped something inside his shirt. He then left the cage. The investigator confronted Sonny, identified himself, and asked him to take off his shirt. Sonny attempted to run. They got into a scuffle and rolled on the floor. The certificates fell out of Sonny's shirt. A crowd gathered in the hallway, the police were called, and Sonny was placed under arrest on a complaint signed by the brokerage house. The police case was assigned to Lieutenant Fred Short.

The lieutenant unsuccessfully questioned Sonny. Short believed Sonny was too young to be involved by himself in the theft. He examined Sonny's address book carefully and found Dom's name and telephone number. He felt sure that Dom was implicated in some way. Short decided his detectives could handle Sonny — he personally would deal with Dom. He called Dom and they arranged to meet in a restaurant deep in a subway station.

They renewed their old acquaintance and conversed about Fred's first arrest of Dom. Since then, Fred had been making his way up in the police department. He was married, had three children and recently received a college degree after going to night school. Dom didn't have much to talk about, except for several arrests and stretches in prison. He told Fred that he could not afford any more prison terms: any more convictions could send him away for a long stretch ... even for life. Fred got down to business. He told Dom that Sonny had been arrested, caught in the flagrant act of stealing bonds. Fred told Dom of his suspicions of Dom's involvement and mentioned that a lot of securities were still missing. Dom wondered to himself if Doc still had the securities, whether Sonny would eventually give him up, how much Fred really knew. He knew Fred was all cop but that he would try to help him. Dom begged off and asked for time, telling Fred he would call him the following night.

Dom then went to see Doc and asked if he still had the securities. Doc said he was in the middle of a deal to unload the securities. Dom told Doc to scrap the deal and return the securities to him. When Doc protested, Dom grabbed him by the neck and threatened strangulation. Doc agreed to get the certificates. Dom then told Doc he was going to get the certificates back to the company in order to short-circuit the possibility of being arrested. Doc unhappily produced the certificates which Dom took and hid.

The following day, Dom and Fred met at the subway restaurant. Dom told Fred that while he thought he could help him recover the securities, he had nothing to do with the theft. Although Fred knew Dom was lying, he had nothing on him and was anxious to recover the securities. Sonny, who could only be charged with attempted grand larceny, might get a suspended sentence and never talk. Consequently, Short replied that if Sonny didn't implicate Dom he would make a deal with him; if, however, Sonny confessed and involved Dom, he would have to be arrested. In the event of an arrest, Fred assured Dom a good deal. Dom stipulated that any deal would have to wait until Sonny's case was closed. They agreed.

Sonny pled guilty and was given a suspended sentence with three years probation. He never talked or implicated anyone else.

Dom then met with Fred and arranged for the return of the securities. Fred volunteered to convince the insurance company to reward Dom. Dom was delighted when Fred was successful in getting several thousand dollars for the return of the securities. Dom tried to give Fred some of the money, but Fred refused, saying he was only interested in getting information on any crimes committed in the city.

Dom decided he would give Fred any and all information he could get as long as he wasn't involved in the caper. In the meantime, he shared the reward money with Doc and Sonny. Doc took his money and left town to begin a new life somewhere else. Sonny was now working as an elevator boy in a large building and soon became the numbers runner for his building and those nearby.

Dom continued his relationship with Goldie, and selectively handled stolen property that she bought. He met Fred frequently and gave him valuable information that came mostly from Goldie who managed to get the story behind each bit of swag she purchased. Dom became privy to both Goldie's clientele and to her ramblings. On several occasions the suite was raided by local plainclothes police. After each arrest, Dom notified Fred, and arrangements were made to release Goldie.

Fred finally was promoted to Captain of another command. Dom felt as though he were losing his only friend. Fred reassured him and told him the new job gave Fred jurisdiction all over the city. He told Dom to continue giving him information and he would see to it that Dom was rewarded one way or another.

In the ensuing years Fred managed to keep Dom out of jail and Dom made sure that Fred got the latest information on stickups and robberies. They were both pleased with their relationship.

When Fred was promoted to Deputy Inspector, he called Dom and spent most of the day with him. He urged Dom to be careful about his dealings with Goldie since she was becoming too well known as a madam. Dom laughed and responded that if he led an exemplary life, he couldn't possibly be in a position to get information for Fred. No one understood that better than Fred, but Fred worried that Dom would get in trouble sooner or later and that he might not be in a position to help.

One day, Goldie showed Dom three $20 counterfeit bills that a client had brought to her. She said she could buy all she wanted at $13 a hundred and asked Dom if he wanted to handle some. Dom said he would look around for some customers and let her know. Goldie purchased one hundred dollars worth of bills and quietly passed them to trades people and clients. I was assigned to the investigation and, after interviewing the victim of the three bills, Goldie became a suspect.

When it looked like I had a good case against her, I went to her hotel and interviewed her. Goldie explained that she must have gotten the bills from a client. She agreed to keep her eyes open and report anything she learned. I told her it was no deal. She was going to be arrested, and could tell her story to a judge. Goldie claimed she needed time to think and asked me to return the following day, when she might have some information for me.

I returned the next day and questioned her about the source of the notes. I instructed her to introduce me as an old friend to anyone who entered her suite. Dom arrived and Goldie introduced me as "Nick," an old friend. When the phone rang she excused herself and told us that she would be back shortly.

Once we were alone, Dom asked me what I did for a living. I told him that I had owned a jewelry store with my brother,but we had had a falling out and he had given me several thousand dollars for my share of the business; he now owned the store by himself. I explained that I was bitter over the small amount he paid me and I wanted revenge. Dom asked what kind of revenge. I said, "Since I have the keys and the combination to the safe, I'd like to break into the store and steal everything!" Dom then volunteered to help me for a share of the proceeds. I told him I'd have to think it over. Then Dom told me he could get me all the funny money I wanted for $20 a hundred. I said, "That sounds like a good deal, do you have a sample I could look at? Maybe if I like what I see we can do business." He said, "I don't have any right now, but I'll try to get one for you later today." We agreed to meet later at the hotel.

When Goldie returned, Dom left. I was positive Dom was a big dealer in counterfeit money and was undoubtedly Goldie's source.

I asked Goldie if she had any information for me. She said she needed time to work things out; she wanted a promise of immunity. I told her I would agree if she consented to let me search the suite. She agreed as long as I didn't bother with anything except counterfeit money. I said okay and made a complete search of the suite. There was no counterfeit money there.

I asked Goldie about Dom, who, she said, was a harmless old man; she called him her errand boy. She said he had been in jail off and on for many years and she was giving him an opportunity to make an honest living. I asked her not to reveal my identity to Dom, since I would want to talk with him from time to time.

I met Dom later in the hotel lobby. He told me he had not been able to get any sample notes on such short notice, but that he would have some in a few days. In the meantime, he was interested in my brother's jewelry store and asked if we could make a deal. I said I still had a lot of planning to do, but I would let him know.

He walked me outside to the corner where he kept me in conversation. He kept moving around in circles and it occurred to me that he was setting me up. He wanted to be sure that someone was getting a good look at me. I didn't go to my car. I left Dom and decided to see if I was being followed. I walked to the subway, ran down the steps and stepped behind a vending machine. Sure enough, two men came running down and frantically searched the platform for me. When I stepped out to the platform, they saw me. After the train arrived I got on through the center door; they both stepped on the end of the train. Just as the doors were closing I stepped off; they didn't. I still didn't know who they were and what they wanted. I met my covering agents on the street and we returned to the office to try and put the pieces together.

There was no doubt that Goldie had a connection for counterfeit money. Her source could be one of many people. Her "Johns" or "clients" were numerous and varied. Her record showed several arrests for prostitution and nothing else. Dom also was still a mystery. One knew from his conversations that Dom had spent a lot of time in prison, but he did not act like a big-time hood. Undoubtedly he, too, had a connection for counterfeit money. Goldie denied that Dom was her source and it appeared that Dom didn't know that Goldie was under investigation. We could arrest Goldie for the three notes that were traced to her. There was no guarantee that she would cooperate, though there was always the possibility that she wouldn't go to jail. She could take the stand, admit she was a prostitute, and claim the bills were given to her in the normal course of business. She didn't have to worry about legal assistance since there were a few attorneys on her client list. We decided to present Goldie's case to a Grand Jury and give her a chance to testify if she so desired. In the meantime, we would learn all we could about Dom and see if he could lead us anywhere. He had made some damaging statements, but we didn't have enough to arrest him.

The investigating agents identified Dom and in a day or so we had his complete record. Two days later Goldie came to the office with her lawyer. I told her that since she had been identified on three separate counterfeit transactions, either she cooperated and told the story, or the case was going to the Grand Jury for indictment. Her lawyer took me aside and explained that Goldie would like to cooperate, but she was afraid. If her cooperation became known, she might as well go out of business. I assured her lawyer that her business did not concern me and that I had every intention of seeing her shop closed up. The attorney stated he would have her waive immunity and testify in her own behalf before the Grand Jury. He felt she could explain the passing of the notes. I asked Goldie if Dom were still around. She said she had not seen him since my last visit.

Three days later the case went before the Grand Jury. Goldie appeared, waived immunity and testified. The Jury apparently did not believe her story and indicted her. She was arrested and pleaded not guilty. Again she told me that she had not seen Dom since our last visit. She began to believe that we had hidden Dom and were going to use him to testify against her.

We were not successful in locating Dom. We found a rundown hotel where he had lived some time before. He had not paid his rent, so the hotel kept his belongings. I went through his old suitcase and found old photos, a few letters, some address books and old clothes. The address books provided some leads. One entry in particular was a surprise: a telephone number listed to Sergeant Fred Short.

Police Headquarters told me that Sergeant Short was now an inspector and one of the most respected senior officers in the Police Department. I called the inspector and we met later in a restaurant. He was cordial and anxious to cooperate. When I mentioned "Dom," he smiled and said, "I guess you're the guy who was going to rob his brother's jewelry store." I said, "No. I was the guy who was supposed to buy counterfeit money." The inspector said, "If you have the time, I'll tell you the whole story," which he did. He puffed on his pipe, looked up and said, "The bum really gets under my skin — if he ever had a chance he might have made the grade." Short mentioned that he also was an orphan and could have gone either way. Explaining further, he said that every time he had helped Dom, it was done legally and always with the District Attorney's approval.

He then told me that Dom had told him about a man who wanted to rob his brother's jewelry shop. The inspector had sent two of his men to try to identify the culprit. After Dom met the man on the street, the detectives tried to follow him but were given the slip. I told the inspector I was that man and that I had had the distinct feeling that Dom was parading me on the street for someone's benefit. The inspector asked me if I had a good case against Dom. I said I wasn't positive, but I was going to try to get one. The inspector said nothing for a few moments and then remarked that he was going to do something he had promised himself he'd never do - turn Dom over to go to work for another agency. He said he doubted that Dom was heavily involved and was sure Dom would cooperate with me. He promised to make Dom available to me in a couple of days.

The inspector kept his promise. Dom, Short, and I met. Dom swore he never handled counterfeit money. He said Goldie had the connection, a customer of hers named Sam. Dom thought Goldie made only one or two buys from Sam. Dom knew most of the shady characters in Sam's neighborhood and could come up with some information if he had time. I asked him where he had intended to get the sample notes that he had promised me at our first meeting. He said he hadn't really intended to get me the samples; he had only wanted to get enough information about the jewelry store to report it to the inspector. I had to try to use Dom to get the counterfeiting information for me. He promised to contact me daily.

When the trial date was set for Goldie's case, she became upset. She told her lawyer she was guilty and would be found guilty by the jury. She asked her lawyer to try to cop a plea and she would cooperate with the government. After her lawyer made the necessary arrangements, both of them appeared at my office for another interview.

Goldie knew I had the upper hand and she began: "First of all, I'm no big dealer. I only bought once, and that was a thousand dollars worth. I passed a few, sold a few, and loused up a lot when I tried to age them by dipping them in coffee." I asked, "Who'd you score from?" She said, "A guy named Sam. Sam's a burglar and a pretty rough guy. He's been a customer for the last nine months. He'll be back again and probably will want to sell me some more." "Next time he comes," I said, "I want to be introduced to him as a guy interested in buying large amounts. Does anyone know you've been busted?" She answered, "No, I didn't tell anyone."

I instructed her how to approach Sam and how to introduce us. She said she would arrange it. A week later Goldie called me and said Sam was at her place. I was there within the hour. The introduction was made: she introduced me as "Nicky," a good customer.

Sam was a middle-aged hood who looked like he might have been a boxer at one time. In spite of extra weight around his middle, and his graying hair, he looked as though he would still enjoy a good old-fashioned brawl.

After we were introduced he eyed me suspiciously and asked, "Who do you know who can vouch for you?" I asked, "Why do I need a voucher?" "Goldie said you were interested in buying some 'queer.'" I replied, "What's the big deal with the 'queer'? Why do I need references? I know Goldie and if that's not good enough for you, forget it."

Goldie then told Sam that she vouched for me 100 percent and would be responsible if anything went wrong. Sam said, "If anything goes wrong, I'll break your goddamn neck." She laughed and said she'd take care of him later on. Sam cooled off and asked, "Okay, Nick, how much you want?" I countered, "What's your price?" He said, "$15 a hundred." I told him, "I'll take 25 big ones if you can get it for me at $10." We haggled over the price and finally arrived at a price of $11 a hundred. I ordered $10,000 worth of the phony money.

If I gave him the money in advance, he said, he could make the delivery in one or two hours. I told him I would need a day or two to get the money together and that, anyway, I couldn't advance it to him because the money wasn't mine. I had to play it safe. Sam said he'd see what he could do and would let Goldie know. Dom came in at that moment and I left. Goldie called the following day to say that Sam wanted me to call him at a number he left. When I called, Sam told me he had the merchandise. We agreed to meet at eight that night outside the shuttle stop at the airport.

The plans for making an arrest at the time of delivery were made. I was to be arrested with Sam, but would make bail and keep Sam uninformed for as long as possible. Goldie was instructed to say that although I was her customer, she knew very little about me and had only one of my phone numbers. At seven o'clock, we deployed agents at the airport. They would move in only when I gave the signal that Sam, in fact, had the money and was ready to make the delivery. Sam was spotted riding around the airport parking lot with another man, looking, obviously, for anything that resembled the law. I was inside the terminal waiting for Sam. Finally he came into the terminal and we had a drink. He asked me if I was ready to do business. I said I was and that I had brought the money; he told me to follow him to his car. There, he introduced me to his friend and then asked his friend for the package. His friend reached down and gave Sam a small suitcase which he then handed to me. I opened it and saw that it was full of counterfeit money. I told Sam to walk over to my car so I could get my money. He was annoyed that I didn't have it with me.

I signaled to the covering agents and, within seconds, they appeared from every direction and placed Sam, his friend and me under arrest. We were immediately taken to the Secret Service office for processing. Sam and his friend had both been arrested previously and knew enough to stand on their right to remain silent. Their car was seized and the contents were well noted. Sam had an address book in his wallet that was perused very carefully. The three of us were kept in a locked room together. I told Sam that I had never been arrested before and asked him what I should do. He advised me to "Keep your damn mouth shut and get a lawyer." I told Sam that since the counterfeits were in my possession, I couldn't see how I could fight the case.

Sam again warned me to keep silent. I became indignant and accused Sam of setting me up. Sam lunged at me and I shouted for help. When the agent opened the door, I told him I was ready to talk. Sam shouted obscenities at me and swore he'd kill me. We had a conference and decided that, since we wouldn't get anywhere with Sam or his friend, we'd try to make them believe that I was getting preferential treatment because of my cooperation. They were carted off to jail to face arraignment the next morning.

The following day I told the Inspector what had happened. He suggested that he and I meet Dom later that evening.

Dom showed up right on schedule and confessed disappointment. He had snooped around but hadn't come up with any real information. He said he had had a talk at Goldie's with Sam that night, during which Sam spoke freely about handling counterfeit money. Dom thought he was one of the principal distributors. He learned that the money came from a legitimate print shop and that "The printer is some kind of a pervert who married his daughter." Dom said he was still digging and would contact me if he found anything else.

Several days later, Dom contacted me with the information that the printer had been arrested during the war for counterfeiting ration stamps. The list of previously arrested printers indicated four who had been arrested for counterfeiting ration stamps. A quick check revealed one died several years back. Parole records were examined and one entry sewed up the case:

"The defendant, Edward Polstis, is white, male, 36 years of age, 5 feet 8 inches tall, 165 lbs., brown hair, brown eyes; is a printer by trade and resides in a one-family home with his wife. This is his second marriage. His first marriage was to a widow who was eight years his senior. She died five months after the marriage. The defendant then married his wife's daughter, who was twenty-one years of age at the time of the original marriage. The defendant has two children as a result of this union."

Eddie had to be our man. The fingerprints on the money were checked against Eddie's - they matched.

Eddie's home was located without any particular problems but it was difficult to find his shop since it wasn't listed anywhere. Following him was the only way we could find his plant, although tailing would be dangerous. If he "made" the tail he might be in a position to destroy the evidence. The men working on the detail were given specific instructions to play it safe, lose him if necessary, but don't burn him. It took six days before they were able to follow Eddie to an area that could be considered suspicious. He generally took a subway to the last stop, and then walked apparently aimlessly, always checking for a tail. He would enter a block and while the agents were giving him plenty of leeway, he would suddenly disappear. It was decided to park several cars in that block to see exactly into which house he went. This used up considerable manpower, since Eddie did not make this trip every day.

One morning, he left on schedule, took his train, got off at the last stop, searched for a tail, and walked to the block where he previously disappeared.

This time he was seen slipping into an alley between two houses. Further investigation revealed a house at the end of the alley, the basement of which was being used for some sort of business. Since the shades were drawn throughout the structure, it was impossible to see into it. The premises were kept under surveillance and the matter was taken up with the U.S. Attorney. Based on the information obtained from Dom and the fingerprints on the bills, arrest and search warrants were obtained.

The day after the warrants were issued, Eddie entered the house at the end of the alley. We went to the house and announced ourselves but Eddie wouldn't open the door, which finally gave way under the pressure of several beefy agents. Eddie was then trying to dispose of a load of counterfeit notes that he had just finished printing. The press, the plates and all paraphernalia used in the printing were seized. From that point, the case's wrap-up was routine. The only problems were Goldie and Dom. Goldie was charged with possession of counterfeit money. She pleaded guilty and received a suspended sentence. We didn't have a case against Dom, so he was never charged. I called Fred to tell him that Dom's information had been responsible for the capture of the plant. I also told Fred that Dom should get a reward for supplying us with that information. Fred then arranged for Dom to accept several hundred dollars reward money.

About a year and a half later, I was working undercover and was about to meet a suspect. On my way, I accidentally met Dom, and we renewed acquaintances. He seemed to be down on his luck and appeared quite dejected. He told me that Fred had retired, and was living about forty miles outside of New York. He heard from him occasionally. He said Goldie had to move out of town since her probation officer wanted her out of the city. He heard she was working as a receptionist at a hospital.

I asked him what he was doing; he said "Nothing." I told him I was going to meet a guy and perhaps he could help me. He said he'd he happy to. I then briefed him about my meeting and told him it would help if, while I was talking to the suspect, he would accidentally run into me, call me Nicky, and ask when I got out of jail. He could then imply that we served time together in prison. Dom was in his element — he liked playing the game.

My appointment was at three o'clock in the afternoon at the intersection of two main streets. The suspect was a bookmaker called Morty who had recently made a connection for counterfeit money and was anxious to sell. Although I had gotten an introduction to Morty through an informant, Morty just didn't trust me. Morty needed to be convinced that I was "one of the boys."

I met him as planned and we spent some time chatting on the street. About ten minutes later, Dom came along. He walked over to me, slapped me on the back and asked, "Nicky! When did you get home?" I answered,

"About eight months ago." He picked it up and continued: "Did you meet the board before me or after me?" I said I made it on the second try. He said he had been out about five months. I then introduced him to Morty. They quickly engaged in a conversation about people they knew or served time with. I excused myself ostensibly to make a call at a nearby public booth. My absence enabled Morty to ask Dom a few questions. When I returned, Dom said he had to go but would call me.

Morty was in a better frame of mind and wanted to know how long I had known Dom. He wondered if Dom would be interested in buying some counterfeits. I told him to lay off Dom as I expected he would be one of my customers. From that moment, Morty was no problem. The following day he supplied me with samples. He quoted a fairly good price and I agreed to buy a package of $50,000 worth of counterfeits. Morty didn't ask for money in advance; he was either well trusted or had enough of his own money to pay for the merchandise. The delivery was scheduled for 8 o'clock the following night in a parking lot behind a restaurant.

The timing was good, the parking lot would have enough activity and could easily be covered. Morty was closely watched. He went about his daily activities, taking bets and meeting people. About 5: 15 he went home and at seven he left and got into his car, driving to the designated parking lot. When he spotted me, he got out of his car, opened the trunk, took out a package, and walked over to my car. He handed me the package casually and told me the count was good, and that he would replace any bad ones. I opened the package, and after I saw that it did contain a quantity of counterfeit money, I gave the prearranged signal. The covering agents immediately placed us both under arrest and took us to U. S. Secret Service headquarters for the usual processing. When we had an opportunity to be alone for several minutes, I opened the conversation by saying, "Morty, I don't know you too well, but something here stinks. This whole deal was too pat. They were conveniently waiting for us. It was like taking candy from a baby. I don't know about you, but I owe the state a lot of time and I'm dead if I don't find a friend. So don't expect me to be a stand–up guy. I had the stuff on me when the bust came, and I can't con my way out of it. So, if they ask me where I got it, it could only be you. I'm sure they saw the whole thing. You don't have to cover for me, because I ain't covering for anyone. In sixty-four hours I'll be on my way back to the state can." Morty was already in a state of shock and my soliloquy didn't help him any.

After we were separated, Morty told the whole story. His source was a long distance truck driver who arrived in New York once a week. The driver had a connection with a plant in the midwest and delivered counterfeit money to New York on a regular basis. Morty explained that he had purchased $100,000 worth of the money and was ready to place another order when he had made my sale.

He then played it straight and cooperated with us by ordering another $100,000 from the driver. In eight days, when the delivery was made, the driver was arrested. The printer was the driver's brother-in-law. His small print shop in the midwest was captured on the basis of the information provided by the driver. It was a good case because while there was no real organization behind the plant, the truck driver was in a position to distribute the notes over a large part of the country. For a small operation, they were fantastically successful for awhile.

Not long after that case was closed, I was told that Fred Short had died of a heart attack and was going to be buried the following day. I went to the church and attended the services. Dom was sitting alone and wet-eyed in the last pew. He was a pitiful figure — his clothes were old, he needed a shave, and appeared to need a good meal. When the services were over, I asked him if he needed a lift back to the city. He said he did and we had an excellent opportunity to talk.

There was no doubt that he was distraught over Fred's death. He had read of Fred's demise in the paper and took a bus to Fred's hometown. He had spent the night in the church and was ready for the funeral the next morning. He was broke and completely down and out.

I told Dom I had some money for him, but hadn't been able to locate him. He told me to use the money for flowers for Fred or give the money to his widow.

A week before Christmas, a police sector car got a call about a burglary in progress at a pharmacy. Two officers proceeded immediately to the location where they found the front door had been smashed in and heard the alarm ringing. The officers entered the premises cautiously, flashing their lights all over the store. Finally, one flashlight centered on a pitiful figure sitting under the counter. It was Dom. He submitted to the arrest meekly. He was handcuffed, thrown into the back of the radio car and carted off to the precinct. The officers turned the prisoner over to the detectives and then settled down for a smoke, accepting the congratulations of their fellow officers.

Half an hour later, one of the detectives came out and told the officers that they had made an excellent arrest. He told them, "This guy has a record as long as your arm. He was first arrested over forty years ago. He served time with the best of them, and most of all, he opened up and told us everything we wanted to know." The cops were elated and went back to their radio car. One said to the other, "You know, that bum could have easily escaped. The alarm was ringing for five minutes. It's almost like he wanted to be arrested. Probably just another nut." "Yea, a born loser."

The author as a New York State Trooper in 1938.

JUST PALS . . . Marine Lt. Carmine J. Motto, of Valhalla, N. Y., shows this native boy on Okinawa the mysteries of an American field ration can. While neither can speak the same language . . . kindly gestures are understood . . . and friendship's made . . . quite easily.
International News Photo from Marine Corps
New York Journal-American ★ Wed., April 18, 1945—1

The author in the Marine Corps during World War II.

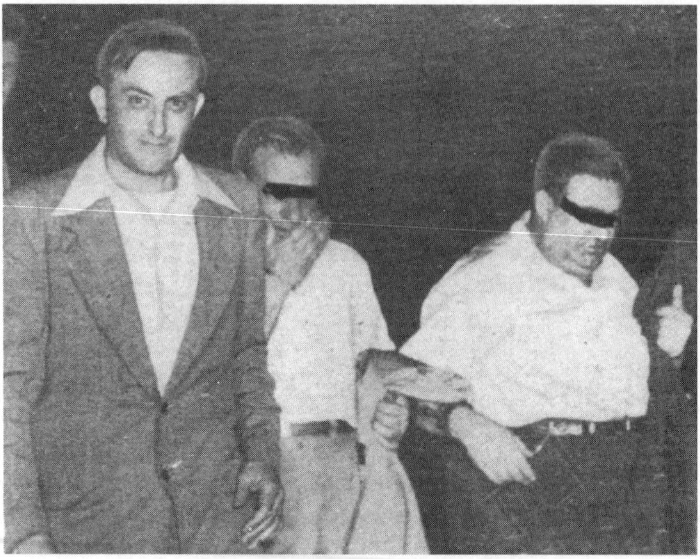

The author arrests suspects involved in a drug and counterfeiting case.

President Harry S. Truman on a whistle stop in New Rochelle, N.Y. during the 1948 campaign. The train had been scheduled to make a five-minute stop with the President speaking for only two minutes; however, the crowd grew so large that it became necessary to make it a major stop The author quickly arranged for a flatbed truck, had it covered with borrowed bunting, and placed into the town square for use as a platform. The President was delighted with the reception he received and the author got a pat on the head for his quick thinking.

The author arrests Mrs. Collazo after her husband's unsuccessful attempt to assassinate President Truman in 1950.

118—NO. 51 NEW YORK, THURSDAY, NOVEMBER 2, 1950 FIVE CENTS

ASSASSIN ADMITS PLOT TO KILL TRUMAN WAS HATCHED IN BRONX

Assassin's Wife Defiant at Her Arrest

By ROBERT H. PRALL, *Staff Writer.*

The stony-faced wife of a quiet little man who wanted to kill the President of the United States found pride last night in the shame that has come to her family.

This was Mrs. Rose Collazo, 42-year-old wife of a fanatical Puerto Rican nationalist who turned assassin overnight. There were no tears, no humiliation for Rose Collazo. Her defiant, black eyes gave her face the look of an eagle. Her head was high, her body erect as she strode last night from a filthy Bronx tenement for whatever destiny awaits the wife of a murderer.

Around Rose Collazo cringed her three frightened daughters. A swarm of Secret Service agents and police officers escorted them from their $35-a-month apartment after three long hours of constant questioning. The daughters covered their faces and Rose Collazo reproached them.

"You do not have to do that," she snarled.

Down three darkened flights of stairs they walked in grim silence, like actors coming onto the stage of a great tragedy. And there was a great audience in the paper-littered pavement of Brook Ave.

Thousands of Neighbors.

This little block between 135th and 136th Sts. in the Mott Haven section of the Bronx has seen excitement before in the street warfare of the slums but never before was there the excitement that last night had brought.

Thousands of neighbors of a man who tried to kill his President had roamed along the block all the late afternoon and evening. And then suddenly the eerie scene was electrified by the floodlights of press and police. The throng surged forward through police lines to the doorway of 173 Brook Ave., the home of an assassin. The curtain was going up on the last act of the stark drama that had come to their block.

In the doorway, Rose Collazo's daughters cringed again at the sight of the photographers.

'Lift Up Your Heads.'

"Lift up your heads," commanded their mother. "Do not cover your faces. Let them take their pictures. We are proud because we are fighting for an ideal. These people here, they were born in this country. But we were not and so we must fight. We are fighting for an ideal."

And Rose Collazo's daughters obeyed their mother. They, too, stood erect and proud. But their eyes could not match the fire of the great tragedienne. She looked aloft, to the darkened sky, to the staring faces that peered through the night from the tenements on both sides of the block.

This was the block that had sent a killer on a ghastly mission to Washington and no one wanted to miss a moment of this Caribbean finale.

A Mask of Scorn.

Rose Collazo, cold and stern, stood there, her face a ghastly mask of scorn. And then the Se-

(Continued on Page 2.)

ROSA COLLAZO ... the questions.

MRS. COLLAZO *After the questions.*

Wife Is Held, 2 Sought as Accomplices

Related news and pictures on Pages 16 and 17.

Mrs. Rosa Collazo of 173 Brook Ave., Bx., defiantly proud of her husband's bungled attempt to assassinate President Truman, was held in $50,000 bail early today as a partner in a Puerto Rican Nationalist plot.

She was the only one held ... up last night by Secret Service ... swiftly to crack the conspiracy ... Puerto Rican sections were bein... two other conspirators ...

From his closely guarded hospital bed in Washington, her husband, Oscar, in good condition despite a chest wound, confessed that the plot had been hatched in his Bronx home.

"We decided to kill the President and start a revolution in this country and independence for Puerto Rico," he said.

Truman Guard Reinforced.

But letters found on the body of Collazo's slain accomplice, Griselio Torresola of 1239 Ward Ave., Bx., indicated the possibility that the assassination might have ...

Truman Takes Walk as Usual

By the United Press.

WASHINGTON, Nov. 2.—President Truman took his usual early morning walk through downtown Washington today, unperturbed by yesterday's attempt on his life.

Shaw's Last Words: 'I Want to Sleep'

Playwright Dies At 94 in Cottage

Last Traces Go

Workmen with a bucket of soapy water scrub the bloodstains at the steps to Blair House after two gunmen had tried to kill President Truman.

2 GI Units Out Of Red Trap, 3rd Still Ringed

More Chinese Reported Joining North Koreans

By EARNEST HOBERECHT, *United Press Staff Correspondent.*

'Heck' He Said

"I would have taken the gun away from him, shoved it up his gullet and pulled the trigger." That was the reaction of President Truman to the attempt on his life. He is shown here attending unveiling ceremonies in Arlington National cemetery shortly after yesterday's shooting at Blair House.

Lynch Won't Comment On Dewey Accusations

By RAY GHENT, *Staff Writer.*

World-Telegram and Sun Index

St. Louis to Guard Truman Well

'Dastardly Act,' Says Barkley

THE WEATHER

Today's Scratches

Newspaper headlines following the attempt on President Truman's life.

The author and other agents display a $2 million counterfeit seizure.

The author meets with E. Villea, Chief of the Cuban Secret Service, and his assistants after a successful counterfeit investigation in Havana.

The author searches a counterfeiting plant.

Director James Rowley congratulates the author after his promotion to Special Agent-in-Charge of the Special Anti-Counterfeiting Detail in New York.

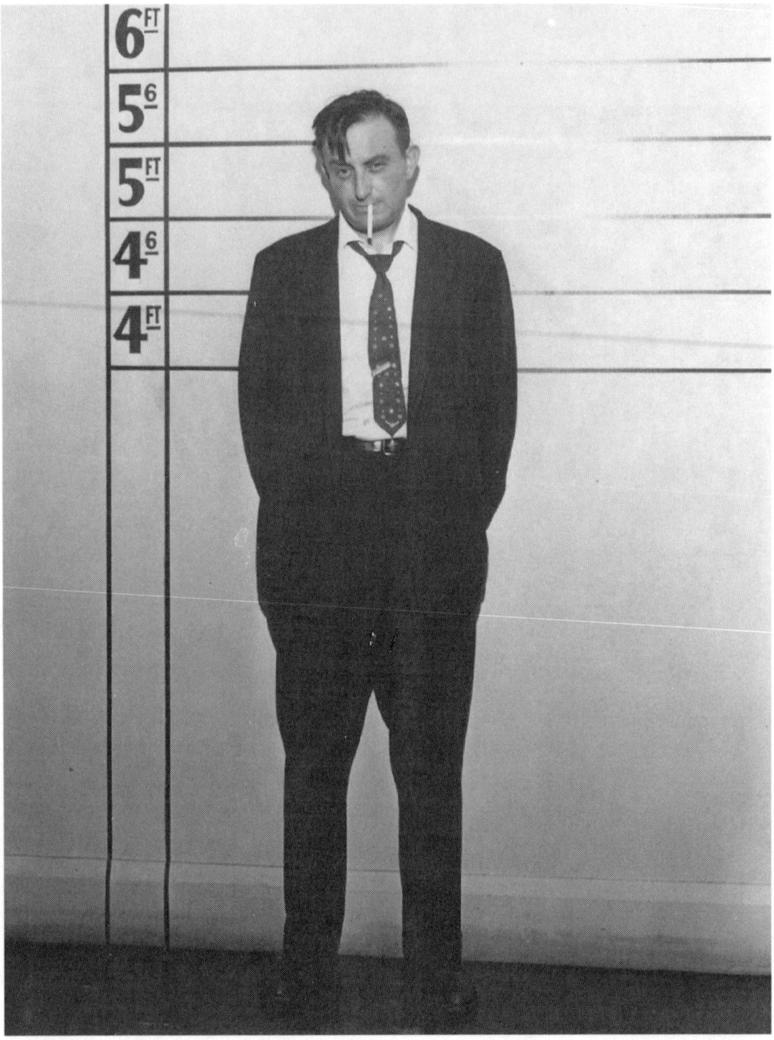

The author was "arrested" along with the suspects in order to keep his cover from becoming known.

The author meets old friend Joe Medina in Havana. Joe had been head of the Cuban Secret Police under Machado. When Batista overthrew the Machado regime, Joe fled to the United States and subsequently became a U.S. citizen and a vice-president of American Express. Joe was an excellent investigator and was very helpful in our investigations in Cuba.

Working undercover on the streets of New York City

The author and SAIC Al Whitaker survey a $2 million seizure of counterfeit bills.

Smiles all around over the seizure of $5 million in counterfeit stamps.

The author examines a $175,000 seizure of counterfeit notes.

The author is sworn in as Deputy Commissioner of White Plains, New York Department of Public Safety — a post he held for 16 years.

President Ford greets the author at a function in White Plains, New York.

Wasting a Day with Joe Valachi

Joe Valachi's name had popped up in several investigations I had handled. He was never mentioned as anyone important, but rather as someone who was on the fringe of neighborhood criminal activities. His territory had been under heavy investigation because of counterfeiting movement and I had arrested many of his friends and associates.

In 1963, some time after the McClelland Committee held public hearings on the Mafia, during which Valachi testified about organized crime and illicit narcotics traffic, I was called to Washington to interview Joe. He had already spoken to the Federal Bureau of Narcotics and the Department of Justice and our headquarters decided that he should be interviewed for any information that would be beneficial to our agency.

It would have been easier to receive permission to interview the President than to interview Joe. He was under heavy guard and in maximum security. After obtaining all the necessary clearances from the Justice Department and other officials from the Attorney General's office, a date and time were set for the interview. I arrived at the jail at the appointed time. I was checked, rechecked and double checked, then I was taken through a series of locked doors and corridors. Finally, I arrived at Joe's chambers, a sort of double cell at the death house in a Washington, D. C. jail.

Joe was sitting at an old wooden table with a sheaf of lined yellow paper in front of him. He was dressed comfortably in a pair of gray slacks, slippers, and a T-shirt. The cell looked like the average room in a tenement -— a few old chairs, a radio, a portable television, with "rabbit ears" antenna with aluminum foil twisted on the ends, a small dresser, and an adjustable hospital bed. Another table had a two-burner hot-plate on it. The air was heavy with the unmistakable fragrance of spaghetti sauce. When I entered, Joe walked over and held out his hand.

He said, "Hi, I'm Joe." I said, "I'm Carmine. Remember me?" He said, "Carmine, that's a good start." He then told me my last name and said he knew of me from ten or fifteen neighborhood cronies of his, whose names he recited, all of whom I had arrested. I reminded him that we had met on several occasions in an East Bronx candy store. He said he'd rather forget that. He then asked about a lot of his friends. I told him who, among them, had been arrested and who was taking over the neighborhood. I gave him a couple of good rumors and some innocuous information he was anxious to hear. He told me he was making some spaghetti and we had a tasty luncheon. He apologized for the lack of wine and promised one day we would get together and split a bottle. I told him the next time I'd take him to a good Italian restaurant. Joe laughed and said, "You're playing it pretty safe. I ain't getting out of here in your lifetime." I said, "Why, you figuring on dying?" He said, "I'm writing my book. Not for myself because I'm gonna rot in here. Maybe if I get some money, I can take care of my family. I never did anyone any good in my lifetime. Maybe when I die I can do a good turn."

Then, before I could begin to ask him specific questions, he launched into a monologue about how he became involved in a murder while he was in the Atlanta Penitentiary. He talked about being in the same cell with the kingpin, Vito Genovese. Vito wielded as much power inside the penitentiary as outside. One day Vito kissed him on the cheek. Valachi interpreted this as being the kiss of death and was certain someone had been badmouthing him.

The next day in the prison courtyard, Joe felt that someone was going to kill him. He saw a man he thought was Joe Beck, a henchman of Vito's, who was behaving suspiciously. Valachi thought that he was going to be hemmed in by a group and killed. Out of desperation, he claimed, he picked up an iron pipe and bashed in Joe Beck's head. Valachi was overpowered by the prison guards and placed in a solitary cell, after telling the authorities he had killed Joe Beck in self defense. He said he was amazed to learn that the man he killed was Joe Saupp and not Joe Beck. Saupp was not connected with the Cosa Nostra and certainly was not a member of Vito's Mafia.

Valachi assured me that Joe Beck and Joe Saupp were physically identical. I said I knew them both and agreed that they could pass for twins. Valachi was delighted; he jumped up and rang for the guard. The guard opened the door and Joe shouted, "Here's a man who knows. Tell him, Carmine! Tell him how much Saupp and Joe Beck look the same." It was not my intention to lend credence to any story that Joe Valachi told the authorities; but in good conscience I had to agree that both men resembled each other.

Without my asking, Joe then settled down and began telling me the history of organized crime in New York City. It struck me as being a bit incongruous. He was the man who had told the world about the dreaded secret society of crime — the "Cosa Nostra" — while I knew him to be a man who obeyed the syndicate's orders of "omerta" (silence). Here he was, talking faster than I could listen. Several times I tried to interrupt him to ask a few questions. There was no stopping him; he talked like a condemned man with little time. It was like he was verbally writing and rehearsing his book.

He started at the beginning. He was born in 1903. He left school at age 15 and got a job on a scow in New York harbor; how he worked for a year. I thought to myself, "Joe, if you worked for a year, that was the only year you ever worked at a legitimate job." He started to tell me that he joined the Cosa Nostra in 1930. I interrupted and asked if it was actually called the Cosa Nostra in those days. He was a bit indignant and said, "Of course, we always called it the Cosa Nostra." He said only the outsiders still called it the Mafia.

I prodded him with, "How come I never heard of it?" He whipped right back and looked me in the eye: "Because you didn't do your homework!"

He said he started out with the 107th Street gang in 1922, working for Big Dick Amato, who was slain in 1931. He said his entry into the LCN (La Cosa Nostra) was handled by Ciro Terranova, the Artichoke King. Then the names came fast and furious: Al Brown was a member, got out and came back; Pip the Blind was a member — he was found hanged in a cell in jail; Charlie Bullets started the "Minutemen." He said this group threw milk cans through store windows. After the break, the group would steal the merchandise, take it to the getaway cars that were waiting to take them away. They figured they had five minutes before anyone responded to the various alarms. He told how they disposed of their loot through three characters named Al Alonzo, Big Dick and Vincent Rao.

He told about how he was shot in the back of the head in 1923 by the police when he attempted to escape from the scene of a burglary. The gang took him to a doctor who removed the bullet — Joe claimed the only anesthesia he had had was a bottle of Scotch. Several gang members then smuggled him into a hospital on 86th Street in New York City. He stayed there for three months.

I lost track of his ramblings until he talked about his being a soldier in the Cosa Nostra. I judged the year to be about 1930. He said he didn't really make much money as a member. He had to earn his own living by the takes from his pinball machines, juke boxes and shylocking. Valachi then spoke about the much-discussed Castellmarese War, which involved two separate groups vying for complete control of the crime syndicate. Joe Masseria ran things until Salvatore Maranzano challenged him and his group. This set off the war. Masseria was murdered in April 1931; all his succeeding heirs were also murdered, including Al Mineo and Steve Ferrugio — killed on November 5, 1930 — and Joe Catania, murdered the following February. Maranzano emerged as the ruling power until he was murdered in September 1931. His heirs also met their demise in rapid succession.

Joe gave me a rundown on the murder of Tom Reina and how an underboss named Guy Gagliano tried to avenge his death. He ran through a list of names and events that I could not and did not want to follow. He then mentioned the names Nick Paduano and Salvatore Shillitani, as people who had been recruited to perform some killings. I stopped him and asked him to tell me more about Shillitani, whom I had known as a counterfeiting suspect years ago.

He paid no attention to me and continued his stories until he was almost current. He then described the five ruling families of New York under Vito Genovese, Carlo Gambino, Joe Bonanno, Gaetano Lucchese and Joe Profaci. He continued to ramble and insisted on detailing how he was inducted into the Costa Nostra: the oath he took and the ritual that was followed to pick a godfather for each member.

I finally blew up and said, "For Christ's sake, Joe, will you shut up for a minute? You could go on all day. I'm not the McClelland Committee or Bobby Kennedy or the television audience. I saw that show, I know all about it. Everyone is now an expert on crime in America. I'm not interested in who killed whom. They're all dead, may they rest in peace. I'm interested in the people who are around now and are still committing crimes. Do me one favor, answer my questions and save your recitation for your book."

Joe said he wanted to fill me in on the whole picture. I told him he was about 20 years too late.

Finally, I said, "Joe, you admitted handling ration stamps during and after World War II." He said, ""Yes." I asked if they were counterfeits. He said "No, they were stolen stamps." I reminded him that years before, I had talked to him about counterfeit stamps. He brushed it off by saying, "I don't remember." I asked him where he got the stolen stamps. He said from various people around the neighborhood. I asked him if he was associated with Vito Genovese in the 1930s when Vito was handling counterfeit money. I reminded him that Vito had been picked up and questioned about counterfeit money. Again he denied knowing anything about it. I told him this time he hadn't done his homework properly. He again attempted to tell me in great detail about crimes that took place thirty-five years ago. I urged him to save it for a better audience.

I tried again: "In the late forties, I arrested a group of your close associates in the Bronx for distributing counterfeit three-cent stamps"" He lit up and said, "Yeah, I remember. You cleaned out the neighborhood. For awhile, things were getting pretty bad; no one knew who was going to be picked up next." Then he laughed and said, "There was even talk of getting you." I told him that was street talk and no one hated me that much. He said, "Okay, I'm gonna tell you a story."

"Remember Vinny from the Bronx?" I said, "Yes, I locked him up." "Okay, here's what happened. When I'm finished call me a liar. Vinny was arrested for passing one counterfeit note. Right?" I said, "Right." "He went to trial and was convicted. The judge gave him six years. He figured you gave him a dirty deal. You pushed and pushed and got him six years for something he should have gotten thirty days for."

I reminded Joe that although Vinny had been wheeling and dealing in counterfeits, the one note was all we could prove. It also came out in court that Vinny had threatened the storekeeper, to keep him from testifying. The case involved more than just the one pass.

He then went on about Vinny and said that while he had been in prison, his wife had left him. When he got out of jail, he had threatened to kill her if she didn't come back and he took to walking around with a gun in his pocket. Vinny became a sick guy, physically and psychologically.

Valachi continued: "Then one day, you came into the candy store, snooping around. We were all playing cards. Vinny was there too. That was the first time he had seen you since the trial. He still had the gun and he started an argument with you about being framed. He was getting pretty steamed up and you were giving ground. I remember you were backing out of the store and he was still calling you a rotten cop. Vinny wasn't sure if you had a gun and he was trying his best to find out." Joe stopped and then said, "Who saved you that day?"

I said, "I didn't figure I was saved, but I recall that Vinny's cousin stepped between us, grabbed Vinny by the neck and dragged him to the back of the store. He apologized for Vinny's actions and hoped I wouldn't make trouble for him."

Joe interrupted and said, "I was right! You remember it all." I wanted to say, but didn't, "Yeah, Joe, I remembered very well. I did have a gun; stupidly I had locked it in the glove compartment of my car parked three blocks away. I promised myself that I would never again be without it."

Vinny, in fact, had tried to kill his wife. She reported him to the probation office and Vinny was arrested and eventually returned to prison for parole violation. After two weeks in prison, he sent for me. He said it was very important. I went to the prison to see him, an entirely different Vinny. He appeared quiet, contrite and expansive. He told me that he forgave me for taking away his liberty, but that he certainly got too long a stretch for passing one counterfeit note. I reminded him that he was a dealer in counterfeit money and the one counterfeit note was all we could prove. The jury found him guilty and the sentencing judge thought the sentence was just. I asked him why he sent for me. He said he had Hodgkins' disease and didn't have long to live. He said he didn't want to die in jail. He suggested that if I could get him out on the street he could work for me and supply me with information on counterfeiting. I couldn't tell him that the warden had told me that the doctors had given him less than a month to live. I told him that being an informant would be out of character for him and that it wouldn't work; there really wasn't any information he could supply. However, I lied and said that I would try and help him get back on the street. He begged me to do something so he wouldn't die in jail. We shook hands and I left. He died as the prison doctors had predicted, 28 days later.

While I was daydreaming, Joe was still talking. He insisted on telling about some murders he was involved in, back 30 years ago.

A little later, the guard came in on a routine check and I decided it was a good time to leave. I was ready to say good-bye, when Joe said, "Have another cup of coffee; I want to ask you something."

He asked, "Did you ever give a guy a dirty deal?" I said, "Not knowingly." He said, "What about Renaldi?" I was a little perplexed and asked, "What about Renaldi?" He said, "You remember him?" I replied, "Yes, I do. I locked him up about fifteen years ago." Joe taunted, "What did he do? What did you lock him up for?" I said, "He was involved in a counterfeit deal." Joe interrupted, "You gave him a dirty deal. He got a ten-year bit for doing nothing." I said, "What do you mean, for doing nothing?" Joe smiled and said, "Listen, and I'll tell you the whole true story."

"Renaldi was a knock-around guy. He was arrested for everything on the books. He spent more than half of his life in jail. He had good connections and could get anything he wanted." I said, "Okay, Joe, so he had good connections, but what about the bad deal you said I gave him?" Joe raised his hand, signaling me to shut up. He said, "See, you think you know everything. Listen and you'll learn something." He continued, "Renaldi made a good score and he wanted to parlay his money on a good deal. Someone told him the Lupo Brothers had a load of "queer.' He got in touch with the Lupos and put in an order for 25 grand in phony $20 bills. He was told when to pick it up. The deal was set up for the following Tuesday in one of Lupo's restaurants. When Renaldi got to the restaurant, Mickey Lupo tells him he'll have to wait; that they had another deal to take care of first. He promised as soon as they took care of the other deal, Renaldi would get delivery of his money. Renaldi waited around the restaurant for awhile. He got nervous, started walking in and out of the joint. He sure must have looked suspicious to you guys who were covering the joint."

I had to break in again. "All right, Joe, I know the rest. I was working undercover and managed to get next to the Lupo Brothers. I had ordered twenty grand in counterfeit notes that day. There were a lot of our guys on the street covering everyone going in and out of the joint. When Lupo finally made the delivery to me, we busted him and Renaldi, who was right there at the time of the delivery. As a matter of fact, Renaldi had over three grand in good money when he was grabbed — and from what we could see, he was the man behind the whole deal."

Joe said, "That's where you're mistaken. Renaldi came there to buy, not to sell. Everything he did, you guys turned around to make him look guilty. As God is my judge, I tell you that Renaldi was innocent. Not only that, but he goes to trial, he's convicted, and the judge throws ten years at him. I tell you, Carmine, it was a rotten deal."

I said, "You finished, Joe? How come you don't tell the rest of the story? The fact that he appealed the conviction and it was upheld. How come you don't talk about the trial? Not one man said anything about Renaldi, except how he was acting before and after the delivery. No one gave him a bad deal. No one lied. Everyone called it as they saw it. The jury chose to believe it. Don't forget, the Lupos also said they were innocent and that they were framed. They went to trial. They had the best lawyers. They used every trick they knew and they still were convicted. Joe, I'm sorry, but my conscience is clear on Renaldi."

Joe shook his head and said, "Renaldi was a good friend. He served a lot of Goddamn time. Now he's dead; Lord have mercy on him. That's one guy I felt sorry for." I said, "I could think of a lot of other people you could be sorry for. I just can't see you brooding over Renaldi." Joe gazed at the floor and said, "You know, sometimes you can be awful thick." I said, "Okay, Joe, I'm thick and I also have a one-track mind. Now that you're such an expert on the Renaldi case, how about telling me who printed Lupo's counterfeits?"

Joe laughed and said, "You're right, you do have a one-track mind." Standing up, I said, "Joe, I'm leaving." He asked if I would return. I said, "Only if you have something to tell me." He insisted that I return on another day, that perhaps we could talk about old times. I told him I would try. We shook hands, he leaned over and whispered, "Do me a favor. Go back to the old neighborhood and tell the boys I'm no stool. I had to do what I had to do." I said, "Joe, no one can ever accuse you of being a stool. From the way I see it, no one will ever serve a day as a result of your talking." He smiled, I said good-bye and under my breath I couldn't help but think, "Joe Valachi, you're the biggest fraud ever perpetrated on the American public."

Suicide in Panama

During his early youth, Joel Serly was always in trouble. He was a truant and a thief and had come to the attention of the local police on many occasions. His first arrest had been for shoplifting a pair of leather gloves. At a subsequent appearance before a family court judge, Joel was sentenced to a youth home. His parents had told the judge that Joel was incorrigible and that they could do nothing more with him. Joel spent over a year at the youth home and was released on his promise that he would go to school and behave himself. For awhile he did just that; but as time went on, he reverted to his old ways.

His second arrest was for breaking into a church and stealing the poor box. Joel was held in custody at the police station until his mother came. The probation officer assigned to his case recommended that Joel be sent to a state school for an indeterminate period. The judge agreed and Joel spent most of his teenage years in an institution.

By the time he was released, his mother and father had died. He tried several jobs unsuccessfully and then decided to work illegally. Several of his friends lived by robbing people in parks and other lonely areas so Joel joined with them two or three times. The proceeds of four muggings netted him about $60. Joel decided to go out alone to a lover's lane he knew. The victims would be at a disadvantage, and many would not report the robbery because of the circumstances. During the next several weeks, Joel pulled about ten jobs and got about $400 in cash and some assorted jewelry.

One particular night, Joel spotted a late-model car parked in a lonely wooded area. A middle-aged man was in the car with a woman. They had a bottle of liquor and were having a good time. After awhile the man removed his jacket and trousers and placed them in the back seat. Joel waited patiently until the couple were completely oblivious to their surroundings and so entwined as to make a fast move impossible. Joel then went to the car, casually opened the back door, took the man's pants and jacket and ran off with them. When he examined the contents of the clothing, he found a wallet with a gold badge that said "Detective: Police Department" and $82 in cash. A .38-caliber revolver was in another pocket. Joel threw away the badge, the empty wallet and the clothing, but could not throw away the gun. He had never had a gun before and he liked it; it gave him a warm feeling. He felt he could handle any situation as long as he had the gun in his pocket.

In the ensuing weeks he used the gun often. He pointed it at his victims and his robberies became relatively quick and simple.

Joel had a small apartment on the west side of town. A very attractive girl named Elsie lived in the apartment above him. Joel learned that Elsie ran a one-woman whorehouse. He became a steady customer. He didn't tell Elsie much about himself, but she saw he always had his revolver on when he visited her. Elsie quickly realized that Joel was a cheap thug who could only bring trouble and though she secretly wished that Joel would take his business elsewhere, she felt an attachment to him.

At the start of a busy weekend, Elsie picked up a client in a midtown bar and took him to her apartment. She had just disrobed when the man pulled out a badge and arrested her. Elsie was quite upset and asked the officer if there wasn't some way she could straighten the matter out. The officer told her if she were talking about a bribe, he would add that to the prostitution charges. The only way she could help herself was by giving him information on any felonies that she might have learned about. Elsie then told the policeman about Joel. She said she knew he was some kind of a stickup man because he never worked, had money and always carried a gun.

The cop called his office and received permission to postpone Elsie's arrest and to concentrate on Joel. Another officer from the local precinct was sent to assist in Joel's arrest.

Joel came home about one in the morning. As he was about to enter his apartment, the two officers stopped and frisked him. They removed the gun from Joel's belt and then searched his apartment, finding quite a bit of loot. They were elated to learn that the gun they took from him had been stolen from a brother police officer. Joel received a hard time at the precinct, not only for stealing a policeman's gun, but also for stealing his trousers and his dignity. After several hours in the squad room, Joel admitted several crimes and was charged with multiple counts of robbery, assault and larceny. He thought he would "cop out" and get a break. He pleaded guilty to one count of assault, larceny and possession of a revolver. The judge gave him a ten to fifteen year sentence.

Joel was philosophical about his arrest, figuring that his depredations had caught up with him. He was sent to a state prison and after the usual quarantine period, was assigned to the kitchen. Joel adjusted quickly to prison life, knowing that if he hoped to make parole in decent time, he would have to obey the rules.

Joel decided to write to Elsie; her part in his arrest was unknown to him. Surprisingly he received an answer from her and soon correspondence became regular and meaningful. She was secretly happy that Joel had been arrested and had apparently changed his ways. She told him she had given up her private business and had found a job in a bakery. Joel was happy believing that he would have a place in the world when paroled. The couple continued writing and Joel got Elsie on the visitor's list. She saw Joel every visiting day, bringing him up to date on the neighborhood happenings.

Years passed routinely and uneventfully until Joel finally met the parole board. The board refused parole the first time, but Joel continued his exemplary conduct, did his job and met the board again. He convinced the board of his good intentions and possibilities and his parole was granted.

The train arrived at Grand Central Station. Joel rushed to phone Elsie at work and that night they had a grand reunion. Joel had a restaurant job that paid well enough for him to save enough money to make two proposals; one to the parole officer to get his permission to marry and one to Elsie: both acquiesced. Joel married and soon became the father of two children.

Some of Joel's former prison pals occasionally stopped by the restaurant where he worked to get a handout, or to offer a proposition. Having decided to be legitimate, Joel sidestepped all the deals.

One day Alex walked into the restaurant. Alex had served time with Joel and was then with the merchant marine. He told Joel that going to sea paid well and that the "fringe benefits" were good. Furthermore, Alex said he had had no trouble getting permission to sign up with the Merchant Marine from his parole officer, and that he had a friend in the union who could get him a card. The idea intrigued Joel and he discussed it with Elsie. Elsie said she would not interfere, just as long as he kept out of trouble. Joel's parole officer also offered no objections. Alex got him a union card and Joel was hired aboard a luxury liner as a mess attendant. He made several trips to South America and was soon promoted to a "glory hole steward;" that is, Joel waited on the crew, but more importantly, he ran the gambling games in the crew quarters. He loaned money, supplied the cards and dice and cut every game that was running below the decks. The "glory hole steward" was also in a position to buy and sell any item, regardless of its source. He also loaned money to anyone who went broke during the game.

Joel became a very sought after man, involved in many shady deals. He was doing well financially and found himself more than willing to become involved in any deal, as long as it was lucrative. Jerry, an old prison pal, had heard that Joel was going to sea and asked him to handle a counterfeit deal. He told Joel that he had a connection for counterfeit money, and could let him have all he wanted at ten dollars a hundred. Jerry was sure Joel could sell the stuff at $25or $30 a hundred. Jerry figured Joel could put some in a game, sell it to other seamen and even peddle it to overseas contacts.

Joel agreed, took the $10,000 in countrefeits aboard ship, and dispersed the bills among the crew, even before the ship left port. Joel became one of Jerry's regular customers.

Just before the last cruise of the season, Joel ran into Eddie in one of the waterfront bars. Eddie, a seaman who had sailed with Joel, worked as a waiter on another vessel. He told Joel he needed some 'queer' for his own overseas contacts who were interested in American counterfeits. Eddie wanted about 20 grand, if the price was right, so Joel quoted a price of $22 a hundred. Eddie blew his top and said, "Remember Uncle Solly? He's my mother's brother. He supplied me with twenties for years. I only paid $15 and the stuff was beautiful. Too bad Uncle Solly's connection is dried up." Joel interrupted, "Don't give me that crap, Eddie. Uncle Sol is a three-time loser on the 'queer' and he won't touch it at any price." They finally settled on $20 a hundred and Joel got the notes to Eddie.

En route to South America, Eddie tried to peddle some of the counterfeit tens to his fellow crew members. For some reason, no one bought. He didn't try to pass them in the game at night because he was a "built-in" suspect. Eddie tried a few contacts in South America but unloaded only $5,000 worth. Not wanting to bring the notes back into the States, he decided to pass as many as he could on the return trip.

The first port of call was Panama. When he made liberty he went to a fairly large department store in town and purchased about $92 dollars worth of goods. The normal thing to do would be to include one or two counterfeit tens in the purchase money. Eddie was hungry, threw caution to the wind and gave the clerk ten counterfeit $10 bills. It so happened that the clerk who waited on him was a relative of the owner, had been educated in the States and had worked part time in an American bank. When he was given the money, he immediately noticed that it didn't look right and then saw that all the bills had the same serial number. He tried to stall Eddie until he could notify the police. Eddie became suspicious, dropped the merchandise and ran from the store. He got as far as the street. A cop heard the clerk's shouts, took out his automatic and fired a shot at Eddie. Eddie froze. Half an hour later, Eddie was in a cell in a Panamanian jail.

Panamanian authorities notified the Insular Police and eventually our headquarters was apprised of Eddie's arrest. At the time, I was working in New York in a particularly happy frame of mind. My wife was expecting the birth of our first child and I was looking forward to taking a week off to celebrate.

I was in the field when the agent in charge asked me to return to the office. It was December 31. It had started snowing in the early afternoon. I reported to the boss as quickly as possible. When I entered his office he said,

"Glad you got here in time. I got a hot one and I want you to handle it." He then showed me the teletype message. After reading it I asked, "What do you want me to do?" He said, "Get home, pack a bag and get down to Panama as quickly as possible and talk to Eddie — maybe he'll cooperate."

I said, "Tonight is New Year's Eve. My wife is expecting a baby any day — it's our first one. We were planning a party for tonight. Is there any way this could be put off for a couple of days — or could you assign someone else?"

He said, "You read the teletype. Washington wants you to go and I'm not suggesting anyone else. You don't have much time. The quicker you leave, the sooner you'll get back."

Before I left, he suggested that maybe Eddie got the notes from Uncle Solly and he supplied me with Solly's picture. I did a lot of thinking on the drive home. How do you tell your wife on New Year's Eve that you're going out of the country — especially when she's due to deliver any day?

I made it to the airport early the next morning and got my flight to Panama. It was uneventful; however, the airlines tried to make it as cheerful as possible. I arrived in Panama fairly early on New Year's Day. Several American officers from the Insular Police took me to see Eddie in his miserable cell. The food was bad, there were no visitors and he was depressed about spending the holidays in jail. He was not cooperative and refused to answer any questions. I told him that we were positive that he got the bills from Uncle Solly and unless he could change our minds, we were going to proceed on that premise. Eddie swore that Solly had nothing to do with the counterfeits. He begged me not to involve him. He said he was ready to take his medicine and was not going to fink out on anyone. I was becoming impatient with Eddie and was not looking forward to a long interrogation since all I wanted was to get what information I could in Panama and then get back home as quickly as possible.

When I was convinced that Eddie really was a "stand-up guy" I terminated the interview. The examination of Eddie's personal effects disclosed a bill for the hotel he stayed at before going on the trip, a small address book listing all his friends and their phone numbers, and a small piece of paper with notations indicating he purchased $30,000 worth of notes at $20 a hundred.

The next morning I boarded Eddie's ship. His locker contained an old shoe box concealing a package wrapped in brown paper. I opened it and found several thousand dollars in counterfeit $10's — the same kind he tried to pass in Panama. I questioned most of the crew members, but came up with a big zero. No one admitted that they knew Eddie had brought counterfeit money aboard the ship.

I spent the afternoon conferring with the local police. They planned to prosecute Eddie and figured he would get a substantial prison sentence. That evening I went back to see Eddie. I said, "Eddie, you're in a mess. I found the remainder of your stash aboard your ship. The case against you here is all sewed up. I don't know when they intend to try you, but you're not going to get the same treatment that you'd get in the States. No bail, no visitors, no nothing — you'll sit here and rot. I'll go back to the States and sure as shooting we'll make a case against Solly. I can see you trying to protect Solly, but if it isn't him, why not go along with me? No one is going to raise a finger to help you. Five years from now you'll still be sitting here wondering if you can make the whole bit and if you do make it, you might have another surprise waiting when you come home. Why? Why sit when someone else is walking? Give me the story and let me decide how to use it."

Eddie shook his head and said, "No, no, no! Everything is not as simple as you try to make it. Are you trying to make me believe if I cop out you're going to square everything with me? Save that for a square. You're like the rest of them. You'll take everything and give nothing. If we are parasites, what are you?"

"Since you have to trust someone, why not try me? You're a loser now. Who knows, maybe I can do you some good." He buried his head in his hands and said, "The best way you can help me is by leaving Uncle Solly alone. He had nothing to do with this mess." I told him his lack of cooperation did not put him in a bargaining position. There were no two ways about it. I knew I was not getting anywhere with Eddie, so I said "so long" to him and told him I had no intention of coming back. He looked up and said, "Thanks." I said, "Thanks for what?" He said, "Just thanks, that's all." I left the jail, took care of some loose ends and made arrangements to return to the States.

The flight back seemed eternally long. When I landed, I telephoned my home and learned that my wife was in the hospital, but had not yet given birth. I rushed directly to the hospital and managed to be there when our son was born.

The following day, with much of the pressure off, I wrote a report and then took several days leave. The leave was interrupted by a phone call from the office. Eddie had hanged himself in the Panamanian prison cell.

When I returned to work, I went to the hotel where Eddie usually stayed. No one at the hotel could give me any information other than the dates he lived there and a list of the calls he made on his last two visits at the hotel.

Then I went to see Uncle Solly. Solly was an old "pro" who had seen better days but was still respected in the underworld. I knew Solly would not be of any help since he had never been known to assist any investigative agency. Solly invited me into his apartment and let me know that I was wrong. He was ready to answer any questions. He was bitter about his nephew's death and wanted to avenge it. Eddie's parents, he said, went to Panama to claim their son's body. I said, "Solly you've been suspected of handling counterfeit notes for years. You have taken many falls, but none for handling queer. When Eddie was arrested I knew you had to be his source. The counterfeits are getting a pretty good distribution and I feel you're the man behind it." He waved his arms around and said, "C'mon, stop with the garbage already. You people start with someone and you never let go. 'Solly's a counterfeiter' — someone told you that twenty years ago and so Solly becomes the King of the Counterfeiters. Sure, I handled some stuff years ago. It was a lousy item. I didn't make a penny and after that I stayed away from it. Some schnook told you about it and when you need something for your reports, you say Uncle Solly is the guy, especially since Eddie had some of the garbage. To you it adds up. Well, listen to me. I wouldn't handle it with a ten-foot pole and I would have broke Eddie's head if I knew he handled it."

"Solly," I said "are you telling me that you don't know anything? Do you want me to believe that Eddie was an innocent victim?" "I don't want you to believe anything. It makes no difference to me or anyone else what you believe. All I know is Eddie's dead. No one can bring him back. I want revenge. Solly was never a stool and no amount of money could make him one. So, listen, maybe you'll learn something."

He settled down and lit a cigar before continuing, "You know, Mr. Motto, it's been a long time since I've been arrested. I'm over seventy now and don't have the stomach for jail. I got a little goulash joint downtown. I pay who I gotta pay and I make ends meet. I got a lot of time to myself and I used to stop in and see my sister. She always told me she was worried about Eddie. He used to get into a lot of trouble and she was always afraid someday he would get into big trouble. She asked me to talk to him. When he was around, he stayed at the hotel and I used to go to see him. Everybody was happy when he got a job on the ships. He brought back gifts. He used to tell stories and his mother was happy. Listen carefully now. The last two times I went to the hotel there was a guy named Joel there. He was an ex-con or I miss my guess. While I was there they don't say too much, but I make believe I was looking at the magazine and I heard them mention 'queer.' Eddie asked Joel for his number and Joel gives it to him and Eddie wrote it in his little black book. When Joel left I put it right to Eddie. I asked him if he was buying 'queer.' He lied and said no, not to worry, he wasn't going to get into any trouble. He almost had me convinced that I heard wrong so I didn't give it no more thought till we hear that he was arrested and then the sad news." Solly's eyes were welling up, and he continually blew his nose and wiped his brow. It must have been a terrible strain for him to talk to me because talking to the police was just not his shtick.

After Solly described Joel I left, telling Solly I would return when and if I needed more information. Solly said he'd keep his ear to the ground and would get in touch with me if he heard anything. I thanked him and left.

At the office I picked up Eddie's little black book. Solly was right. In the middle of the book was a written notation "Joel S." with a local phone number. The phone company gave me Joel Serley's name and address. Joel's name appeared in our files as a counterfeit handler. He had been the subject of several anonymous squeals. A complete background on him was in the files, but no case had been made.

The following day I went to see the parole division supervisor who supplied me with Joel's current information. He said that if we could prove that Joel was consorting with known criminals he could send him back to prison. According to the supervisor, Joel was presently aboard a ship and was due to return in three days. He agreed to get a warrant against Joel based on the notation in Eddie's notebook and the fact that Solly could put them together.

When Joel's boat arrived, another agent and I went on a Coast Guard cutter to the quarantine zone where the ship was awaiting its turn to dock. We quietly boarded the ship and arranged for the captain to send for Joel. When Joel arrived at the captain's quarters, the captain left and I identified myself to Joel. He asked me what I wanted and I told him about Eddie's arrest. Joel immediately replied: "That son of a bitch gave me up!" I indicated he was right. Joel threw out his hands and said, "Okay, put the cuffs on; remember you only have me for conspiracy." I told him to put his hands in his pockets. Perhaps we could do business. We sat down on the captain's bunk and Joel looked like he was ready to do anything for a break. He said, "Look, I'm sure you guys got me right, but don't screw things up or I'll never be able to help. You have to let me leave the ship and get paid. A lot of guys owe me money and we square up right after we get paid. A lot of these people don't ship out again and I'll never see my money. If I don't go, someone will get suspicious. They already know that the captain sent for me and I'll need an answer for them. Believe me, I don't have any of the 'queer' in my locker, you can search it if you want, but a search will louse things up. Give me a couple of hours to get things squared away and I'll go along with you."

Although it was a surprise to hear Joel 'cop out' so quickly, I didn't like the idea of trusting him and I really wanted to search his locker. After I decided to gamble and go along with him, I suddenly remembered that the parole officer was on the pier with a warrant. I had the other agent take the cutter back to shore and attempt to get the supervising parole officer to delay serving the warrant until we had a chance to see what we could do with Joel.

The senior parole officer was very understanding and he notified his man at the pier to return to the office without serving the warrant.

Joel took care of all his business without anyone getting suspicious. We later made arrangements to have Joel meet us and continue the investigation.

Joel went home, saw his family, did all the things that were necessary and then met us at a pre-arranged spot.

When Joel tried to do a little verbal fencing at first, I became impatient with him. I reminded him that we lived up to our part of the bargain and that as soon as I figured he was double-talking me, I would toss him in the can. I made no bones about getting the whole truth.

He said, "Okay, but it's like someone handing you a rope and saying: here, go hang yourself.'" I chilled. Had he learned of Eddie's suicide? If he did, he must know I didn't have a case against him. I let him talk and he came through beautifully.

He told about his release from prison, the restaurant job, going to sea, buying and selling queer and the sale of notes to Eddie. It disturbed him that Eddie gave him up. I asked if he would go all the way with us, work and give information, until we captured the plant. He said it would be dangerous. I agreed but told him to weigh it against the time he owed and the federal time he would get. He gave it some thought and asked if we would protect him and his family if he went "all the way." I said we would and he continued. "Well, it all started when I ran into Jerry the Prince. You know him?" "Yeah" I said. I could hardly contain myself. Just about every law enforcement officer knew of Jerry the Prince and his family.

His father was a hood and had died in prison. Even his mother had a record. Jerry and his two brothers were known as the "Three Jays." Jerry, the Crown Prince was the oldest and had the longest record. Julio was the next and he was known as the "Duke." His record was also quite long. He also had the distinction of beating two murder raps and was suspected of several more. Jackie was the youngest and was known as the "Count." His record was not so long, but he had followed his two brothers into crime and it wouldn't be long before he had a substantial record.

Joel continued. "I meet Jerry – you know he and I pulled time together. I ain't seen him since he got out of prison. He asks me what I'm doing and I says I'm shipping out. He says he's got a good deal for me, 'shoving the queer'. He gives me a good price so I make a deal with him. Then I run into Eddie. He's anxious to pick up some of the stuff. I made a deal with him and you know the rest." I sure did know the rest. Just knowing that "Jerry the Prince" was involved made the whole case exciting.

We had voluminous files on the family but had never made a case. This was the first time we had heard directly from a man who had actually made a "buy" from one of the Three Jays. I thought if we worked this one right, we would get Jerry and possibly his brothers out of our hair.

But there were problems. If we made a buy from Jerry, we probably would go no further, since Jerry wouldn't talk. His brothers would probably take over the distribution of the counterfeit money. Then we'd have to do something with Joel. His life wouldn't be worth two pins if they found out he set them up.

A review of the files indicated that the district attorney was investigating Julio and Jackie for several murders. I arranged to see the assistant district attorney handling the case. He had a similar dilemma. He figured he could wrap up a murder case against Julio and Jackie if he could get a certain federal prisoner to cooperate. The prisoner was held on bond forgery charges. The assistant D.A. said he was in the midst of working out a deal with the federal authorities and he estimated that within a month he should be able to indict the two brothers. At this point, I told him of our plan. I would try to get Joel to introduce me to Jerry and make a "buy" of counterfeits.

We worked out a plan where we would not arrest Jerry until the district attorney was ready to arrest the other two brothers. Hopefully, we would do this simultaneously. With all three brothers in jail we could use Joel's services a little longer and possibly locate the plant.

I felt that the Three Jays would eventually know that Joel set up Jerry, but as long as they were all in jail and separated, nothing would happen to Joel.

The District Attorney's office worked out a deal with the bond forger and he agreed to testify. The District Attorney also promised to hold up any arrests until we made a buy from Jerry.

Joel and I then had a heart-to-heart talk. He realized that if and when it became known that he was an informant, he would have to move and move fast. The brothers had many friends and it would only be a matter of time before they caught up with him. He certainly couldn't go back to prison since the brothers had plenty of contacts in several state and federal institutions. I spent a lot of time with the U.S. attorney and the parole authorities, making plans to get Joel off the hook and on his way after the arrests were made. After obtaining all the necessary commitments we were ready to try and make a case against Jerry. It was necessary for me to be seen constantly with Joel, to pose as his shipmate. Jerry had a piece of several downtown bars and Joel saw to it that I was in Jerry's company quite often. Jerry loved foreign-made miniatures and asked me to bring some back after my next trip. I got to know him well enough to hint that I was anxious to make an extra dollar on anything.

One night, Jerry asked me point blank if I ever handled any "queer.' I told him that on one or two occasions Joel had supplied me with "some stuff" but that I wanted to get out of the "penny ante" class. He asked me how much I could handle. I said "About 25 grand." He agreed to give me a special price of ten dollars a hundred for the $25,000. I told him it would take a few days to put my money together. Our strategy was to give the twenty-five hundred in genuine money to Jerry, take delivery of the counterfeit and not arrest Jerry until we felt that the time was ripe. We would then coordinate that arrest with the arrests of his two brothers and anyone else who became involved.

A couple of days later when I told Jerry I was ready to do business, he took me aside and said, "The only reason I'm talking and doing business with you is because Joel put the OK on you. If anything goes wrong, you go. There are no excuses. This game is for keeps." I swallowed hard and said, "Right, Jerry, and remember that goes both ways. No one takes me or sets me up."

Jerry asked for the buy money in advance. I refused by saying that I trusted no one when it came to money. He was a little peeved and said that his family was honorable and no one could accuse them of beating anyone out of his money. I told him it wasn't personal, but that I never "fronted" my money.

He told me to get a hotel room and give him a call. When the hotel was properly covered by the assisting agents, I telephoned Jerry. After I gave him my room number he said, "Wait for a call."

About two hours later a man calling himself "Chuck" rang me from the lobby and said he was coming right up with the "package." As he walked through the lobby he kept his suitcase close to him and continually looked over his shoulder to see if he was being followed. When I admitted him into my room, we shook hands. I took the suitcase, opened it and found that it contained several outdated telephone directories. When Chuck saw the expression on my face he laughed and explained that the telephone books were being used for a "dry run" to see if the delivery would smoke out any coppers who might be watching. He then told me to wait in the room until I was contacted again. He left, not taking the phone books with him.

About half an hour later, Jerry came to my hotel room without any advance notice. He assured me that a delivery would be made in a short time. He demanded to see my buy money. I took him to the main desk in the lobby where I had a safe deposit box and showed him the genuine money. When we returned to my room, Chuck was in the hallway. He checked to see if we were being followed. He was carrying a small bag. When he was satisfied that we were not being followed, he came into the room right behind us.

We shut and bolted the door. Jerry opened the suitcase and showed me the twenty-five thousand in brand new counterfeit ten dollar notes. I examined the money and satisfied myself that it was all there. Jerry told Chuck to remain in the room with the counterfeits. He and I went back to the lobby where I got the $2,500 in genuine money and gave it to Jerry. He was so hungry for the money that he took it in full view of the agents covering the lobby. We returned to the room. Chuck and Jerry left immediately. After I got word that they left the area, I returned to the office with the counterfeits, the two suitcases and the telephone books.

We were in a pretty good position. Jerry and Chuck were our prisoners anytime we wanted to get the warrants. The district attorney was presenting his case and was in the process of getting indictments against Jerry's two brothers. It looked as though our crime family could be put out of business at any time. There was just one problem. We were no closer to the plant than we were six months before.

Joel continued to be of great help. He assisted us in setting up "buys" from other people he knew, but we were never in a position to make an arrest. We felt that when the first arrest was made, Joel would be exposed and we would have to go through with our plans to put him in protective custody and get him out of town.

Further investigations indicated that the plant might be a good distance from the city. Before stowing the evidence away in Jerry's case, the outdated metropolitan directories that Chuck used on his "dry run" interested me. I knew that very often I made notations on the covers or anywhere in the book when I was in a hurry. One day I found myself a nice quiet spot and started to go over the directories page by page. Special attention was given to all notes and writings anywhere on the books. After about ten days, I had compiled quite a few notations gleaned from the directories. Of course, much of what I copied was useless: proper names, some graffiti and a lot of doodling. I did get quite a few telephone numbers that appeared to have been hastily written on the covers and, in some cases, underlined. Tracing these telephone numbers was not a tough job, but it was time-consuming. When I finished I was able to deduce that the telephone books came out of the office of one of Jerry's bowling alleys; that most of the writing was done by Jerry; that most of the telephone numbers were of Jerry's friends or business associates. There were about a dozen out-of-town numbers that needed further investigation.

About the first ten turned out to be people who knew Jerry and did business with him. The next one I checked was a printing company. This was too good to believe. The number to the shop was listed. It was located about a hundred ten miles from the city. I made arrangements to go to that city and meet an old friend who was in charge of the detective bureau. He assigned a lieutenant to work with me.

We learned that the printing shop was owned by Art Cross, a lifelong resident of the community. He had learned the printing business while he was in the service during World War II. After his discharge, he opened a shop in the middle of a decaying residential neighborhood and tried to make a living. He was the only printer in town and had a fairly good reputation. He did a lot of civic and charity work and was considered a leading citizen until he had some trouble several years ago. He was arrested in an adjoining community for issuing worthless checks.

Business had not been too good, he had been drinking more than he should and found himself in financial straits. After he was arrested, he was able to get a loan from the bank, paid off the checks and the charges were dropped. A little more snooping indicated that while business did not appear to be any better, Art seemed to be doing well financially. He drove a new car, was recently married to a widow, had set up an apartment in town and was making frequent visits to the race track.

We decided to watch the shop. We couldn't use any of the local detectives as they were all known, and we couldn't tail Art or watch the shop without attracting attention. At the end of a week all we could prove was that Art led an exemplary life. He worked every day, closed the shop at 5 o'clock in the afternoon and rarely returned. He spent the weekend with his wife and, as far as we knew, he was not in contact with any known hoods. Art employed two people at the plant — a pressman and a clerk. We couldn't contact either one as they were both distantly related to Art.

We decided to take some direct action. If our suspicions were correct, and Art was responsible for printing the counterfeits, we had to do something to get him printing again.

I got in touch with Joel and told him that I wanted him to set up a meeting for me with Jerry. We met at Jerry's bowling alley that night. Jerry was affable and happy to hear that I had disposed of the last batch of phony bills with no trouble. He kidded about raising the price. I told him that I had an opportunity to dispose of $150,000 if the price was right. This raised Jerry's eyebrows; he took out a pencil and said, "I can give it to you for 9 cents on the dollar." I said, "Jerry, I can't make anything on the price you're giving me. You're killing me here. You're squeezing me out of the play." Jerry laughed and said, "Nick, you're full of crap; you're probably getting 20 cents for the stuff." I said, "If I get 10 cents, that's a lot. I'll tell you what, get me 200 big ones and I'll pay you 14 grand for it." He thought a bit and said, "Nick, come up with 15 grand and you got a deal." I said "Okay," we shook hands and he said he should have the merchandise ready in a week.

That was good news because I figured if he had $200,000 worth of counterfeit money readily accessible, he would have done business within 24 hours. If it was to take a week, it was logical to assume that he had to put in an order for it.

We all had a drink and Jerry asked Joel why he wasn't buying these days. Joel thought fast and said he was "on the beach" and besides he was charged too much for what he was buying. Jerry said, "That's what you get for dealing in peanuts. Give me a big order and you'll get the same price."

We left and I promised to call Jerry in six days to finalize the delivery. Joel and I got into my car and drove one block before I called Joel's attention to the fact that our friend Jerry saw fit to send one of his hoods to follow us. Joel said, "Let's go to a church and sit for awhile." It sounded like a good idea, but instead we went to a restaurant, had supper and then headed for the midtown section of the city where we had no trouble in shaking the tail.

We renewed the surveillance at the print shop and identified most of the people coming in and going out of the shop. After two days we were seriously doubting whether Art was really our man. If he wasn't then we had big problems. Tailing Art was a ticklish proposition because whenever it appeared he was becoming suspicious, it was necessary to drop him. We could not take any chances. Again the surveillance was reduced to watching the premises for what we could see from the outside. Manpower was always a problem, so I was elected to go up again to the shop to keep a night surveillance. I decided that I would watch the place beginning from four in the afternoon. At about 5 o'clock on the second night of my surveillance, the snow began to fall quite heavily. Art and his two employees left the square brick one-story building, but Art did not get into his car. He walked several blocks to a nearby bar, sat at a table and apparently intended to have supper. This gave me enough time to call my local detective contact and have him meet me. About 45 minutes later, Art was observed leaving the bar and returning to his plant. There were no windows in the front of the building and the back windows were either painted black or were equipped with black shades. As the hours slipped by, the detective and I were beside ourselves with frustration trying to find out what was happening.

Art was working. It was very late, and he was getting phone calls. He didn't have anyone helping him. He undoubtedly was involved in something shady. He could be printing checks, pornography, phony licenses or most anything. We preferred to believe he was printing counterfeit money; but how to make the case legally? Sure, we could kick the door in and catch him in the act, but that was no good. The case would be kicked out of court on an illegal search. We didn't have enough probable cause to get a search warrant and the payoff was that Art could come out of the shop with a big package and we couldn't legally search him or look in the package.

By this time, four or five inches of snow had fallen. It was getting near midnight and we knew that Art would soon be leaving. I made a closer examination of the building and noticed a very small window on the side of the building about twelve to fourteen feet above the ground. There was no way of telling whether the window was clear or if it would give a good view into the shop. We didn't want to look for a ladder or do anything that would create suspicion; however, it was most important that we look into the shop. A quick search of the neighborhood produced three garbage cans. We placed one on top of the other and I managed to get to the top without breaking my neck or making a lot of noise. I could look down and see Art working, but from the position I was in, I could only see the back of him. I suspected he already had a set of negatives and a set of plates. The press was being prepared for use. Unfortunately, the action was away from me and I could not see what he was doing. The cold weather and falling snow prevented either one of us from looking in for more than five to ten minutes at a time. Eventually Art started the press and he was rolling something off them. We stretched and strained, but could not make out what he was doing. We prayed for any kind of break we could get to help us make the case. At about two in the morning, it appeared that Art was about finished with his work and was wrapping it in packages. I still couldn't see what he was printing. I was taking a last look when Art took a piece of paper off the top of one of the filing cabinets and held it up to the light to examine it. I almost fell from the cans with excitement. I could clearly see that he was examining a piece of paper that had two counterfeit $10's printed on it. I quickly jumped to the ground and announced to my frozen buddy that we had a counterfeit plant. He was elated that this miserable detail was over. He wanted to bust right in and arrest Art.

By now, it was now 2:15. I told him to wait until I contacted my boss to get an okay. After kicking around all the possibilities, the boss agreed that Art should be arrested as soon as he left the premises. He prefaced his remarks with, "Since there is no doubt that you saw the counterfeits…"

At about three o'clock, the lights went out in the shop and Art walked out onto the snow-covered street. I stepped behind him quietly and told him I was a federal agent and he was under arrest for counterfeiting. His first inclination was to run. However, when the local detective confronted him from the other side, Art recognized him and meekly submitted to the arrest. He unlocked the front door, turned on the lights and was told to sit on a chair in a corner of the premises. The plant, at first glance, was absolutely clean. I told him that I knew he had printed the counterfeit $10's and suggested that he tell me where they were. He denied that he had printed any tens. We asked him to show us the work he was doing during the night. He looked around the shop and showed us some old work. I kept insisting that the machine had been filled with green ink and what he showed us was blue. He shrugged his shoulders and said, "Go see for yourself." We had expected to see counterfeit money all over the shop. No dice. It was as clean as a whistle. I began to wonder if I had actually seen the counterfeit money.

After we had searched fruitlessly for 20 minutes, I decided it was time to have a talk with Art. I told him I knew the "stuff" was in the shop and again asked him where it was. He professed not to know what I was talking about. I then made a very solemn promise to him. I said, "Art, I will take this building down, brick by brick, if necessary. I intend to search every nook and cranny of the shop until all the counterfeit money is found." Art was not impressed.

The search continued. The lack of evidence was becoming disconcerting. There should have been at least $100,000 or more in counterfeit notes, several sets of plates, negatives, and wipings from the press.

Art's shop contained a large supply of paper stock, neatly wrapped and stacked. It seemed foolish to tear each package open, but I had promised Art that I would meticulously take the place apart so I kept my promise.

The first 55 packages or so contained what they were supposed to — high-grade bond paper. Then I hit pay dirt! The next package I opened contained the newly printed $10 bills, two to a sheet, just as I had seen from the window. After all the packages were opened and I was satisfied that all the counterfeit notes were accounted for, I again approached Art. This time he was visibly shaken and more amenable to talking. He wanted to strike up some sort of bargain in exchange for the negatives and the plates. I explained that he was not in a very good bargaining position. He faced a maximum of fifteen years and while the plates and negatives were important, they did not put him in any driver's seat. I reminded him that anything he did to make my work easier would be brought to the attention of the court.

Art, realizing the futility of the situation, decided to cooperate. He took me into the dark room and removed several loose floor boards. He reached down and extracted several sets of negatives and the plates. During the next half-hour, Art cooperated fully.

Art was then taken to police headquarters for processing. His arrest caused a problem for the police department since Art did all the printing for the city, including the traffic summonses, one of which was on my car parked several blocks away. Since Art's arrest flushed out the plant, there was now nothing holding up the arrests of the "Three Jays."

The District Attorney's office took care of Julio and Jackie and our office arrested Jerry. His arrest did not go smoothly. He tried to run two agents down when they attempted to arrest him in his car. Several shots were fired. Jerry rammed his car into a light pole and wound up in the prison ward of the city hospital.

Julio and Jackie were held without bail on the homicide charges. After the arrests of the "Three Jays," a meeting of the clan was held to determine what went wrong. Nothing could be found out until Jerry made bail. It took three days for Jerry to post the necessary $100,000 and make the street. Jerry wasted no time in putting the loose ends together.

On the night he was released, there was another family get-together in Jerry's home. Only the closest and most trusted associates were there. While the get-together was to be informal, it became almost like a board meeting. When Jerry came into the large living room, everyone stood up and congratulated him on his release and then they all sat down to hear Jerry's words of wisdom. He was brief and to the point: Joel was the informer and he had to be taken care of. Everyone knew what he meant. There was a lot of small talk and contracts were handed out and, before long, everyone knew what they were supposed to do.

In the meantime, the government also had a job to do. Joel expressed a desire to go out West with his family. We received excellent cooperation from the parole authorities. In a matter of hours, they were able to arrange for Joel's parole to be transferred to the other state. Joel was moved quietly and efficiently. Joel got a job and was quite proud of the fact that he was able to earn a comfortable living in an entirely new field in his new surroundings.

I felt I owed old Sol some sort of explanation as to what happened. I went to his apartment late one afternoon. Sol hadn't been well and I wasn't sure if he was at home or in the hospital. He answered the knock on the door and told me to come in, He was sitting in his rocking chair and looked more like a doting grandfather than a racketeer. It suddenly dawned on me that Sol was old — very old. He looked tired, worn, and listless. When he saw me, he told me to sit down and to pour myself a drink from the bottle which was close by him. I bypassed the drink but refilled his small glass, which he left untouched. He was smoking a cigar. The ashes were all over his chest and small holes had been burned in his sweater. I doubted he would show any interest in the story I was about to tell. I was wrong. The deep hurt from the suicide of his nephew was still there, and Sol wanted to hear all the details.

I wasn't going to tell Sol that Joel had been arrested and cooperated with us. I thought it would suffice to tell the old man that Jerry was the man who was responsible, that he had been arrested, and that he had many years to serve. I told him of the plant capture and then I noticed that he was falling asleep. He muttered, "It's good, it's good." I took the cigar from his fingers, put it in the ashtray, and quietly left the room. Shortly thereafter, Sol was felled by a stroke and passed away.

The "Three Jays" all went to trial. The legal battles were long and bitter, but fortunately ended with guilty verdicts. The "Three Jays" all served long sentences and were never again considered a threat by law enforcement agencies.

Some years later, I received a note from Joel. He was happy to tell me his oldest son had graduated from college and had been accepted at a prestigious medical school. The return address on the letter was a state prison out west.

Dennis — A Real Menace

Anytime a new counterfeit hits the street, there is much speculation on where it originates, who's behind it, how much was printed, and how long it will take for the first suspect to be identified.

One fine spring day, one of these new notes appeared. Three days later I received information that the notes were being passed by a man called Dennis. I spent most of the week trying to find out all I could about Dennis. The fact that he married a policeman's sister didn't bring him any closer to being a law-abiding citizen. His past, like that of so many other criminals, was sordid and apparently without rhyme or reason. His folks came from Chicago and had settled in New York when he was a child. There was a new addition to the family every year, and soon there were more mouths to feed than the family could afford. Aside from the obvious, Dennis' father had but one interest — drinking. The odd jobs he worked at kept him in "drinking money." The welfare bureau handled the actual support of the family.

Dennis dropped out of school as soon as he was old enough and tried, at first, to earn a living legitimately. But he soon learned that there were other ways of making money. He started out as a member of a street gang that specialized in burglarizing neighborhood stores. On his second burglary job, Dennis was caught breaking into a neighborhood candy store after it had closed for the day. This escapade brought him before a judge who felt that he would benefit from doing some time in a state school.

The school proved to be an institution of higher learning in the crime field. The older boys taught him how to pick pockets, shoplift from department stores, and snatch purses. When Dennis was released, he went straight back to the old neighborhood with his newly acquired smarts. After several weeks on the street he managed to impress his older associates with his willingness to try bigger and better scores. They tried Dennis out on several jobs: residential burglaries in the city's suburban areas. It was agreed among his friends that while Dennis was short on brains and wit, he had a lot of guts and could be expected to do what he was told. When it came to doing any original thinking, Dennis failed miserably. Dennis enjoyed the jobs although he didn't make any great amount of money. The other boys always found a way to cheat him out of some of his share.

Those who said, "Dennis is a little nuts" weren't far off the mark. Psychiatric reports from the state school indicated Dennis had undergone some psychotherapy during his confinement.

Dennis started attending neighborhood dances and met Marjorie at one of these functions. She apparently saw something in him that she liked and agreed to go out with him. The relationship soon grew into a full-fledged love affair. After six months they were discussing marriage.

There were several reasons why Dennis had to get a job. First of all, his nocturnal "second-story" jobs weren't bringing in enough money to support a wife; second, he had to impress Marjorie that he was an honest working man; and third, Marjorie had a brother, Tim, who was a police officer and didn't like Dennis very much. If Dennis didn't have a job, Tim would have a good reason to urge his sister to break off the relationship with him. Marjorie's parents weren't impressed with Dennis either and they were opposed to their seeing each other exclusively. While Dennis was still pondering his situation, Marjorie announced that she was pregnant. Dennis was ready to run to the preacher, but Marjorie decided to try to get the family's blessing.

When Marjorie announced she was going to be a mother, there was an ugly scene at the house. Tim threatened to kill Dennis. Her father threatened to throw her out of the house. Her mother fainted and her younger sister thought it was wonderful. There wasn't time for likes or dislikes. The matter at hand was to get Marjorie married and avoid a neighborhood scandal.

Although the animosity was still there, Dennis was half-heartedly accepted into the family. He managed to get a tenement apartment for himself and Marjorie. He continued to work part-time and occasionally went out to make a score with the boys. He was careful not to let Marjorie know that he was doing anything illegal.

A son was born and not too long after that, Marjorie became pregnant a second time. Dennis was having trouble making ends meet. After some thought, he decided to quit his legitimate job and concentrate on stealing on a full-time basis. The gang was happy to have him around since he could be counted on to do anything.

Someone in the group had information about a local supermarket keeping the weekend receipts at the store instead of making a deposit. The group decided that early on a Monday morning they would break into the market and take the safe. Dennis was asked to go and this time his friends presented him with a .38-caliber revolver that was stolen from another job.

Dennis was pleased with the gun and felt that he was finally getting somewhere within the organization. He wanted to do a good job. "Chick", one of the men in the group, had other ideas.

He owed a local detective a favor. Some time before, Chick had been picked up by a police detective on suspicion of burglary. During the search, the detective found several marijuana cigarettes in his possession. Instead of arresting him, he told Chick, "You owe me, so don't forget." Since Chick wasn't going on this caper, he thought he'd give the detective the information and get square with him. Perhaps he could make a few bucks too. He also figured it would be nice to have a friend at the precinct.

Dennis had a hard time explaining to Marjorie why he had to leave the house at one o'clock in the morning. He mumbled something about getting a job loading trucks. Marjorie didn't believe him, but there was nothing she could do about it. There were times when she thought about telling her brother that she thought Dennis was a burglar, but she knew that it would cause a lot of trouble. With the family growing every year, trouble was the last thing she wanted. Dennis left and met the boys. They went over the plans and proceeded directly to the supermarket.

The parking lot was empty. They cruised around the area and nothing suspicious was noticed. They parked in the back of the building where they couldn't be seen from the road. Dennis had no trouble in jimmying the door and bypassing a very obvious alarm system.

The safe was in the manager's office, so the group went directly there. They were working on the safe when someone thought he heard a noise. They all left the office to investigate. At that moment, several police officers appeared from behind the aisles and ordered them to put their hands up. Dennis ran and was chased by an officer. Dennis then pulled his gun, wheeled around, and fired a shot. The man in blue slumped and fell as Dennis continued running. Another officer saw an opportunity to get Dennis and he did — with a well-placed shot just below the spine. Dennis was stopped dead in his tracks, he stumbled, and fell in a heap. The rest of the group was completely outnumbered. It wasn't necessary to fire any more rounds. The whole area was covered with police officers. Escape was futile.

Dennis came to in the hospital ward of the local jail. The bullet had been successfully removed and he was going to recover. The police officer also recovered; however, his wound was more serious and his convalescence took even longer.

Dennis could see that the police had been supplied with excellent information. He had no doubt that there was a stool pigeon in the group. It didn't make much difference who it was. Dennis knew he was looking at a long prison term; the fact that he had shot a cop would make things a lot tougher for him. Dennis spoke to his court-appointed lawyer and after several meetings with him, decided to "cop a plea" and throw himself upon the mercy of the court. Dennis knew he had no defense. He had been caught on the premises and there was no doubt he was the one who had shot the police officer. He figured that the sooner he went before the judge, the quicker he would start serving. The time he spent in the local jail would not be counted toward his ultimate sentence.

Several weeks later in court, Dennis pleaded guilty to all the counts in the indictment — burglary, possession of burglar's tools, attempted grand larceny, atrocious assault, and carrying a dangerous weapon. He told the judge he had nothing further to say. The judge already had the benefit of his prior record and sentenced him to ten to twenty years in the state prison.

This was about all the information I could learn and while it was well documented, it didn't tell me what I wanted to know. The obvious question that had to be asked was: How could a cheap thug like Dennis make a connection for a new counterfeit note so soon after his release from prison? He had served twelve years of his sentence and was conditionally released. He went back to his wife and children, got a night job delivering newspapers, and in five days we had received three anonymous phone calls that saying he was passing counterfeit money. He had never appeared in our files and his history had no information to indicate that he was involved with counterfeit money. There appeared to be only one approach: to tail him and try to catch him passing the bogus bills.

Dennis worked late and did not leave the house till early afternoon. We would tail him from three o'clock in the afternoon to eight o'clock at night, when he was on the loose. This would be the ideal time for him to pass the counterfeit bills. We started tailing him on a Monday afternoon. We followed him to a movie, then checked the bill he used to buy the ticket. We did the same for all the stores where he made purchases. We had no luck the first week. All the bills he spent were genuine. On the second week Dennis bought a flashlight at a downtown hardware store. He paid for the purchase with a $10 bill. Soon after he left the store, we checked the bill. It was a counterfeit. We had the clerk initial the bill for identification purposes. Dennis didn't spend any more money that day. It took several more days before we got him passing another counterfeit bill. This time it was at a movie house. When it was apparent that we were not getting much return for our efforts, I decided to get a warrant based on the two passes. Usually, it would have been a routine case except for the fact that Dennis was now known as a man who would kill a cop if he had to. We could arrest him on the street with no problems, but instead we decided to arrest him at his home where we could legally search his apartment. We felt that if he had any counterfeit money left, he would undoubtedly have it at home.

We took more precautions than we normally would. We used about eight agents to arrest one passer. On the day we obtained the warrant we arranged for two agents to be on the fire escape of his apartment house, two on the roof, two in the basement and two to enter the apartment.

I had the warrant and decided that I would be one of the two to approach the apartment. After all the men were at their appointed places, we knocked at the door. Marjorie opened the door. While the other agent kept Marjorie occupied, I slipped by her and looked in the rooms and finally found Dennis asleep in his bedroom. I quietly walked across the room and tapped him on his nose with my .38. He awoke and was ready to jump out of his skin. I identified myself and threatened to blow his head off if he made a wrong move. The other agents entered the room through the windows and in a very few seconds, everything was under control. Fortunately, the children were in school.

We started to make a very systematic search of the apartment. This, of course, didn't meet with Marjorie's approval. She tried to prevent the agents from making their search and at times appeared almost hysterical. I managed to get her and Dennis into the kitchen. I told her to make a pot of coffee and we would try to salvage a bad situation. She told me I would hear from her brother who was a police sergeant. I urged her to get in touch with her brother since I was sure he would give Dennis some good advice. Marjorie tried to get her brother on the phone, but was unsuccessful. In the meantime, I poured myself a cup of coffee. I reached for the sugar bowl. Dennis jumped up and tried to grab the bowl. We struggled for the bowl for a few seconds. I retained it, lifted the lid, and saw the roll of counterfeit bills inside the bowl.

It seemed a bit corny and not very original, but that was probably the only place that seemed handy and safe to Dennis when he wanted to stash the bills. It probably was a playback to his childhood when he remembered his mother hiding money from his drunken father in the sugar bowl.

I now had a better position at the bargaining table. I told Marjorie that unless Dennis did some fast talking she was rapidly becoming involved in the case. At about that time, Tim the police sergeant brother called. I explained to him what had transpired. He told me he'd be right over. He said he had no concern for Dennis, but that he certainly did not want to see his sister become involved.

While waiting for the sergeant to arrive, the agents searching the other rooms had found several hundred dollars worth of counterfeits hidden in a dresser in the bedroom. Under the mattress in the same room they found a .38-caliber revolver. Dennis could see the charges mounting and he was becoming increasingly agitated. He accused us of framing him and swore he'd kill us all. About this time, Tim arrived and he had a talk with his sister. She then urged Dennis to cooperate with us. He was reluctant at first, but then decided to tell us the story.

He said that one of his newspaper delivery stops was at a restaurant and candy store in the north end of the city. The store was owned by two brothers, Al and Fredo. The brothers controlled several numbers runners, handled stolen goods, and had their fingers in a little of everything that was shady.

One day, Al asked Dennis to handle counterfeit money. He offered him $10 and $20 bills at 25 cents on the dollar. Dennis had saved a little money and decided to buy $4,000 worth. The cost to him was $500 down and $500 later. Dennis said he went up to Fredo's house to buy the counterfeits. After he ordered the notes, he stayed with Al, while Fredo left. When Fredo returned he told Dennis to look at the base of the tree about 50 feet from the house. Dennis said he went to the tree and saw a brown paper bag hidden near the base of it. He picked it up and found it contained the counterfeit money.

Accounting to us for the notes he bought, Dennis said he had passed several hundred dollars worth, destroyed some because the workmanship was poor, and that, together with what we recovered at the house, accounted for almost all the notes he had purchased.

I then asked him if he would introduce me to either one of the brothers. He said, "No! No, absolutely not!" There was no way I could persuade him. So I then asked him if he would make another "buy" from either of the two brothers. He wasn't happy about it, but finally agreed.

I told him I would give him $500 in genuine marked money to be used for the buy. I reminded him that this was Uncle Sam's money and that if it got away from him, I would personally find an excuse to shoot him through his miserable head. I felt that Dennis had to be convinced to play this one straight and that at all costs he had to level with me. I continually reminded him that his demise would be a reality if he double-crossed me. Dennis was visibly shaken and, after some thought, decided to cooperate fully. We carefully laid out the plans for him to follow. Since he was not too bright, we had to rehearse his part over and over again.

When we were satisfied that he knew what to do, we drove him to the vicinity of Fredo's house. We took up surveillance in the area and searched Dennis before we gave him the $500 in genuine currency. We searched him so that if necessary, we could later testify in court that when he entered the house, he didn't have counterfeit money, but did have it when he came out. This would help in establishing circumstantial evidence against the brothers, Al and Fredo. It would also give us probable cause to obtain a search warrant for Fredo's home. I threatened him again before he left. These threats appeared to have a visible effect on him.

Al and Fredo each had extensive criminal records, so we had pictures of them. We waited for some time. After an hour we noticed Al leave the house. He walked one block to a parked car, looked up and down the street, got into the car and drove away. We didn't follow as we fully expected that he would return.

Nothing happened for several hours. The next thing we noted was that a small panel truck arrived on the scene. Fredo and his wife came out of the house carrying some personal belongings. They got into the truck and left the area. We noted the license number of the truck but again made no effort to follow it. It was another hour before Dennis came out of the house. He seemed awfully excited.

I asked him what was wrong. He said he didn't know if anything was wrong. He said he went to the house and told Al and Fredo he wanted to buy another $2,000 in counterfeit money. Al said okay and left, presumably to get the counterfeits. After Al did not return, Fredo and his wife decided to go out and look for him. Dennis claimed he waited around in the house for an hour or so and then decided to report what happened.

I asked him if he had the "buy" money. He said he did and handed it over to me. You didn't have to be a genius to realize something was wrong. I thought that perhaps either Fredo or Al got a phone call warning them that Dennis had been arrested. Rather than argue with Dennis, they figured "forewarned was forearmed" and decided to leave.

We waited around for several more hours but there was no activity at the house. A crew of agents was covering the candy store and they also reported no activity. We returned to Dennis' home and learned that Marjorie had told several people of his arrest. Since it looked like Dennis' arrest was no longer a secret, we put him in jail for the night. The following day he made bail and let it be known that he was no longer cooperating. In fact, he told the Assistant U. S. Attorney that he didn't know anything about the counterfeit money. He insisted that I had planted the counterfeits in his home. He said that I had suggested the names of Fredo and Al as the suppliers and that they had nothing to do with counterfeit money. When he finished, it was clear that we would have to get to the brothers from another source. Sergeant Tim attempted to get Dennis to change his mind, but Dennis wouldn't budge. The one night in jail convinced him that it wouldn't be safe to set up the two notorious brothers.

The following day the Motor Vehicle Bureau identified the owner of the truck in which Fredo and his wife left the apartment. The owner was Felix Darlow, also known as the "Shark," a well-known hood in New York City. Several attempts had been made on his life and there were quite a few people who were sorry the attempts failed. The "Shark" made a fairly good living shaking down storekeepers, buying stolen property, and loaning money at excessive interest rates. Those who were unfortunate enough not to pay were generally ruthlessly beaten up. The "Shark" had been arrested on several occasions and his latest escapade, involving a jewelry store burglary, landed him a stiff prison sentence.

The police records showed that the "Shark" should have been currently in prison, although the man driving the truck was positively identified by the surveilling agents as being the "Shark." I went to the "Shark's" last known address and was surprised to find him at home. He was completely uncooperative. He was evasive and wouldn't answer any questions regarding why he wasn't in prison where he should have been, why was he and his truck seen picking up Fredo and his wife, and what was his involvement with the suspected counterfeiters. In exasperation, I threatened to lock him back up. He still didn't budge. When he decided that I was losing patience with him, he cryptically suggested that I look up a certain police lieutenant who might be able to help me.

I managed to locate the lieutenant who was very annoyed at the mention of "Shark's" name. He asked me if I could forget the whole matter. I refused and suggested we level with each other. We left the precinct and went to a nearby restaurant.

I volunteered all the information I had regarding the counterfeit case and told the lieutenant of the small part the "Shark" had played. He reluctantly told me that he was in charge of an investigation involving several brutal serial type slayings. He was under a lot of pressure to solve these murders, since the victims had been good citizens and no motive had been found for the killings. Whereas the murders had apparently been committed by the same person, the police couldn't find a common thread. Finding a motive was the first order of business.

In connection with the homicide investigation, the police had reason to interview the "Shark" at the state prison. The interview convinced the lieutenant that the "Shark" was not involved. However, the "Shark" told the lieutenant he would make a deal with him. Since the "Shark" thought that, if given the opportunity, he could learn the identity of the killer, he offered his complete cooperation in return for a release on appeal and $150 a week while he worked for the police. Normally, the lieutenant would have told the prisoner to go to hell, but this homicide case had aroused too much public indignation. The lieutenant agreed to the "Shark's" terms and promised to do his best to get the "Shark" back on the street. The "Shark" also insisted that he would play it on the level and get the case solved. However, he cautioned the lieutenant that it must never be known that he was cooperating or his life wouldn't be worth a "tinker's dam," regardless of who committed the murders. The lieutenant finally succeeded in getting the "Shark" sprung and put to work.

The lieutenant then looked at me and said, "Tell me, do I need you and your headaches?" I agreed that I did present a problem, but he had to admit that I had a job to do as well. I said I would be satisfied if the "Shark" would just answer my questions and supply me with intelligence about the brothers. If the "Shark" wasn't involved in the counterfeiting case, it wouldn't be too much of a problem. The lieutenant listened and, although visibly distressed, he agreed. He insisted that he be kept advised of the kind of information the "Shark" was giving me and he wanted to have a veto power on any active participation by "Shark" in my case. He wanted to be sure that nothing happened to his newly acquired friend. We shook hands and he made arrangements for me to talk with the "Shark" again the following day.

When I met the "Shark" again, his whole personality had changed. He had a sense of humor, he smiled and appeared to be anxious to answer any questions I put to him. He told me he had known Al and Fredo Adamo for several years and that they had been engaged in many illegal activities. Their candy store was just a front for a numbers drop. One of the Adamo's was involved in union activities, he said, setting up paper unions and engaging in "sweetheart" contracts with some of the people who ran the shops. I asked him why he had gone to Fredo's home and why he had practically moved Fredo and his wife out. He laughed and said, "I had a truck and they had a need for it, so I helped them. I brought them to their parents' home."

He then asked me if I wanted to know what had happened with Dennis in the Adamo apartment. I didn't need to answer; he knew the answer just by looking at me. It was obvious that he was going to enjoy telling the story. The "Shark" smiled and gave a small chuckle as he sat back, took a long pull on his cigarette, poured himself a drink and started out by saying, "You sent a guy by the name of Dennis up to Fredo's house to make a buy of counterfeit money. You must be some kind of a nut. He was a minor leaguer trying to play in the major leagues." I cautioned the "Shark" about trying to practice psychiatry without a license. He laughed again and said he stood a better chance of being a headshrinker than Dennis did of making a buy of counterfeit money again from Al and Fredo.

"Dennis told Fredo he wanted to make another buy of $500 worth of money. Fredo asked to see the money and Dennis showed it to him. Fredo then snatched the money from his hands saying, 'This is what you owe us from the last buy.' Dennis nearly had a heart attack. He pleaded with Fredo to get him the counterfeit money. But Fredo wouldn't budge; he kept insisting that Dennis get some more money if he wanted to buy more 'queer.' When everything seemed hopeless, Dennis told Fredo that the money belonged to Mr. Motto of the U. S. Secret Service. Dennis was immediately pounced upon by the Adamos. While Fredo throttled Dennis, Al took out a revolver and threatened to blow Dennis' brains out. Dennis begged for his life, admitting that he had been arrested by the Secret Service the day before and that he was forced by Mr. Motto to try to make another buy, this time for the government. Dennis said that Mr. Motto was downstairs with a group of agents waiting for the buy to come off. He said that Mr. Motto threatened to kill him if anything happened to the government's $500. Al was all for killing Dennis. Fredo insisted that they not be too hasty, especially because Fredo's wife was with him. They could always catch up with Dennis and knock him off at their leisure later. Besides, with the Feds in the area, it was dangerous anyway.

"Fredo told Al to leave the house and look over the neighborhood to see if he could notice any law around. Al left and did his job well. He called his brother and said that Dennis had been telling the truth there were Feds all over the neighborhood. Fredo told Al not to come back and that they would meet later. He told Al to call me and have me help move some belongings that Fredo and his wife would take with them. Fredo then turned to Dennis, again poked a gun in his face and said, 'Listen, you fink, me and my wife are leaving. You stay here for at least an hour after we go or I'll catch up with you and take care of you for good. So just go home and forget that me or Al ever existed. I don't care how you do it, but change your story to the Feds and change it quick.' Dennis said he would and thanked Fredo for not killing him. He then asked Fredo for the $500 that belonged to Mr. Motto. Fredo thought for a minute, took the $500 out of his pocket and threw it in Dennis' face. Fredo then grabbed his wife and some belongings and left before I arrived with my truck."

The "Shark" concluded the story by laughing and saying, "This poor schnook was really on the spot. He damn near blew his life for a measly $500. Look at the squeeze he was in ... if he let Fredo keep the money, you would pounce on him. In order to get your $500, he had to level with the Adamos and damn near get killed. No, sir! No one needs this kind of headache." I saw what he was talking about but I didn't share his sense of humor.

The "Shark" then said he didn't know if he could help me out any further. I looked at him and said, "You can sure help a lot by testifying in court to what you told me now. On top of it, I could arrange to get you five hundred dollars." The "Shark" started to scream until the significance of the five hundred dollars sank in; then he laughed when he realized that I did have a sense of humor and said, "$500, $500,000 or $5 million dollars, I couldn't ever afford to go into any court and testify." I assured him I understood and asked him to keep his eyes and ears open for any information I could use on Fredo and Al.

I reported back to the lieutenant who was relieved to hear that the "Shark" and I had gotten along well and that I wasn't going to arrest him. What the "Shark" gave me was very nice for intelligence purposes, but it wasn't helping me with the investigation. It looked like the case against Fredo and Al was going out the window.

Dennis was becoming a problem. He definitely wouldn't testify against the brothers. The case against him was good enough to get a conviction but the government lawyers didn't want to prosecute a man with a history of mental illness. A state parole violation warrant was issued for Dennis and he was picked up and returned to a state institution. He became completely unraveled there and was then transferred to an institution for the criminally insane. The government didn't take any further action against him and the complaint was dismissed.

Three years later, a large number of stolen government bonds were cashed in a midwestern bank. The bonds had been stolen in a string of burglaries in New York, New Jersey, and Connecticut. They had apparently been sold to a fence who, in turn, had lined up a number of people who were interested in disposing of them. The agents handling the investigation in the Midwest did a brilliant job of identifying several of the forgers. They had been arrested and, like all defendants, they had been given an opportunity to cooperate with the government. Several of them availed themselves of the opportunity and named their suppliers. Warrants had been obtained and the suppliers had also been arrested.

Dan, a known handler of stolen bonds, said he had obtained his bonds from a New Yorker by the name of Fredo who had been introduced to him by another party. He said he had met with Fredo in a New York City restaurant and that they had made a deal whereby he would be supplied with all the stolen bonds he could handle. Dan stated he purchased $100,000 worth of the bonds. He said the delivery was accomplished in a matter of hours. The price was good, the merchandise was marketable, and Dan and Fredo parted. Fredo told Dan he could call the restaurant whenever he was in town again. Dan stated he made two buys from Fredo, both of which had gone without any problems. Dan agreed to cooperate further by setting up Fredo for another buy. He also stated that he had taken a good look at the man who had brought the bonds to Fredo and would be able to identify a photograph of him.

Dan's information was put into a report and forwarded to New York. An agent working bond cases was given the assignment of identifying Fredo. The following week, at a regularly scheduled office meeting, the case of Dan and Fredo was discussed in an effort to get a "make" on Fredo. Fredo and his brother, Al, immediately came to my mind. Fredo fit the description provided by Dan. We obtained Fredo's and Al's photos and sent them to the office handling Dan's case. A teletype came back advising that Fredo was Dan's connection and that Al was the man who had delivered the bonds. This put us in good but not great shape. There was nothing to corroborate Dan's story. We could only hope that Fredo and Al wern't aware of Dan's arrest. If Dan played it cool, he might be able to make another buy of bonds — this time for us. We pitched the idea to Dan and he was agreeable.

Dan was brought to New York and after getting a hotel room, he called for Fredo at the restaurant. Someone there said he would deliver the message. Nothing happened that night. The next day Dan again phoned the restaurant and again was told that the message would be delivered. I was in Dan's room when Fredo finally returned the call. He said he had been out of town and had just received the message. He invited Dan to meet him at the restaurant. Dan was fitted with a listening device so that their conversation could be recorded.

Dan and Fredo met and we monitored and taped the conversation. Fredo was surprised that he hadn't heard from Dan for some time. Dan made good excuses and before long they were talking about "tickets." Dan told Fredo that the tickets had sold well and that he could use some more. Fredo tried to raise the price, but Dan held him to the same price as the previous deals. They agreed and Fredo said that he would need two days to make another delivery of $100,000 in bonds. He said he would meet Dan at the same restaurant then. They shook hands and parted company.

At the appointed time, we saturated the area with surveillance personnel. We observed Fredo arrive at the restaurant. Dan was supplied with buy money and he also arrived at the restaurant promptly. After Dan showed Fredo that he had come prepared to do business, Fredo made a phone call. About twenty minutes later, his brother, Al, arrived, carrying a package. Al joined Fredo and Dan at the table. When we heard Fredo invite Dan to take the package and examine it, we moved in and arrested Al and Fredo.

The prisoners were taken to the U. S. Secret Service office for questioning. When Fredo was brought in, I introduced myself to him. When I said my name was Motto, Fred lit up and said, "Was it a long wait?" I said, "Yeah, three years, but it was worth it.' He said, "You didn't win yet." I said, "I'm optimistic." I had reason to be. As far as I was concerned, it was an open-and-shut case. Eventually the jury saw it the same way. The brothers were found guilty of handling stolen bonds and were sentenced to serve a total of fifteen years each.

That ended my concern with Fredo and Al until one day I read in the newspapers that a body had washed up on the shore near Coney Island. According to the paper, the body had been horribly mutilated. After much difficulty, it was identified as the body of a notorious hoodlum named Felix Darlow, also known as the "Shark." I didn't bother to call the Lieutenant to find out what happened.

The Corsican's New Life in America

The Corsican's life was complicated. So complicated in fact, that the best efforts of several governments could not unravel it. He was Phillipe, commonly known as "the Corsican." Was he the incarnation of a famous pirate, or was he one of the best con men to come to America in many a year? Our government believed the latter and so the Corsican found himself on Ellis Island ready for deportation back to Corsica to face a multitude of charges ranging from desertion from the French Foreign Legion to passing bad checks.

He had exhausted all available legal channels and deportation appeared imminent. While waiting for the actual deportation, he was being held on Ellis Island where he became friendly with a group of fellow detainees that was responsible for smuggling narcotics into this country. The group had worldwide connections and was able to operate through couriers without ever leaving the island. Phillipe saw an opportunity to turn this information into a ticket from Ellis Island back to the mainland, perhaps permanently.

He spent time with the group and learned their operation. He memorized times, dates, places, names, and cities. He made notes and before long was a walking central file of narcotics and smuggling information. He managed to get word to the Federal Narcotics Bureau that he had important information and, in time, was interviewed by a federal narcotics agent. The agent was warned by other agents who had had contact with the Corsican, that he was not to be trusted and that anything he said was probably a lie. But, Bart, the narcotics agent, was a meticulous, careful, and insightful investigator. He spent hours with the Corsican — probing, questioning, and testing.

After many interviews he was convinced Phillipe was telling the truth and that there was a group on Ellis Island responsible for large amounts of narcotics coming to this country from overseas and for its eventual distribution throughout the States. He promptly attempted to get Phillipe off Ellis Island and put him to work. It was not easy. The officials handling the deportation felt sure this was another "smoke and mirrors" attempt on the Corsican's part to avoid deportation. Bart was frustrated; convinced that he had developed a potential valuable informant, he eagerly sought help from any quarter.

In one conversation with the Corsican he learned that the Ellis Island gang also handled counterfeit money. Certain visitors acted as couriers and placed orders and arranged for delivery for all sorts of contraband, including counterfeit money and bonds.

In desperation, Bart briefed me on the whole case. He thought that through the combined efforts of the Federal Narcotics Bureau and the Secret Service we might be able to arrange for the release of Phillipe, enabling both agencies to profit by his cooperation.

I put the proposition to my supervisors and was surprised when I was given the go ahead. They suggested I try to settle the matter on a local level. In the event I couldn't swing it, they would contact the Immigration authorities in Washington.

I began by immersing myself in the Corsican's files. He was indeed a colorful character. The date of his entry into the United States could not be documented, but he first came to the attention of the authorities when, at the age of fourteen or fifteen, he was arrested for stealing some clothing from a hotel. He pleaded guilty to a misdemeanor and was deported. His European escapades were legend. He joined the French Foreign Legion and promptly deserted. He was later found impersonating an army officer in Corsica. He had at times passed himself off as a great painter, a fencing master, a security consultant, and a health expert.

Several years later he reappeared on the American scene posing as the son of a famous Contessa who was a leading manufacturer of cosmetics. Phillipe became the darling of the "Hollywood set" and a sought-after consultant in the art of cosmetology. His masquerade might have gone unnoticed for a longer period, except that the Contessa came to the United States and announced that she did not have a son. The Corsican, undaunted, moved on to other pastures and became involved in the sale of some questionable stock in the West. When the venture was exposed, he escaped and returned to the East Coast.

He soon passed as a famous portrait artist to the prominent and wealthy. He received several commissions, was paid in advance and absconded. With each exposure he simply moved his base of operations to another city and took on a new identity.

Phillipe became known as a great French chef, and was fairly successful, catering to the more fashionable trade. For awhile, it seemed the Corsican had settled down, then one night a mysterious fire destroyed his restaurant. In the meantime, the government was quietly following his activities and decided to pursue a deportation case against him. It was a long hard fight. The government proved his criminal record with the conviction on the clothing theft when he was a teen-ager many years before. He was arrested and placed on Ellis Island pending routine deportation paperwork and perhaps an appeal. That is where his story was when Bart and I came into his life.

Everyone who knew about Bart's and my plan were skeptical and quite sure the Corsican would disappear as soon as he was released from the Island, and that his cooperation was just a sham.

My first step was to spend some time with Phillipe. He was completely charming, a captivating continental con man. We spent several hours discussing what he could do for the government and what the government could do for him. I could not make any promises, but after I was convinced that he could produce, I said I would take the steps to try to get him off the island.

He spent many hours trying to convince me that he was a U. S. citizen by virtue of being born in the United States. His story was that he was orphaned at an early age and a relative took him to Canada. After a short stay, he was farmed off to other relatives in Corsica. He ran away to France and, with the connivance of some French seamen, he hid aboard a ship headed for the United States. When the ship arrived, they helped him to get ashore. He was alone in New York and without friends. He managed to get a job as a dishwasher at a hotel in the city. One day he walked by an open room in the hotel. He went in and stole a fur coat from the closet. When he tried to leave with the coat, a hotel detective stopped him. He was arrested, pleaded guilty and was deported. He insisted to me that he was pressured into pleading guilty on the misdemeanor charge; that he was young; did not have counsel and did not know the consequences of his plea.

When I asked him about his long criminal record in France, he replied: "All that you officers worry about are criminal records. Doesn't the person mean anything to you? Records are bits of paper and what is written on paper could be all lies. You say I have a long record in France. They say Phillipe did this and Phillipe did that. I say no one has my prints or my picture and there isn't anyone in France who could point a finger at me. Don't worry, I can take care of things in France. Besides, I don't know if I ever want to go back there. I was born in America, I am a U. S. citizen and some day I'll prove it; then everyone will know that Phillipe told the truth. You believe me, don't you?"

Phillipe's performance was worthy of the best Hollywood actor and could have won an academy award. However, I was not trying to prove or disprove his nationality, I was interested in counterfeit money.

The first big problem was to fend off his pending deportation and to get him off Ellis Island. He swore he would be our slave once he was released. There was no doubt in his mind that he would succeed.

My next visit was with the immigration authorities. They listened with a sympathetic but cynical ear, saying they had been playing cat and mouse with the Corsican long enough and were now in a position to get rid of him.

They were not amenable to letting him get off Ellis Island. My argument was simple — I wanted to gamble with the Corsican. The only way he could double-cross me was by running away and leaving the country, which would accomplish what the government had been trying to do for years. The argument got me nowhere. It was apparent that I would have to go to higher authority to get him sprung.

Amazingly, somehow through the maze of diversified channels in Washington, the Corsican was paroled. Phillipe was required to report to either Bart or me on a daily basis, and could be returned to the Island any time it was felt that he was not leveling with the government. Then we laid down our ground rules. The Narcotics Bureau was satisfied that he could produce. However, I also had to be assured that he not only had counterfeiting information, but that he would work with us according to our instructions so there would be no aura of entrapment. We had to be sure the information he had was something he picked up and not something he engineered.

We had more interviews and I used every means I could to check on his story. He convinced me that the same syndicate he had come into contact with on Ellis Island was selling narcotics and counterfeit money. The kingpin of the group was a fellow Corsican called Duchon. Duchon had a long criminal record in Europe and was a man with worldwide connections. He was in his middle forties; a big strong man suspected of many killings in his homeland. Duchon was also awaiting deportation, but his confinement on the Island did not prevent him from transacting business. This he did through contacts and friends who visited him and other members of his group on the Island.

Phillipe learned that Duchon used one contact for narcotics and another for counterfeit money. The contact for counterfeiting was a rough, crude, and dour-faced man called "Happy." Happy had direct contact with the counterfeit manufacturing plant and had several underlings who handled the distribution for him in the East. Phillipe named four of Happy's contacts and talked about sales that were made in the past.

I listened to Phillipe for some time and questioned him to see if he knew anything about counterfeiting or was simply repeating what he had heard. I became convinced that he only knew what he was told. All the information he gave me checked out and I soon became one of his staunchest allies.

While I wasn't familiar with the Ellis Island group, the name Happy meant a lot to me. Happy was out of state prison only two years after doing a long term for robbery. Having been denied parole, he completed all of his time, came out and immediately became the head of a small group that would handle anything as long as there was money to be made. It was not clear how Happy became involved with Duchon. Somewhere along the line, there was a common denominator, but the Corsican could not help us. We weren't even sure that Duchon and Happy knew each other. The Corsican would have to stay on the Island for awhile longer to give us a better picture of the setup.

In the meantime, Bart and I had to work out a system of priorities. Neither agency would be satisfied to see the other make the case. Also everyone is stat conscious and must have the numbers to give to those who control the purse strings. We had two problems. First, who was going to make the case? Second, where was the buy money going to come from? It's difficult for people to believe a federal law enforcement agency could run out of money, but it happened every year.

We agreed to try to make several conspiracies rather than a lot of substantive counts of possession and sale of narcotics and/or counterfeit money. To make the substantive counts would require investing a lot of money in making buys and we just didn't have it. We would proceed as soon as we could get Phillipe off the island. We would have him introduce undercover agents to as many people as possible. They would get as much information as they could. Several buys could be made and we could then round up all that were involved. This would require a minimum of expense to the government and could result in a number of arrests. We then saw Phillipe and had him pass the word that his lawyers were attempting to arrange bond pending further appeal.

The Corsican's performance before Duchon and his cohorts was excellent; so good in fact that Duchon saw great possibilities in Phillipe, and asked him to act as intermediary between the couriers and the suppliers. Duchon's love, Yvette, was also on Ellis Island. She was a large, attractive woman who was the confidante of many mobsters in the French underworld. Convicted of prostitution in France at the age of 16, she had decided she would pick her man and live with him. She had gone through three men in less than ten years — two died violently and one was serving a long penitentiary sentence in France.

She had met Duchon shortly before the death of "husband" number three. There were rumors that Duchon arranged for his liquidation when he met Yvette at a nightclub and all his amorous efforts met with negative results. Duchon made inquiries and learned that Yvette was well known in the French underworld. He viewed Yvette from two different angles. On the one hand, she was a smart, attractive woman of the world whom he wanted as a paramour to replace his wife, who died six months before. Secondly, she would be an asset to his group. She could be a courier; she could be an "entertainer"; and she could entice customers to buy Duchon's contraband. Duchon wanted Yvette and he meant to get her.

Husband number three was found one morning in the trunk of a stolen car. He had been shot in the head, stuffed in the trunk and driven to a spot in a wooded area outside of town. Yvette, with Duchon's help, took care of the funeral arrangements. Then Duchon set her up in an elegant apartment, gave her all the clothes and jewelry she needed. She responded by obeying his orders. She spent weekends with important clients, she acted as a courier and delivered packages to mysterious people at all hours of the night. She was also expected to entertain at the apartment as often as Duchon brought guests. The combination worked. It appeared that Duchon's business would be international in scope, and they eventually made connections with their counterparts in America.

Duchon could supply unlimited amounts of narcotics and through American connections, make sales of unlimited amounts of counterfeit money, stolen stocks or bonds. He went merrily on his way buying and selling and making frequent trips all over the world, sometimes traveling with his two principal aides — Marcel and Jacques. On one of his trips to America, Duchon and his group decided to make New York their base of operations.

They rented two apartments in New York, continued their operation and overstayed their visas. The French authorities had been ready to close in on the group when they left France, but had to be satisfied to wait until they returned. When it was apparent that the group was in no hurry to return, the French authorities contacted the Americans. This resulted in the group being confined on Ellis Island to await deportation. However, Duchon soon found ways to conduct his business while on Ellis Island by having his orders filled through third parties whom he trusted.

Phillipe spoke with Duchon often before his release from the Island. He convinced Duchon that he had the connections which would enable him to return to the Island; presumably to handle paperwork in connection with his appeal. Duchon was pleased.

The day came when the Corsican left the Island and became Bart's and my personal ward. That night he told us that Duchon wanted him to contact a man named Mike. He was to give Mike the name of a ship that was due to arrive in five days. Mike knew who Phillipe was to contact. The Corsican understood that Mike would receive two kilos of heroin. The purchase price would be paid to one of Duchon's henchmen who would see to it that the people overseas received their money and the remainder would be sent to a friend of Duchon's in Paris. Phillipe called Mike, met him and delivered the message.

We had a hurried meeting to decide what to do with the delivery of narcotics to Mike. We agreed to let Mike take the package, give him a tail and play it by ear. If we could make an arrest without using the Corsican, we would do it; otherwise, we would have to let it go and hope to get Mike later.

We struck a lucky streak at about that time. Another narcotic agent reported that an informant had introduced him to a man named Mike; that he had ordered a kilo of heroin and was expecting delivery any day. We had Mike's phone number and a complete rundown on him. We obtained his picture and showed it to the other narcotic agent. He identified the photograph as being the Mike he knew. This took care of what otherwise could have been a sticky situation.

The Corsican had made his first contribution, and did his job well. The Narcotics Bureau not only had an undercover buy set up, but now knew what ship it was coming in on and the man who would probably make the pickup. Mike was arrested at the time of the sale.

None of this roused the suspicions of the group on Ellis Island. They figured the narcotics undercover agent ratted on Mike. While Mike's arrest disturbed them, it did not make anyone suspicious of Phillipe who was still gathering information from Duchon.

Shortly after Mike's arrest, Yvette was released on bail from Ellis Island pending appeal. She rented an apartment in midtown New York and carried on Duchon's work. She visited him frequently, received her orders and carried them out. This was ideal for Phillipe. He visited Yvette frequently and was brought up-to-date. He often performed innocuous tasks for the group and was slowly finding himself in a position of trust.

Phillipe was becoming anxious to square away with us. Our deal was to get him off the Island. There was no promise of reward. He was in continual need of money and it became apparent that if we did not subsidize him, he would have to find some other way of supporting his family. However, supporting him was not a part of the original deal. Money for informants was scarce and we were rapidly approaching a crisis. We either had to support him or let him earn a living the best way he knew — and that frightened us. We decided to force the issue. We would set up a "buy" of narcotics and counterfeit money and make both cases at the same time.

The Corsican was not happy with the arrangements since after the case was made he still had to face his deportation problems. Nevertheless, he went along with us.

Phillipe could contact Yvette and tell her to get the word to Duchon that he had located a buyer who was interested in a kilo of heroin and another buyer who wanted a hundred grand in counterfeit money. The buys would have to be set up so each agency could make a case without investing too much money or spoiling the other agency's case.

The Corsican was a real pro. He convinced Yvette that his buyers had shown him their money; that he had checked up on both of them and was convinced that they were well-connected people who meant business.

Duchon wanted to discuss the deal with Phillipe personally and in two days Phillipe was back on Ellis Island. Duchon had not liked receiving the message second hand. Phillipe replied, "My friend, you don't understand. These two men come to me with a proposition; they want a deal in a hurry. I just can't take the ferry to Ellis Island anytime I want. There are some people that have to be taken care of. You know how it is, you can't do it too often or someone will smell a rat. So, I know Yvette is coming to see you and I tell her. I know you trust her with anything."

Duchon listened and said, "Okay, shut up. Who are these people?" Phillipe answered, "Two very good people whom I have done business with for years. I mean big business. Both are well connected and I would trust them with my life." Duchon growled, "You know you are trusting them with your life! You are responsible if anything goes wrong. No excuses." Phillipe assured Duchon that nothing could go wrong and he would accept responsibility for the transaction. Duchon dismissed Phillipe and told him he would be contacted by Yvette.

On her next visit to the Island, Yvette was instructed to contact two men — Pepe and Happy. She was to put them in touch with the Corsican and personally tell them that Duchon okayed any deal that the Corsican set up. She was to have the meeting at her apartment, be the good hostess, keep her ears open and report back to Duchon as soon as possible.

Our plan was to have Bart buy the narcotics and I would buy the counterfeit money. The meetings went well. Bart could speak some French and he did a good job of impressing Pepe with his flashy sports car and jewelry. (Bart made good use of a friendly car dealer and jeweler). Pepe agreed to get a kilo for Bart as soon as he was able. He promised to meet Bart the following day to supply him with an ounce as a sample.

Later that evening, I met with Happy. He was a suspicious sort and not buying introductions too easily. He first questioned the Corsican on who his people were. Phillipe said he represented Duchon and Yvette worked for him. Happy then insisted on the names of people who could vouch for me. I refused; I told him the Corsican was my man. Before Happy would go any further, Phillipe told him that he had done business with me for years; that Duchon was satisfied with the deal and personally okayed it. Happy didn't like doing business that way, but he would handle it. He wanted ten cents on the dollar for the hundred grand lot. I insisted that ten cents did not leave a margin of profit for anyone else and tried to get it down to seven, but Happy wouldn't budge. He insisted that the quality was excellent and was worth far more than his asking price. When we left the apartment, he told me confidentially that this money was perfect. "You know, we were lucky. We managed to get hold of an old engraver who worked for the government. He lost his job because he was an alcoholic. We have him under our control. He is practically a prisoner and he works only for us." I said, "Gosh, that's great." I thought to myself, "Here we go again." The story about the alcoholic engraver is a witch's tale that's been going around for years and I was hearing it from a bum who probably had no idea who was responsible for making the money. He agreed to supply me with several hundred dollars as a sample.

The following night, I met Happy at a pre-arranged place. We had a drink and it was obvious that Happy was putting me on display for other people who were involved in the deal. I apparently passed the test because after fifteen minutes he told me to go outside alone and I would be contacted. I walked outside and after a minute or so a car pulled up. A man wearing glasses rolled the window down and handed me a small brown paper bag. I knew the covering agents got the license number of the car and I concentrated on the man with the glasses who gave me the package. I walked back into the bar, went into the men's room and opened the bag. It contained several hundred dollars of fairly deceptive counterfeit money. I then returned to the bar and told Happy that the merchandise looked pretty good; I would show the samples to my people and would give him an answer in a day or so. I made another attempt to get the price down, but Happy wouldn't come down. We engaged in a little small talk and then I left.

When I got outside I decided to take a walk through the neighborhood. I barely got down the street a short distance when I noticed two men following me. Happy wasn't completely sold on me. I did a lot of window shopping and took the boys on a merry chase before getting into my parked car. They made no attempt to follow me. They wanted to see if anyone met me after I left Happy. When I was positive I no longer had a "tail," I met the other agents. We examined the counterfeits and exchanged notes. The car that delivered the money to me was registered in the name of Olga Benton, the girlfriend of Les Stoler. Les was the man with the glasses and he was suspected of being a plant connection for several years.

It seemed incredible that Les would make the delivery himself. He had any number of flunkies that would have been happy to make deliveries for him. Phillipe was undoubtedly responsible for having Happy and Les do business directly with me.

Time was running short and the boys from narcotics and our bunch had a quick meeting to coordinate our activities. I would put the order in for one hundred thousand dollars in counterfeit notes and Bart would put his order in for a kilo of heroin. We would try to engineer the buy for the same day so that the arrest on one case would not hurt the other.

The Corsican knew that after the arrests were made he would be in a precarious position. He would have to leave town and certainly would have to have the deportation order stayed, as he could not return to Ellis Island. Nevertheless, he was anxious to get the case rolling and he was able to have Bart meet Pepe again. Bart put his order in for the heroin and insisted that delivery be made in three days. With a spread of three days he could control the delivery pretty much to coincide with the counterfeit money delivery.

Happy and I arranged to meet in a midtown bar. I told him the sample notes were acceptable to my people; that we were in a position to use one hundred thousand dollars in counterfeit notes; that the people buying the notes had to have it in time to get it on a certain ship that was leaving the United States. Happy was pleased to hear that the money was leaving the country. We spent several hours trying to agree on a place for delivery and a suitable method of payment. Happy, like the rest of his ilk, wanted to make things as safe as possible and naturally wanted payment in advance. I refused. I insisted that I would not pay until I saw the merchandise and satisfied myself that the quantity and quality was correct. This time Happy was on the spot because I wasn't budging. He tried to drive a hard bargain but his lust for money made him eventually agree to do business my way.

On the appointed day I registered at a midtown hotel under an assumed name. I called Happy and let him know that I was ready to do business. He advised me to sit and wait for a call. In the meantime, the narcotic boys had made their contacts and were proceeding successfully with their case.

About four in the afternoon. I received a call on the house phone, and a man who called himself "a friend" said he was coming up. I alerted the covering agents in the adjoining room. There was a knock at the door and I opened it. It was Les. He introduced himself as Happy's friend and wanted to know if I was ready to do business. I told him I was, and asked if he had brought the stuff. He examined the room carefully. He looked in the closet, bathroom, under the bed, tore the bed apart and looked between the mattresses and finally convinced himself that the room was not bugged. I suggested that "If I were that suspicious, I wouldn't bother to pull a deal."' He ignored that and asked to see the 'buy money.' I asked to see the counterfeits. We were clearly not getting along too well. I wanted to talk with Happy. I said we went all through this money business before; that Happy agreed to a hand-to-hand delivery. I would have to be out of my mind to give him 10 grand; especially since this was only the second time I had seen him.

He asked, "When was the first time?" "You were the guy who gave me the samples." "Then you should know you can trust me." "No dice. Bring the stuff and you'll get paid." He said he would call Happy and be guided by what he said. It was obvious that this was some kind of a stall.

He left and spoke to three men near the entrance to the hotel. One was Happy and the others were not known to the agents. It later developed that they were Marcel and Jacques, friends of Duchon. Happy took a suitcase out of the trunk of a nearby car, gave it to Les, and accompanied him to my room. Les said that the suitcase had an extra $20,000 in it. He claimed that he couldn't break up the lot and that he would wait a few days for the extra money if I didn't have it.

I opened the suitcase and found it neatly packed with stacks of counterfeit money. Les was becoming impatient and wanted to be paid. He said, "For Christ's sake, you're not going to sit there and count each one?" I said, "No, I don't expect "o, but I just want to be sure of the quality." He replied, "Don't worry about it! Come on, let's get going! I told you there was an extra 20 grand there. If there are any bad ones, just deduct them from the extras." This conversation was being overheard by the agents in a nearby room. They now had enough information to make the arrest at any time. I suggested that Les stay with the package and Happy accompany me to another room in the hotel where I had a buddy waiting with the 'buy' money.

Happy agreed and he and I left the hotel room. As we walked down the hallway toward the elevator several agents were waiting nearby and attempted to arrest Happy. He pulled out a gun, but never got a chance to use it. The agents were too quick and arrested both of us without further incident. They took us back to the room where Les was waiting. Les was arrested while he was repackaging the counterfeits. The two men waiting by the car were also taken into custody and the car was confiscated.

Meanwhile the narcotic boys were equally successful. Bart got his kilo of heroin and Pepe and two of his cohorts were arrested while making the delivery.

We applied for warrants against Duchon, Yvette and the other members of the group. Yvette's apartment was raided. There were a lot of names and addresses in her telephone book that gave the Narcotics Bureau a better picture of their operation.

Les was getting the counterfeits from out of town. We had an idea who the printer was, but could not make a case against him.

All of the people arrested stood on their rights and refused to give a statement. They all elected to go to trial.

Some months later a trial was held. Everyone was anxious to see if the Corsican would take the stand against his friends and countrymen. He did testify and underwent many days of intensive cross-examination by a battery of defense lawyers. In an effort to discredit Phillipe's testimony, some of the lawyers went to France and Corsica with an eye toward gathering information about his background. They were disappointed. While there was plenty of information, it was muddled, incomplete and no one could get a decent police record on Phillipe that could be used in court.

Phillipe took the stand and the only arrest they could talk about was the clothing he stole many years before. After a long and bitter trial, all defendants were found guilty and received substantial prison terms. The plant was not captured until a year or so later when the printer decided to go back into the counterfeiting business.

What of the Corsican? Shortly after the case was made, he left town and went to work for several other law enforcement agencies. He had fantastic success and became one of the most sought-after and controversial informants of our time. One agency needed the Corsican for a series of cases. Phillipe was assigned to work with an agent who previously practiced law. He suggested to Phillipe that he enter a motion to have his conviction on the theft of the clothing set aside on the grounds that he was not represented by counsel at the time.

The Corsican hired a prominent attorney to handle the matter for him. He was successful, enabling Phillipe to remain in this country.

Phillipe exposed several crooked politicians. His services were eagerly sought by many public and private organizations. He recovered stolen property and exposed thieves. There were times when he found it necessary to hire help. He handled matters throughout the United States, Mexico, and Canada. The money rolled in. He soon built a beautiful home in the suburbs, owned several large limousines and even had domestic help at home.

After several years, he became interested in the investment business. He joined several businessmen who were going public with their company.

Phillipe became a principal. He sold stock in the company and before long took complete control. He then spread out into several other stock deals which were pouring quite a bit of money into his pockets.

Quietly, the government began looking into his questionable investment practices. Phillipe found himself indicted in federal court. While the case was on the calendar, Phillipe applied for and was granted permission to go overseas to handle his company business and protect the interests of the stockholders.

By the time his case was called for trial, Phillipe had sold everything he owned and disappeared. Over the years, he was spotted in Africa, Paris, Rome, London, and Israel, among other places. Eventually, information was received that Phillipe was running a very successful restaurant in a remote part of the United States. The lead resulted in his arrest. Unfortunately, many of the witnesses against him were long gone and Phillipe found himself back on the street as a free man. He pled guilty to some minor charges and was given probation. After completing his probation he disappeared from official and public activity.

Wherever he may be, Phillipe, will undoubtedly get the urge to operate again. No one can predict which side of the fence he will be on, but one thing is clear — he will be a formidable adversary for the opposing side and it will make for another interesting story.

Adrian — A Mafioso's Son

The police officers bent over the body. A call from a passing motorist had brought them to a wooded area about a quarter mile outside of town. At first it appeared that the victim had been struck by a passing car, but closer examination revealed a vicious murder.

She was in her mid- to late-twenties. She had been raped, strangled, and mutilated. And she had been dead only a few hours. There were multiple stab wounds on her body and her stockings had been used around her neck as a garrote, either of which might have caused her death. She had no purse, no identification and no indication of where she had come from. There were no missing person alarms out on anyone who fit her description. She was just another statistic Jane Doe.

Halfway across the country, Butch, the owner of several after hour joints in a midwestern city, had just made a connection to purchase counterfeit money. Butch had been a target of police for many years, but always managed to stay one step ahead of them. He had a finger in many different rackets, but always made sure he did business with well-recommended customers. His lottery business practically ran itself. The after-hours clubs gave him a comfortable income. He was always on the lookout for anything that would give him a quick profit.

When he was first approached on the "funny money" deal, his inclination was that there wasn't enough profit in it. Then he had second thoughts. He had enough contacts to handle it and make a decent profit. He saw the samples, liked what he saw and ordered a package of $25,000. The investment cost him $3,000 in good money, which he was sure he could double. He wanted to sell the whole package in one deal rather than having a bunch of punks bothering him for small 'chump change.' He knew what it was like selling to cheap punks. When he handled narcotics the small buys gave him more trouble than they were worth.

For some reason, it wasn't easy to dispose of the package locally. He tried hard, but there were no takers. Times were tough and money was tight. When he realized he couldn't sell the $25,000 in one package, he found a buyer for a $10,000 lot and made up his mind that the remaining $15,000 would have to go in one sale.

Then there was Adrian. His father was a well-known crime figure and an old friend of Butch's. Adrian came to Butch to arrange for the sale of some stolen jewelry. The jewelry was too hot in Adrian's area so he traveled 350 miles to peddle it through Butch, who was always a good outlet as long as the price was right. Just before Adrian left, Butch remembered the counterfeit money. He told Adrian that he had some "queer money" and would let it go at a good price. Adrian was not interested but said he'd let Butch know. The plane left and Butch couldn't help but think how different Adrian was from his father, Albert.

Albert had great plans for Adrian. After high school, he sent Adrian to college and had hopes that he would eventually become a lawyer. These hopes went up in smoke when Adrian was arrested on a burglary charge. The arrest was miles away and the only thing Albert could do was supply his son with the best counsel available.

Adrian returned home and got the thrashing of his life from his father. The lawyer that Albert had retained made a complete investigation and told Albert that his son had been caught in the act. Attempting to fight the case was ridiculous. He suggested that Adrian plead guilty to a lesser charge. The lawyer would play heavily on the fact that this was Adrian's first arrest. Albert listened and finally gave the lawyer permission to plead his son guilty.

The judge gave Adrian a long lecture and sentenced him to five years, suspended the sentence and put him on probation for ten years. He warned him that if he were ever brought before him again, no matter the charge or regardless of when, one year, ten years, or fifteen, he would go to prison for a long time.

Returning to school was out of the question. He didn't have any interest in school and the school didn't want him. He married a local girl and ran a small business that his father set up for him. This satisfied the probation officer and gave Adrian plenty of time to run errands for his father.

But Adrian had no patience for legitimate business and was always looking for a quick buck. He had a reputation for being a tough guy, and would fight at the drop of a hat. His temper got him into many local scrapes; but he was always able to convince the victims not to testify against him.

When Adrian returned home from his trip to Butch, he told his father that Butch handled the jewelry sale. He didn't mention the counterfeit money. He felt sure that his father wouldn't approve. However, he made it known to his friends that he could get counterfeit money at a good price. Several weeks later he was approached by "Corby."

Corby had moved away several years ago, but made a point of returning two or three times a year to see what was going on and what he could pick up. Corby told Adrian he could handle the counterfeits if the price was right.

After the usual haggling, they agreed on $10,000 of the counterfeits with Corby planning to buy more as soon as he disposed of the first batch.

Adrian immediately got in touch with Butch and said he would take the entire $15,000 package off his hands. Butch quickly got the counterfeits to Adrian and Adrian made the sale to Corby. After the deal was completed, Corby left town. He went to New York where he was sure he could make a quick sale to his friend Whitey for a three-point profit. What Corby didn't know was that Whitey had recently been arrested. He cooperated with the authorities and promised to let them know the next time he did business with Corby. He was back on the street when Corby approached him about buying the package of counterfeit money. Whitey set up a deal and notified the police. They, in turn, notified the U. S. Secret Service. We covered it and intercepted the transfer of the notes from Corby to Whitey.

It was a most inopportune time for Corby to be arrested. He had used all his money to get the notes from Adrian. His pregnant wife was ready to go to the hospital at any time. Corby, needless to say, was ripe for a deal. He was anxious to set up Adrian if it would help him. He was released on very low bail.

We let a few days pass and had him call Adrian to set up a meet. Adrian suggested a diner and the meet was set for the following evening. Corby and I and a young agent went to the diner.

We arrived there first, and waited half an hour for Adrian to arrive. Corby introduced me to Adrian and I, in turn, introduced him to the agent working with me. Without a word, Adrian walked out. I motioned to Corby to see what was wrong. Corby chased after Adrian and they had an animated conversation outside.

After about five minutes, Corby returned and said Adrian did not like the young agent. He was sure the agent was some kind of cop and he would not talk in front of him. I told the agent to wait outside in the car. I went out with Corby and spoke to Adrian. I told him my friend just got out of jail; that I was paying him a few dollars a day to drive me around; that he was now depriving this man of making a day's pay. Adrian said the man made him nervous; he just felt that the man was heat. I said, "If he is heat, then I must be heat and you probably are heat." Adrian settled down and we returned to the diner. He insisted that the other man stay outside.

Corby told Adrian that I was an old friend of his; that he had sold me a package of notes and that I was anxious to get more. Adrian said he had made a couple of sales and only had $2,500 left. I said I could use it for starters as lunch money, but I needed much more to take care of people who had orders. Adrian said he wasn't interested in staying in the counterfeiting business. He would arrange to get me the money in half an hour, but that's all there would be. I asked him if he could put me in touch with his connection; then I could make future buys without involving him. He said he'd think about it. In the meantime, he made a phone call (presumably to have the counterfeits delivered). After the call he began probing. He asked me questions about myself and my relationship with Corby. He received several calls and finally was able to say that the notes would arrive in a few minutes. A car pulled up to the diner and Adrian got up and walked outside.

The agent waiting outside watched Adrian go to the car and get a package from the driver. He got the license number of the vehicle. Adrian returned and motioned me to follow him. We went into the men's room where he turned the package over to me. I opened it and found about $2,500 in counterfeit $20's. I paid Adrian and we went back to the table. He was in a better mood after the deal went down. He announced again that he wouldn't be dealing in counterfeits anymore but, at my urging, he agreed to call his connection for me.

He called Butch. When I got on the phone, Butch wanted to know where I was from and who I knew. I mentioned a few names. I'm sure he didn't know the people, but he tried to make me believe he knew a lot of connected people. I asked him if I could get some 'paper.' He said he didn't have any available at the present time, but expected more in a couple of weeks. I asked for his phone number. He obliged and I told him he could expect a call from me in two weeks. When I finished talking to Butch, I asked Adrian for his number in the event I ever came to town again. He gave me the number of his business. He said he was sorry he had chased the other man, but he wanted to be careful and play it safe. I told him I understood and we left.

Back at the office we decided to wait it out and see if we could score from Butch. We could arrest Adrian at any time. He wasn't much of a problem and it looked like he was out of the counterfeiting business.

Several days later, Adrian was summoned by his father who told him, "Your sister is having trouble; go to her and see what's wrong and let me know." Dutifully, Adrian made the trip to see what was wrong with his sister, Marie. He found her almost hysterical. Her husband, Jimmy, hadn't been home in over two weeks. The police had been to the house on several occasions and wanted to know where he was. They wouldn't tell her what they wanted with him, but she knew it was serious. She said Jimmy called her at her girlfriend's house most every night, but he wouldn't tell her what was wrong.

Adrian called his father and told him what was happening. Albert told Adrian to wait there until Jimmy called and he had a chance to speak to him. He was to find out from Jimmy what was wrong and if it was necessary to hide, he should be put in touch with Butch. He also told him to close up the apartment and bring Marie back home with him. Adrian told him not to worry, that he would take care of everything.

The next night Adrian and Marie waited at Marie's girlfriend's house hoping Jimmy would call. The call came. Jimmy told Adrian that there had been a murder and the police were looking for him in connection with it. He said he was innocent, but was afraid the cops might pin it on him;, so he was hiding out. Adrian told Jimmy to take a plane and go to Butch's home. He was sure Butch would take care of him until things cooled down. He added that Marie was going back to her father's house, but under no condition should Jimmy go there until he was told. Jimmy said he understood and would immediately make plans to see Butch.

In the meantime, Albert made the necessary arrangements with Butch to hide Jimmy until it was safe for him to return home. Butch was happy to be of service to the 'old man.'

After two weeks had passed, I called Butch to see if he had the counterfeits; he said they weren't ready yet and to call back in another week or so. The phone calls continued for several months, always with the same results. I thought perhaps it would be best to drop in on Butch to see if he really meant to do business or was stalling me.

When I got to Butch's town I gave him a call. I told him I was an hour away; that I had some business to handle and I would drop in to see him. He said fine. Several hours later I called him again; this time he gave me the address of his club and directions. I rented a car and went to the address. The club wasn't open. A man answered my knock and let me in. I told him I wanted to see Butch. He introduced himself as "Rocky." He poured me a drink and said he expected Butch to be back in half an hour. Rocky had a patch on his nose. I asked him if he was a fighter; he said, "No, I recently had a nose job to clear up a problem and it is just healing." He talked a lot about New York and New Jersey and seemed to know quite a few people there. I told him I was from New York and knew some of the people he mentioned. The conversation was pleasant enough and the time passed quickly.

Butch finally came in about an hour later. He was a big powerful man in his forties and he was tough. His face was marked with scar tissue and there was a four inch scar on the left side of his neck that looked like the wound that caused the scar should have been fatal. Butch greeted me and told Rocky to pour me a drink. After serving the drink, Rocky disappeared. Butch said he was anxious to get a plant started and wanted to know if I knew anyone who wanted to finance the printing operation. I asked him "How much are you talking about?" He never blinked an eye and said, "Forty or fifty grand." I said "That's way out of my league. I'm only interested in buying maybe $10,000 or $20,000 worth of stuff." I got the feeling that Butch was trying to take me for a sucker. I figured that I'd get as much conversation from him as possible and if he admitted selling to Adrian, perhaps we could book him for conspiracy later. During the conversation he finally mentioned selling $25,000 worth to Adrian. He said, "The printer isn't around any more so to get more counterfeits I would have to set up a whole new printing operation." I again told him that I wasn't interested in the manufacturing, but I was willing to purchase any notes that were still around. He suggested that I call him from time to time. When it was apparent that I couldn't get any more information from Butch, I said good-bye and left.

I knew Butch could now be included in a conspiracy indictment. His own conversation had implicated him. I returned to New York and called him from time to time. He never indicated that he was setting up a plant or that he was ready to do business. We weren't getting anywhere on the case so it was time to wrap it up. I returned to my district and went about the daily load of cases assigned to me.

Several months later I was working out of town on some routine assignments. The local state troopers were assisting me on these particular investigations and at the end of each day I relaxed at the barracks in anticipation of a tough day to follow.

One night the sergeant and I were in the office playing two-handed rummy just before turning in. Some time during the game a clipboard of "wanted" notices hanging on the wall caught my eye. The picture and notice on the top bore the legend 'Wanted for Homicide.' The poster included the fingerprints of the man, his name, and record and a mug shot showing full view and profile. There was something disturbing about the photograph. It looked like someone I had met and yet there was something different. I took the board down to examine it more closely. The wanted man's name was James Deale also known as Jimmy Dino. The name meant nothing to me, but the face did and it bothered me that I couldn't remember. Of course,this made me the butt of many jokes at the barracks. To the layman, the photo of a wanted man always looks familiar. I tried to assure them that I was serious, but to no avail.

That night I slept at the barracks. After tossing and turning for several hours, it suddenly hit me — the face — it was Rocky from Butch's place! I jumped out of bed, went downstairs, took the picture from the clipboard, and studied it again. The trooper on night duty must have thought I was crazy. He came on duty at midnight — here it was almost two in the morning and a guest in pajamas was standing in the office and flipping over a mug shot. The only trouble with the photo was the nose, but then Rocky did tell me he'd had a nose job. Things started to add up. Rocky seemed awfully familiar with the goings on in New York and when I talked with him, he appeared to be hungry for information. He also gave me the impression he was visiting with Butch and came from somewhere else.

The next morning I put in a call to the police department that originated the 'wanted' alarm. The homicide lieutenant was delighted to get any information at all. He said the flyer had been out for several months and mine was the first call. I suggested we meet and discuss the matter. He agreed. I contacted my headquarters and was given the go-ahead to drop what I was doing to meet with the lieutenant.

We met at a local police headquarters midway between our two locations. The lieutenant was accompanied by a sergeant who was working the case. I knew nothing about their case other than the general information given in the flyer so I told them my story. When I got to the part about meeting a man named Adrian, both of them jumped and said, "That's it! You sure you got it right?" "Got what right?" I asked. The lieutenant replied, "Adrian is the brother-in-law of Jimmy Deale/Dino. Dino married Adrian's sister. There's no doubt we are all in the same ball game."

I explained that Adrian wasn't going to handle any more counterfeits, but had introduced me to Butch over the phone and how I eventually went to see Butch and, while in his club, met Rocky.

I went into great detail of my conversation with Rocky and gave as good a description as I was able including his new nose. I was now positive that Rocky was Jimmy Deale also known as Jimmy Dino. I had to admit he looked a little different, but nose or not, Rocky was Jimmy. The lieutenant was delighted and filled me in from his end.

"Several months ago, a dead woman was found alongside a road in the early hours of the morning. She had been strangled, mutilated, and raped. It was believed she was killed somewhere else and then dumped alongside the road just outside of town. It was very hard to identify her as there was nothing at the scene to help us. After a real painstaking, don't overlook anything, investigation, we finally had a tentative identification. A check of the missing persons records and files had been negative. However, there was information about a young divorcee who had a daughter in private school in another town. The young woman visited her daughter every weekend and every holiday. Suddenly, she didn't appear at the school for two weekends. The school authorities made inquiries at the mother's address. No one knew where she was; she didn't answer her phone; she did not make payment on her daughter's tuition. The school officials were sufficiently disturbed to report the matter to the police in the town where she lived."

"The sergeant on duty at Headquarters tried to be polite and explain to the school officials that the woman was over the age of consent and free to come and go as she pleased. It was highly improper to list her as a missing person unless a member of her family made a formal complaint. The sergeant did agree to take the information and distribute it locally and perhaps have an officer make inquiries at the last known address. He insisted, however, that for the present, the information could not go out over the teletype. He assured the school officials that he would notify them if he received any information on the woman."

"When we contacted the detective bureau, it was only a matter of minutes before the missing person information was dovetailed with information on the murdered woman. The next problem was to have someone identify the body. The woman had been so savagely beaten that even close relatives might have difficulty in identifying her and, needless to say, no one in the department was going to bring the little girl in to identify her mother. One of the women at the school who knew the girl's mother agreed to come to the morgue. After viewing the body she was pretty well certain that the body was that of the little girl's missing mother. So, the missing woman, the murdered woman Jane Doe, was now tentatively identified as Lila Freisch, DOA."

"The detectives assisting on the case found Lila's dentist who agreed to try to identify the dental work of the unidentified body. In the meantime, Lila's apartment was searched. Lila apparently was not a 'stay-at-home' type of girl. She had many men friends and was not bashful about having them stay at her apartment for a day or two at a time. She worked occasionally in a nearby town as a cocktail waitress and between her men friends and her job, she managed to make ends meet."

"The husband would normally have been a prime suspect. An investigation revealed that he and Lila were married quite young. After the birth of their daughter, they divorced. The husband remarried and moved to California but an inquiry there revealed that Lila's former husband had been killed in an auto accident a year and a half before the murder. In the meantime, a set of fingerprints was obtained from the corpse and sent to Washington. A return indicated the prints were indeed those of Lila Freisch who had been arrested once as a disorderly person. The dentist was also able to make a positive identification on the dental work."

"The investigation continued and it led the us to the bar where Lila worked. All the employees were close-mouthed and professed not to know anything of Lila's private life."

"Shortly after our unsuccessful and apparently wasted visit to the bar, we received a phone call from a woman named 'Gert'. She worked at the bar and said she had some information but was afraid to talk. She agreed to meet with us at a spot out of town. We met there several hours later."

"Gert said that she knew Lila on and off for almost two years; they were fairly good friends. Lila was 'footloose' and a 'fast stepper' but quite particular about who she went out with, especially when she was sober. She once told

Gert that she went out with a local bookmaker by the name of Jimmy Dino but that Dino was an obnoxious bastard and an abusive pervert. She confided to Gert that she detested the man and was deathly afraid of him. Jimmy never stopped trying to take Lila out but she always came up with some excuse. Gert said that one night just before closing time she saw Jimmy outside the bar, apparently waiting for Lila to finish work. She thought that Jimmy looked wild and she hoped that Lila would manage to avoid him. After she saw Jimmy lurking around, she went back into the lounge and warned Lila. Lila said that she didn't have a date with him and had no intention of going with him. Lila apparently ducked him that night but she noticed that he appeared in the vicinity on subsequent nights. Lila confided in Gert and told her she was scared and intended to quit her job because Jimmy was really annoying her. When Gert didn't see Lila anymore, she assumed that Lila had changed jobs to outfox Jimmy. But now she was certain that Jimmy had something to do with her demise. Gert was able to set the date when she last saw Lila. The date coincided with the date of the murder."

"We tried to find Jimmy Dino but were unsuccessful. His wife, Marie, and kids lived in town but they have closed their apartment and, as far as we know have gone to live with her father, Albert. We tried to talk to Marie before she moved but she couldn't or wouldn't give us any information on her husband except to say she hadn't seen him in some time. We then learned that Mrs. Dino is the daughter of a man who is considered a prominent crime figure in an other city. Inquiries in that city produced nothing."

"As a last resort and in desperate frustration, our department sent out an alarm for Jimmy and continued to try to build a case against him. We have obtained a warrant and are prepared to extradite him in the event he is located in another state."

The lieutenant snuffed out his cigarette and said, "That's the whole story. Where do we go from here?" I said, "The first order of business is to call the U. S. Attorney's Office and see what they did on Adrian and Butch's case."

The call brought disturbing news. The U. S. Attorney told me that the grand jury had met two weeks earlier and had voted an indictment against the two men. They were arrested and arraigned; both pled not guilty, got out on bail, and were back-tracking to see who had set them up. The wording of the indictment indicated that I was an agent working undercover. That information precluded my returning to Butch's club to see if Rocky was still there. This didn't give the officers too much to work on. They could now be sure that Jimmy was using the name Rocky; that he had a new nose and that several months before he was seen in a distant city in an afterhours club. They could take a trip out there, talk with the local police and hope for the best. I promised that I would do all in my power to help; however, I felt that nothing could be done until after the disposition of Adrian's case.

Several months passed with no new information. Then one day I received a letter from Charlie Stone, the U. S. Attorney in charge of Adrian's case. The case was ready to be called to trial and Mr. Stone wanted me there for a pre-trial conference. Adrian and Butch were going to fight the case right down the line. He couldn't understand it, as he felt the government had a perfect case. He said there were various unconfirmed reports that Adrian and his people were going to cause as much trouble as possible. They planned to plant bombs in the cars of the officials connected with the case. They also planned to harass the jurors and their families. Inasmuch as the area was noted for its bombings and other violence, Charlie was concerned. He certainly didn't want anymore violence. He was arranging to have a change of venue to have the case tried in another part of the state. He thought that with Adrian's people away from their home grounds, it would make it more difficult for them to operate.

Charlie suggested that all law enforcement personnel assigned to the case stick closely together during the trial and if it became necessary, he would request more federal agents to be assigned for protection. Charlie said that there was another thing disturbing him. He had received still another report that Adrian had some plans of his own. Adrian was a martial arts expert and it was his idea that if things were looking bad during the trial, he would wait until one of the government witnesses got off the stand, jump up from his seat, attack the witness and attempt to do as much damage as he could. He felt that this would cause a mistrial; that he would be ordered to an institution for a mental examination. He knew he could bluff his way into being declared a psycho. He figured he would do a little time in a state institution and be back on the street again. By doing this, Adrian figured Butch would also beat the rap, because Butch's case couldn't be tried without Adrian's.

Adrian and Butch spared no expense in obtaining the best legal talent. The defense used every means to try to stall the case. Motion after motion was submitted, heard, and denied. Finally a date was set and the judge named the city where the case was to be tried and warned all lawyers that there would be no further delays.

After both sides made their opening statements, the government called Corby as its first witness. Corby, at this time, was serving a long prison term for a robbery he committed on the West Coast. He had no fear about testifying and inwardly he was actually quite happy. He never had any particular love for Adrian and he wanted to see him squirm for a change. Adrian had always been the protected bully in his town and always managed to keep out of scrapes because of his father and their friends. This time Corby was going to raise his right hand and tell the truth. If it hadn't been for Adrian's "funny money" Corby wouldn't have been in a mess. Corby had run to California after the case was made. He had no means of support so he got money the best way he knew how — by stealing. He tried it, was caught, and sentenced.

When Corby took the stand, Adrian glared at him as though daring him to testify. Corby just stared back and told his story. Surprisingly, he made an excellent witness. Adrian sat in his chair cracking his knuckles. His face was red with rage and several times his lawyer had to caution him about making threatening gestures to the witness. The defense spent hours with Corby on cross-examination, trying to impeach him. He stood up well under the ordeal and was finally dismissed. He was whisked away to a jail in another county and arrangements were made to return him to California as soon as the trial was over.

A representative of the telephone company brought in the records that showed calls from my home to Butch's place of business. The agent who accompanied me on the trip took the stand and testified about the original meeting. The next witness was a representative of the Motor Vehicle Bureau. He testified that the car in question from the night of the original meeting was registered in the name of Adrian's wife. Several more witnesses took the stand and each contributed a little more towards convicting the two defendants.

Blinky the bookmaker wasn't happy about testifying. If Hollywood had been casting a typical bookmaker, Blinky could have been the model. He was a colorful, flamboyant character. He was a short, thin man with slicked-down hair parted in the middle, and thick glasses. He always wore a checkered suit, a loud tie with a diamond horseshoe stickpin, and a Panama hat that he carried into court in his hand. When he took the stand and the direct examination began, it provided the only bit of humor in a potentially explosive situation.

We had decided to use his testimony because he wound up with several of Adrian's counterfeit bills in his crap game one night. He couldn't say who put the money in the game, but could say that Adrian was in the game that night. While this evidence wasn't devastating, it was helpful.

Stone: "I call your attention to the night of 17th of April and ask you to tell the judge and jury what you were doing."
Blinky: "Me and a bunch of guys was shooting craps."
Stone: "Would you please explain to the court what you mean by 'shooting craps.' "
Blinky: "You gotta be kidding! You mean there's someone here who don't know what 'shootin' craps' means?"

Everyone laughed. Even Butch and Adrian showed a trace of a smile. The judge rapped the gavel and called for order in the court.

Judge: "All right, Mr. Stone, I think we have all learned all we need to know about dice. Please proceed."

Stone led Blinky through the direct examination revealing that there were ten or twelve counterfeit bills passed in the game and, further, that Adrian was one of the players. Under cross-examination, however, Blinky had to admit he didn't know who put the bills in the game.

By the end of the third day, most of the witnesses were finished. We were still getting reports that there would be violence and we were prepared. On the fourth day, I took the stand and testified about meeting Adrian. I then testified as an expert that the notes were counterfeit and they were placed in evidence.

Cross-examination by the defense didn't accomplish very much. They went over my testimony line by line and only succeeded in having the whole story repeated. The government called several more witnesses and then rested its case. The following day the defense had several witnesses testify to the general good character of the defendants. Neither Butch nor Adrian took the stand. The defense rested. Both sides summed up and the following day the case was given to the jury. The jury deliberated for only an hour and a half and rendered verdicts of guilty against both defendants. At this point we were prepared for some violence, but nothing happened. The judge set the next day for sentencing.

Later that afternoon, I was sitting in a restaurant when Adrian's lawyer approached and said that Adrian wanted to talk with me privately. I had no objection to talking with Adrian as long as it was private and the U. S. Attorney's office had no objections. I contacted Charlie Stone. He said officially he had no objections, but warned me that Adrian might try to pull something at the last minute. I was prepared for that and said it was worth the risk. I was anxious to establish a rapport with Adrian so that he might help me find Jimmy Dino. It was a hell of a long shot.

I met alone with Adrian in a small room in the courthouse. When I entered he was already there. He stuck his hand out and said, "Carmine, I want to shake your hand. You told it like it was." I fully expected him to grab my hand and throw me out the window with a judo throw or break my neck with a karate chop. Thankfully, he did neither. Adrian expected the judge to sentence him to between five and ten years, and, since this conviction put him in violation of his probation when he finished his federal time, he would have to start a state sentence. He said the whole thing was a nightmare and far too much time to serve for his crime. Whether or not I agreed was immaterial. I mentioned he was in the unenviable position of not being able to cooperate with the government as we already knew his source. He shook his head and pounded the table saying, "I know! I know!" He then fell silent and appeared to be in deep thought. I interrupted by saying, "Adrian, you sent for me and you must have had a reason for doing so." He looked up. "I want you to do me a favor." I looked at him. "Tell me what it is and I'll see what I can do."

"I'm being sentenced tomorrow morning. There's very little I can say in my own behalf, but unless I put myself in a decent light I'm going to have the book thrown at me. Carmine, everything you said was true, but you didn't go far enough. Why didn't you tell the judge and jury that I didn't want to have anything more to do with the counterfeits after the first sale? That I just wanted to get rid of the ones I had left? That's the reason I put you on the phone with Butch. I wanted to be cut out and not have a part of any deal you had with Butch. I never asked for a cut or percentage. I gave you my connection and bowed out, and I never saw you again. Why didn't you say all that?"

"No one asked me. In court you just answer the questions." I reminded him that his lawyer had been free to ask any questions he wanted when he was cross-examining me. He was aware of that and he did tell his lawyer to question me on that phase of the case, but the lawyer didn't want to open any new doors because he couldn't be sure that I would tell the truth. I again asked him what the favor was. He said, "I want you to go into court before sentencing and tell the judge about how I tried to get out of the counterfeiting business before I knew who you were." I said couldn't do that for two reasons; one, it would be out of order and, two, I wasn't sure that he was entirely accurate in his recollection of our original meeting. I told him to wait and I would contact Charlie Stone to see what we could come up with.

I managed to get a hurried conference with Charlie Stone. His first reaction was "To hell with Adrian. He had his trial and now he'll have to face the music." I told Charlie that there was more at stake than Adrian's future. I told him the story of his brother-in-law, Jimmy Dino, and how we might get Adrian to give him up if it was worked properly. Charlie listened attentively and then suggested that Adrian's lawyer, at the time of sentencing, include the fact that Adrian was not a part of any other conspiracy; that after he sold the counterfeit notes to me he tried to extricate himself from any further counterfeit sales. He said he would not object to anything the defense counsel said as long as it was the truth. He considered convicting Adrian a victory for law enforcement and would do anything to make Adrian cooperate with the authorities.

I returned to the room where I had left Adrian. He was pacing. The reality of his conviction and the prospect of a long prison term were sinking in and it showed. I told him that I had reviewed my notes and while he wasn't completely accurate, I would go along with him. The U. S. Attorney would not object if his lawyer told the judge that he and Butch had no further business in counterfeiting after my buy in the diner. I stressed that this only could be done at the time of sentencing and by his lawyer. It was the easiest and best way. Adrian smiled for the first time and said he appreciated it and hoped that some day he could repay me. He offered his hand. We shook and I said, "Good luck tomorrow." He said thanks, turned his back and started toward the door. Just as he was about to leave, I called him and said, "Adrian, I do have something I want to ask you." He turned around and said, "What?" I said, "Where's Jimmy Dino?" At that moment his face flushed, his hands clenched, he roared, "What the hell you asking me for? You're a Fed, why are you interested in Jimmy? Don't I have enough trouble without being grilled about Jimmy? You guys are all alike. You do a favor and you think you own a person. Well, forget it, you don't own me." When he finished I said, "Just remember I asked you and maybe I have a reason." He left still ranting. Trying to make a deal with him wouldn't be easy.

The next morning both defendants appeared before the judge. Butch was found guilty of conspiracy and was given a five-year maximum sentence. Adrian was found guilty of conspiracy and a substantive count — he faced twenty years. His lawyer made an eloquent plea for leniency saying that Adrian had renounced all counterfeiting activities after the last sale. The plea was good but the judge had already made up his mind. He listened and when the lawyer was finished, the judge sentenced Adrian to eight years and he was ordered remanded immediately.

It was quite a shock to Adrian when he figured eight years with the government and then eight years with the state — sixteen years was a long time. Adrian was to be kept in a local jail until the marshal could transport him to a federal penitentiary. I decided to try to talk to him again. Perhaps at this time he would be in a more receptive mood. I made arrangements to see him in a private room where he could talk if he wanted to.

We were left alone in the room. I started by saying, "Sixteen is a tough stretch." He stared and said, "How would you know? Have you ever done time?" I said, "No, I'm on the other side of the fence. What makes you guys think we're a heartless bunch of bastards; that we will lie, cheat, steal, do anything to put a guy in jail? Listen, Adrian, I'm made of the same stuff as you are; there's nothing different about us but our way of life. You decided on the so-called easy road and when you did, you took a calculated risk. You had to know that you'd have to pay sooner or later. Now, you're looking at sixteen years in prison for crimes that didn't involve violence. Sixteen years is a long, long time. Especially when you have kids growing up. There's a way you can help yourself, but you won't listen. You got a bastard of a brother-in-law who is charged with committing an atrocious crime, the worst type possible — strangling and chopping up a young woman. He's walking around free and you're caged up like an animal. Does that make any sense to you?"

He looked up and said, "What did you say about a young woman?" I said, "He raped, strangled, and mutilated a young woman he was dating." Adrian looked shocked. He muttered almost incoherently, "He said it was some bum who tried to beat him in a game. The rotten bastard, the no-good son of a bitch! I'd like to get my hands on him."

When he had recovered somewhat, he turned to me and said, "Carmine, even if I were facing a hundred years and if Jimmy killed ten women, I couldn't give him up. My father would cut my throat if he ever found out that I worked against the family." I understood, but I still felt he could help himself without letting anyone know. He said he appreciated my interest but it was out of the question. I told him that I was leaving and that there was no reason for us ever to meet again unless he sent for me. He knew my name and number; anytime he wanted to see me, I would be available, but only for one reason — a deal on Jimmy Dino. He said, "You mean you'd be the go-between?" I said, "Right." He stood up and said, "I guess this is it. So long, good luck, and be a good cop." I wished him luck and we parted. The next move was up to him.

The following morning I returned to New York and got in touch with the sergeant and lieutenant who were handling the Jimmy Dino investigation and brought them up to date. I told them about my private conversations with Adrian and how I tried to work out a deal with him. I told them how Jimmy passed the word that he was wanted in connection with the killing of some guy who beat him out of money; that he apparently told no one he was being sought for a rape–murder that involved a girl he was going out with. This meant he was cheating on Albert's daughter and Adrian's sister. Now that this word was out, it might make a difference. I wasn't sure how, but I felt we might get a break. They had nothing new to tell me.

Spring became summer and it was time to get away for a little vacation. The work that needed special attention was taken care of and it was 'so long' to the office on the first Friday in July. The following day we left for the cottage in Connecticut. My wife kept saying it was too good to be true. The first two days were paradise — lying in the sun, pretending to fish, and not caring whether I caught one or not. Just the idea that the line was in the water and I was sitting on a rock waiting for the cork to bounce was enough to make me happy.

On the fourth day, we planned an outing. We were busy making sandwiches and lemonade when a car pulled up in front of the cabin. A man got out and started walking up the path. I recognized him as one of our agents from the local office and I knew it had to be something important that usually meant bad news for a vacation. He was sorry to interrupt my vacation, but the warden of the penitentiary where Adrian was serving his time wanted to speak with me. We drove to a nearby phone and I called the prison.

The warden told me that an inmate named Adrian wanted to see me as soon as possible. If I could let him know when I expected to arrive, he would arrange a private meeting. I told him I would leave right away and would arrive at the prison the following day. I thanked him and hung up. Then it struck me that I was letting the family down for the one hundred millionth time. I returned to the cabin and tried to explain. Every cop's wife has to be someone special; she has to be able to take a lot of things; and my wife is no exception.

She said only, "How long do you think you'll be?" I said, "There's really no way of telling. Could be two days or two weeks." She wanted to return to the city with me. I protested and tried to get her to stay, but she was adamant. It was a long, silent trip. We were both lost in our thoughts.

I called the lieutenant and sergeant, and told them that Adrian wanted to see me. I suggested that they stand by and be ready to join me if need be.

The long ride to the penitentiary gave me plenty of time to reflect and also time to be apprehensive. I guessed that what Adrian wanted to tell me would take two seconds, but he would want something in return and it would surely be something that would be impossible for me to deliver. Then the haggling would begin and perhaps no one would gain anything. No sense worrying about it; in a few hours it would be over — one way or another.

It was quite late when I arrived at the penitentiary and I was taken to the warden's home. He was a real "pro": a man who knew his business and wasn't afraid to extend himself in the interest of justice and common sense. I apologized for arriving so late. He understood. He felt that any man who canceled his vacation and traveled a full day to handle a matter of this sort shouldn't have to apologize for being late. He was having a late snack and asked me to join him. When the meal was finished, he offered me the guest room and suggested that I get a good night's sleep. I tried to explain my interest in this particular case. He shrugged me off saying he preferred not knowing anything unless my seeing Adrian was going to cause problems at the institution. I told him I didn't believe my interview would cause any problems, but if I felt differently afterwards, I would certainly let him know. There weren't any other ground rules and he was arranging the interview in such a way that no one would know who spoke with Adrian. I thanked him and took advantage of his hospitality.

The next morning after breakfast, I went to the warden's office. He was already at work and told me that he decided to make his own office available to me. He arranged to make it appear that he was sending for Adrian because of an emergency in the family. When Adrian arrived, the warden left us alone. Adrian had lost a great deal of weight and looked like a beaten man. We shook hands and each waited for the other to start talking. He broke the silence.

"Carmine, I can't do this time; it's killing me. You've got to get me out right away." I said, "Come on, Adrian, you didn't send for me to tell me that. You've been around enough to know that I'm not magic; I don't run the whole goddamn country." He said, "You promised that if I went along with you, you'd get me out." This was too much for me. "Look, Adrian, we never got close to making a deal; nothing was ever said about getting you out. You never wanted to listen to any deal. When I first mentioned Jimmy Dino to you, you damned near walked on the ceiling. Why don't you come off your horse and listen to me for a change? You're so used to giving orders that you can't take any. Remember, I'm a Fed. There is nothing in this deal for me except headaches. Your probation is a state matter and so is homicide. You'd better decide what you want to do and stop reaching for the moon. Okay,? You sent for me, tell me what you want."

He looked straight at me and said, "I'm in your hands, I'll do whatever you ask." I said, "Are you ready to tell me where Jimmy Dino is?" He nodded. I said, "Don't tell me, I don't want to know until we lay down the ground rules."

"Now, let's analyze the situation. First, Uncle Sam has no interest in Jimmy Dino, so don't figure on any help on your Federal sentence. The probation violation is what we have to work on. We have to get the sentencing judge in the state court to drop the warrant that is filed against you. All we can offer is that you will give up Jimmy Dino. The whole matter is up to the judge. If he promises to go along, you can hope to get out in minimum time on the federal sentence. Maybe two, two and a half years if all goes well. That's the best you can hope for. On the other hand, if the state judge doesn't go along, then you don't make a deal on Jimmy and you'll have to do your time. Do you understand?"

He did and asked, "Who do I trust?" I said, "I'm up to my neck in this deal and I might as well go all the way. Don't do anything till I give you the word." He said, "Okay, where do we go from here?" "Unfortunately, you're not going anywhere. As for me, I'm going to meet with the lieutenant and sergeant who are handling this case and then we are going to see the judge. Keep your fingers crossed and I'll be back in a few days." He made a feeble attempt at thanking me and I told him to wait until we had something to be thankful for.

I left, took time out to thank the warden for his splendid cooperation, and got in touch with the lieutenant. I suggested that we meet somewhere along the way and go see the state judge. We planned to meet at a hotel about halfway, make some decisions, and then try to see the judge the following morning.

Later that evening, we met as planned and I brought the officers up to date on what happened at the penitentiary. They felt that real progress had been made and were looking forward to arresting Jimmy Dino. We decided to lay our cards on the table when we met the judge and hope for the best. If he would give us a commitment on vacating the warrant, we could go back to Adrian and continue from there. We were up early the next morning.

We drove several hours to the city where Adrian had first been sentenced. Before seeing the judge we went into a restaurant for a snack and while there, we got our first break. Sitting at another table was a state police lieutenant - the man who was a sergeant when I first spotted Jimmy Dino's picture in the barracks. We joined him and discussed our problem. The lieutenant was not optimistic. He knew the judge; and the judge was tough. Since there was strength in numbers, he agreed to join us and try to swing things our way. His help was most welcome.

The judge was sitting on a case when we arrived at court and we decided not to interrupt. We would wait until he was finished for the day and then front the lion in his den. He sat until after five in the late afternoon. When he left the bench, the state police lieutenant contacted his bailiff and asked him for an appointment with the judge. At seven o'clock we were escorted into his chambers and introduced to the judge. He was a big, burly man with a deep voice who could just as easily have been a police inspector. He said, "Gentlemen, to what do I owe this extraordinary visit? Two men from a city police, one from the state police, and one from the federal government."

I was elected the spokesman. I told the judge I wanted to start at the beginning and then present him with our problem. For what seemed like the hundredth time I told the story of buying counterfeit money from Adrian; of meeting Butch; of meeting Rocky at Butch's club; of discovering Rocky's picture on a wanted notice; of learning that he was really Jimmy Deale also known as Jimmy Dino, wanted for a particularly gruesome murder; of learning that Jimmy Dino was Adrian's brother-in-law; of the trial and conviction of Adrian; and of the recent interview with Adrian in which he said he would give up Jimmy if we could get the probation warrant killed.

"Your Honor, that's the story. We are here to ask if you will vacate the warrant and put us in a position to apprehend the fugitive."

The judge bowed his head in thought. After a moment he looked up and said, "I remember this Adrian very well. He came from out of state and was attending college here. He quit school and one night broke into a supermarket. He was caught in the act. Halfway through the trial he pled guilty. He was represented by the best lawyer available. The probation report indicated that his father was a criminal with quite a reputation and that Adrian did not seem to have any redeeming qualities. He was a bully and the chances were that he would follow in his father's footsteps. My first inclination was to send Adrian away to a state prison. However, I was deluged with letters from friends, the clergy, and politicians asking for clemency for this boy."

"While he had been arrested on several occasions, this was his first conviction. I put him on a long probation. Unfortunately he lived in another state and we had to depend on them for the supervision, which I suspect was lax. I promised myself if he was ever brought before me on a new charge, no matter what it was, be it within a year, ten years or fifteen or for a probation violation, I would give him the maximum. Gentlemen, it looks like that time is arriving. I have no intention of vacating the warrant and I have every intention of sending him away when he comes before me."

This was a shock none of us had expected. We had built our hopes on the fact that the judge would go along with us, and I guess we never thought he would turn us down. He noticed the dejected looks on our faces. He said, "Come now, gentlemen, you are all grown men; surely in your official lives you've had greater setbacks than this one. I am sure through your combined investigative talents you'll be able to locate Jimmy Dino. Perhaps you'll find him without making a deal with Adrian, and then we'll all be better off. Now, if you'll excuse me, gentlemen, I must get off to supper."

Before leaving, I admitted to the judge that we didn't expect to be turned down but since we were, I wanted time to make an appeal, possibly the following morning before the court convened. He laughed and said we were now acting like a bunch of lawyers. I assured him our appeal would be brief and to the point. He agreed to hear our appeal the first thing in the morning.

We returned to the state police barracks and tried to map out some sort of strategy. We all agreed that the judge was determined to send Adrian away and it would take nothing short of a miracle to change his mind. We stewed about it all evening. The only thing we decided was that there was no way we could go over the judge's head. He was the court of last resort. The sergeant and lieutenant were studying the file on the case. For want of something better to do, I picked up a folder marked 'photos.' This was the first time I had seen the official photos of the homicide. The first one was a long shot of the highway showing the approximate spot where the body was found. The next was a closer shot showing a partially-clothed woman in a clump of bushes. A still closer shot showed the twisted body bent and contorted into an unnatural position. The head was turned upward, the eyes were still open, the entire face was covered with cuts and bruises and completely swollen. The mouth was open and the front teeth were broken. The lips were torn. She looked like she might have been dead for months. The destruction was complete. The pictures that followed were just as revolting. Each part of the body that was mutilated was photographed in detail to keep a permanent record of man's inhumanity to man. The pictures were too much for me and I put the folder down. In that instant it came to me! I jumped up and yelled, "I've got it!" The other officers looked at me as though I had flipped. I said, "Confucius or someone said it a thousand years ago: 'a picture is worth a thousand words.' These pictures will make our case. We'll show them to the judge tomorrow. I don't care how tough he is. When he sees these pictures, I'm sure he will go along with us." The others were inclined to agree.

The whole matter was building up in my mind and even after I went to bed, I found it difficult to sleep. The night was a mishmash of disconnected dreams. Old Bailey, powdered wigs, long robes, endless days of pleadings, the tower, clanging doors, men in masks carrying axes, the escape, the chase, recapture, the chopping block, chanting priests carrying crucifixes, electric chairs. And I woke up. The time – 3:15 in the morning! The situation was crazy. Why should this case and the appointment with the judge bother me so much? Perhaps I had gone too far with something that was not really my business; but violence and murder should be everyone's business. Since sleep was out of the question, I managed to kill most of the early morning hours catching up on some reading.

The lieutenant and sergeant apparently had no trouble sleeping and at eight o'clock I had to give them a call to get them going. By 8:45 we were ready to see the judge. He looked pleasant, but unbending. He reminded us that time was short I said, "Your Honor, our appeal will be very short. I, sir, have a folder here. If you will take it and look at the pictures we will be satisfied. We would like to trade a man who broke into a supermarket for a maniac who destroyed the person in these photos, your Honor." The judge examined the photos in silence and halfway through he closed the folder, adjusted his glasses, and said, "Gentlemen, you made your point. If Adrian can give you the man who committed this murder, I'll vacate the warrant. I believe it was the Chinese who said 'one picture is worth a thousand words.'"

We parted company with the state police lieutenant who had been so helpful, and left in a better mood than we had arrived in. I phoned the warden of the penitentiary to let him know I was coming back to see Adrian.

The trip back to the penitentiary was uneventful and I managed to get some of the sleep I missed the night before. We arrived at the institution in the late afternoon. I would see Adrian first and try to pave the way for the lieutenant and/or the sergeant. In ten minutes I was face-to-face with Adrian. He asked me how it went. I said, "It wasn't easy, but I believe we got what we wanted." I told him that there was a lot of work to be done, and a number of questions to be answered, and I had taken the liberty of bringing two men from the local police who were familiar with Jimmy Dino and the facts surrounding the crime. This didn't set well with Adrian. He said he didn't want to talk to anyone; that I had promised to handle all the details; that if anyone else knew he was cooperating he wouldn't get out of the prison alive. He said he'd rather do all his time than let anyone know he had talked to the cops. He went on to say that he should have known better than to trust anyone. Halfway through the diatribe I interrupted.

"Adrian, I've been on a merry-go-round with you since that day in court when we disposed of your case. I told you once before that this whole matter means nothing to me; I am ready to take you at your word and walk out. I came off my vacation to see you. I came as quickly as I could. I brought two officers with me whom I know and trust. It's their case, not mine. I spent time convincing the judge that you're a worthwhile swap for Jimmy Dino and he agreed to go along. Now you are acting up. Why? Because you're trying to get off an eight year bit and you want it done smoothly, without any bumps or waves. Right now, you're the only one making waves. I can't make you give us the information. But neither do I have to face our friend, the judge. It's your decision, but remember, when I leave, I'm not coming back. You have to make up your mind what you want to do and hope like hell that you make the right decision. Sure, you're gambling that someone might find out you gave us information. No one is going to broadcast it and we are certainly doing all in our power to try to plug up all the holes. But to do this thing, we have to take certain people into our confidence. No one person can swing this deal. Now, if you have any better plans or ideas on how we can do this, tell me now and we'll try." I had to stop for a long breath.

Adrian was filled with mixed emotions. On one hand he wanted to tell me to take a walk; on the other hand, he didn't want to alienate the one man he could turn to for some help. He finally said, "Carmine, with you something is either black or white. Sure, I need help, but I don't want to save a couple of years just to wind up with a hole in my head. I've got to trust someone, not with money or anything, but with my life. I want to trust you and you tell me I've got to see a couple of police officers and I've got to trust them. After them, who else do I have to trust? I'm in the position of not being able to turn to anyone — not my lawyer; not my family; and, certainly, not my friends. So I find myself trusting the guy who sent me to jail. Figure that one out and tell me how you would feel if you were me."

"Adrian," I said, "you're looking for a patsy to blame if something doesn't turn out right. I'm not going to be that patsy. We are wasting time; for all I know, Jimmy Dino may be arrested by now and if he is, all bets are off. Remember, anytime Jimmy comes to the attention of the police, we don't need you. Sleep on it. Tomorrow morning we're going to settle this matter once and for all."

"Okay," he said, "Are you sure the judge said he'd pull the warrant if I gave the information?" I said, "You have my word." He said, "Okay, I'll sleep on it." I said, "But keep in mind I'm leaving tomorrow morning after I see you."

My two companions were a little upset about the turn of events but, of course, they were going to see it through, no matter how long it took. In any case, the officers would proceed to Butch's city and touch base with the local police. We also decided that Jimmy Dino's wife should be re- interviewed at her father's home. She should at least be told that Jimmy wasn't involved in a simple gang slaying, but was the perpetrator of a gruesome sex murder. Perhaps the adage "Hell hath no fury like a woman scorned" would be prophetic. At the end of the evening all of our eggs were still in Adrian's basket.

The following morning the lieutenant and I saw Adrian in the privacy of the warden's office. Adrian was visibly nervous and wouldn't sit down. I started, "Adrian, the lieutenant and I want to ask a few questions. Make yourself..." He broke in, "I'm not answering any damn questions." Then he shouted, "Feed your cheese to some other rat. I'm not staying." He reached into his pocket, took out a book of matches, threw it in my face and stormed out of the room. The lieutenant and I looked at each other in bewilderment. I picked up the book of matches and opened it. Inside the cover was Rocky's name, address, place of employment, and social security number.

Things started to make sense. Adrian was putting on an act for someone; I didn't know who, and I didn't really care. Perhaps he thought the room was bugged, or the guards outside the office were listening. He had answered most of our questions by writing the information on the matchbox covers. The lieutenant and I thanked the warden for his cooperation and we then went outside to meet the sergeant who was cooling his heels on the front steps.

The lieutenant asked me what my plans were. At this point, I could have bowed out, but I said I would accompany him until we either proved or disproved the information we got from Adrian. I had no desire to get involved in the case itself. Whether Jimmy Dino was guilty or not was no official concern of mine. I did feel, though, that I had the responsibility of seeing that Adrian got a fair shuffle. After that, I would be satisfied to follow the progress of the case in the newspapers.

Enroute to the city, we decided to look over the place of employment named on the matchbook cover. Then, we would check the home address. If it appeared that our man was there, we would enlist the aid of the local police.

It was late when we arrived at our destination. Still, after supper, we couldn't resist driving by the home address that we had, just to see if it was really there. Even the cab driver had trouble locating the street. We got out of the cab several blocks away from the actual number. The neighborhood was run down. The houses were mostly old multi-family dwellings badly in need of repair. The number we were looking for was in an old housing project that consisted of ten buildings with thirty or forty families in each building. We tried checking the building directory and mail boxes to see if we could recognize a name that could be our quarry. The boxes and directory were in bad shape and we learned nothing. There was a rental office in the complex, but we didn't want to approach anyone until we were more sure of ourselves. We returned to the hotel and decided to get up early the next morning and check out the place Jimmy Dino was working in. After that, we would decide what to do.

We got up at the crack of dawn, ate and then arranged to get to the employment address that Adrian provided us with. This was a six-story loft building and had about twenty different tenants. We were there early enough to place it under surveillance. At about eight o'clock, people started entering the building. We could not get a good look at each one and for all we knew, Jimmy could have walked right past us. Suddenly I had a disturbing thought. What if Jimmy did walk right past us, saw me in the back of the car and remembered me? I suggested to the lieutenant that I thought we were doing things wrong. We were taking unnecessary chances. Waiting outside the building in the hopes of getting a glimpse of Jimmy might cause problems, not the least of which would involve the police. If someone became suspicious of three men in a car they could very well call the local police and we would then be in the embarrassing position of trying to explain what we were doing. We decided to check in at police headquarters and do the job properly.

We introduced ourselves to the chief and he turned us over to the captain of detectives, Captain Long, a veteran of 25 years on the force. After the introduction we explained our mission to the captain. He said he would brief several of his detectives and said he had some sources of information that he would contact. Perhaps he could learn whether or not Jimmy was working at the address we had.

Several hours later, he was able to tell us that a man using the same alias was employed on the second floor of the loft building. The captain said his information indicated that the man was now living with a woman in a three-room apartment in a housing project on the East Side of the city. I got a funny feeling, knowing that our man had taken up with another woman and I felt a sense of urgency about arresting him as soon as possible — before there was another horrible murder. The others shared my apprehension. We wanted to work as quickly as possible.

Jimmy had not shown up for work that morning; he had called in sick. We decided that inquiries would be made at the apartment. At about eight thirty that night, two detectives armed with a cover story went to the address and knocked at the door. No one answered. We set up a surveillance.

The Captain, meanwhile, was busy gathering information. He learned that the apartment was originally rented to a man and wife, Arthur and Evelyn Sempter. Both were in their early thirty's when they first moved into the apartment several years before. He was a sickly man who had worked as a painter before he was injured in an accident. Evelyn was a rather attractive woman who supported her husband by working as a waitress. It was said that she had a child, but the baby died in infancy from pneumonia.

Arthur died a few years ago. After the death of her husband, Evelyn started going downhill. She drank more than she should have and started running around with all kinds of strange characters. There was a rumor that Evelyn was either married to or living with a man called "Rocky." The captain's information just about convinced us that our man was there. Everything fit into a neat pattern; perhaps just a little too neat for comfort. I just hoped that nothing would happen to Evelyn until we had Rocky safely in custody. The wait was long and irksome. It was almost impossible to scrutinize everyone who was entering the building.

At two in the morning, a cab pulled up in front of the building. A man and woman got out and started arguing in front of the building for several minutes. I strained my eyes in an effort to identify the man. I felt reasonably sure that it was Rocky or Jimmy Deale, known as Jimmy Dino or whatever he was calling himself.

They entered the building. We had a conference and decided that nothing would be lost by knocking on the door of the apartment. If no one was at home, nothing would be lost. If someone answered, we could wrap up the case in a hurry. We proceeded to the apartment and knocked at the door. A woman asked who was there. One of the detectives said, "I'm the cab driver, Ma'am, you left something in the cab." She opened the door and the detectives brushed passed her into the bedroom where the man was undressing. It was Rocky. The detectives told him they had a warrant for his arrest for murder. He made no attempt to resist. He said, "You know, I'm glad it's over" and meekly submitted to being searched and handcuffed.

When Evelyn realized what had happened, she passed out. A neighbor agreed to stay with her until she recovered.

I had promised myself that I wouldn't be involved after the arrest was made. I returned to the hotel and went to bed. I got up early the next morning and left a note for the lieutenant and sergeant who were still sleeping. I arrived at the airport in time to catch a plane for New York.

When I got to New York, I called the office and told them I was back. The boss asked if I enjoyed my vacation. He said things were piling up and he had a couple of out-of-town assignments for me. I told him I'd call him back. I put a coin in the phone, dialed my home phone, and held my breath. "Hello?"

Ellen and the Dead Woman's Bonds

Mrs. Elizabeth Candless had lived in the same apartment for years. She was old and had been widowed for years. No one in the neighborhood had known her husband, but it seemed to the neighbors that he had been fairly well off, since Mrs. Candless paid her bills promptly and was never known to lack for anything. She was friendly and well liked in the neighborhood. She occupied a three-room apartment on the second floor of a two-family house in a residential neighborhood. She only had one known relative; a married daughter who lived in California and who visited her once a year.

Her landlady, Mrs. Leonard, a middle-aged woman who worked in a local dress factory was also a widow. Her salary and the rent from Mrs. Candless' apartment allowed her to get by. Mrs. Leonard had a son and a daughter, neither of whom lived at home. Mrs. Leonard was in touch with her elderly tenant at least once or twice a day and ran errands for her when she finished work. A time came when Mrs. Leonard became concerned about Mrs. Candless' health. She wasn't well and it appeared that she was rapidly going downhill. The doctor came three times in one week, but just as they were preparing to move her to the hospital, she died. Mrs. Leonard discovered the body at about 7 o'clock one evening when she went upstairs to see if Mrs. Candless needed anything. At the time, Mrs. Leonard's daughter was visiting and they promptly called the authorities.

Mrs. Candless' daughter was notified and she took care of the funeral arrangements. The public administrator, Arthur Taylor, sealed the apartment pending settlement of the estate. Mrs. Candless died without a will and the estate had to be handled through the public administrator's office and the surrogate's court. While the matter was being settled, Mrs. Candless' daughter had a final interview with the administrator before returning to California. When she was shown the final inventory of her mother's belongings she pronounced it incomplete. She advised the administrator that her mother also had a substantial number of Series E Savings Bonds. Mr. Taylor called various Treasury agencies to report the possible theft of bonds and inquire if duplicates could be obtained. The inquiry reached my desk and we made arrangements to meet the following day to see whether I could be of any assistance in the matter.

At the meeting, Mr. Taylor told me about Mrs. Candless and that her daughter felt there were a number of bonds missing from her mother's apartment. A detailed search of the apartment had been made and the inventory prepared, but no bonds were found. According to the daughter, the deceased had kept them in the apartment. He had not been able to locate a bank safe-deposit box where Mrs. Candless might have kept the bonds, so he wanted to know if the existence of the bonds could be proven. I said it could and if the bonds existed, we would locate them.

First, it would be helpful if we could learn when and where they were purchased and how they were inscribed. The daughter had told Mr. Taylor that she believed her father had originally purchased them at a bank. She supplied the name and location of the bank and the approximate time period they were purchased and further said they were inscribed in her mother's name with her father as beneficiary. I told Mr. Taylor that I would have a search made and if there were bonds due the estate, we would find them.

Several months later I received a report from the Division of Loans and Currency that Mrs. Candless did have bonds totalling $11,500 which were purchased at the bank the daughter had mentioned. The report also said that the bonds had been cashed several weeks after she had died.

Copies of the bonds were attached with the report, together with the forms needed to allow duplicate bonds to be issued. An examination of the back of the bond copies showed that they were all forged by the same person and that they were cashed in various banks within a 50-mile radius of Mrs. Candless' apartment.

The case was assigned to me and I furnished Mr. Taylor with he information contained in the report. We met again that week and I learned additional details of the case. I showed Mr. Taylor the copies of the bonds and told him that we had opened an investigation. The first order of business would be to take handwriting samples of everyone who may have had access to the bonds. Since he and his assistants had been at the apartment, their handwriting samples were required as well. He said he understood and did the necessary writing for me and was immediately eliminated as a suspect. His handwriting did not resemble the forged endorsements. He called in his assistants and both their handwriting samples also eliminated them as possible suspects. I told Mr. Taylor that I would arrange to get Mrs. Candless' daughter's handwriting sample from our office in California and make the necessary arrangements to get duplicate bonds issued.

I then went to Mrs. Leonard's house and talked with her. She told me all she could about her late tenant, from the time she moved into the house until she died. Mrs. Leonard had no objection to submitting handwriting samples, and a quick examination of her writing eliminated her as being the author of the forged endorsements. She said she didn't know anything about the bonds and she couldn't think of anyone who might have taken them.

In the usual stolen bond case, the registered owner generally is the first person to be interviewed. He or she can supply the circumstances under which the bonds were stolen and how many there were. The owner can supply the investigator with an inventory of other property that was also taken. He can account for certain identification which might have been used in negotiating the bonds and can express any suspicions he has. If the theft was the result of a burglary, the local police can be interviewed to see if their investigations produced any worthwhile suspects. In this case, however, the registered owner was deceased and even setting the time of the theft was difficult, if not impossible, and nothing had been reported to the police.

The next move was to visit all the banks where the bonds were cashed and interview the bank officers who had handled the transactions. Since quite a bit of time had passed since the transactions took place it was unlikely that anyone would have any specific recollections.

The stop at the banks served two purposes: to see if there was any information about the forger; and to see if the banks had taken the necessary precautions in cashing the bonds. The government normally does not take the loss on forged government checks or counterfeit securities; however, in the case of Series E bonds, banks are only the paying agents. If the government held the bank responsible for forged bonds, it would create a real problem. Banks get paid very little for handling bonds and in the event the banks decided to discontinue the service, the public would be less willing to buy them, since cashing the bonds would be such a problem. Therefore, the government issued a set of suggested procedures for the banks to use for cashing Series E bonds. If the bank can prove that it followed the government's suggested rules, the government takes the loss on the forged instruments.

Most banks ask for identification at the time of the transaction and the bank officer will either describe the identification on a special form or note it on the back of the bond.

The bonds in question were cashed at a dozen different banks and visits to each location turned up empty. At the first bank, $2,000 worth of bonds were cashed on the basis of a social security card in the name of the registered owner. The number was not recorded. At the next two banks, accounts had been opened in Mrs. Candless' name in the amount of $50. Four days later, the bonds had been cashed on the fact that the negotiator, supposedly Mrs. Candless, had an account at the bank. At the time of my visit, the accounts were still open and still had the initial $50 on deposit.

At three banks, the bonds had been cashed on the basis of some document that bore the legend "DISC 803922." No one could recall what the identification was or what the numbers meant.

After several days of visiting banks, I had learned that the forger had used a social security card, an insurance policy in the name of the registered owner, and a piece of identification with the number DISC 803922. It wasn't much to go on. A check with the insurance company revealed that the deceased was insured by that company and a policy was still outstanding. The policy was undoubtedly stolen at the time the bonds were taken. The social security card most likely was also stolen. But I couldn't figure out what the DISC 803922. number was all about.

I decided to go back to see Mr. Taylor, the public administrator, and bring him up-to-date on the investigation and to let him know that the deceased had an insurance policy in effect, the proceeds of which might be included in the estate. Taylor was happy to get the information and he made a note and placed the paper in a neat thick folder. That folder represented all his notes and reports on the Candless case. He asked whether there was any information I wanted from it. I said "Yes, everything." I didn't know what I wanted as I didn't know what information it contained. I wanted to sit with the folder, read it, and perhaps pick up some new leads. I was quickly getting near the end of my leads and needed some new ones or the case would become an unsolved investigation. He handed me the folder. I opened it and on the top was a handwritten letter addressed to him. Staring right at me was the same handwriting that was on the bonds! The letter was dated three weeks earlier and said:

Dear Mr. Taylor:

I am the former landlady of the late Mrs. Elizabeth Candless. If you recall, after her death you sealed the premises, and it was several weeks before everything was moved out. Therefore, I feel the estate owes me one month's rent. I would appeciate it if you you would send me $80 from the estate.

Sincerely,

Mrs. Leonard

I didn't have to look any further. I told Mr. Taylor that as far as I was concerned, the case was solved. I thanked him and left him with a puzzled look on his face.

My next stop was at Mrs. Candless' apartment address. Mrs. Leonard was working and I waited until she returned. She remembered me from the first visit and tried again to be helpful. I asked her if the estate owed her any money; she replied that it did. She felt the estate owed her one month's rent because they tied up the apartment for a month after Mrs. Candless died. I then asked her what she was doing about it. She said, "I had my daughter write a letter to Mr. Taylor asking for the money." What a relief. I knew that Mrs. Leonard hadn't forged the bonds as her handwriting samples had not been similar to the writing on the bonds; yet the writing on the letter which bore her name was identical to the forgeries. Now it was obvious that her daughter had written the letter and was the thief. I had to be careful with my questioning.

I wanted to learn all I could about her daughter without arousing suspicion. Her name was Ellen; she was 30 years old, divorced, had served an enlistment in the Women's Army Corps, and lived in a nearby town. She was employed part-time as a relief telephone operator in a furniture factory. She normally visited her mother once or twice a month, and had visited the day Mrs. Candless died. I determined that during the excitement of discovering the body, she had plenty of time to "case" the apartment and take what she wanted. I further learned that she was living with a man at the address her mother provided.

It appeared that Ellen was a real swinger. While she didn't have a criminal record, the juvenile authorities had taken numerous complaints from her parents that she was an incorrigible child. She had been a habitual truant and a high-school dropout. Several times her parents reported her as a runaway. When Ellen turned 18, there were no further complaints. It was believed she had finally outgrown her juvenile problems.

There was no use in wasting time. Ellen was undoubtedly the thief and forger. I didn't have enough information to obtain a warrant, but I felt that I was close to it and perhaps an interview with Ellen would supply the necessary additional information.

The following day I went to see Ellen. It was 11 o'clock in the morning, but she was still sleeping when the doorbell woke her up. She came to the door in her nightgown and looked like she had been out drinking all night. While only in her early thirties, she gave the impression of being much older. She might have been an attractive girl once, but now she just looked burned out. When I identified myself, she invited me in. The apartment, while quite messy, was well furnished and the furnishings seemed quite new. She excused herself, put on a pot of coffee, and went into another room to get dressed. She came back several minutes later, poured us a cup of coffee, lit a cigarette, sat down, and said, "Okay, Mr. G-Man, what do you want to know?" I told her that I was conducting an investigation regarding the theft and forgery of some bonds that had belonged to her mother's former tenant. She remembered the woman quite well, and recalled being there the day the body was found. I told her that everyone who was at the apartment that day was considered a suspect and it would be necessary to obtain a personal history and a handwriting sample from everyone.

First, the usual pedigree questions: name, date of birth, height, weight, social security number, etc. Then, military service? She said she had served in the Women's Army Corps and received an honorable discharge. Serial number? She immediately replied "803922." Then she said, "Why do you need that?" "Routine." Suddenly it hit me! "803922!" That was the number on the back of some of the forged bonds! DISC was the word preceding it and I knew now that it meant discharge, or discharge number, or the number appearing on the discharge. To me, it meant Ellen's army number was used as identification.

The fact that the discharge was in the name of Ellen Leonard didn't mean anything. There were cases where forgers used their own military discharges by erasing their own names, inserting the name of the registered owner, and having a reduced copy made and laminated. Most alterations wouldn't be noticeable on the smaller copy. Ellen was becoming increasingly nervous. She lit one cigarette after another and poured herself a stiff drink of something other than coffee, which she downed in a single gulp. I asked her if she would give me a handwriting sample. "Is that on your idiot form, too?" she asked. I replied, "You're a suspect like everyone else who was at the house the day Mrs. Candless died." She replied, "Do I have to give you samples?" I said, "No, as a matter of fact, you don't have to do anything. You didn't have to answer any questions; you didn't even have to let me into your house. But I'm sure you wanted to know how close we were to you. Well, for your information, we're pretty damn close." She lit another cigarette and said, "What are you accusing me of?" I said, "You're a suspect in the theft, forgery, and negotiation of almost $12,000 in U.S. Government bonds and the next time we meet, I'll have an arrest warrant. So, I suggest you get yourself a good lawyer, because just as sure as God made little green apples, you're going to need one; and for goodness sakes, when you do get one, tell him the truth or don't bother getting one."

I gave her my name and telephone number in the event she got a lawyer and either he or she wanted to contact me. I then left the apartment. Before leaving, I noticed a man coming out of a bedroom. He undoubtedly heard everything we said.

Tying up the loose ends only took a few more more days; at the end of which we had a good case. The handwriting analysis confirmed Ellen was responsible for the forgeries and the army supplied us with documentation that Ellen had been assigned number "803922." during her stint in the Women's Amy Corps. That was enough to obtain an arrest warrant.

On the morning that the arrest was planned, I received a call from an attorney who said he represented Ellen. I told him there was a warrant issued for her arrest and that he could surrender her at my office that morning. He said he would bring her down immediately.

She was processed before the arraignment — mug shots, fingerprints, and personal information were obtained. She was taken before a U. S. Commissioner and bail was set at $10,000. A bondsman arranged the bail and within hours she was on her way back home. She made her appearance in court alone. She was living with a man called "Spooner." She didn't want him to be seen in court for fear he might somehow be implicated.

She had been living with Spooner for over a year. She supported him while waiting for him to make the "big score." Stealing the bonds was not a chance theft. Several times while visiting with her mother she saw Mrs. Candless and knew that she had the bonds in the apartment. She mentioned it to Spooner who wanted to burglarize the apartment and take everything. She had a very difficult time stopping him. When she did manage to steal the bonds, he tutored her on how to cash them. She learned her lesson well and was successful in disposing of the bonds after which she dutifully turned the money over to Spooner. He told her the money was going to be used to finance an operation that would make them both wealthy. He refused to go into detail with her.

In the meantime, Spooner didn't deny himself any of the luxuries that this new-found cash could buy. He bought himself a new wardrobe; a new car; had the apartment stocked with the best liquor and new furniture. He was doing fairly well for himself since his release from jail. He was in his early thirties, tall, and fairly good looking. He looked like the all-American "Joe College" type instead of the creep he really was. His first arrest had been for burglary and the next two were for "living off the proceeds of a prostitute." He had tried to get Ellen to work for him as a prostitute. Ellen loved him and would do whatever he said, but even she had limits. So she worked as a telephone operator, she waited on tables, tended bar, and even tried show business to earn a living.

Soon after meeting Spooner she agreed to share her apartment with him. He was a smooth talker and had no trouble in persuading Ellen that one day he would go out and earn some money. Ellen knew she was a sucker for loving him and doing anything for him. Now that she was in trouble she thought they should decide together what the next step should be. Her lawyer told her the government had a solid case against her. He wanted her to plead guilty and hope that since she didn't have any previous convictions, she would get a short term perhaps even a suspended sentence. He also told her that he wanted $2,500 in advance as a retainer to handle the case. She promised to discuss the matter with Spooner and get back to him the following day. She knew she had to stall the lawyer until she found out where the money to pay him was going to come from.

When she got home, Spooner was waiting. He was anxious to know what had happened. Ellen brought him up-to-date. Spooner just nodded until she got to the part about the lawyer's fee. He told her the money would present a problem. He just couldn't lay his hands on that kind of money. Ellen stared in disbelief. She had given him over $10,000 from the proceeds of the bonds. She couldn't believe that it was all gone. He saw that she was getting angry and started soft-pedaling her. He told her that a business venture was eating up all the money; that, as a matter of fact, he needed more for his own use.

Ellen was incensed, she couldn't believe that there wasn't even enough money for the bondsman or the lawyer. She knew that Spooner had spent at least $5,000 for the things she could see — the furniture, the car, the clothing. She demanded to know where the rest of the money went. She wanted to know what kind of business he was getting into and how much it was costing. His reply was a hard back-hand across her face that sent her sprawling across the room. He followed it up with a vicious blow to her stomach. She collapsed on the floor. He made no attempt to help her up and when she finally managed to pull herself up on the couch, he made another motion to kick her, but changed his mind. He walked over to the table, picked up the liquor bottle, and poured himself a drink. He told her that she had just gotten a small sample of what she could expect if she stuck her nose into his business again.

Between the appearance at court, the prospect of going to jail, and the beating from Spooner, Ellen felt sick to her stomach. She managed to get to the bathroom before she threw up. Ten minutes later she heard the door slam and was relieved to know that Spooner had left. He would probably be gone half the night. That would give her time to think. She walked over to the table and poured herself a drink. She lit a cigarette, sat down, and tried to take stock of her life.

Here she was, barely 39 years old, looking like a burned-out 50 year old, in love with a bastard who beat her and who wanted to make a whore out of her. Sometimes she felt she wasn't any better herself, supporting a bum like Spooner who would never get an honest job. She faced an uncertain future and it was obvious she couldn't expect any help from him. She knew it wouldn't bother Spooner if she were sent away for 10 years. He'd simply find another sucker to support him.

She tried to explore the avenues that were open to her. She could continue to live with Spooner and support him. At this moment, however, the thought of continuing to live with him was out of the question. She could pack up and go live with her mother until it was time to dispose of her case, and accept the penalty and the time she would have to serve. Spooner would probably come after her and give her a hard time. She wasn't sure her mother knew of her arrest. If she didn't know, that would be fine. She really wasn't sure that she could go back to living the quiet life with her mother, although right now peace and quiet looked awfully good. She could leave, get herself a room, and try to make a new life without Spooner. This seemed to be the best idea and the sooner she got started, the better.

She went through the motions of packing. She found herself looking through everything, hoping against all odds to find the money Spooner may have stashed in the apartment. Spooner kept his suitcases in a closet in the bedroom. That seemed like a good place to snoop. She opened the suitcase and found it stuffed with the meager possessions of a "drifter." There were several pieces of pornography with Spooner as one of the participants. She knew he was rotten, but this was disgusting. She was starting to feel nauseous again. She then found and read every word of three or four recent letters from women who professed their undying love for him. Then there were several $20 bills that were printed only on one side. This stumped her for awhile, then it became clear. Of course! The big business venture that Spooner was talking about was undoubtedly counterfeiting. Someone else was printing the bills and maybe Spooner was financing the operation. Her anger over finding out that Spooner was two-timing her slowly subsided and the thought of revenge was creeping in. With thoughts of revenge came the idea that if perhaps she played her cards right, she could use Spooner and his operation to make a deal with the Feds. The more she thought about it, the easier it was to justify. There wasn't any doubt that when Spooner got his counterfeits he would use her to dispose of them. That was how it had worked with the bonds. Then after she got the money he would keep it and all Ellen would have to look forward to would be a beating and, eventually, a jail term. Ellen wouldn't let it happen twice. She knew what she wanted to do, but needed to make sure she handled it right. She had no doubt that Spooner would kill her if he ever found that she had turned him in. She couldn't confide in her attorney since she couldn't pay him. She had to find someone to confide in; someone who could advise her.

For the present, her only course of action would be to continue to live with Spooner as though nothing had happened. She would get as much information as possible on the counterfeiting operation and then try to make a deal with the government. Above all, she had to think straight. She unpacked her things, had a few more drinks, and went to bed falling into a deep alcohol-induced slumber. Spooner returned home in the early morning and slipped into bed as though nothing had ever happened. She woke up, and staring at the wall as though she were still asleep, was thankful that he was drunk.

The next morning, Ellen decided she was none the worse for the cuffing she had received from Spooner, although there were still some bruise marks on her face and her stomach was sore. She went over things in her mind again: stay with Spooner; learn about the counterfeits; and give the information to the Feds. It was still the best way and she was determined not to "chicken out."

Later she received a phone call from her attorney who wanted to know when she was coming in with the fee. She promised to call him back soon.

Spooner got up late in the afternoon. Ellen prepared a snack for him and told him that the lawyer had called looking for money. Spooner reminded her that he had already discussed that and had no intention of going over it again. Ellen knew that if she pressed it any further she was likely going to receive another slap, so she kept her mouth shut.

She had to buy as much time as possible and make it work in her favor. She called the lawyer and told him she didn't have any money and the prospect of getting any was slim. He promptly informed her that he would withdraw from the case. Perhaps the court would appoint a public defender. He gave her the number of the bondsman and suggested that she call him and make a deal on payment for the bond.

Ellen's call to the bondsman was more trouble. He wanted $600 or he was going to back off the bond. She had two days to come up with the money. She gave the matter some thought and realized there was only one person who could help — her mother. She got dressed and was about to leave when Spooner asked her where she was going. She told him she needed money for the bondsman and was going to see her mother. Perhaps her mother could lend it to her. Spooner thought it was a good idea and told her to get enough for both of them. He laughed and said to tell her mother he'd pay her back with interest when he struck it rich.

By now, lying came easily to Ellen. Lord knows, she had told enough of them. As a matter of fact, she couldn't remember the last time she was truthful with her mother. She waited for her mother to finish work and then drove her home. Mrs. Leonard was happy to see her and in no time there was a hot meal on the table. Ellen told her mother that she was working part-time, but was having trouble making ends meet. She said she had fallen behind in her rent and car payments because of illness and other problems. She didn't have any trouble convincing her mother that she was very sick and under a doctor's care. After listening to Ellen's tale of woe, Mrs. Leonard insisted on helping her with her finances. Before she left, she had $250 in cash and the promise of a $500 check.

In the required 48 hours, Ellen had made her peace with the bondsman and satisfied his payment demands. However, she was now without counsel and had no prospect of getting another. Her hatred for Spooner was as intense as ever. She decided that the best way to keep away from him would be to get a full-time job. She realized that she must spend some time with him if she was going to go through with her plans, but it would be as little as possible.

She got a job as a waitress in a nearby restaurant. The work was tiring, but there were enough wolves around to make the job financially rewarding.

The next few weeks brought little information from Spooner. His absences were more prolonged and she felt certain that something was going on. She hoped she could get the information in time. She checked his suitcase periodically and found that the counterfeit notes were still there. She didn't find anything new around the house to cause her to believe the scheme was coming to fruition.

One evening, Kayo, a friend of Spooner's, stopped at the house. Ellen had known him for about a year. Kayo was a former fighter who had never quite made it, and that, of course, was how he got his nickname; he was always being knocked out. He and Spooner had been involved in a lot of shady deals in the past and he had served time for assault and for selling dirty pictures. Lately he was seeing a lot of Spooner and Ellen felt that Kayo knew something about Spooner's deal. She figured he might be a part of it. Kayo told Ellen that he was supposed to meet Spooner in the city, but he couldn't keep the appointment and he thought he would stop and see him at home.

Ellen poured Kayo a drink and engaged in small talk, asking what kept him busy. He said he managed to make a buck here and there. He was buying and selling anything he could get his hands on. Ellen made sure that Kayo's glass was always filled and with each drink he became more talkative. Ellen had been around long enough to spot a two-timer. It would take about five seconds to convince Kayo to continue the conversation "under the sheets." It was a dangerous game. If Spooner came in while they were frolicking, someone was bound to get hurt. She tried flirting and had to discard it immediately. Kayo had to be held at arm's length; he was ready, willing, and able.

The phone rang, a welcome interruption. It was Spooner. She told him Kayo was there. Spooner got Kayo on the phone and told him to wait; that he'd be home in half an hour. Ellen poured Kayo another drink and then put on a pot of coffee. When Kayo was "four sheets to the wind", she asked him if he figured on getting rich on this caper. Kayo looked up. "You know?" She laughed and said, "Sure, I know everything." "Did you see them?" he asked. "Not yet, are they out?" He said, "No. The printer is having trouble with the paper, but he'll have them ready soon and when they come out they'll be beauties." He said the printer was spending a lot of time on the job and was waiting until they were perfect before going into production. Ellen hoped and prayed that she could pump Kayo for all the information she could before Spooner got home.

Kayo was feeling frisky. He got up, grabbed her, and asked for a little kiss before the old man got home. Ellen teased and said "OK, but just one." Kayo revolted her, but he was going to be her best source of information and her ticket to the Feds and she hoped, her "get out of jail free" card. She had to make him believe that she was amenable to extracurricular activities. Kayo told her when he made his bundle he was going to steal her away from Spooner. He said he would set her up in a really swell pad and show her how to really live. She laughed, "How are you going to get rich on this deal?" "You kidding? Me and Spooner are going to handle all the output. Nobody gets any unless it's through us. We can pass it, sell it, exchange it, do anything we want. Spooner's got the printer under his thumb, and he doesn't do anything until Spooner tells him. Me and him and two other guys bought the equipment, rented the store, and staked the printer a year's salary. After he does our stuff, he can own the shop. Then the four of us are going to split everything that comes out of the plant. This bum ain't doing too bad for himself from making dirty pictures — now that he's in partners with Uncle Sam." Kayo laughed wildly at his own joke and slapped Ellen on the back so hard he almost knocked her over. Ellen heard Spooner coming down the hall and suggested that they keep their secret to themselves. What Spooner didn't know wouldn't bother him. Kayo liked the idea of being a part of anything that involved Ellen. He said he'd give a week's pay for a weekend with her.

Spooner came in, said he was hungry, and told Ellen to fix him something to eat. He then poured a drink and sat down with Kayo. Ellen went into the kitchen, but kept her ears wide open to hear the conversation.

Spooner: "More damn trouble."

Kayo: "What's the matter now?"

Spooner: "That bastard of a printer is giving me fits."

Kayo: "What now?"

Spooner: "Now he's saying the job is going to take a few more weeks. He is afraid to work nights because it might look suspicious and he says he has to be careful in the daytime because he doesn't know who might come in."

Kayo: "So what's he gonna do?"

Spooner: "I don't know. I tried to get the son of a bitch to set the plant up in his cellar, but he wouldn't do it. He figured after our job he would have a going business for himself."

Kayo: "Did you talk to him?"

Spooner: "Talk ... I'm done talking. You, me, Frank, and Charlie are going to pay him a "piss call" and do a little arm twisting."

Kayo: "If we break his arms how are we gonna get him to finish the job?"

Spooner: " I don't know; I don't know! All I know is we're going out to see him. We've got to scare him somehow. He's stalling us. He never had any trouble at his other plant. He turned out porno pictures like crazy. He never worried about someone walking in on him."

Kayo: "Maybe he figures we ain't giving him enough. Maybe he wants a piece of the action; like a guarantee or something."

Spooner: "I'd like to guarantee that punk a six-foot hole in the ground and put him in it myself. First it's the paper; then it's the ink; then he needs more equipment; then he says he could use a better press. All we've been doing is giving him money. He's worse than a woman. The crippled bastard, I think he's going loco."

Kayo: "Okay, so it's all set. Let's call Charlie and Frank and pay our friend a visit."

Spooner: (sarcastically) "Oh no, we can't go at night. Our friend will be nervous. We gotta go in the daytime so he won't be frightened." (angrily raising his voice) "Ellen, where in the hell is the food? I could starve my ass waiting for you to feed me!"

Ellen quickly fixed a sandwich and a beer and set it down in front of Spooner. Kayo promised to see Spooner the next morning. He left, giving Ellen a big wink. Spooner told Ellen to get dressed; he wanted to take her to a movie. Ellen was in no mood to go out. She just wanted to review everything she could about the conversation between Kayo and Spooner. She cursed the day she dropped her shorthand class in high school; it sure would have come in handy this evening. She made an excuse about a headache. He swore and muttered something under his breath and went out alone.

Ellen took the opportunity to scribble a few notes so that when the time came she could recall what she had heard.

Several days passed without any further developments.

One morning she went out to get the mail and there was a letter that made her heart jump. It was from the U. S. District Court. She tore the letter open. It said something about an indictment and a date for pleading. She was in a turmoil. This was the letter she had been fearing. While she knew it was coming, she had tried to put it out of her mind and hoped that it would go away. It was time to make her move. She still didn't have a lawyer. She still didn't have money. The only thing she had was information. She desperately hoped that the information would be worth something to someone.

I had just returned from an out-of-town trip and was in the office trying to get caught up on the paperwork when the phone rang. "Mr. Motto, this is Ellen Leonard. Do you remember me?" I said, "Yes, it was a bond case." "That's right. I'd like to talk with you." "About your case?" She said, "Not really. It's about something else." I pondered that one. "Okay, you name the time and place." She said, "I have to be careful. No one must know I'm talking with you. I have a letter to be in court on Thursday. How about if I meet you there?" I said I would see her in court and make arrangements for an interview in private.

On Thursday morning I went to the calendar part of the court. I waited until Ellen came in. She was alone. I got a seat beside her and told her I had her case postponed; that she should follow me to a room where an interview could be held without any interruptions. She followed me to the designated room on the same floor.

I asked her if it had anything to do with her case. She said it was something new and had nothing to do with the bonds. I asked her about her lawyer; she said she didn't have one, nor did she want one at the present time. She preferred not to have anyone else around because she didn't feel she wanted to trust too many people. I tried to assure her that I would keep her confidence and try to keep the information on a "need to know" basis within the service. It was obvious that she was frightened and would need a lot of reassuring. She was nervous, pale, and looked like she was ready to pass out. I got a couple of cups of coffee and suggested that if the information could wait, perhaps we could arrange the interview for another time. She said, "No, I've gotten this far and I ain't turning back now."

She calmed down and said she had information on some counterfeiting and wanted to know if I could handle it. I told her counterfeiting was my department. I asked her what she wanted for her information. She asked if everything was that simple. I explained that people always had a motive for cooperating. She interrupted, "You mean stooling?" "You heard me — cooperating. You have a right to explore the possibility of cooperating with the government. You have a right to find out what will happen. Make a deal, if that's what you want to call it. Try for the best bargain you can get. Before we get started, I also have some rights. I have the right to expect the truth and get your full cooperation. In return, I'll make sure any bargain we make is kept. Do we understand each other?"

She said, "It's pretty clear. Okay, I want some help on my case. I don't have any money, I don't have a lawyer, I don't want to go to jail, and I don't want to get killed. I am willing to do anything you ask except testify in court or be exposed in any way. Can you promise me that?" I replied, "I can really promise very little. You are entitled to anonymity. You are entitled to a lawyer and you have a right to live. I can't promise that you won't go to jail. I can only promise that your cooperation will be brought to the attention of the court and it will be done in such a way as not to be public knowledge." This appeared to mollify Ellen.

She spent twenty minutes outlining her relationship with Spooner, stealing and cashing the bonds, stumbling on the counterfeiting operation, and her desire to see Spooner put away. When she had finished I asked her if she brought any of the counterfeits with her. She said she had thought about it but was afraid Spooner might get suspicious if one was missing. Under the right circumstances she might get one long enough to show and perhaps it could be copied. I asked her what she could specifically do on her own. She said she could listen, report and try to follow instructions. I asked her to wait in the room until I spoke with the assistant U.S. Attorney handling her case. She said she would wait. She had nothing better to do. The assistant U. S. Attorney said he'd be as helpful as possible. I suggested that Ellen's case be postponed and that we get her a lawyer. We'd work the counterfeiting case with a view to keeping Ellen as cool as possible. If we were successful we could dispose of Ellen's case, making sure she got credit for whatever she accomplished. He agreed and I was able to tell Ellen that we would handle her legal problems.

We arranged code names, meeting places and everything necessary for easy communication. I told her the first order of business was to see one of the counterfeits. I arranged to meet her later that day, provided she could get away from Spooner.

Several hours later she called. Spooner had left the house and would not be back for quite some time. It was the right time for her to bring me one of the bills. She selected a spot not too far from where she lived that she knew would be safe, and she showed up at the precise time. She brought the counterfeit. It was the back of a $20 bill. The counterfeit was well executed and, if the face were done as well, it would be a real problem for us when it hit the street. On the back of each bill in the lower right hand corner is a back plate number. In this case the number was "82." It would give us some indication of the source in the event they were completed and distributed. After I made a copy of the bill I returned it to Ellen and she put it back without arousing any of Spooner's suspicion.

After that, information was slow in coming. Spooner wasn't saying much and Kayo hadn't shown his face at the apartment. They were making frequent trips, but she didn't know where. From what she could learn, Spooner's printer was still having problems and was trying to overcome them.

Three weeks later I put in a hurried call to Ellen. We met at the usual place. I told her some new counterfeit $20s had hit the street and they had number "82" as a back plate. It looked like Spooner's operation was on its way. The news upset her terribly. She desperately wanted to be first with the information so she could get credit where it counted. I told her our investigation had produced some pretty good leads, but not enough to stop the notes from hitting the street. I told her to wrack her brain for any information, however slight, that might not seem important to her but might help the investigation. She tried to repeat the conversation between Kayo and Spooner that night at her apartment. She recalled the names of Charlie and Frank as people who invested money with Kayo and Spooner and, after some deep thought, she recalled that in a fit of anger Spooner referred to the printer as a "crippled bastard." She didn't know if the man was actually crippled or if it was one of Spooner's expressions. This was welcome information.

Ellen felt she could do more if she were free to see Kayo, but right now it was impossible. I asked her what Spooner was doing. She said he left fairly early in the morning; generally going to the races. She suspected that the evenings were spent with his cronies on the counterfeiting setup. She then remembered something else. Spooner had wrecked his car and he was now riding around in a stolen car that he kept in the parking area behind the apartment house where they lived. She had made a note of the license number of the car and gave it to me.

I verified the stolen car. This opened a new avenue of approach. We would have the police cover the car and place Spooner under arrest when he got into it. This would give Ellen an opportunity to contact Kayo and, perhaps, have an opportunity to get up-to-date on the activities of the group.

I asked Ellen if Spooner knew me, specifically referring to my original interview with her at her apartment. She said she didn't think so. Spooner was just waking up when I was leaving. She agreed to call me just as soon as Spooner left the apartment to go to the car. The police were happy to cooperate and watch Spooner's car.

The following day the car was spotted in the parking area. About one o'clock in the afternoon, Ellen called to report that Spooner was leaving the house. Five minutes later, he was observed entering the car. As soon as he drove onto the main street, he was stopped by a radio car. He had no papers for the car. He was promptly placed under arrest. Ellen knew what to do from that point. We could only hope that Spooner's arrest would hold him long enough for Ellen to work on Kayo. The hours dragged and the only report we received was that Kayo had gone into Ellen's apartment. Time was not on our side.

Spooner was held for a hearing set for the following day, at which time bail would be set. At eight o'clock that evening, Ellen called and said she had some information.

Ellen said that at two o'clock in the afternoon, she received a call from Kayo. He told her that Spooner was arrested for driving a stolen car. He wanted to see her in order to get Spooner out on bail. When he arrived at Ellen's apartment he was agitated and extremely nervous. He couldn't understand how Spooner could be so dumb as to ride around in a stolen car. He fixed himself a couple of double shots and calmed down. Ellen had made sure she looked her very best and was dressed "properly" for his visit. Kayo didn't notice the flimsy nightgown, the plunging neckline, or the heavy scent of perfume. He only noticed the bottle and wasted no time trying to empty it. Ellen tried to act concerned about Spooner. She begged for details. Kayo said he didn't know too much about what happened except he had gotten a call from Spooner who said he was arrested for possession of a hot car and that he expected bail to be set the following day. The counterfeits had just come through, and he and Spooner had a sale planned for that night. Now he didn't know what to do. He was going to sell a $20,000 bundle to a buyer for $2,500. Ellen asked why he couldn't make the sale. Kayo said he had to make the sale in order to get the bail money for Spooner, but didn't like going there alone. Ellen gambled and said she could go with him. Kayo was pleased. He'd be happy to have her come along. After the sale, perhaps he could stay over at the apartment — he had noticed the nightgown and the plunging neckline. There were no excuses, since Spooner would definitely be out for the night.

The sale was set up for midnight just across from the railroad terminal. He wanted her to drive but wanted her to stay in the car. After the sale, they could go out and make a night of it. He said if everything went okay, he would pick her up at her apartment at 11:30.

I told Ellen that we had to move quickly. My plan was to have some men in the area and cover Kayo's car at the railroad station. When he got out, I wanted Ellen to give us a signal that Kayo had the money. He would be followed until he met the buyer and when the sale was about to be consummated, we would arrest both of them. I told Ellen we'd use her as a pawn. If Kayo didn't talk, we'd threaten to arrest his girlfriend in the car. From that point on, we would play it by ear and hope Kayo would go along with us. Ellen said she'd play her part and keep her fingers crossed. I suggested that she turn the ignition key and step on the brakes after Kayo left the car with the money. The flashing lights would be a good signal.

Things went according to schedule. At 11:30, Kayo arrived at the apartment. He locked his car, went upstairs, and came out with Ellen fifteen minutes later. Ellen drove to the vicinity of the railroad terminal. Kayo got out of the car, opened the trunk, looked around, then took a small package out. He closed the trunk, gave the keys to Ellen and walked toward the terminal. A man who had been under surveillance at the terminal walked toward Kayo. When they met, Kayo handed the other man a package. Two agents came from opposite directions and restrained Kayo and the other man. They relieved the man of the package and opened it. They found that it contained counterfeit money and placed both of them under arrest.

They were separated and taken to the office for questioning. Kayo's friend was "Lefty," an old thief. Lefty verbally fenced with the interviewing agents for a few minutes and then admitted that he had made a good score and tried to parlay it by buying a bundle of counterfeit money from Spooner and Kayo. He said he'd take his medicine, but would not testify against his suppliers. He didn't relish going back to jail, but at the same time, he wanted to stay alive.

Kayo denied he knew anything about the package. We told him that Lefty had already talked and that we picked up Ellen and intended to hold her. Kayo pleaded with us to let the girl go, and said she had no part in the deal. He was obviously distressed at the possibility that Ellen would be arrested. It would be tough to explain to Spooner. We made it appear that she was arrested and brought to the office. Kayo was a good candidate to be a cooperative defendant. After he learned that I was the man in charge, he asked if he could speak to me privately.

When we were alone in the room I started to recite his rights. He joined me in the recitation and quickly convinced me that he had gone this route before. He wanted to make a deal, but wanted to be sure he was protected. His first request was to cut Ellen loose, swearing that she was not part of the deal. He insisted she just came along for the ride and had no idea what was going on. After much haggling, I agreed to let her go. Then he wanted me to help him with a story to tell his people. I told him I could not help him with a story until I knew the truth.

He said, "I'm cutting my own throat, but here's the way it goes: there's a guy named Spooner who lives with Ellen; that's the girl you picked up. He made a good score not too long ago and he decides he wants to set up a counterfeiting operation. He's got a few grand and is willing to invest it. I tell him I know some printers and I'll try to get one of them interested in a deal. I talked to a couple of guys I know. I give them the proposition, they said they'd try, but it wouldn't be easy. I got Spooner to part with some of the dough. I kept a couple of hundred and gave the printers a couple of hundred. They fooled around, but didn't really get off the ground. These guys weren't printers, they were butchers. I told Spooner I put some money in the deal. I wanted him to be sure to cut me in on anything in the future. He kept looking around and finally found some people who could really get the operation off the ground, 'cause these guys had experience. Two of them, Charlie and Frank, are employed by a legitimate outfit as photographers and plate makers. They make a good buck, but they're always in debt to the bookies and shylocks. They're looking for a chance to make a good score and they jump at the idea to set up a plant. They know a printer who has a press in his cellar. He knocks out a living by doing odd jobs. He can't really work too much because he's some kind of cripple. He needs a cane to walk and he gets tired pretty quickly."

"They all get together and agree to go into production. Charlie and Frank figure they can use their boss's equipment to make the plates and the printer could finish the job. Spooner meets the guys and he puts up the money and we all agree to take a cut of the stuff when it's finished. All except the printer; he's gonna get a flat price. Charlie and Frank have to be real careful. During the day, Charlie shoots a few negatives and has to make sure that no one knows what he's doing. Then he and Frank wait for the opportunity to make a plate. The chance comes one night when the boss asks them to work late to finish a couple of special jobs. They are the only two working. They finish the boss's work and then they spend half the night making plates for the twenties. They have a few problems, but they manage. They turn the plates over to the printer and wait for him to do the job. The printer tells them that his press broke down and that he can't do the job. He don't want to do the job at home and wants us to open a shop for him. Spooner blows his top, but they get a store and put a down-payment on a press. He manages to print a few samples, but he never gets the job going. We finally pay him a visit and threaten to bury him. He knows we mean business and he decides to get busy and go to work."

"Once he gets started, he gets the job finished. He gets in touch with Spooner and tells him he's got $2 million ready. Spooner picks up 100 grand and stashes it somewhere. He promises he'll cut me in on the profits when the big pie is cut up. In the meantime he says he's got a deal lined up to sell Lefty $20,000. He gives me the 20 grand and asks me to handle the deal with him. I get everything lined up and what happens? Spooner gets busted for riding around in a stolen car. The goddamn dope thinks he's so smart. He buys a hot car and uses it with the stolen plates still on it. What did he expect ... the cops would give him a medal? Anyhow, the deal is still on. I know Spooner needs bail so I figure I'll go along on the deal with Lefty and bail Spooner out. I ask Ellen to drive the car so I could make the sale quick and get it over with. She don't know what's going on, except I tell her I'm arranging to get bail money for Spooner, so, naturally, she goes with me. In the middle of the deal, you guys bust us and so here we are. Now you got the whole story."

I said, "No, I don't. I still don't know who the printer is or how I can locate him." Kayo laughed and said, "I don't know either. I met him a couple of times, but always away from his house or the print shop. He don't want us near the place 'cause he's scared. Every time we meet, Spooner does the talking and I sit in the car. Spooner plays it cute and don't want me to know too much. Maybe he's afraid I'll steal the guy. I know the guy is in his forties; he's crippled; uses a cane and I'm sure he's done time. Charlie and Frank will be able to tell you about him. Just give me some time and I'll line them up for you."

There was no doubt the case was progressing well; but we had to move quickly. Spooner had the answers to all our questions and unless he talked, we had troubles. We also had to think about all the defendants who were cooperating and we had to make sure no one got hurt.

The prospect of several million dollars in bogus bills hitting the street was frightening. They were good looking bills and would be all over town in no time. Investigating that would tie up the office for months.

I had Lefty brought in to see if he changed his mind about cooperating. He didn't have any particular love for Spooner; however, he just didn't want to tell the world he was an informer. When it was all over, he still had to make a living. I asked him if he would appreciate a "break." He said a break was always welcome, as long as he didn't have to go to court to testify. "Okay, Lefty, here's the deal. Tomorrow morning you will be arraigned. We will have you released on very low bail. I want your word that you will not tell anyone about your arrest, especially not Spooner. As a matter of fact, avoid Spooner for a couple of weeks, if possible. If my plan works out, you'll get some consideration when the case is disposed of." Lefty smiled. "There must be a catch. This is the first time anyone helped me for doing nothing." "On the contrary, stay away from Spooner and that will be plenty of help," I replied. He didn't understand it, but it was a deal.

Then I brought Kayo back in. I laid it out for him. "Listen carefully. First of all, I am going to cut the girl loose because I believe your story. She won't even be on record as having been arrested. Okay?" Kayo was pleased. "Okay, shoot." "Ellen is cut loose." I said, "The next thing is to get rid of Lefty. We'll arraign him quietly, give him low bail and tell him to get lost for a couple of weeks. He has agreed not to tell anyone about his arrest, okay?" Kayo nodded. I continued, "You will waive immediate arraignment. That means we are going to postpone your arrest until another date, okay?" Kayo nodded again. "The next thing you do is make bail for Spooner. I will have it lowered so you can get him out. You'll have to do it the first thing in the morning. Now, here's where you really have to do your part. You tell him that after he was arrested you felt that something was wrong and you were sure you were being tailed. You were worried about the 20 G's in phony money you had in the car, so you shook the tail, and threw the package in the drink when you crossed the bridge. After you drove around for a while and were sure you were not being tailed, you went to keep the appointment with Lefty at the railroad station to tell him that there would be no deal that night because

Spooner was in the can. You met Lefty and his friend, Nicky, who also wanted to buy some stuff. You told them to come back in a couple of days; that there would be enough for everyone. Lefty said Nicky would be back to make a good-sized buy."

"Nicky actually will be back to arrange for a $75,000 buy from Spooner or whoever might handle the sale. At the time of the transaction, all three will be arrested. When it's time to go before the judge, you will be quietly arraigned before a judge on the notes that you were arrested for tonight. Spooner won't know it, but you will. We accomplish everything we want and, hopefully, Spooner will want to get on the bandwagon and maybe go along with us. You got it now?"

Kayo said, "Yeah, but who is this guy Nicky and where is he?" I said, "I forgot to tell you, I'm Nicky." "You?" He thought a minute and then he lit up when he figured it all out. He said, "Suppose it does work and you get the rest of the 100 grand? What about the $2 million and the people that made it?" I said, "You're jumping the gun. That's the next part of the plot. As soon as the deal goes down and we are bagged, I'll open up on you and Spooner. I'll give the impression that I want to save my own hide and will try to do it at your expense. After that, it will be your job to convince Spooner that you both should cooperate with the government."

"When he sees everything collapsing around him, he might be ripe for a deal himself. It looks like a long shot, but we have to take our chances. If it doesn't work out, we can always go after our crippled printer. Either way, we have got to get this show on the road. We got to move before the city is flooded with these bills. Now, Kayo, do you understand everything?" Kayo said, "Sure, I'm no dope, but you're a conniver. You know, I think I might like the idea of being a part of something exciting like this and knowing in advance how it's gonna turn out. Are you sure Spooner don't know you?" I assured him that I never had any business with Spooner. I didn't tell him that maybe .... just maybe .... Spooner got a quick peek at me the first time I talked to Ellen. I was worried, but there was no sense in worrying Kayo.

I obtained permission from the U. S. Attorney's office to release Kayo. We went over some of the details again and he was allowed to go home. While it looked like a big gamble, I figured Ellen was still on our side and she could let us know if Kayo didn't play it straight.

The next morning Lefty was quietly arraigned in Federal court and was bailed out in record time. He kept his part of the bargain and disappeared as soon as he hit the street.

It took a little longer to get the bail reduced on Spooner. It was late afternoon when Spooner was finally sprung. His problems were in state court and we couldn't call the shots as easily. Kayo was there when Spooner got out and drove him home. Ellen was on the scene to keep on eye on Kayo.

She didn't know what our plans were, but she was told to report anything she heard.

At five in the afternoon, I received a call from Ellen who was quite excited. "Listen, this is what I found out. I don't know if it makes sense, but Kayo told Spooner that he had to get rid of 20 big ones. Spooner blew his top and it looked like they were really gonna come to blows. Kayo says what the hell is twenty big ones compared to a collar by the Feds? Spooner settles down and finally agrees that maybe it was the best thing to do. Mr. Motto, does this make sense?" "Yes, Ellen, go on — then what happened?" Ellen continued, "Well, Kayo tells Spooner that there is a guy named Nicky who wants to buy a load. Kayo says maybe this will be a way to get a stake and take care of the lawyers and bondsmen. Spooner wanted to know how well he knew Nicky. Kayo said not too well; that Nicky was a friend of Lefty's and that he only met him once. He thought Lefty and Nicky were good friends. From the way Spooner was acting, it looks like he might do business with Nicky because he needs money in a hurry and for all kinds of lawyers and bail for him and he even said to Kayo that he might have to get a lawyer for me. How's that for a report? Now do I get my badge?" I said, "You did your job well and I'm going to see that you get out when your time is up." "Drop dead." "Thanks, keep in touch."

The men on the street had come up with two printers with deformities. One had a wooden leg and was in a veterans' hospital. He had been there for over a year so he was eliminated. The other was a man who walked with a limp. He lived about 30 miles out of town; his record was mostly for pornography. There was a rumor that he had a press in his cellar and a shop somewhere else. His name was Norman Stevens but everyone called him "Nooby." He was the best suspect we had, so the men kept digging and put a loose tail on him.

At about ten that night, I received a call from Kayo. He wanted to meet me as soon as possible. He picked a safe spot and we met. He reported what happened and it was pretty much the same story as Ellen told us. Kayo thought that Spooner was hungry enough to sell what he had on hand, providing he was satisfied that everything was safe. He wanted to meet Nicky before he went through with any deal. Kayo told Spooner that just as soon as he heard from Nicky he would set up a meet. Spooner said he also wanted Lefty there. I asked Kayo if he had any idea where Spooner was stashing the money. He said he wasn't sure but he knew Spooner's folks had a house in the city and that it would be as good a spot as any to hide a bundle. He was sure that it wasn't in the apartment. I asked Kayo if Spooner had any other customers lined up. Kayo didn't think so. He figured Spooner wanted to unload one big bundle so he would have some money to tide him over. I told Kayo that the best thing was to tell Spooner that he had gotten a call from Nicky and had arranged for a meet the following afternoon at a bar in a local hotel. I insisted that Kayo not give any information to Spooner except that which he could have learned on the first meet. Kayo asked what he should say about Lefty. I said, "Tell Spooner Lefty is out of town, but if he gets back in time you would be sure to get him to come to the meet." Kayo said he would take care of everything and would report as soon as he was able.

At two in the morning, Kayo reported that he had met Spooner and a meet was arranged for the following day. I told him the name of the hotel I would use and suggested they be in the bar around 4:30 in the afternoon.

At the appointed time, I went down to the bar and in about ten minutes Spooner and Kayo arrived. Kayo introduced me to Spooner and we sat down. Spooner lit a cigar, looked at me and asked, "Where's Lefty?" I snapped, "This is my deal and Lefty doesn't have anything to do with it." Spooner interrupted, "Hey, slow it down. Don't get mad at me. Remember, Lefty's my friend. I know him and I don't know you. I'm not doing business with any Tom, Dick, or Schmoe. I want Lefty to put an Okay on you." I said, "Then you don't want to do business with me. Anytime I need a reference from Lefty, I'll find someone else to buy the stuff from." Spooner calmed down a little and said, "Don't get so goddamn uptight. I'm entitled to know who I'm dealing with. If you don't like Lefty, give me the names of some people you know who can put the O.K. on you."

I figured I'd gamble and really test him. "Now you're playing goddamn games. First of all, you're not going to check on me. You think I'm gonna give you the names of connected people and have you ask if Nicky is okay to do business with? They'd spit in your goddamn face. Maybe you'd like to have my picture so you could really check me out. I'm not sure that you can handle a big deal. You better stick to passing your stuff on blind news dealers." With that, I got up to leave. Kayo jumped up and asked me not to be too hasty. Spooner sat and sulked.

I went off to the men's room and in a minute or so, Kayo came in and told me to come back. He thought that I was pushing Spooner too hard. I went back to the table and told Kayo and Spooner that I was in room 467; that they could join me there so we could talk without worrying about the waiter who looked like he should be wearing a badge.

I went to the room and ordered a bottle. Spooner and Kayo came up. We had a drink and we all felt a little more comfortable talking in private. Spooner opened the conversation by saying, "Look, Nicky, I have to be careful. I just got busted on a State rap and I'm not looking for a Federal rap; that's all I need." "I'm not interested in getting busted either. If you're that hot maybe you shouldn't get involved. Look, Spooner, I am not in any hurry. I buy and sell if the price is right, if it's not, I can wait."

Kayo chimed in, "Nicky, there's nothing wrong with being careful. I am sure after the first deal we can relax a little and maybe we can handle the deal by phone." I said, "Okay, where do we go from here?" "How much are you interested in?" Spooner asked. I appeared to think about it. "About 100 grand if the merchandise is good and the price is right." Spooner said sharply, "No one has any better stuff. It will pass anywhere. I got one with me — take a quick look and I guarantee that's the stuff you'll get." He took out a crisp new $20 from an envelope in his pocket. I wanted to shove it down his throat. It was a genuine bill! Spooner was playing games, but I had to go along.

I examined the bill and handed it back. "You're right, it's pretty good but I've seen better. How much?" Spooner thought a minute and said, "Well, right now I can give you about 80 grand. The price is twelve points." "You were only charging Lefty ten points." He replied, "Lefty promised to give Kayo two points for handling the deal." I insisted that the price was too high, besides I was buying more than Lefty and that should bring the price down. I said, "How much can you deliver tonight?" He answered, "I can get $80,000 right away. After that, all you want." I said, "Okay, I'll give you $6,500 for the package." He said, "$7,500 straight cash." We haggled and finally agreed on a price of $7,000. He then told me to give him $2,000 in advance to show good will. I told him he was crazy; I wouldn't advance two cents on a deal where I only saw one sample. He insisted that the whole batch was excellent and if I didn't like it at the time of the buy, I could turn the deal down. "And then you'd refund my money," I sneered. "Don't make me laugh. You bring the 80 grand here tonight and you'll have your money." He said he'd think it over. He then got up to leave and motioned Kayo to follow. Kayo told me to stick around for a call. I told him I'd wait around for a couple of hours, but I didn't intend to stay on the hook indefinitely. Spooner said, "Don't worry, you'll hear."

They left. Spooner was not in a very good mood. I wasn't sure I hadn't overplayed the part, but he needed money desperately and wanted to take advantage of a fast deal.

Kayo called and said he spent some time with Spooner at the apartment; that Spooner was furious. He was toying with the idea of coming back to the hotel and sticking me up for my money. Kayo told him to calm down and simply go through with the deal. Spooner said he didn't trust me; he was sure I was a thieving son of a bitch and wasn't too sure that I wouldn't stick him up and take the counterfeits. Kayo told him that he would see to it that nothing went wrong and would make sure that Nicky was alone in his hotel room. Spooner finally agreed and told Kayo to call me and tell me to wait for further information. He figured that they could make the delivery at about three in the morning. Kayo didn't think that anything would change, so we set up for a delivery at that time.

We had a late conference at the office. If and when Spooner and Kayo made the delivery, we would arrest them. When the notes were delivered, I would ask Spooner to come with me to get the money in another room. Kayo would stay with the counterfeits. As soon as we left the room, the arrest would be made.

At two o'clock in the morning, I got a call from Kayo who was calling for Spooner, who wanted to know if everything was okay. I said I was still waiting. Kayo said he would be up in half an hour.

Right at 2:30, Kayo knocked. He told me Spooner was parked near the hotel in a rented car. He wanted Kayo to make sure that I was alone and had the money. Spooner had the package and was ready to make the delivery. I told him to reassure Spooner. Kayo left and ten minutes later he returned with Spooner. Kayo was carrying a small suitcase which he put on the bed. Spooner told me to open it. I fully expected that this would be a test run, so I was pleasantly surprised to find it full of counterfeit twenties. I took out a few and started to examine them. Spooner was impatient. "For Christ's sake, Nick," he said, "are you going to look at each one? We'll be here all night. I'll guarantee the count. Give me my money and let me get going." I asked why he was in such a hurry; he was acting like a new young bride. He said, "Never mind the crap, let's get it over with." I said, "Okay, come on down the hall." He said, "Down the hall — for what?" I said, "For your money. I have it in another room. I guess I didn't trust you." He exploded and finally yelled, "Nick, you don't go for sweat, do you? Why the hell didn't you have the money ready? Why do we have to go parading all over the damn hotel for the money?" I said, "We're wasting time arguing." He decided to go with me to get the money.

We stepped outside and were immediately intercepted by four men who announced "Federal agents!" and pushed us back into my room. There they found Kayo sitting with the suitcase. I said the room was in my name, but I knew nothing about the suitcase. Kayo interrupted and said that neither Spooner nor he was involved; that they had merely come to the room to see someone and were apparently in the wrong place. Spooner agreed. I stared at them. "Are you guys gonna let me take the whole rap? You can go straight to hell by yourself. If it's every man for himself, then I'm going to think of myself." I turned to the agents and said, "I guess you know I am on parole and I owe a lot of time. I want the best deal I can get. These two guys brought the bundle here. They can tell you where it comes from." Spooner jumped up and shouted, "Keep your mouth shut, you stupid bastard!" Kayo joined in and I was taken out of the room by the agents. We were hustled down to headquarters where we were questioned.

Kayo asked that he be left alone with Spooner. Kayo told Spooner he thought they were sunk and figured it would be better if they cooperated.

"The whole deal is dead; why not tell them what they want to know. Maybe we'll get a break." Spooner was not inclined to admit anything. Then Kayo told him he would go along with anyone he thought could help him. He didn't see any prospect for bail or lawyer's fees and didn't want to sit in the can. Kayo admitted he didn't know much, but figured if both of them talked, maybe they would get a break.

Spooner was still mad about my giving up as soon as we were arrested. He told Kayo, "Your bastard friend was a real stand-up guy — as soon as someone said 'boo' he folded." Kayo said, "You can't blame him. If he owes any real time, he's got double troubles. So why should we take the rap for a couple of creeps who made the notes." Spooner agreed and after rationalizing it in his own mind, said he would try to make a deal.

Kayo, of course, really had nothing to say. It was obvious that Spooner didn't like talking with the police, but too much was happening to him too soon. He started by telling the agents that there were only four more people to arrest — Nooby the printer, Charlie, Frank and Nooby's brother-in-law, Artie. Charlie, who worked as a photographer for a printing concern, had dreamed up the whole thing. He was in debt to the shylocks and needed money desperately. An excellent photographer, he got the idea that he could put enough people together to start a counterfeiting scheme. His first thought was to feel out Frank, who worked in the same company as an offset plate maker. Frank, while not in debt, liked the things money could buy — such as the attentions of a certain blond divorcee. Charlie said he would shoot the negatives right in the plant. No one ever bothered him while he was working in the dark room. Frank had some platemaking equipment in his house and could buy the few pieces more he would need to complete the job. If he couldn't do it at home, he would do it at the plant where he was working overtime. Both men knew who they wanted for a printer. Everyone called him Nooby.

Our file on Nooby was quite complete. He had polio when he was young and it left him with a bad leg that needed a brace. He walked with a cane. He managed to pile up quite a criminal record that included several arrests for pornography and making counterfeit checks. In one prison he ran the print shop and when he finished his bit, he was better than the average printer. Released from prison, he obtained several jobs as a printer, but in each case he was fired for using the boss's equipment for his own purposes. He eventually bought himself a press and went into business for himself. He came to the attention of the Secret Service on one occasion when he printed some advertising circulars that bore a replica of a dollar bill. He was not arrested, but was warned about printing anything that looked like U.S. currency.

When Nooby was approached, he was happy to be a part of the group. Naturally, he needed money for supplies such as ink, paper and other incidentals. He also wanted money to keep him going while he was doing the job. He suggested that his brother-in-law, Artie, buy supplies and help him with the printing. Spooner admitted he financed the operation and expected to get the lion's share of the output. He also elected himself the principal distributor of the bills.

The job went slowly at first, but eventually was finished. Spooner decided to let Nooby keep the bills in his house until they were needed for a sale. Spooner admitted he passed a few to see how they would go and then began to look for customers. Lefty was the first prospect, but no deal was consummated. Nicky was Lefty's friend and he wanted 80 or 100 grand. Spooner made the delivery and they were arrested.

After Spooner told his story, he seemed to enjoy being the center of attention. He was quick to answer all questions and even volunteered some suggestions. He supplied the agents with enough information about each conspirator to enable us to identify and locate him.

Surprisingly, Spooner didn't have an objection to signing a statement. He only asked that he not be used as a witness unless it was absolutely necessary. Fair enough.

After Spooner and Kayo had been put in the detention cell, I was able to get back to planning the raids for later that morning. We decided that Nooby was to be arrested at his home. I obtained an arrest warrant and a search warrant for his home and shop. I made arrangements to have a truck available so that all the equipment used in the operation could be seized. Artie, Nooby's brother-in-law, was to be arrested at his home on a warrant, his home to be searched incident to the arrest. Charlie was to be arrested at his place of business on an arrest warrant. I obtained a search warrant for his place of business. Frank also was to be arrested at his place of business on an arrest warrant, and I got a search warrant for his house, where some of the plate work was done.

Everything had to be accomplished before noon the same day so that there would be no chance that anyone would learn of Spooner's arrest, thereby giving them a chance to dispose of any evidence. At about nine o'clock in the morning, teams were sent out to effect the arrests and searches. Each team was assigned local police to assist them. Nooby's place was already under surveillance. When the warrant was issued, they moved in.

At about 10 o'clock the first report came in. Frank and Charlie were arrested. Both protested their involvement. In Charlie's locker there were several sets of negatives that were used to make the counterfeit plates. This just about sewed things up for him.

Frank's house produced a lot of equipment used for making the plates. At first it looked like the cellar was clean; however, a detailed search turned up some plates for counterfeit money hidden in the upholstery of an old stuffed chair in the basement.

Artie's arrest came off without incident. He had no contraband at home and immediately told the officers of his involvement in the scheme. He surrendered all the receipts he had for the purchases of inks, paper, chemicals, papercutter, and plates. He estimated that Nooby had printed over $2 million of the counterfeits. He had stacked the money neatly between the studs on the cellar walls and then nailed sheetrock to the studs, completely hiding the money.

The agents at Nooby's house didn't need this information. They arrested Nooby, found the press and other equipment in the cellar and spotted the phony wall. They removed the sheet-rock and found the money. There were nearly $2 million in counterfeits in the cellar. Nooby was in the unenviable position of not being able to offer any cooperation except to admit the part he played. He admitted he did a little cheating on the rest of the group and sold two $10,000 packages to friends. This was his own deal and he kept the money for himself.

He identified the men for us. They were arrested. One man still had $9,300 in counterfeits in his possession. The other man surrendered $8,700 that he had hidden.

At three in the afternoon, just about everything was wrapped up. Searches and seizures were completed. All prisoners were arraigned. The press had their pictures and stories. While the investigation of the case was complete, the prosecution still had to grind to its conclusion.

Months later, the final chapter was written:

Nooby: 5 years in custody 3 years probation
Artie: 3 years custody 2 years probation
Frank: 3 years custody 2 years probation
Charlie: 3 years custody 2 years probation
Spooner: 5 years custody 2 years probation
Lefty: 1 year custody 2 years probation
Kayo: 3 years suspended and 5 years probation

Quietly, in another courtroom, Ellen was given a year and a day on the bond charges which was suspended in consideration of her help to the government.

The last time I saw her was on the courthouse steps. She left arm in arm with Kayo. As she got into a cab she looked over her shoulder and said "Thanks." I smiled, waved, and quietly said, "Thank you for writing the letter."

"Postmarked for Prison

One of the most interesting cases I ever worked on started with a three-cent stamp. Before it reached its climax, we had arrested sixteen defendants. All pleaded guilty and were sent to prison. Hollywood, at its best, couldn't create the characters or story that marked this case. It played out like a spoof of a Mickey Spillane novel.

It was late one afternoon on a fairly busy day at the office. Most of the agents were out and I was busy trying to get caught up on some paperwork. The door to the office opened and an attractive middle-aged woman walked in. She took a couple of steps, then turned around and started to walk out. I called to her and asked if I could be of any assistance. She came back in and sat at a chair by my desk. She stated her name was Bonnie, she opened her purse and extracted a three-cent stamp. She handed the stamp to me and asked if it was counterfeit. I looked at the stamp and my first impression was that it looked genuine. I kept examining it under a magnifying glass and matching it with a known genuine stamp. I finally decided it was a counterfeit. This was my first experience with a counterfeit stamp and it baffled me as to why anyone would put the time and effort into something that was worth only three cents. I told Bonnie that the stamp was bogus and asked her where she got it.

She said it was a long story and she got up to leave. I told her: "You walk into the U. S. Secret Service office with a counterfeit three-cent stamp and then you decide to leave. Bonnie, you have a story to tell and I have the time to listen, so sit down, have a cup of coffee, pull yourself together, and let's get to the bottom of it."

She took a sip of the coffee and grimaced, "You'll never get anyone to talk with serving that awful coffee — cruel and unusual punishment went out a long time ago." I promised to send out for a fresh cup of coffee as soon as we got to the story.

She said, "O.K. here's how it happened. My older sister Brenda is recently divorced, she's a knockaround gal. She has been arrested several times and in the last several months she's been hanging around with a real tough bunch and I'm concerned that she's going to get ino some serious trouble. The night before last, she came to my apartment and asked if I knew anyone who might be interested in purchasing some counterfeit postage stamps. She said she would sell them for $1.50 for a sheet of 100 stamps. She said she could get thousands of sheets and would split the profits with me. She gave me a sheet of stamps, I tore one off, and that's the one I brought with me. The rest of the stamps are in my apartment."

I asked her if she thought her sister would cooperate with us. She said "No, my sister is stubborn and it would take months of rotting in jail before she'd decide to cooperate. She lives in a fleabag hotel downtown. She buys and sells anything that's illegitimate. She's not really getting by on her own. When she needs help, she turns to a 70-year old widower who just adores her. He lives in the same hotel. Everyone there knows him as "Blind Irving." He's not really blind, he just wears thick glasses. He's always in the lobby waiting for Betty to come in."

I asked Bonnie if she'd introduce me to her sister as a prospective buyer of the stamps. She said, "No, it would cause too many problems." As the conversation continued, I noticed that she was getting more and more angry at her sister. She called her every name she could think of, and at one time she said she wished her sister were dead.

I finally said, "Bonnie, you're not telling me the whole truth. You come here with a counterfeit three-cent stamp. You say your sister gave you a sheet of stamps and asked you to peddle them. Your sister is now hanging out with a tough crowd and you don't want to see her go to jail. What did you think I was going to do with her? She's violating the law and somewhere along the line she'll have to pay. If there's more to this story, tell me now so we can get an investigation started."

Bonnie thought for a while and said, "O.K., here's the story again. Everything I told you is the truth except for one thing. I hate my sister and I don't care if you send her up for life. Why do I hate her? Simple enough. She is playing around with my husband and ruining my marriage. Tell me what you want me to do and I'll do it." I told her to go home, get in touch with her sister, and tell her she had one or two prospects in mind and perhaps she could get rid of a couple of thousand sheets of stamps. Then I told her to call me at nine that night to set up a plan. She agreed and said she would call later that evening.

I went in to see the Agent in Charge. I told him about my interview with Bonnie. We notified the Postal Inspectors and had a meeting that evening. No one could understand why anyone would want to counterfeit three-cent stamps. The boss said, "Go investigate so we'll find out why they did it." He reminded me that we didnt have any money to blow on this case. I gave the matter a lot of thought and devised a plan that I relayed to Bonnie when she called that night.

I told her to call her sister and tell her she had a friend at the General Post Office in Manhattan, who had expressed a lot of interest in getting some counterfeit stamps. He was friendly with a shady character who could set the whole deal up.

Brenda wanted to meet with the shady character at eleven that evening in a restaurant near the General Post Office. I became the shady character, with the name Nicky Spina.

The meeting with Brenda came off promptly at eleven. She entered the restaurant with two characters who looked like they were fugitives from the radio show "Gang Busters" or the pages of a Damon Runyon story — George Raft, James Cagney, Humphrey Bogart, or Sheldon Leonard. Stereotypical Hollywood "Guys and Dolls" hoods. Dark suits, dark shirts, white ties, and hats pulled over the eyes. I even expected them to say, "You, you dirty rat!"

Brenda was a 50-year-old, tough-talking, bleach-blond — every word she uttered was preceded by an expletive. She did all the talking and she drove a hard bargain. She continually reminded me that if things didn't go right, someone was going to get hurt. She said she had 1,000 sheets of stamps and wanted $1.75 a sheet, with the money paid in advance. After the first sale, she was prepared to sell any amount of stamps.

I told Brenda that my plan was to pay $1.50 a sheet for the stamps, then I would give them to my friend in the Post Office who would sell them over the window and also use them to fill overseas orders. I assured her she would never become involved if anything went wrong.

Brenda finally agreed to my offer of a $1.50 a sheet. She argued against waiting several days for her money, but finally agreed to it. She insisted on meeting the employee at the post office. I told her that the meeting would be set up at the General Post Office at eleven-thirty in the morning the following day. Fortunately, I had a brother, Robert, who was a postal employee at the time and the Postal Inspectors arranged for him to be at the Post Office to meet Brenda the next day.

We met as planned. Bob told Brenda that he would be free for lunch in fifteen minutes and they could continue the conversation. Bob had been schooled on everything that happened and was able to convince Brenda that he could handle several thousand sheets of stamps.

Brenda was thrilled with the idea that the stamps were going overseas, and before the lunch period was over, she had agreed to everything we wanted. Brenda left with her two lumbering "Guys and Dolls" bodyguards tagging along like "Tweedle-dee and Tweedle-dum," and agreed to meet me later that evening with the thousand sheets of stamps. Before she left, I told her that I would meet her Friday evening with the money for the stamps, and I suggested she should bring an extra 5,000 sheets that I had a buyer for.

This deal would be cash on delivery. Brenda agreed after warning me that there were some big people behind these stamps and everything better go as planned.

On Friday evening, Brenda arrived with her two cronies and insisted I get into the car. I told her I was double-parked and didn't want to get a ticket. I showed her a phony roll of bills and directed her to my car that was just up ahead. I opened my trunk and directed that they put the stamps in it. She told her friends to put the stamps in the trunk and just as I was about to pay her, we were all arrested.

True to her reputation, Brenda would not talk. She threw all the blame on me and insisted she was innocent. Her two friends, Moonie and Peter, said they were only giving Brenda a ride.

Brenda languished, or rotted, as she described it, in jail for several weeks thinking someone would bail her out. She learned that Moonie and Peter made their bail but the only person that ever visited her was Blind Irving. He brought her candy, sandwiches and whatever she asked for. He was a regular figure outside the jail.

In the meantime, we had 6,000 sheets of stamps, with the possibility of millions more in the city. The Postal Inspectors had detected many of the stamps on Christmas cards. We followed up on each card and the person who mailed the cards said he or she found the stamps on the street. In some cases it was true, and in others they insisted they got the stamps at vending machines in the Post Office.

The next job was to see if the gummed paper could be identified. I had a meeting with the Director of the Gummed Paper Institute. He felt he could be of assistance. He requested that sufficient stamps be given to him so that they could be forwarded to the laboratories of the gummed paper manufacturers. He stated that there were about ten companies involved. I gave the Director ten sheets of stamps and he said he would contact me when he received any information.

Early one morning about three weeks after the arrests, Blind Irving came into the office. He said he had visited Brenda at the Women's Detention Bureau. He said she was fed up with her friends and was ready to make a deal.

I didn't lose any time in visiting her. She was in a foul mood, wanted to get the whole matter straightened out, and was willing to go to court and testify. She said, "There's no need in me telling you about Moonie and Peter. You played your part and you have the three of us cold."

She said the first time she heard of counterfeit stamps was from an old friend who was known as Chet. He said he had a connection to get any amount of phony stamps at half price. Brenda knew a friend in Connecticut and she thought she might interest them in the stamps.

Chet drove her to Connecticut and took along a friend called Red who was also involved in the conspiracy. The deal in Connecticut fell through and no sale was made. On the way back to New York, Brenda learned that the principal person behind these stamps was a Mafia soldier called "The Mouse." I almost stopped breathing when she mentioned the Mouse. He was suspected of handling counterfeit money, narcotics and illicit alcohol. Brenda said she didn't know the Mouse, but Chet and Red used his name when talking about the source of the illicit stamps. She said that both Chet and Red supplied her with the stamps that she sold me.

Chet and Red were immediately arrested and as expected, they did not answer any questions.

I visited Brenda at least once a week and each time she recalled a little more about the case. I convinced her to stay in jail until the case was disposed of. She was making a lot of enemies and we could not guarantee her safety. From the information she supplied, there were many more arrests to be made and an awful lot of stamps to be seized.

It wasn't too long before Chet and Red decided to talk. They gave information that their source of the stamps was Natie Lavin, also known as "Little Mo." They didn't think he was the manufacturer, but he did have the connection for obtaining them. Based on their statements, Little Mo was arrested. He claimed not to know anything about the stamps.

The prosecutor in this case was Roy M. Cohen. He had just started in the U. S. Attorney's Office and was a real 'firecracker.' He had a photographic memory and drove a hard bargain.

A day came when I got a call from the Director of the Gummed Paper Institute. He said he had information regarding the paper used to print the stamps. Within the hour I was at his office. He said he had sent the stamps to each of the ten companies that manufactured gummed paper. Nine reponded that it wasn't their paper and the last remaining manufacturer identified it as theirs. The paper was known as 'Perfection White.' They not only identified the paper, but in this particular run, they had put a chemical in the glue and since the sheet of stamps contained the chemical, they were in a position to send us a list of everyone who had purchased it.

Eventually, the company sent me the list. After looking at the list, I could see my work was cut out for me. All the people on the list appeared to be legitimate paper suppliers and users. There were over 100 purchasers in our area and some were out of town. I informed the Agent in Charge that the answer to who our printer was lay somewhere in the list. He told me to stay on the case and to see everyone who purchased that particular paper.

I started to make the rounds and soon found out that the hundred purchasers were large paper houses who sold to smaller printing supply houses. The number of purchasers grew to well over 300.

A typical day of interviewing the purchasers was met with these results: "Yes, we did buy 100 reams of this paper. Here are the names of the purchasers." I would then add five or six more names to the list. The other answer was: "This item was sold over the counter. It was a cash purchase, there's nothing else we can tell you." This went on for days and days. The list was getting larger and I wasn't getting any closer to the printer.

I still managed to see Brenda at the Women's House of Detention and the longer she stayed in jail, the more information she had for me. She gave me information on stolen goods, narcotics, and illegal aliens; however, she could not help in identifying the manufacturer of the stamps.

It was a hot, humid, generally miserable summer day so typical to New York in August. I found myself on the lower East side of New York City in an area they called the "ghetto." I walked into a printing supply house. It was called "Front's Supplies." It appeared to be a shop that had seen better days — the counter was broken, there was paper all over the floor, empty coffee cups, dust, and cobwebs all over the place.

The first thought was "I'm not going to get anything out of this place except maybe some strange and exotic summertime disease."

There appeared to be no one in the store but way in the back the owner was dozing off. I woke him up, showed him my credentials and asked him what he did with the "Perfection White" paper he had purchased sometime ago. He said "Wait, I'll check my records." I couldn't imagine that he would come up with any records, let alone one small receipt. His whole desk area was a cluttered mess like a grenade had exploded on the desk top.

After about twenty minutes of rummaging and shuffling, he found an invoice and said he sold all of the paper to a printer in New Jersey. He also said he was paid by check and the check bounced. He said "Wait, I'll find it." This time, I had confidence in the man and sure enough, he came up with the bounced check. The name of the shop was Hart Press and was located in Jersey City, New Jersey. The owner was Manny Epstein. I spent an hour or so with Mr. Amen, owner of Front's Supplies. He told me that he made several trips to Jersey City but was unable to collect on the bad check. He gave me a description of the owner. I thanked him for this cooperation and got back to the office without visiting any more supply houses.

I had a feeling that this was going to be our best lead in the whole case. After arriving at the office, I called our Newark, New Jersey office. They made a quick check and stated their files had no record with respect to Hart Press and its owner, Manny Epstein. I then proceeded to Jersey City and was able to find Manny at his print shop. He was just cleaning up before closing his shop for the evening. I showed him my credentials and asked him what he did with the ten reams of Perfection White that he had "purchased" from Front's Supply house. He stuttered and stammered and denied even knowing where Front's Supply was. I showed him a copy of the "bounced" check that bore his signature. He looked at the check and almost fainted. I told him that several persons had been arrested, that there were many more to be arrested before the case was closed, probably even him. I told him right now the odds were in his favor as there were a lot of details that I had to iron out. If he gave me the whole story, I would not have to get the details from anyone else and I would make sure the U. S. Attorney was advised of his cooperation. He said he needed time to think about it. I suggested that we go to a restaurant, have a bite to eat and perhaps he'd see fit to tell me the full story about the counterfeit stamps. He agreed, we ate at an out-of-town diner, and he told the following story.

He had owned his present shop for the past five years. Anytime he needed printing plates, he used Henry and Donato who owned a plate making shop in downtown New York City. One day, Henry and Donato came to his shop and asked him if he would print up some counterfeit postage stamps. They produced several genuine stamps and wanted one hundred stamps to each sheet. Manny said he would have no trouble printing the stamps but he could not do the perforations. Henry said it would not be necessary to perforate them as they had someone who could do it. Manny then ordered the paper from Front's Suppliers. He purchased the necessary purple ink and as soon as Henry and Donato delivered the plates, he started printing.

He worked on the project day and night and finally, printed 12 million counterfeit three-cent U.S. postage stamps. The stamps were picked up by Artie Bosca who also had a print shop in the Bronx. Manny later heard through the grapevine that there were some arrests in the case so he was not surprised at my visit.

I told Manny to not leave town and I would meet him in Roy Cohn's office the next morning. After giving the facts to Roy and after questioning Manny, Roy obtained arrest warrants on Manny, Henry, Donato and Artie Bosca. Artie was arrested in his shop and held on high bail. Henry and Donato were arrested in their plate making shop, which was about one-half block from our office. While searching Henry, I looked through his wallet and found a rent receipt for a place which was not his home or his office. I went to this address. The superintendent let me into a very small room. The place was about twelve by twelve feet. It had a multilith press and a waste paper basket. It was very clean, no telephone, no desk, the search took about five minutes. There were some rags in the waste paper basket and about six sheets of paper. The printing on the paper was a lot of colored balls. I took the rags and paper and returned to the office. I showed the Agent in Charge what I had found. He examined them carefully and said, "You just broke the American Express Traveler's Check Case!" He explained that officials from the American Express Company had contacted him and told him that someone had counterfeited their American Express traveler's checks. The checks were being passed all over the country, and the American Express officials were requesting his help in running down the counterfeiters. The information was turned over to the FBI. By this time, Henry and Donato were cooperating and before long, they were in Roy Cohn's office admitting their guilt in the three cent stamp case and the American Express Traveler's checks.

Soon after the arrests, a bunch of young kids found about eight million counterfeit three-cent postage stamps in an empty lot in the Bronx. Needless to say, I was elated with the turn of events, but I still had to make a case against The Mouse or Mousey as some called him. He was the big man in the Bronx. The only one who could put him in the case was Artie Bosca. I tried several times to get Artie to cooperate. He always refused, saying he feared for his family. I explained that we didn't get this far on the case without someone cooperating, and since the case was coming to an end, perhaps we wouldn't need his help.

After many visits from his family, he decided to send for me. I saw him and after talking with him, we were back in Roy Cohen's office. He began talking and quickly implicated Mousey, his two friends, the Mariano Brothers, one known as "Bull" and the other as Mugsy. He stated it was the Mariano Brothers who first approached him about the stamps. All the money was put up by Mousey and there was a third man who was close to Mousey. His name was Felix Abbonda, also known as "The Student." He was called The Student because apparently he was the only one in his neighborhood who made it to college. Our guess was that The Student would be the easiest to approach.

I asked Bosca who perforated the stamps. He said he took the stamps to his home and tried to perforate the sheets. He had purchased a foot-operated perforator and after several hours, he realized it was too tough on his back and legs. He got in touch with The Student who obtained the necessary funds from Mousey to purchase another perforator. The original perforator was thrown into the Long Island Sound. He later showed me the spot. After listening to Bosca, Roy Cohn said he was prepared to issue warrants for the arrest of Mousey, The Student and the Mariano Brothers. The warrants were issued; Mousey and The Student were arrested. They stood on their right to say nothing and were held on $75,000 bail. Mousey made bail, but The Student didn't. The Mariano Brothers fled town and became fugitives along with some minor characters whose role, though small, was big enough to cause them considerable inconvenience.

After the arrests were made, the real work began. We were able to get the original invoices for all of the paper and all the inks that were used, all the invoices for the first and second perforators, and the invoice for the multilith printing press found in the office of Henry and Donato. The recovered stamps had to be inventoried, and the complete history of this case had to be supplied to the U.S. Attorney for prosecution. We had Navy divers recover the perforator from the Long Island Sound.

One day while I was trying to put together the lengthy and complex case report, I received a call from The Student's wife. She said that The Student wanted to talk to me. I had him taken over to the Courthouse where I interviewed him. He said he had given the whole matter a lot of thought and decided he would testify for the Government. He said he had one favor to ask — I tried to assure him that his cooperation would be brought to the attention of the sentencing judge. He said "Look Carmine, I am not looking for any breaks. I came from a proud Italian family. They tried to give me a good education but somewhere along the line, I decided to team up with the gang. I did well with them but now everything has crumbled. I have a wife and two kids who will have to shift for themselves until I get out of this mess. Ten days from now, my kid sister will be getting married; the reception will be at my parent's home. There will be relatives and friends coming to the wedding. Most of them do not know of my arrest. I desperately want to go to the wedding. If you can arrange it, I will testify for the Government." It was that simple! I relayed the information to Roy Cohen, he immediately said, "Step outside while I make a phone call." After the call, he said "No problem, you and a prison guard will take The Student to the wedding. Be careful; if he manages to get away, a lot of eyebrows could be raised." I talked with The Student again and told him that he would be granted the opportunity to attend the wedding. I said I would do nothing to embarrass him, just so long as he did not try to escape. We shook hands. The wedding day came; he was turned over to me and a prison guard. We attended the wedding reception. I don't know how many people thought we were guests, but the bottom line was that The Student was happy and by midnight, when the ball was over, we had him back in his cell.

The word must have reached the gang that The Student was cooperating. We had not located any of the fugitives, and yet, Roy Cohen was preparing for a trial. He called me one day and said Mousey's lawyer had relayed the following message to him. "Mousey will have all the fugitives in court in forty-eight hours. Everyone in the case will plead guilty and they all want three to five year sentences." I said it sounded good to me. At the time, we didn't really have the necessary personnel to locate the fugitives and do our normal work. In 48 hours, true to Mousey's promise, all the fugitives appeared in Court and pleaded guilty.

Sentencing was the following week. On the day of sentencing, I looked around a pretty crowded courtroom.There were wives, children, parents, lovers and informants. The Judge took his seat and said to Roy Cohen, "You have sixteen defendants here, they all pleaded guilty. Will you please advise the Court of the facts in this case so that I can properly dispose of the matter."

Roy jumped to his feet and for the next hour and fifteen minutes, he related every single detail that made up the case. He was able to describe every criminal act that each individual was involved in, and then went on to recite the criminal records of each of the defendants. He did this without a single note in his hand. He was able to get the sentences for each defendant that he had agreed to. The Judge made the remark that the call from the Mouse was louder than the call of the police sirens.

I stayed around to collect the evidence that was in Court. I finally slumped into a chair in my office and thought about the case in general. We had a lot of good breaks in the case. I felt good because I had done ninety-five percent of the investigative work. I picked up a stamp from the desk and wondered what would have happened if we had decided that the stamp was genuine.

A lot of these defendants became good informants for other cases. The case made the front page of the New York Times; Roy Cohen was riding high, and of course went on to greater glory and recognition in the political/legal arena. Many years later, when I read of his demise from AIDS, it struck me hard, as we made many more cases together. How could a prosecutor as brilliant as this man lose his license and die so tragically? My brother, Robert, left the post office, joined the Secret Service (where we successfully worked many other undercover cases together) and eventually retired as Assistant to the Special Agent-in-Charge in Chicago.

Some years later, I ran into Mousey; we shook hands and he invited me to have a cup of coffee with him. During the conversation that ensued, I asked him if he could tell me why they had printed twelve million counterfeit U.S. postage stamps. He admitted that it was not a smart thing to do and it was almost impossible to make any real money. He looked at me and laughed and said, "I served my time, everyone in the case has served his time, a lot of them are dead, so I guess, there is no harm in talking about it." He went on to say that "During World War II, there was a lot of money to be made. Everything was rationed and you needed a card and ration stamps to buy anything. In our group of guys, we had some pretty good printers and it wasn't long before we were printing stamps for just about everything. Gasoline stamps were in great demand. Without the stamps, you couldn't get any gasoline. We sold the counterfeits to just about everyone; we had butchers, bakers, candlestick makers, doctors, lawyers and even policemen who were our customers. Things were so good that we just didn't bother with other crimes during the war. The money was rolling in and we were all happy. When the war ended and rationing was over, we were looking for new ways to bring in some money. One of the group suggested we print counterfeit money. It sounded like a good idea, but I had been arrested before by the Feds and I kind of knocked it down. Then he said how about counterfeiting postage stamps. They were worth $3 for a sheet of a hundred. We probably could make $1.50 on each sheet. The idea didn't sound bad to me and I said, 'Okay, try it, and let's see how it goes.' Somehow, I didn't think the Feds would get involved. I even thought about borrowing money and putting the stamps up for collateral. Somehow, I didn't think this would be a big deal. Now that I look back, sixteen of us did time and no one earned a nickel!"

All this over a measly three-cent stamp that no one even used! After a while, we parted and I kept thinking he was right. So much trouble was caused by one three-cent stamp that became obsolete in no time as the postal rates continued to rise.

The Rogue

Probably the toughest assignment in police work is to weed out a "rogue cop" — a federal officer, state policeman, city, town, or village officer. The assignment is distasteful to the group who must investigate or arrest the person suspected of being a rogue. Some departments prefer to handle the matter administratively; others will pursue the rogue with every weapon at their command.

I've had my experiences with rogue cops; not only those in various police departments, but right within my own group. It was our policy to investigate these cops in exactly the same way we went after any other violator. Since the man was an insider — one of us — we had to be doubly vigilant because of the suspect's expertise in knowing how we operated, and his own experience with firearms and other equipment.

When information was received that a suspect was a law enforcement officer, a preliminary investigation would be made to try to determine if the person was an innocent victim of a counterfeit note, simply being "setup" or "framed" or if he was, in fact, knowingly becoming involved in a counterfeit operation.

In the larger police departments there are special Internal Affairs units whose duties are to investigate complaints on "wrong cops." Their role is generally something akin to a "devil's advocate." They, out of necessity, proceed on the premise that the accused is wrong and then they must try to prove it. To feed information to any of these special units, on the basis of an unconfirmed accusation by an informant or anyone else, would cause the officer a great disservice. The accusation, true or false, sooner or later would find its way into an official folder and become a permanent record forever, to haunt the officer in his future years with the department.

I was the Special Agent-in-Charge of a U. S. Secret Service Special Detail in New York. This was an anonymous and autonomous group of Special Agents, whose principal duties were to investigate major counterfeiting cases in New York, New Jersey, and in any area that the Director felt needed help. The men working on this detail were chosen for their particular talents, their ability to work undercover, and to handle complex investigations. This detail, out of necessity, had to be a cohesive group of agents with different ethnic backgrounds who could acclimate themselves to every changing condition that existed in our type of work.

As the man in charge, I made it my personal business to become involved in any information that involved a brother officer. I'd make sure that there wasn't any chance of a "white-wash" and to make equally sure that the officer got a fair shake.

We had our share of cases. We won some and we lost some, were in doubt on some and had to remain in a sort of limbo, until the weight of evidence could push them on one side of the fence or the other.

My first experience was a simple enough case. A police detective purchased six new tires for his personal automobile. The man who sold him the tires was a friend who had a shop in the neighborhood. The detective paid for the tires with five $20 bills. When the deposit was made, two of the bills were determined to be counterfeit. The bank forwarded the counterfeit bills to our office. The tire man told us that something had to be wrong; the bills couldn't be counterfeit, because a friend who was a police detective gave them to him.

The following day I interviewed the officer. He was an amiable fellow. He admitted giving the tire man five $20's but couldn't be sure if the two counterfeits were his. I asked him where he got the five $20's and wasn't prepared for the answer he gave me. He said, "I paid a visit to a 'goulash game' and I was paid off in the dark." That terminated the very brief interview and was the subject of a report to his superior officer. He never came to our attention again. It was possible that he did not know the bills were counterfeit, but to walk into a governmental agency and admit he was "on the take" was more than I could stomach. This was a loser I would have preferred not to lose.

There was the detective who was the leader of a group of bandits terrorizing a whole community. His own department was quietly putting the pieces together to form a noose that would forever rid the city and the department of this vicious rogue. At about the time when their case was coming to a head, we arrested a known burglar who passed several counterfeit notes. He eventually cooperated and named the detective as his source for the bills. This dovetailed with the information that the City was working on, and was helpful in convicting the detective for robbery and burglary. He was given a substantial sentence in state court and then a consecutive sentence on the counterfeiting case.

I had an opportunity to talk with our burglar witness after the case. I asked why he agreed to testify against the rogue. He said, "We pulled a lot of jobs together and handled a lot of loot. On one particular job, I asked him what I should do if a cop surprised us while we were doing the job. He said, 'take out your gun and shoot the bastard right between the eyes.' I knew then that this was a madman and I wanted nothing more to do with him." If this case had to be rated as a "winner or loser," I would say this was a winner that I was happy to win.

Another case that came to our attention was a little disconcerting. Ted came to the incorporated village right after the war. He joined the small police department soon after and was a popular officer. He married a local girl and slowly grew with the department. He became a sergeant and five years later became the lieutenant. Now he was one step away from becoming Chief. Normally, this would have taken years to attain, but an unfortunate accident in the line of duty created the opening, and the good village fathers promoted Ted to Chief. He was quite popular with the village people and with the men in his own department. As Chief, he made it his business to delegate much of the responsibility of his office to subordinates; thereby freeing himself for extracurricular activities.

He was seen in the neighboring cities in the company of questionable characters. If asked about it, he could shrug it off by saying it was part of an investigation. Those activities became more varied and his absences were more protracted. He took up with a showgirl and his marriage was going on the rocks.

He came to our attention as the result of the arrest of a counterfeit note passer called Kurt. Kurt wasn't an ordinary passer; in fact, passing counterfeit notes was only a minor part of his depredations. He was a good con-man, swindler and check forger. His introduction into counterfeiting was almost accidental. A fellow swindler owed him some money and offered him counterfeits to clear the debt. Kurt accepted the bogus bills and used them in connection with his con games. When he wanted to impress a potential victim with his affluence, he would light a cigarette with one of the counterfeits. This never failed to impress the "mark."

On one occasion, Kurt attended a cocktail party given by a man who was anxious to enter a "business deal" with Kurt. There were fifteen or twenty people at the affair, which was at a local motel. Kurt, as usual, tried to impress the people by lighting his cigarettes with the $20 bill. Soon after one of his displays, he was quietly approached by Ted, who introduced himself to Kurt. He made no bones about being a police chief and told Kurt that he could see the bills were counterfeit. Kurt was frightened at the prospect of an arrest. His fears were allayed when Ted told him he had no intentions of arresting him. He asked Kurt how many bills he had. Kurt said about "About $700 worth." Ted convinced Kurt that it was in his best interest to surrender the notes immediately. Kurt got the notes and gave them to Ted. Kurt asked Ted what he'd tell the Feds. Ted laughed and said, "The Feds aren't getting these bills. I know what to do with them."

Kurt, of course, didn't surrender all of the counterfeits and was arrested when he continued to pass them. After his arrest he told his story, but identifying Ted was a tough job. We did not know if he was, in fact, a police chief and if he was, we didn't know even what state he worked in. The name Ted helped in running down the suspect. We didn't expect to find many "Chiefs" with that first name. It was a long investigation but we came up with several possibilities, and Kurt picked out the right one.

We only had Kurt's word that he gave the counterfeits to Ted. We had absolutely nothing else to corroborate his story. Ted didn't contact the U. S. Secret Service to surrender any counterfeits. Our investigation showed that he did, indeed, spend little time on his job and did considerable running around with women.

Every one of the particular counterfeits that was passed was worked to see if it could be traced, in some way, to the chief. The results were always negative. We wired Kurt and had him accidentally run into Ted. There was no doubt that they had previously met, but Ted wouldn't say anything that would incriminate himself or would corroborate Kurt's story. To challenge the chief on it would be foolhardy as he could then destroy any counterfeits he might have in his possession. We continued to work every possible angle on the case — but to no avail.

It was decided that Kurt would tell his story to the grand jury and we would be guided by what they decided. Before Grand Jury date, Kurt was stricken with a blood disease and confined to a hospital. He told me on a visit to the hospital that he believed the chief had heard that he had been arrested for counterfeiting, and Ted naturally would avoid any conversation with him. Kurt never got to the grand jury. His illness became worse and he died within a month.

Ted, one morning soon afterwards, walked into the village hall and tendered his resignation to the village fathers. He and his wife had separated. He stated he was anxious to try earning a living in another part of the country. His resignation was accepted and he quietly left the area.

We kept track of him for many months. He managed to get a job and earn a fairly decent living. The notes never hit the street again. There came a time when it was necessary to statistically close the case; always with the reservation that it would be reopened if a lead, however slight, was received on the ex-chief.

I had mixed emotions on this one. If the Chief were innocent then we were certainly not responsible for doing him any harm. If he were guilty, then he would not be the first man to beat us. We felt secure in the thought that he could only do it once.

"El Techo" was a large Latin dance hall in the heart of one of America's largest cities. This establishment catered to the many Latinos who lived and worked in the city. While it did a brisk business every night, the weekends brought customers in from all over the state. The attraction was usually a popular Latin band and a lot of single women who patronized the hall, hoping to find suitable partners.

One morning we received two counterfeit $20 notes from the bank. The transmittal slip indicated that the notes were taken in over the weekend at "El Techo."

This would have been a routine case if the original inquiry had indicated the management had no information on the source of the note. Instead, the manager said he had some information. He believed a police officer passed the notes at the establishment.

I interviewed the manager and learned that no one really knew who took in the notes, but the word among the employees was that an officer who frequented the dance hall passed the notes. It became apparent that no one was going to point a finger at the suspected officer, so the next best thing was to try to at least identify the officer and proceed from there. We made several appearances at the club to try to have someone pick out the police officer. It was necessary to work with the police department's Special Investigations Squad in order to properly handle the case if/when the officer was identified.

On the fourth night, a well-dressed dapper man of Latino extraction entered the dance hall, and paid for his admission with a genuine $20 bill. Several minutes later, one of the employees told us that this man was the police officer.

We confronted the officer, identified ourselves and questioned him about the counterfeits. He admitted he was a plainclothes police officer, and that he patronized the club on the night the counterfeits were passed. He even recalled changing a $20 bill at the bar. He said everyone at the place knew he was a police officer, and that his only source of money was from his paycheck and no where else. All his checks were cashed at the bank. He was irate, annoyed and angry, and resented our approach.

The police officers working with me made their report to their supervisor. It was decided that the officer would be called before a board of inquiry. When I heard about it, I spoke to the supervisor and tried to assure him that we had nothing on this officer. He was merely identified as an officer who was a steady customer; not as the man who passed the bills. I was against taking any kind of action against the officer. The superior used the classic cliché, "Where there's smoke — there's fire."

Several days later, an arrest was made of a Latino who not only was an active distributor, but was also a passer of counterfeit notes. While he was being questioned, I looked through his effects and found an imitation police badge. I picked it up and couldn't help but think that it could fool someone in the dark. It suddenly hit me — perhaps this man was our "cop."

I went into the room where he was questioned and interjected a few questions of my own. The prisoner sidestepped and avoided answers to most of the incriminating questions. I lied and told him that one night we followed him to El Techo. I asked if he went there often. He said yes, he liked the place and generally went on a Friday night. He admitted being there on the night the notes were passed. His description and that of the police officer were quite similar.

I immediately dispatched two men to El Techo to get the owners and the cashiers to come down right away. I also had a representative of the police department Special Investigations Squad join us.

When they all arrived, I had them view the prisoner and asked each employee if they knew the prisoner. One person did not know him and the other three said, "He is the policeman who comes every Friday." Then the city officer who was working with us joined me in questioning the prisoner. The prisoner admitted passing the two notes at El Techo.

I was overjoyed at the prospect of telling the superior officer that his cop was cleared. At our meeting the next day we did a lot of talking and when I left police headquarters, I wasn't sure that the combined efforts of myself and the city officer were sufficient to convince the superior officer that his officer was clean. I left his office with the cliché still ringing in my ears: "In this business, where there's smoke, there's fire." Anyhow, this was another loser that I was happy to lose.

During a particular busy period of counterfeit note passing, our agents identified a man named Dave who had passed counterfeit notes in three different places. He owned a record shop but was not around when the agents stopped at his shop. Since he lived near the police precinct, the agents stopped at the detective bureau and asked the officers there to pick up Dave in the event they could locate him.

They found him on a Friday afternoon and notified our office. Two agents had the warrant. A detective turned Dave over to the agents, and the agents proceeded to the office to process him. En route, the conversation went like this:

Agent: "Dave, we have you identified passing notes in three places. You gonna tell us where you got them?"

Dave: "No."

Agent: "Why?"

Dave: "You guys are all alike."
Agent: "What do you mean?"
Dave: "Cops are cops and you all stink."
Agent: "Since I'm accused of stinking, what's your beef?"
Dave: "You don't trust a cop. I learned that years ago and if I stuck with it, I wouldn't be in trouble."
Agent: "C'mon Dave, you sound like you want to say something."
Dave: "Everyone wants to know where the notes came from. They beg me to tell and when I do, they tell me to keep my mouth shut."
Agent: "Who told you to keep your mouth shut?"
Dave: "You want to know? Well, I'll tell you. The detective who locked me up, that's who. You want to know why? Well, I'll tell you, and you might as well fall off the chair and then tell me to keep my mouth shut. He asked me where I got the counterfeits. He really wanted to know. He wanted to be a good cop. Well, I told him. I said your captain gave them to me, yeah, your boss, Al, the famous cop who keeps on getting medals."
Agent: "Hold everything. You had better go in and see the boss and tell him what you just told me."

The agent came into my office and brought me up-to-date on what happened. I talked with Dave and he got around to telling me the whole story. He had known Captain Al for some time. They went bouncing around together. Things weren't too good at Dave's shop and he found himself in financial straits. He told the captain about his problems and was quite surprised when the captain said he might be able to help him. He met him one night and asked Dave if he would be willing to pass some counterfeit notes. He went on to say he had about $5,000 worth of the stuff that he would let Dave have for $1,000. He figured Dave could double that for himself if he got rid of them. Dave said he couldn't buy them as he didn't have any money. Captain Al agreed to wait for the money until Dave got rid of the counterfeits. Dave agreed and Captain Al went into the station house and came out five minutes later, carrying a package. He gave the package to Dave who looked into it and found it full of counterfeit $20s.

Dave stated he decided he would try to pass the bills instead of trying to sell them. In this way, he figured he could make far more money. There came a time when he decided to go out passing. He went out of town and was quite successful in disposing of some of the counterfeits. The following day he decided to get rid of some of the notes locally. He passed about a half a dozen notes in the neighborhood on people he knew. When the notes were returned, most of the victims identified Dave.

I asked Dave if Captain Al knew of his arrest. He said he didn't know but felt sure that the detective who arrested him would tell the captain. If the captain had found out, we felt we would never be able to corroborate Dave's story. I immediately notified the Chief in Charge of the Special Internal Investigations Bureau, who handled complaints about police. He made inquiries through his own sources and learned that Captain Al was off duty and would not return for a few days.

In checking the captain's name through our files, we found we had a card on him. This card indicated that our office questioned him several years before when he tried to change a $100 at a bank. The bill was counterfeit and he insisted he received it from another bank when he cashed his paycheck. This could not be proven as no one at the bank could remember the transaction. Nothing further was done at the time. Here again, we faced the "where there's smoke, there's fire" routine.

It was agreed that Dave would contact Captain Al the next day at his home and tell him he had some trouble. He would then try to make a meet with him. We would wire Dave and then be guided by what we heard on the tape.

Dave called Captain Al, the next morning. Al agreed to meet Dave at a local bar. This meeting was covered by our people and members of the police internal investigation unit, all of whom were unknown to the captain. The meeting went off as scheduled, after which we played back the conversation between the two men:

Dave: "Hi, Captain."
Al: "Hello, Davey boy."
Dave: "Boy, have I got trouble."
Al: "What's the matter?
Dave: "I got busted on those bills."
Al: "Did they get them all?"
Dave: "No. Some guy fingered me and I got bagged."
Al: "So, what are you worried about? Nothing is going to happen."
Dave: "Nothing? How come?"
Al: "The Feds will be notified. An agent will come to see you. Tell him to go screw. Tell him you're a businessman and you got the bills in connection with your business. Don't worry, they don't have a case. They can't do a thing."
Dave: "Al, are you sure? You make it sound so easy."
Al: "Because I know how these things work. I worked with the Feds before. I'm telling you there's no case, so stop worrying. The case will be closed. You can't help it if you get stuck with some bills."

Dave: "Al, you know I had to destroy all the rest of the bills."
Al: That's okay, don't worry. "
Dave: "What do you mean, don't worry. How am I going to pay you for them?"
Al: "That's all right, pay me when you get it."
Dave: "But Al, a thousand dollars is a lot of money. I'll never be able to get it. "
Al: "Pay me a little at a time. Before you know it, you'll be paid up. "
Dave: Okay, Al, thanks. Do you have any more bills?"
Al: "Not right now. You'd better lay low till this case is over with. "
Dave: "Thanks Al. I'll see you."
Al: "Okay, Dave, take it easy. Remember, they don't have a case."
Dave: "Okay, so long."
Al: "I'll see you."

After the tape was played, we knew it was all over for Al. I couldn't help but think of the countless times he was decorated for heroism, of how we had worked together over the years on various assignments of mutual interest. He was arrested later in the day, arraigned and made bail. He was suspended from the department and vowed he would fight the case through all the courts. We allowed his attorneys to listen to the tapes, after which they decided to have him plead guilty.

Several months later, Captain Al was in the courtroom. This time, on the other side of the fence. He heard them sentence him to a term in the Federal penitentiary. Now he'd have enough time to reflect on what makes a respected police officer throw away a lifetime of hard work and accomplishment, to make a fast buck on something that could only be a one-way ticket to oblivion.

It's bad enough in this business to have to investigate or arrest a brother police officer. The only worse thing is to get information that one of the men in your own group is "wrong." This has to be a specter that haunts every police supervisor.

We had just finished working a very difficult and very successful case. An agent working undercover with an informant was successful in making a $100,000 purchase of counterfeit notes. It was a very difficult case because the people handling the notes were suspicious. They came a long distance and were accepting the agent on the basis of the recommendation of the informant. Since there wasn't any money paid in advance, and since the original order was for a quarter of a million, the counterfeiters decided to change their plans. They planned to deliver $100,000 on the first delivery and after they were paid, they would arrange to deliver the remainder of the notes.

As the evening wore on, we could only hope to get the hundred thousand and gamble that after the arrests someone would tell us where the rest of the money was.

Practically the whole squad was working on the case and everyone was putting in extremely long hours. The delivery finally came off in the early morning hours. The $100,000 was seized, four prisoners were arrested and a mock arrest was made of the undercover agent and the informant. Later in the morning, one of the prisoners cooperated and gave us the address of where the other $100,000 was. We went to this apartment, which was empty, and secured the premises; we left an agent there to make sure no one entered to take the money until a search warrant was obtained.

It takes two things to make a thief — there has to be the opportunity and the desire. Unless the two are present at the same time, the crime is not committed.

Due to a shortage of manpower, I left the agent at the apartment longer than I wanted; but I did not have anyone to relieve him, so he stayed at the apartment for ten or more hours. The agent was nicknamed "Sparks" for his knowledge of electronics.

Sparks was married, had two children, had about five years service and was transferred to us from another federal agency. He was raised in a depressed part of the country; in spite of a tough life, he was able to get through high school, and through the generosity of a family friend he was able to make it through college.

He had a natural talent for police work and was considered a better than average agent. He was well paid for the work he was doing, and managed to support a family and also did a little cheating on the side. Nevertheless, if he was so inclined to cross over the line, he found himself in an excellent position. There was an unspecified amount of counterfeit money in the apartment; he was alone with it and there was no one to say how much there was; he had a car on the street and could have moved the money very easily. There certainly was the opportunity — was there the desire?

Later that afternoon, a search warrant was issued for the apartment. The counterfeits were found and it appeared that there was well over a hundred thousand dollars secreted on the premise. The seized money was taken to the office, and the prisoners were processed and placed in jail pending arraignment the following Monday morning.

On Monday morning it was necessary to pick up the prisoners early to get them to court. The informant also had to be present, to make it appear that he was also being arraigned.

Vince, the informant in the case, stopped in my office right after everyone left for court. He looked like he had something on his mind and I was afraid he was looking for more money. It took him a few minutes to get started.

Then he casually asked me if I hand-picked the men on my detail. I said, "Yes, I do. I try to pick a certain type who can do this sort of work." He didn't say anything else. I waited and then said, "Why do you ask?" He said, "Oh, nothing. Maybe some day I'll tell you, it can wait." I said, "Vince, you have something on your mind and I'm not waiting till some day. You and I are going to leave this building, go out for a cup of coffee, and you're going to tell me what's troubling you and, above all, you're going to level with me." We left and found a secluded spot in the restaurant.

Motto: "Okay, shoot. What is it?"
Vince: "I don't know where to start. "
Motto: "Start at the beginning."
Vince: "Do you know you have a thief in your outfit?"
Motto: "No, of course not!"
Vince: "Well, you do. "
Motto: "Who?"
Vince: "Sparks."
Motto: "What are you saying?"
Vince: "Sparks is a thief. You want it from the beginning? Here it is. The beginning was only yesterday. After all the arrests were made, I was put into the back room by myself. Sparks came in and said, 'Did you get any?' I said, 'What do you mean?' He said, 'Any of the stuff.' I said 'No, did you?' He said 'I grabbed a bundle for myself. Will you help me get rid of it?' I said, 'Yeah.' He said not to mention it to anyone, and gave me his home phone number saying, 'Give me a call tonight and we'll make a deal.' Vince then took out a piece of paper with Spark's home phone number on it."

I 'm not easily shaken , but I have to admit that this really got to me. The thought never occurred to me that one of my own men could be a thief. I needed time to think. I told Vince not to speak to anyone about it and not to talk with Sparks until I could work something out. I asked him how far he would go. He said "All the way. I don't owe Sparks anything. You and me have done a lot of jobs, and I can't figure out why Sparks couldn't realize that my loyalty is to you and certainly not to him." I said, "We might have to make you go through with a deal, and then arrest him when he delivers." Vince said, "I'll go all the way, and you can depend on me." I then asked Vince to disappear for several hours until I could make some plans.

I was now in a turmoil. Was it possible that there was someone else in on it with Sparks? If so, who? This was a close-knit outfit of men who spent long hours together, who traveled all over the country together, who visited each other with their families. How could you investigate one and not let the others know?

The first thing I had to do was notify headquarters. I had a conversation with the Deputy Director who gave me the answer I expected. He said "Treat Sparks like any other case and we'll supply all the help you need. If you can prove he's wrong, lock him up!"

The next person I told was my assistant. He was as shocked as I was. He was ready to do whatever was necessary to learn if Sparks was the victim of an overzealous informant, or if he was really wrong. We agreed that we would have to work alone with Vince after hours until we saw the whole picture. We would have to handle our routine work in the usual manner, be very careful about what assignments we gave Sparks, and then try to work the case without any help until we were sure Vince was leveling with us and could be sure that Sparks was a rogue.

We arranged to meet Vince late that night and we told him to call Sparks at his home. We brought a recorder with us so we could get the conversation down on tape. Inwardly, I was hoping that Sparks would vindicate himself right from the start.

Vince made the call and the results did not need any explanation. While it didn't last but a minute or so, it told a whole story:

Vince: "Hi, buddy."
Sparks: "That you, Vince?"
Vince: "Yeah, buddy. This is the first chance I got to talk with you. Can't be too careful."
Sparks: "That's right."
Vince: "You say you got some stuff from the other night?"
Sparks: "Yeah. They're real good."
Vince: "How much did you get?"
Sparks: "About 30 grand, take or leave a few."
Vince: "Boy, that's great. I got some friends from out of town that could sure use some."
Sparks: "Well, you got the man who can handle it"
Vince: "Let me call my people and firm up a deal. I'll call you just as soon as I know. "
Sparks: "Okay, make it snappy. I can use some 'bread.'"
Vince: "I can too. I should have a deal in a few days"
Sparks: "Don't mention anything to any of the guys. I know you're friendly with some of them."
Vince: "No chance, baby, I'll see you."
Sparks: "Right. Take care."

Vince hung up and said, "You convinced now?" I guess I must have had tears in my eyes. He knew the answer without my saying anything. I then called the Deputy Chief at his home and told him that I was ready to bring the case to a head. I said it would be necessary to bring agents in from out of town. Each agent would have to be questioned to determine whether or not he knew or had ever worked with Sparks.

The list of agents who went to school with Sparks would have to be examined, and these agents would have to be eliminated. We figured now that the die was cast. Sparks would be extremely vigilant. He would look for any sign that would indicate that Vince was double-crossing him. He would undoubtedly be carrying his gun. We could only speculate whether he would try to use it if he were cornered. It was something that had to be considered and since time was on our side, we had to take every precaution.

On Wednesday, we had our plans pretty well made. Vince would contact Sparks on Thursday and would make a "meet" for Friday night at which time Vince would get delivery of the counterfeits and the case could be wrapped up.

Vince called Sparks and told him he had made arrangements to swap the counterfeit $30,000 for a kilo of heroin. He asked Sparks if he could handle it. Sparks seemed delighted. He said he had connections that would take it off his hands. Vince said that after he got the counterfeits he would take them out of town to a relative and would return with the kilo of "H." He expected he could finish the deal in about three days. Sparks was happy and suggested that they meet at a sidewalk cafe in the downtown section of the city at eight o'clock Friday night.

I arranged for a suite of rooms in a midtown hotel that we could use for a command post and a place for the out-of-town agents to check in. It was necessary for my assistant and I to carry on our normal duties for another two days. It was obvious that Sparks was looking for anything at the office that would seem out of the ordinary. He listened to every conversation and spent an awful lot of time at the office, supposedly doing paperwork.

On Thursday afternoon, some of the men went to lunch together. Generally they ate in a neighborhood restaurant and sometimes left their weapons in their desk. As soon as they left, I checked Sparks' desk and found his service revolver in the upper drawer. I took it out, went into my office and filed the firing pin down to a point where the weapon would not be able to shoot. When this was accomplished, I returned the weapon to his desk and was thankful that it was done without anyone seeing me.

The next day I got to the hotel early and made the final plans. Each man was shown a photo of Sparks and had an opportunity to visit the area where the exchange was to take place. I then returned to the office and tried to run the shop as casually as possible. Sparks seemed very nervous and tried not to miss a word that was said around the office.

In the afternoon I had reason to leave my office for a few minutes. While I was gone, Vince wanted to contact me. He called my number; a senior agent, Jim, answered my phone and immediately recognized Vince's voice. He asked Vince what he wanted. Vince said he had some problems and had to contact me. Jim hung up and said he'd give me the message. Jim then located me and gave me the message, then added, "Carmine, what the hell is going on around here? Something is wrong and I can't put my finger on it. You have not been yourself and we can't figure it out." I said, "We? Who else feels that way?" He said, "Eddie and I." This really threw me. I couldn't bluff any more. If any of the other men started talking, Sparks would hear about it, become suspicious, and the case would go out the window. I said, "Jim, something is wrong — very wrong. Nothing involving you or Eddie, mind you. Just do me a favor, grab Eddie and get out of the office; go somewhere and don't talk to anyone. Call me at six o'clock tonight at the Avon Hotel. I'll have you and Eddie come up and give you the whole story. Remember, grab Eddie and not a word — just leave like you were heading out on an assignment. That's all I can say right now, so get moving." Jim left, grabbed Eddie, and they were gone in a flash.

I was extremely disturbed that the men could recognize that some thing was wrong. I felt that I was running the shop the same as always and couldn't understand why my feelings were showing through.

Just before five o'clock that afternoon, I walked into the squad room and said I was leaving and would be home in an hour or so. I left and met my assistant and the out-of-town agents at the hotel. Vince came up and after a final briefing, he called Sparks, just after six o'clock. Sparks assured Vince that he had the stuff and would meet him at the appointed place.

At seven-thirty the men were all at their assigned spots, covering the sidewalk restaurant. At five minutes after eight, Sparks drove by and a few minutes later he double-parked his car, got out and talked to Vince. Vince accompanied Sparks to the car. There was another man in the car; a narcotics agent who was a friend of Sparks. After a short conversation, Sparks went to the trunk of the car and took out a package and handed it to Vince. At that moment, agents closed in from several directions. Sparks saw them and immediately announced that everything was all right; that he was a U. S. Secret Service agent. One man said "*Was*, is right!" and put the cuffs on him. The other man was also arrested — a counterfeit note was found in his pocket.

They were brought back to the office. I had Sparks brought into my office. He had tears in his eyes. I asked him if he had anything to say. He said, "Nothing, just that I know I let you down." I said, "You sure did. Not only me, but your wife, kids, relatives, and everyone who believed in you."
Everything that happened after that was anticlimactic. The loose ends were quickly tied up. There wan't any way that Sparks or his friend could offer any cooperation with the government. We knew how he got his notes and were successful in preventing him from distributing them.

He and his friend chose to go to trial separately. We tried Sparks. Even he knew it was an open-and-shut case. He took the stand, lied, and tried to make all the wrong things right. His defense was a sham and the jury saw through it. One hour after they got the case, they found him guilty. His friend went the same route with the same results. In due time, both men were sentenced to prison terms.

It could only be described as a shallow victory with everyone losing and it spelled the end of a case, a career, and two families.

There was the usual publicity that comes when a rogue cop is arrested. In this case, the underworld reaped extra dividends. Both men had been very active agents and were involved as undercover agents and witnesses in many cases. Practically all these indictments had to be 'nolle prossed' as each of these men were now tainted. Several prisoners requested to have their cases reviewed because Sparks or his friend was the principal witness against them.

Many a drug peddler and counterfeiter walking the streets today owes their freedom to opportunity and desire that come together in the mind of an officer at precisely the same moment, making him a rogue.

The Fruit Basket

I had been assigned to accompany Richard M. Nixon on his campaign swing through New England as he was running for re-election as Vice-President. Keeping up with him was quite a challenge, as he made a whirlwind tour of the entire New England area: a stop here, a long speech somewhere else. His last day in New England was spent in and around the Boston area. After shaking hands with practically everyone in the suburbs, he headed for his main and final appearance in the city of Boston proper.

He gave a rip-roaring address and when he was finished, a man carrying a large basket of fruit asked for permission to present the gift to the Vice President. We examined the basket and allowed the man to make his presentation. Mr. Nixon thanked the man, and we took the basket from Mr. Nixon and placed it in the trunk of my car for safekeeping.

Shortly thereafter, we began the drive back to New York City where Mr. Nixon was to attend a St. Patrick's Day dinner. Upon our arrival in the city, my day ended, and I asked the Special Agent in Charge about the fruit basket which was still in my trunk. He said, "You may as well take it home and enjoy it."

By the time I finally arrived home, my family had gone to bed for the night and everyone was sound asleep. I placed the basket on the kitchen table.

The next morning when I walked into the kitchen, everyone was happily dipping into the basket for his or her favorite fruit. My wife asked me where it came from. I told her it was presented to the Vice President in Boston. She asked, "How did it end up here?" With a straight face I replied, "You don't think we'd let him have it, do you? It could be poisoned!"

At this point she said, "Why in heaven's name did you bring it here?" For the next several minutes I was dodging oranges, apples, grapes, kumquats — even a pineapple.

Sometimes you can learn more at home than in all the sophisticated training sessions. I wouldn't trade those minutes of laughter, smiles, and love for anything!

"Tiki"

Every so often, someone comes to the attention of the authorities and becomes a police matter; yet they remain very much of an enigma. They walk a thin line, managing to keep one step ahead of the law and from arrest. One such man was Turendino Edward Sanchez, better known as "Tiki." Tiki invariably claimed Puerto Rico as his birthplace whenever he was questioned by the police; however, most of his close friends and associates knew he had actually been born in a small village in Colombia. The authorities were never quite able to determine just how and when he had arrived in New York City. He didn't have any family or relatives there, and his name wasn't on any of the official records, except for the few entries in the police blotter for minor arrests. Tiki was young, brash and handsome and had a reputation as a ladies' man in the neighborhood. He was equally fluent in English as he was in Spanish, his native tongue.

Tiki had close ties with the Latino population in the Bronx and was a much-feared man among his peers. They feared him for good reason: he carried a .45-caliber semiautomatic handgun and he had a bad temper. He didn't hesitate to use the gun if sufficiently incensed. He was also quick with his hands and was continually getting into fights with people who disagreed with him or incurred his displeasure. He always seemed to have enough money for his own purposes, which included being a familiar sight at the neighborhood gambling games, though he was never known to hold a regular job.

Tiki maintained an apartment in the Fort Apache section of the Bronx. The building looked dilapitated on the outside, but inside, his apartment was well furnished and appointed. He owed the appearance of his apartment to his current "love interest," Elena. Elena was a girl he had known back in Colombia and Tiki had sent her a ticket and some money to join him in New York. She was an excellent seamstress and earned a decent living working in a local garment factory. Elena would have been happy to settle down with Tiki, work hard, raise a family, and perhaps buy a house someday away from the stresses and temptations of the city. Tiki had other ideas.

He told Elena to have patience because he would make her rich one day, so she wouldn't have to work so hard. He resolved that one day he would organize the Latinos into a syndicate that he would control. With him at the helm of his new powerful syndicate, Gringos would no longer be able to push him or his people around. His plan was to have his people steal, then dispose of the loot among their own people, keeping the profits — not only from thefts but also from narcotics, street lottery, and any other kind of illegal operation. He said the trouble with his people was that they did not stick together and they all, in one way or another, worked for the hated Gringo. The Latinos took most of the chances committing crime, but they gave "the play" to the "Yonkees," and when it came time for someone to go to jail it was always his people who went; never the Gringo.

Tiki tried desperately to put an organization together, but he only got lip service from most of the people he approached with his plan. They said they thought it was a good idea and would consider it; not because they believed in him, but because they feared him and were not anxious to incur his displeasure by disagreeing with him.

One day Tiki bought a car from a group of local youths who had stolen it from a parking lot. It was this action that set into motion a series of events that eventually brought Tiki to my attention. Tiki gave the thieves very little argument over the time and expense he would have to incur to legitimize the vehicle. Tiki hid the car in a friend's garage until he could arrange for a buyer who could supply him with a counterfeit bill of sale. When he wasn't successful in his neighborhood, he broadened his search. He heard about a fellow countryman in New Jersey who operated a printing business and who was known to undertake some shady requests on the side. Tiki figured that this was exactly what he was looking for. He was certain that he could obtain whatever bogus paper he needed from this man.

Tiki stuffed his .45 into his belt and headed for the print shop, which was located in a single-family house in a lightly populated neighborhood. At first, he had some difficulty finding the address because he expected that it would be in the business sector of the town. He approached the house and rang the doorbell. He was pleasantly surprised when it was answered by Tomaso, a man he had met at a dance several months before in New York City. Tomaso invited Tiki into the residential part of the house where he offered him a drink. During their long conversation about old friends and current endeavors, Tomaso invited Tiki down into the cellar to show him the shop.

The shop was cluttered with papers, inks, and machinery. Tomaso was proud of his shop and took great pains to explain the workings to Tiki, who had never been inside a print shop before. Speaking in their native language, Tomaso told Tiki he was equipped to do almost any kind of printing, since he made his own negatives and plates and did the printing himself. He continued, saying that he didn't have any employees other than his wife who occasionally assisted him with a large printing order. He then took Tiki to a corner of the cellar that had been partitioned off to make a darkroom for processing of the negatives. He explained that the first step in printing was to make a negative. This was done, he said, by taking a picture of the item to be copied. He had a large copy camera in the corner of the room and proceeded to demonstrate how it worked.

Tomasso tore a page out of a magazine and snapped a picture of it. He then led Tiki into the darkroom and showed him how the film was developed to produce a negative. He removed a paper-thin sheet of aluminum from an envelope, placed the negative on top of it, and exposed it to an extremely bright light. He then dipped the plate in a chemical solution for a short time. Removing it from the solution, Tomaso cleaned and dried it, and then stepped over to an offset printing press. He wrapped the plate around a cylinder on the press, checked the ink supply, stocked the machine with paper, turned a switch, sending the whells in motion. The machine bounced into action, spewing out copies of the magazine page faster than Tiki could count.

When Tiki compared the printed page and the original magazine page, he was astonished, He couldn't believe copying and printing could be so easy. Tomaso was beaming. He was pleased that Tiki admired his craftmanship. Tiki removed his hat, wiped his brow, and continued to examine the copy. It occurred to him that this was the set-up he had been looking for. He asked Tomaso about the type of work he did.

Tomaso replied that he printed a lot of business cards, fliers, and brochures. Tiki was in deep thought even as he listened to Tomaso and asked his questions. The ideas were just racing through his head. This machine, this set-up, Tomaso doing the printing with no one else involved…lottery, identification, birth certificates, army discharges, driver's licenses, vehicle registrations and bills of sale, dirty pictures, maybe checks and even, who knows, maybe even the gringo's own dirty dollars. This was the kind of thing Tiki had dreamed of all his life! An operation run for and by Latinos with Tiki at the head! There was, however, the practical side that had to be dealt with right away. Could he get Tomaso to go along with him? Could he control Tomaso? Who else would have to be brought in? Could they handle the marketing and distribution? How much of a cut would Tomaso want? Could he be trusted? He would have to feel Tomaso out to find out if he would go along.

Tomaso interrupted Tiki's reflections by asking him the purpose of his visit. Tiki laughed and said he had been so interested in Tomaso's operation that he had completely forgotten about why he had come in the first place. He told Tomaso about the stolen car he had purchased and that he didn't have a bill of sale or a title for it. He said he had an old title certificate for another car and wondered if Tomaso could copy it for him. Tiki watched Tomaso closely for any sign of reluctance. Tomaso looked at the certificate and said he could duplicate it very easily. He said he would simply prepare a negative of the old bill of sale then opaque out the typed information describing the vehicle, motor number, color, license number, etc. The print made from the negative then would be blank and Tiki could describe any vehicle he wished. Tomaso said that once he made the plate, he could print as many copies as needed. He said he could do the same thing with the state title certificates. The only problem with the title certificates was they were printed on a special security paper, and that would be difficult to get. He said he knew of some security paper outlets and he would see how closely he could match the paper stock used on the genuine titles.

Tiki was pleased with what he heard. It was even better than he had dared hope for. He told Tomaso to take his time and that he would contact him in a few days to see how things were progressing. Before he left he gave Tomaso some money to cover his initial expenses. Tomaso accepted the money without any hesitation and shook Tiki's hand.

On the way back to New York, Tiki mulled over his meeting with Tomaso. He was satisfied with Tomaso's expertise and knew that this relationship could be the means by which he would become wealthy and be in a position to gain power and influence and help his fellow Latinos. His mind was racing at full speed as he thought of all the ways he could use Tomaso and his shop to full advantage.

As soon as he reached the city, Tiki contacted the controllers of the various street lotteries. His plan was to take over all the ticket printing and make sure that his people were the ones to benefit. He had no trouble convincing some of the operators to use his "company" for the printing — he promised he could do the job for less money and he ensured them of prompt delivery.

Several days later, Tiki went to Tomaso's house again. Tomaso told him that he had found a paper stock almost identical to that of the original titles. He removed a cardboard box from a metal locker. He opened it and showed Tiki several thousand blank auto titles that looked as good as the originals. Tiki was amazed — he couldn't believe his eyes (or his good fortune). He decided to let Tomaso in on his plan to see whether he would be agreeable to it or not. He asked Tomaso if he would be interested in being a partner in a business in which Tiki would obtain the orders and Tomaso would handle the printing. He could see that Tomaso was a little reluctant, but as he offered no objection, Tiki continued, "Tomaso, my friend, listen to me. The old way was to fight the gringo using violence — a gun, knife, club, or a bomb. That was dangerous and stupid. What we have to do is use our heads, and I think

I know how. We fight him with paper — yes, paper. We hit him where it hurts him the most — in the pocketbook. We will make the gringo dog eat his own paper — we will make lottery tickets, checks, driver's licenses, ownership cards — any kind of paper to get the money from the greedy gringo. We choke him with our paper." With a toothy grin, he continued and spoke a little softer and with conviction, "Tomaso, how do like my idea? But we must not be too hungry. We must not involve too many people. I know how to run this deal and I want to play it safe. You and I will work alone. You will print the items and I will get rid of them. We will be partners and no else will be in with us. Or, if you like, I'll pay you a straight salary and I will handle the sales." He stopped talking and looked Tomaso in the face. "What do you say —partners?" He waited for an answer for what seemed an eternity.

Tomaso finally replied by saying that his business was almost paid for and he was clearing about $200 a week without killing himself doing it. He also said he didn't have any particular hate for the gringo. He said the only people he wanted to help were himself and his family. The rest of the people would have to fend for themselves. Although he didn't say so, Tomaso wasn't sure that he fully trusted his new-found friend.

Tiki offered Tomaso another deal. Instead of the 50–50 split, he would put Tomaso on a straight salary — $500 a week, guaranteed. Tomaso would print whatever Tiki requested. In between Tiki's jobs, Tomaso could take care of his usual business. The $500 a week caught Tomaso's attention — he accepted Tiki's offer on the spot.

Tiki said he had three conditions that Tomaso had to adhere to: first, was that Tomaso would only accept legitimate printing assignments from his other customers; two, he would never tell anyone that he was working for Tiki; and three, he must give absolute priority to the lottery tickets which had to be delivered no later than on a Monday night.

Tomaso agreed to the conditions and Tiki gave him $500 to cover his time on the completed titles. Tomaso was delighted to get the money. He felt it was the easiest $500 he had ever earned. They shook hands and Tiki promised to be in touch within in a few days. Before leaving, he told Tomaso to give him the plates and negatives for the titles. Tomaso told him that he had destroyed them the night before. Tiki replied that in the future he expected to have all the materials turned over to him. He explained he did not want them around the shop and wanted to be sure they were destroyed. Tomaso said he understood and any future plates, negatives, or other materials would be saved and given to Tiki for disposal.

Tiki returned to the city, took the box of titles to his apartment, removed a dozen from the box, put them into an envelope, and went to a local bar where a lot of his friends hung out. He let it be known that he had some auto titles for sale, and within two hours had sold the dozen for $100 each.

He could have sold more, but he knew if he distributed too many, the price would tumble. Nevertheless, he took orders and promised future delivery to those who put down a deposit. He didn't want it to look too easy.

Tiki took pleasure in knowing that he had enough blank titles to supply the car thieves for years. He also realized an added prestige, by providing the means for the thieves to make a few hundred extra dollars by including the title and a bill of sale when they sold the stolen cars. It was only a start, but Tiki felt he was on the way to taking revenge on the lousy gringo; some gringos were losing their cars and other gringos were buying them and in the middle were Tiki and his people making the profit.

Two weeks after Tiki went into the "title business," a young man, one of the local "car dealers," had been picked up by the police and questioned about a stolen car. They had been unable to charge him for lack of evidence and he was released a few hours later. When Tiki heard about the arrest, he became very uneasy because he had sold several titles to the young man and he wasn't sure whether he had cooperated with the police. One night soon after the arrest, Tiki stopped the boy and told him to get into the car. Tiki drove him to a deserted part of town. He asked him what he had told the police. The boy said he hadn't cooperated or said anything. Tiki said he didn't believe him because no one could get off that easy selling stolen cars. The boy became angry and started to talk back to Tiki. Tiki took it for a couple of minutes, then pulled the .45 from his belt, cocked it, and placed it at the boy's head. "One more word from you and you die." The frightened boy begged for his life. Tiki did a good job of pistol whipping him and threw him out of the car with a warning that the next time he would kill him.

On his way back home, Tiki thought it would be a good idea to dispose of the remaining titles and his gun. He knew that if the boy had "ratted him out" he would undoubtedly be getting a visit from the police. He stopped and called home. Elena answered the telephone; she said there hadn't been any phone calls or visitors. Tiki was still uneasy so he hid the gun in the tire well of his car and left the car some distance from the apartment and took a taxi from there to within a block of his apartment building. He then called Elena once more to make sure no one was waiting for him.

As soon as he got home he hurriedly gathered the remaining car titles and bills of sale and stuffed them into a box. Elena knew the look on his face; she knew better than to question him when he was like this. She simply accepted his irrational actions, and waited until he decided to tell her what was going on. She was the dutiful wife, ready to obey his every command. Tiki took the box and went up to the roof top, jumped over to the next building, and made his way down through that building and exited through a back entrance, and across several back lots until he reached another street.

Tiki returned to his car and drove around aimlessly. He needed time to clear his head and think. Here he was, ready to embark on a major league caper that would score him a fortune, and one stupid mistake by someone he was dealing with could bring the police to his home and jeopardize the entire setup. He realized that he couldn't use his apartment to store the items Tomaso was printing for him. He needed to find another place, one that was known only to himself. He decided to rent another apartment. Under no condition would he take anyone else there — not even the muchachas that he was seeing on the side.

The next day he spent several hours looking for a furnished apartment outside his own neighborhood. The prices were high, but he knew he could afford it because the lottery ticket operation would be giving him a fairly decent income. He finally decided on a small studio apartment on the east side of town. He paid the required deposit and a month's rent in advance, telling the manager that his job required him to be on the road a lot so he would be gone for days at a time. This apartment was a place to stay when he was in New York.

Later that evening he returned home and told Elena that he had to get rid of some things because some kid might talk to the police about him. Knowing better than to ask questions, she quietly accepted what he said. She tried to caution him to be careful, but she knew her warnings would only fall on deaf ears.

The next day, Tiki went to Tomaso's shop to pick up that week's lottery tickets. Tomaso was busy with some legitimate printing, but was happy to see Tiki. He had printed some blank birth certificates and military discharge papers. Tiki was pleased with the work and gave Tomaso some driver's licenses to duplicate. Tomaso said he would try to have them ready by the following week. Tiki paid him for the completed work and said that he would see him in five or six days. When Tiki left, a new plan was taking shape in his head.

He now had several different ID's. It was time to put his paper to the test. It could be filled out in any name and would be considered excellent identification. But for what? To cash checks? That was it! He would get Tomaso to print checks, and he would make a package deal —counterfeit checks and the identification to go with it. No one could get into trouble if they had the proper identification. How to get specimen checks? He figured that shouldn't be a problem — Steal them? Buy them? Print them up? After some thought, he entered a local bank and asked to purchase a certified check for $60. The check was made payable to him. He then went back to his neighborhood and talked to an acquaintance, Umberto, who worked for a small electrical supply company. He asked Umberto if he could get a couple of the company's blank checks for him. Umberto said he could easily get a couple from the back of the checkbook because the girl who worked in the office generally left everything out when she went to lunch. He promised Tiki that he would have the checks the following day.

In a few days, Tiki had an assortment of checks from various sources, including one of Elena's uncashed paychecks. To complete his plan, he purchased a check writer and typewriter. He left everything at the new apartment and was careful not to let anyone know about his new setup.

On his next trip to Tomaso's, a few days later, he went prepared to give Tomaso enough work to keep him busy for a long time. Tiki showed him his assortment of checks and asked how long it would take to make new checks like them. Tomaso examined each check specimen and shook his head saying that they would need a lot of work, especially the checks that were already made payable. He explained further that the serial and bank numbers on the checks would also have to be replaced, because, if anything went wrong, the police could trace the checks from the original numbers. Tiki understood his point and congratulated him on his attention to detail.

Tiki told Tomaso to do the best work he could on the checks and that there would be extra money in it for him. Tomaso smiled a big toothy grin and said he would have the checks ready in a week to ten days, even if he had to work day and night on them. On his way home, Tiki couldn't help but notice that Tomaso knew quite a bit about checks. He concluded that it might be possible that Tomaso was also working for someone else, since he knew so much about checks.

Tiki spent the next several days making contacts and lining up customers for his counterfeit checks. He was careful to choose customers from among his own people and people he could trust. He asked a price high enough and the quantity low enough to prevent a sudden flooding of the city with bogus checks that would bring authorities swooping in from all sides. He always managed to rationalize to himself that he was being kind and benevolent to his people by affording them such a grand opportunity to purchase contraband from him and not have to steal it. It was rather a complex rationale because, in actuality, he exploited them more than the gringo ever did.

A week later, Tiki was back at Tomaso's print shop. Tomaso had done an excellent job on the checks and driver's licenses. He had made enough to flood, not only the city, but the entire state. Tomaso told Tiki that he had again destroyed the negatives and plates after completing the print run because he didn't want them lying around. Tiki had to accept the explanation, but it still made him uncomfortable.

Tiki took the checks directly to his new apartment and spent the rest of the evening filling them out — putting in the dollar amounts and making identification to match the checks. He ruined a few checks but, in the end, he was pleased with the evening's work. Late that night he returned to his neighborhood and looked up several customers. He was paid for the checks and his customers were very satisfied, putting in orders for additional checks in the future. Tiki took orders, but was cautious about taking too many. He swore to himself that he wouldn't get greedy and would limit the amount that he sold.

That night when he returned home, he had over $2,000 in cash and the prospect of more in the days to come. He was so happy with the way things were going that he told Elena she could quit her job. He now considered what she was earning to be "chump change." Tiki told her that he would take her home to Colombia for a vacation to visit her family and friends.

Plans were set for the vacation and before leaving, Tiki gave Tomaso specific instructions about delivering the lottery tickets. He told Tomaso to place the tickets in a public locker at the bus station and deliver the key to a particular bar where the lottery operators would pick it up. In this way he could keep the business going without anyone knowing each other. He didn't fully trust Tomaso and thought (and it was probably true) that he had ambitions to handle the whole operation himself. He swore to himself that he would kill Tomaso if he ever double-crossed him.

The trip to Colombia was idyllic. They met old friends and relatives, went to the best restaurants, took sightseeing tours, and spent time playing at the beach. But it wasn't all a holiday forTiki. He took time out to line up new customers for his check business and was successful in obtaining local checks and various pieces of identification. His new customers were anxious to do business with him because the local printing facilities and equipment were archaic and the printers couldn't be trusted.

On the return trip to New York, Tiki was flush with good fortune and success. He confided to Elena that he was doing a big business in checks and that if things continued going as well they had, they could be married in a couple of years. Elena was happy at the prospect of marriage and hoped that Tiki would not outsmart himself. She knew that if anything happened to him, she would be alone and in dire straits.

Back in New York, Tiki didn't lose any time in going to see Tomaso. Tiki was happy to learn that while he had been away, Tomaso had delivered the lottery tickets as he had been instructed, and everything had gone flawlessly. Tiki paid Tomaso the money he owed him, and couldn't help but congratulate himself on how smoothly the operation was working. Even while he had been away on vacation, he had made a bundle of cash from Tomaso's printing. He gave Tomaso the job of printing the foreign checks and identification and Tomaso promised that he would have the finished product ready, as usual, in about a week. He asked Tiki why he was getting involved in foreign checks, but Tiki quickly changed subjects with no explanation and Tomaso decided not to press him any further.

Tiki returned to the neighborhood and discovered that while one or two people had been arrested for passing his counterfeit checks, there were still plenty of others who were anxious to buy more checks. He also learned that there was also a good market for blank ID's without the checks.

Tomaso finished the checks on schedule. Tiki picked them up and mailed them to his contacts in Colombia. After the checks were in the mail, Tiki waited in relaxed anticipation of the money and the new orders that would be pouring in from his homeland. As each day turned into another week without any returns on the money from the checks, he began to become concerned. After several weeks had passed with still no money, he made several telephone calls to Colombia and learned that they had all underestimated the ability and interest of the local police in chasing down forgeries and counterfeit checks and passers. Most of the people who had bought checks from Tiki had been arrested very shortly after they had passed the checks. This news was very disturbing to Tiki. Not only was the operation a total loss, but he was sure that some of the stupid people would give him up. There was little doubt in his mind that his foreign business was dead and he would have to concentrate on the local business. He also decided it was time to get some new check specimens since the original ones had been out on the market for some time and were considered "hot."

The arrests on the checks were beoming more numerous in the neighborhood and things were getting very uncomfortable for Tiki. One night as he was returning home, two men in suits were waiting for him in the hallway. They showed him gold badges and identified themselves as detectives. They roughly threw him against the wall and searched him. Fortunately he was clean. They wanted to search his apartment. Tiki asked if they had a warrant. One of them put a gun to his head and said, "Here's my warrant, do you want me to execute it?" Tiki was angry, but was smart enough to know when he was on the losing end. He took a good hard look at their ugly faces so he would remember them and settle the score with them at a later time. He was sure that the apartment was "clean;" he couldn't recall one thing in his place that could be considered illegal. He accompanied them to the apartment. Elena was home. When she was told the apartment was to be searched, she put up an awful fuss, but the men searched the apartment anyhow. They found nothing of a contraband nature and left without anything even resembling an apology. Their only words were a warning: "We'll be watching."

After they left, Tiki had a fight with Elena. She wanted him to give up his check business and try to find a real job. He slapped her across the face. What right did she have telling him what to do. Didn't he treat her well? Didn't he give her everything she wanted? Didn't he take her for a vacation to Colombia? Where did she think the money was coming from? Not from working in the gringo's stinking sweatshops or from some stupid burglary or stickup. No, the money was coming in because he, Tiki, was smart enough to find a way to make a clean dollar, even if he had to take it from the stupid gringos. He struck her again, with enough force to send her flying across the bed to end the argument.

Up to now Tiki had been lucky, but the experience with the cops made him rethink the whole situation. There was no doubt that someone had talked and finked him out. Someone had given him up to the pigs. Why? Why did his own countrymen want to harm him? Didn't he treat everyone right? Why would anyone want to sell him out? To get a break? For money? Who could trust the pigs? Everyone knew that when they arrested you they would promise anything, then in the end they would double-cross you and send you away like the others. Why were his people so stupid?

Tike came to the conclusion that the check operation was dead and he would have to do something else. He had to deal with too many ignorant punks. There was only one thing that he could use Tomaso for — printing money. That was it. He would get try to get Tomaso to print millions of the gringo's filthy dollars. He would have his people pass the money — pass it everywhere. When he got rid of enough of it, he would retire. He and Elena could live in splendor. He would be respected — a big man around town.

A few weeks later, after the heat was easing up, Tiki decided to proposition Tomaso about printing counterfeiting money. He want to the shop and talked with Tomaso, telling him he wanted Tomaso to print a million dollars in $10's and $20's. The work would have to be of excellent quality and pass the closest scrutiny. He would pay Tomaso a handsome bonus if the money could be passed without raising suspicion. Tomaso was skeptical,"Tiki, my friend are you sure you want to make counterfeit money?" Tiki said, "Tomaso, I came here to see you because I know what I am doing and because you are the very best printer. Have I not kept my word on everything? Do you not get your money every week? Have the fat gringo pigs been bothering you? No, of course not. That's because you're doing business with Tiki, not some stupid slob who is going to get diarrhea of the mouth as soon as a fat pig puts a hand on his shoulder. You do good work for me and you get paid well. You will never have to worry about being arrested."

Tomaso continued, " I know everything you say is true. But, bad money is a big crime, it will bring the Feds on us. They are like the leaves; there are thousands of them. Why can't we just go on with the lottery tickets and checks?" Tiki laughed and responded, "The checks are becoming trouble. Too many people are involved, too many stupid rats. They could get Tiki into trouble, but Tiki is too smart. I have a new plan with this bad money. I have made connections with a worldwide syndicate . You know the Italianos? They are willing to take all the money I can supply them with and send it far away to be passed. For you and me there is no risk, no heat, no fat gringo pigs to bother us. That is good, eh, Tomaso?"

Tomaso was easily convinced and smiled as he was relieved to know the bad money would be shipped far away. Of course, Tiki was lying. He didn't have a syndicate to distribute the money for him. But Tomaso had to believe it. After all, the relationship had gone well. Tiki always kept his word. Tomaso received his weekly paycheck whether he worked or not. His legitimate business was doing well and he had recently started to print pornography for some of his old customers and they were paying him well for it. He was careful not to mention the other people to Tiki. He would be very angry if he found out that Tomaso was doing illegitimate work for other people. He knew that if anything went wrong Tiki would insist the other people's work brought the heat.

With a sigh and a smile of resignation, Tomaso agreed to try his hand at printing the $10's and $20's. He told Tiki that he would need technical and physical help in getting started. He would need lots of materials and wanted help with the paper supply. Above all else, he didn't want to be rushed. He told Tiki that he would have to take his time to do the job right and to do trial runs many times over until he was satisfied. Tiki promised he would devote as much time as possible to helping, and he would not push with a deadline. He had a big interest in seeing that the work turned out well — bad counterfeits would be dangerous.

The next day, Tomaso gave Tiki a list of supplies he needed. He wanted a package of offset printing plates. He told Tiki that they could be purchased in any stationary or printing supply store. He also wanted several packages of some special film. The film would not be a problem if he went to a photographic supply house. He needed some green ink but Tiki had to be careful not to order any that was too close to the green used on genuine money. The ink supplier might become suspicious and tip off the police. It would be necessary to buy a similar color and then mix it to get the proper color. The most important item was the paper. He needed 20# bond, 100% rag content paper in large sheets. They would then cut the paper to the proper size. He knew a cash purchase of this paper might raise suspicions on the part of the supplier and he certainly didn't want to buy it in his own name. He thought perhaps buying a box of good stationary paper with 100% rag content might take longer, but in the long run, it would be safer.

The chemicals and other materials Tomaso could buy from his regular outlet without arousing suspicion, because he used them routinely. But Tiki should also purchase a good-sized paper cutter to trim the notes to the proper size once they were printed.

Tiki was a little annoyed at being used as a delivery service boy, but as he didn't want to bring anyone else in on the operation, he dutifully went about buying the supplies in various parts of the city. He carefully avoided conversations with the salesmen. He always admitted he knew nothing about printing, that he was just doing a favor for a friend. He was also always very careful about parking his car at a distance so that any suspicious salesmen couldn't take down his license number.

Within a week, Tiki had purchased all the supplies on the list. Tomaso managed to get the things he had decided to purchase himself. A date was set to start the operation. It was agreed that this particular job would only be worked on at night, so there wouldn't be any chance of someone walking in on them while they were working.

Tomaso was an excellent printer, but he wasn't quite as adept as a plate maker or photographer. He ran into problems right from the beginning. He had Tiki obtain some brand new $10 and $20 bills from the bank. He needed to photograph them to make the negatives. It was only when he snapped the picture that he noticed the serial numbers and seal were in a different color and would have to be printed separately. The serial number could easily be opaqued or blocked out, but the seal was a problem. The denomination of the bill was spelled out and printed over the seal, which was printed in green. Tomaso knew nothing about color separation, so the first night's work was a complete wash. Try as he might for the next several nights, Tomaso shot good negatives but the color problem was causing him real fits. Tiki was growing impatient and started to accuse Tomaso of stalling. There wasn't much he could do but sit and wait, and cuss Tomaso out for his ineptitude.

Finally, Tomaso gave up and said he'd have to talk to someone about his problem, perhaps the clerk at the photographic supply house. Tiki warned him to be very careful not to mention the seal or the bills to the man. Tomaso assured Tiki that he would be careful not to say or do anything to alert the man or to cause any suspicion.

Tiki departed the print shop thoroughly disgusted. He began to wonder whether the job was too much for Tomaso; why hadn't Tomaso prepared for these problems before he began the operation? He called Tomaso the next day, after Tomaso had an opportunity to ask the expert for advice about color separations. But the problem still hadn't been resolved. Tiki was disgusted and slammed the phone down.

Two days later he called again. This time Tomaso told him that he had solved the problem and now knew how to do the color separations. He suggested that Tiki come over as soon as possible. That night Tiki went to the shop and found Tomaso in a very good frame of mind. The explanation was simple enough; all he had to do was put the proper filter on the camera lens to filter out the green. Tomaso looked at his filter/color chart, selected the proper filter, placed it on his camera, and shot and developed the picture.

It worked. The serial number and seal were not on the negative. He made a few contact prints from the negative to see how it turned out.

The detail was fine, but the back of the bill showed through a little on the face. This was another problem to handle. After much thought and experimentation, he worked it out. The bill would have to be split and each side would have to be photographed on something opaque so that the back wouldn't show through. That night he spent most of his time perfecting a set of negatives. He told Tiki that for the next few days he would have to work alone. He wanted to make the plates from as near-perfect negatives as he could produce. He knew it took a good negative to make a good plate; a good plate resulted in a good counterfeit note.

The job was tedious and time consuming, but his patience paid off. He made an excellent set of negatives. Now the next job was to make a set of plates worthy of the negatives. He made several sets, some he exposed too long, some not long enough, but after many tries, he managed to get a set of each denomination that met his high standards. He ran some sample proofs on plain paper stock and was pleased with the results. He called Tiki and told him they were ready for the printing operation.

When Tiki arrived, Tomaso showed him the proofs of the bills he had printed. Tiki could barely conceal his excitement — the bills were excellent. He was careful to restrain his elation lest Tomaso would want more money. That night they decided to print the face of the $20's. They printed for some time, but Tomaso wasn't satisfied with the results. He felt the face was too dark. He made a few adjustments on the press and sat back while the machine printed one bill after another. That night they had enough paper to print about $60,000 in $20's and they worked until they used up all the paper.

Tomaso still thought the face was a little dark and he spent most of the next afternoon mixing the green ink until he came upon what he thought was the proper shade for his counterfeit bills. That night he filled up the ink wells with the new ink while Tiki helped him to load the machine to print the back of the $20's. The printing of the backs was accomplished without any difficulty and Tiki was thrilled with the results. While the press spewed out sheet ater sheet, Tiki fantasized about how he would spend the money.

When the backs were printed, Tiki was ready to take them with him. Tomaso ruined his fantasy by telling him that the hardest part was yet to come. Tiki could barely contain his anger. He thought that Tomaso was trying to pull something, perhaps even steal a few thousand for himself. Tomaso then explained that they still had to overprint the serial number and seal on the face of the bill. That job was very difficult and would have to be put off until another night. Tiki had to agree in spite of his anxiety. He hated to leave all that money with Tomaso for another night. He felt like sticking his .45 to Tomaso's head and threatening to blow it off if he stole so much as one bill.

He decided against it — if things worked out well, he would need Tomaso for many more years. Besides, the $10's still had to be printed before the job was complete.

Tiki wanted no less than a million dollars. But of course, he now had to figure out how he was going to get rid of it. It was one thing to lie to Tomaso that he had a distribution system in place, but it was another thing to find the right people to handle it. He thought they would at least be worth thirty cents on the dollar. He would look for someone to buy a large chunk, but that would include those anglo bastards he called gringos. They were the only ones he knew who had that kind of money. He did all the work and the gringos would reap the profit. He could always sell it in small amounts to his own people, but that would be a slow process and as soon as one of them was arrested, he would probably give Tiki up. After all, they gave him up on the checks. He couldn't understand why anyone would talk to the fat sweaty pigs who were supposed to be the law. He'd like to take his .45 and kill them all. He couldn't make his mind up on how to handle the money, but he was sure he would come up with the right method by the time everything was ready.

The next several nights were busy. Tiki purchased more paper and supplies and Tomaso kept busy making plates for serial numbers and seals and changed the serial numbers often. Then he repeated the whole process with the tens. It took them several weeks to complete the job. Finally, only one thing remained before the money was ready — the job of cutting the sheets of notes and trimming the bills. Tomaso needed Tiki to help him. It was a slow and difficult job. If they had a power paper cutter the job would have been faster and neater, but the old hand-operated cutter Tiki had purchased required a lot of patience and time often resulting in spoilage through sloppy cutting.

When the job was finished, both Tiki and Tomaso were exhausted. Tiki, however, insisted on packing the bills in cartons and taking them with him. He didn'tt want to trust anyone, especially Tomaso, at this point. Tomaso argued and suggested that they should do something about making it appear that the bills had the same silk and rayon threads that the originals had in them. He thought he could simulate the threads by making a plate and printing little marks on the bills. Tiki was impatient and annoyed and wanted to get going with the money. He said that perhaps on another printing they could do the effect with the threads, but for now, he was satisfied and wanted to start selling the money. He was getting fed up with Tomaso's stalling. He figured that Tomaso simply wanted a chance to steal some of the money, so he left and headed for his secret apartment in the city.

He was cautious and made sure he sure he wasn't being followed. He took a circuitous route, carefully checking his rearview mirror and looking carefully at each passing car. He made sure that he lost any car that appeared suspicious.

When he was in close to the hideaway apartment, he parked his car several blocks away and checked the area thoroughly. When he was satisfied that no one was following and it was safe to proceed, he got the cartons out of the car and carried them to the apartment. He locked the door, pulled down the shades, and emptied the cartons on the bed. The sight of all that money sent a tingling through his body. He wanted to pick up the money and caress each bill. This is what he had waited for all his life. This was the big score that would take him out of the peon class and make him somebody. The only problem was the distribution. He hated to sell even one bill at a discount. He wished he could get rid of every one himself, then he wouldn't have to worry about anyone squealing on him to the fat pigs.

He continued to examine the bills closely. They looked a little too bright. Someone had once told him that counterfeit bills could be made to look old by dipping them in coffee or tea. He quickly made a big pot of coffee and dipped some bills in it. He laid them out to dry. When they were dry, he examined them and was satisfied with the result. The newness was gone and the bills looked like they had been in circulation for a while. At last, he was ready to turn the bills into real cash. He decided to sell them in $1,000 lots for $250 in cash.

The next day he contacted several friends and propositioned them about the bills. Two of them pooled their resources and bought $1,000 worth. Tiki decided to sit back and see how it went. The two men went on a shopping spree and were successful. In five days they had passed all of the $1,000. They went back to Tiki and bought another $1,000 worth. In the meantime, Tiki made other sales and the notes began to circulate in and around the city.

Tiki decided to pay Tomaso a visit. It was a good thing for Tomaso that Tiki called first. Had Tiki dropped by without calling, he would have found Tomaso printing a load of the counterfeit notes for himself. When Tiki arrived, Tomaso had already cleaned up the shop and made sure there wasn't any evidence around indicating what he had been up to. Tiki told Tomaso that many of the notes were bad and he had to destroy them. Although this wasn't true, it gave Tiki an excuse to settle with Tomaso for a lower price. He gave Tomaso $500. Tomaso didn't object since he intended to do a little distributing himself. He knew his work was good and he could find a ready market.

When he left, Tiki told Tomaso to be careful and to continue printing the lottery tickets and the tickets for the baseball pool. Tomaso told him not to worry. Tiki left with misgivings about giving Tomaso only $500. He suddenly remembered that he had forgotten to ask Tomaso for the plates and negatives. It was too late to go back and besides, Tomaso would probably say he had already destroyed them.

It was about this time, that the U. S. Secret Service began to notice these particular $10 and $20 counterfeits starting to come into the office with an increasing frequency. The only descriptions we were able to obtain of the passers were that they were either of Puerto Rican or other Hispanic descent. Several passers had been arrested, but all were maintaining a tight-lipped silence. Those that did talk, claimed they got them in a crap game, from storekeepers as change, or occasionally, some would claim to have found the notes. Nevertheless, they all professed to be innocent victims. We knew the operation wasn't a large one, but the money was hitting the street and we needed to get some information. It was particularly irksome to me. At this time, I was a supervisor in of special U. S. Secret Service anti-counterfeiting unit, and it was my responsibility to suppress counterfeiting in the tri-state area and to aid any district experiencing a particularly difficult counterfeiting problem.

Tiki continued making his sales as cautiously as possible. He made sure he knew the buyer and that they were one of his countrymen. He also waved his .45 under the nose of each buyer to warn him of the penalty for talking.

One day Tiki learned that two passers had been arrested. They were quickly released — too quickly it seemed to Tiki. He was suspicious that they had talked. He was aware that some of his stupid friends might give him up and there were times he thought he was being followed. Whenever he was on the street he looked closely at everyone and constantly made sure he wasn't being followed, especially when he went to the apartment where the money was stashed.

He laid off selling notes for about a month. The inactivity made him even more irritable than usual. He knew he had a fortune in counterfeit money and that if he could only unload it, he would be well off. But his stupid friends were being arrested by the police and he knew it was only a matter of time before someone would talk. He needed someone he could trust to not give him up if he was arrested by the "fat gringo pig." But, who? Who would take the rap and not give up the man who was supplying the notes? He couldn't think of anyone.

Just as he was thinking this, Elena came home. Tiki thought, "How about Elena?" He was giving her a good life. Now that she wasn't working anymore she had nothing to do with her time except sit around and get fat or go out shopping and spend his money. Why couldn't she still go out shopping, only instead of using his good money, she could use the counterfeits? She didn't have to pass too much — maybe a $100 a day. The police wouldn't get excited over five or ten bills a day. He knew he wouldn't have to convince Elena that what he wanted her to do was good for them. She did what he told her to do and didn't ask any questions. If she balked at the idea, he'd slap her around. He thought about it some more and decided that he would have her pass the bills, but wouldn't tell her the bills were bad. However, he would warn her to keep her mouth shut if she was asked any questions. After all, no matter what happened, he would handle everything for her and make sure she didn't go to jail.

So, the next Monday morning, he told Elena that he wanted her to go shopping. He explained that he wanted her to purchase one item in each store and pay for it with the $10 or $20 bills that he gave her. He told her he'd park his car a few blocks away and that under no circumstances should she return to it. He would watch her coming out of the store and when he was sure the coast was clear, he would pick her up. Elena said she understood perfectly. She knew she was doing something wrong, but she wouldn't dare question Tiki.

He selected a shopping center several miles away. He gave Elena $10 and told her to go into the drug store and purchase a bottle of aspirin or some toothpaste. He parked across the road and watched her go in and several minutes later he saw her come out carrying a small package. He let her walk for some distance then picked her up. He asked her if everything went okay. She replied that it had. They repeated the same routine several more times. Each time she made a purchase, she gave the cashier the money and they gave her change which she gave to Tiki. At the end, when Tiki decided it was enough for one day, he had netted $117 plus all the merchandise that she had bought.

The following day things went well again. This time he netted $176. On the third day he dropped Elena off at a liquor store in the heart of downtown and instructed her to buy two bottles of rum. She went in, but didn't come out. Tiki knew something was wrong. He wanted to go into the store, but he was afraid he might become involved. A few minutes later a police car stopped outside the store, and a police officer went inside. Tiki went wild with rage. He wanted to take his .45, go into the store, and blast the fat pigs and take Elena away from the trouble. He stayed in the car, however, until he saw the police take Elena away.

Just prior to the arrival of the police at the liquor store, the U. S. Secret Service office received a call from the Albion Liquor Store. The clerk said a girl attempted to pass a counterfeit bill for a purchase of two bottles of rum. The clerk described the girl, matching the description of a girl who had been passing counterfeit $10's and $20's for the last few days. The clerk was told to stall the girl and to call the local police precinct. In the meantime, I dispatched two agents to make an investigation. They proceeded to the precinct house and attempted to question Elena, but she wouldn't answer any questions. It was decided to arrest her and charge her with passing counterfeit money. We knew there were several other storekeepers that could identify her.

Shortly after she arrived at our office, I received a telephone call from a man (later identified as Tiki) who said we had his girlfriend in custody and if I didn't release her, he would blow my head off. I invited him to the office to discuss the matter. He asked my name and I told him. In the next few hours he called me at least ten times. On one call he promised to make it "worth my while" if the girl was released. I asked if he was trying to bribe me over the phone. He said, "No, but I can get you the whole story on the counterfeits and I know that you need the information I have." I replied, "I can arrange to have Elena on the street, but you have to come down to the office and talk — face to face." He would stay on the phone only for a minute or so. He said he knew I was trying to trace the call and said that I was nothing but a "fat gringo pig." I tried to assure him that I would play it straight while reminding him that we had the girl in custody and I had to do something with her — either have her arraigned before the court closed, or she would be taken to the women's house of detention for the night.

He said, "I'll give you valuable information as soon as she calls me and convinces me she's not locked up. Then I'll come to your office and give you the whole story."

He assured me that in no way was he involved and wanted my promise that he wouldn't be arrested. I told him, "If you're not involved then you have nothing to fear and you won't be arrested. I can have the girl arraigned and then released on her own recognizance. After the arraignment, she will be returned to my office where you can pick her up." He said he was going to hang up and think it over. He said he'd call me back because he was sure I was trying to trace the call.

About fifteen minutes later, he called and said he wanted to talk with Elena. We put her on the phone and he told her to call him at a number he gave her as soon as she left the courthouse.

The assistant U.S. Attorney handling the case gave us all the help we needed and he saw to it that Elena was released on her own recognizance. The arraignment was over in 25 minutes and Elena was returned to our office. She was allowed to make the phone call to Tiki. She convinced him that she was out of the courthouse and free to leave whenever she wanted to. Tiki then made a call to the court and learned that Elena had been released a short while before. He immediately called me and said, "You have kept half of your bargain, will you keep the other half?" I said, "What other half?" He said curtly, "About not arresting me."

"I have no intention to arrest you," I told him, "however, if at anytime I receive information that you are involved, you will be arrested."

"Well you sound like you can be trusted, even though you are a lousy gringo pig. I'll be right down, but I want you to be alone."

His insistence that I be alone didn't settle with me. I said, "You are being unnecessarily cautious. You can trust me all the way, but I am running the show here. The sooner you come to my office, the quicker Elena can go home with you."

Two hours and five telephone calls later, Tiki appeared at the office. He was a wild-looking man with a small chin beard and mustache. He was dressed in baggy tan trousers, a sleeveless undershirt, and a wide–brimmed hat, angled over one eye. I ordered that he be frisked before entering my office. He agreed and was found to be "clean." I had several of my agents sit in on the interview. Tiki plunked himself in a chair and began to rant and rave about a gang that had counterfeit money, and Elena had been framed. He jumped up and walked angrily around the office, talking fast and gesturing wildly. I suggested that he calm down, start at the beginning and tell me the story as he knew it. I would try not to interrupt him, but he had to stay on one track so we could make some sense of it. "After you finish your story, I'll arrange to have someone take notes, but for the present, I'll just listen."

He began, "About five or six weeks ago, I wanted to see my friend Tomaso, who is a printer. I wanted to start a foreign language newspaper for my people. They have nothing to read in the stupid gringo newspapers. I know Tomaso is a good printer and perhaps he could show me how to get started. I tried to find his shop in the city but he had gone out of business and moved. Finally, I meet a friend who tells me that Tomaso was operating a shop in the cellar of his home out of town. I decided to go and see him."

"One day I go to his town. I found his house and he showed me the business he was doing from his cellar. He tells me he was printing stationary, business cards, wedding invitations and sometimes he makes lottery tickets for some people. He said he made a good living and never wanted to go back to the city and open a shop. I tell him of my plans to start a newspaper. He says he did not have the machinery to print a large newspaper, but he thought he could print a small one. I was really excited because I felt that at last I was getting started. One evening I decided to go see Tomaso about the paper. I didn't call, but went straight to his house. It was late and he was working in the cellar. I knocked, he opened the door after I tell him it's me, and he lets me in. On the machine I saw what looked like money. I then realize he was printing counterfeit money. I say, 'Tomaso, are you crazy? Do you want to get into trouble?'"

"Tomaso laughed and says, 'I won't get into trouble. I'm printing these for some friends. They're going to send it overseas. The pigs will never see the money in this country. Every time they get an order, I print it and get paid well.' I knew there would be trouble because it looked like he was printing hundreds of thousands of dollars worth, and someone would pass them all over the city. I think I can find out from Tomaso who his people are. I have to be very careful, it'll take time but I know he will tell me. The whole business is in his house. When you look you will find the plates, the negatives, the paper, and everything. Now I suppose you want to know about Elena and how she got involved. This girl does not know what is going on! The money that Tomaso printed didn't go overseas. The people lied to him. It was sold on the streets. Everybody was buying cheap money and passing it all over town. Elena is from Colombia and she don't know good money from bad money."

"One night, Elena and I have a big fight. She gets mad at me and left the house. She and her friend, Maria, decide they would go to a dance. If I know this I would kill her, but I don't. At the dance, she meets this bastard, Chico. Chico must have been one of the people that bought the cheap money. Elena don't come home that night. She stays at Chico's sister's house. Again I could kill her because I am so worried. I don't hear nothing. Chico don't work and he and Elena go out every day and every day he asks her to buy something at the stores. Every time she goes he gives her the money. He keeps the change and lets her keep what she bought. Elena is stupid, she don't know she is passing bad money. She thinks Chico loves her and is buying things for her. Now I want to help Elena because she knows she made a mistake and I want to take her back home with me."

"Now you have the whole story. Chico I will take care of. I know he is running, but I will find him and make him pay for all the trouble he has caused. Okay? So what else do you want?"

I stared at him for a few seconds and said, "Here is a pen and paper, write down Tomaso's address." He looked back at me defiantly, as if to say, "Yea, sure" but picked up the pen and wrote down an address.

I could see that the other agents who had just heard this story were "champing at the bit," anxious to ask Tiki a million questions. I was sure they thought Tiki was lying, but I wasn't convinced that the whole story was a lie. I had Tiki taken out to another room so we could discuss the matter. Each and every agent in the room felt Tiki wasn't telling the truth and there wasn't any doubt he was involved. Some felt he should be questioned extensively and arrested when it was proven he was lying and was involved. I agreed that Tiki was lying, but I decided it was best to go along with him and see how much of his story was true. Up to this point, all we had was a girl who attempted to pass a note and a possibility that she might be identified on one or two more. At best, it was a 50–50 chance we could do anything with her. She was scared to death, and there was a language problem she could throw at us during questioning.

As for Tiki, I decided to play him like a rainbow trout on a line and for all he was worth. We didn't have a case against him and he could leave at any time. In the meantime, he did give us information on Tomaso, which could be checked out. I intended to try to get Tiki to give us a sworn statement. Based on this statement, we would apply for a search warrant for Tomaso's premises. If Tiki didn't want to sign a statement, then it would be necessary to show him as a previously reliable informant. In this way he could remain anonymous and we could still apply for the search warrant.

I had Tiki brought back into my office and asked him if he would sign a statement. He almost jumped through the ceiling. He accused me of double-crossing him and trying to get him into trouble. I managed to get through to him to to explain why I wanted it. I asked him if he could tell me anything that I could check out which would make him reliable. He thought it over and said he would call me the following day and would have something for me. He assured me that nothing would change at Tomaso's providing I didn't put any heat on the place. I told him that we would stay away from Tomaso. He said I wouldn't be sorry for taking his advice.

After a while we allowed both of them to leave. Somehow I was getting the feeling we weren't getting the best part of the deal. Yet, no matter how the pieces were shuffled and put together, it still added up that we started with nothing and anything we could get from Tiki would be in the plus column.

The following day, Tiki called to say that he knew where there was approximately $25,000 in counterfeit money hidden in an apartment that belonged to the counterfeiting "group" and the occupants would be away for several days. The money was stuffed into a mattress in the bedroom of the apartment located in the city. He continued further that any investigation at this address would certainly upset Tomaso's plant. He said the key to the apartment was generally left over the door molding. He said that if the money was taken quietly, it wouldn't affect Tomaso's operation. Tiki wasn't fooling me with this call. I now felt certain that the operation was his and that he was just throwing me a bone. Nevertheless, we were progressing while Tiki was doing a fine job of fouling himself up. I felt sure somewhere along the line we would be in a position to make a case against him and then I could just reel him in.

I immediately dispatched two agents to the address, advising them to take the key from its hiding place, enter the apartment, look in the mattress, remove any counterfeit money that was found, and return to the office without making any further investigation. One of the agents wanted to know what he should do in the event the apartment was occupied. I told him that it was situations such as this that made the job interesting. The other agent assured him that he knew what to do.

About an hour later, the agents contacted me and said everything went smoothly. The key was where it was said to be, nobody was home, they had removed approximately $25,000 of counterfeits from the mattress, and left without being observed. They went on to say that it didn't appear that the apartment was occupied. There wasn't any clothing around, the apartment was sparsely furnished, and there wasn't any indication that anyone lived there.

The men returned to the office with the seizure, which were the same notes that had been plaguing us and the same that Elena had passed. We were now in a perfect position to move in on Tomaso. Just then the phone rang. It was Tiki. He said, "So, am I now, how do you say in pig talk, reliable?" I said, "Yes, you are reliable." He asked, " Will you trust me now?" "It all depends," I replied, not giving him anything. He then questioned, "Are you going to arrest me?" I replied simply, "Should I?" He laughed as he said, "You can never trust a gringo." He then hung up.

I didn't want to concentrate too much on Tiki. There were still an awful lot of questions that remained to be answered; thinking about them and Tiki might move me in the wrong direction. For the present, Tiki had to be taken at face value. There wasn't any doubt that Tiki could be considered reliable and, now, based on information from a reliable source, we could apply for a search warrant for Tomaso's residence and still keep our source anonymous. The men applied for the warrant and got it within hours. A raiding party was formed with instructions to make a complete search of Tomaso's premises, to seize any and all contraband, and to place Tomaso under arrest if the search proved fruitful.

The men went out and several hours later one of the agents called me and reported that they had completed almost half of the search and so far it was unsuccessful. He explained that the place was a real mess. Tomaso had so much stuff around that it would take several more hours before they were finished. My heart sank. This wasn't the news I had been hoping to hear. I began to have second thoughts about how I had handled the case. Perhaps I should have concentrated on Tiki and gambled with losing the plant, but that didn't make much sense either. Perhaps we should have held Elena at a higher bail. Perhaps ...

Several hours later, while I was still in deep thought, the phone rang. It was the agents reporting in again. The agent on the line reported that they had seized a complete plant. They had removed the floor pads on the cellar steps and found about 20 different negatives for counterfeit money. They also found an envelope containing the plates of the $10's and $20's we were interested in, hidden behind a radiator. The utility room had yielded several hundred thousand dollars in counterfeit $10's and $20's, in a box hidden behind the oil burner.

I breathed a sigh of relief and felt good: we had the plant and Tiki appeared to be on the level, at least partially. Also, with the pressure off, we could proceed with other problems that needed our attention.

Tomaso was brought to my office that night and I had a chance to question him. He was advised of his rights and he refused to make any statement regarding the plant. He had a philosophical attitude about the whole matter. He said, "What I did wasn't right. I knew what I was doing. I made money." Then he smiled and added, "In more ways than one." He said no one else was involved and he would take the fall like a man. He was disturbed to learn that we were seizing all the equipment in his place. I told him the law required us to do that. He said, "Some law. You take away a man's only means to make a living and you expect him to be straight?" I said, "Yeah, Tomaso, but you abused the privilege." He was put away for the night.

We needed a large truck to haul all the equipment and contraband from his house. The men also found plates and negatives for checks, driver's licenses, birth certificates, lottery tickets, as well as pornography. It appeared that Tomaso was serving many masters. The information regarding this material was given to the local police.

The seizure and arrest got a lot of publicity in the next day's newspapers. The local police were arranging to file warrants against Tomaso on the basis of the state violations that we turned over to them.

Tiki also read the papers. He figured it was time to make his move. He called me and asked, "I kept my part of the bargain, didn't I?" I said, "Yes." He asked another question, "So then I guess we're even?" "Pretty much," I told him. He then said, "Why do you want to arrest me?" I replied, "What makes you think I want to arrest you?"

"I know some people have been saying bad things about me, right?" he wanted to know. I said, "Tiki, why don't you come down to the office so you and I can talk?" "You are like all the gringo pigs," he said, "you don't keep your word — you are trying to trace this call." He hung up.

Several hours later he called again and said he wanted to make a deal. He said there was another half million dollars of that stuff around; it was going to be moved shortly, and then there wouldn't be any chance of getting it once it was gone. He said he could get it for me for $5,000. I said, "Tiki, I can't do business like that over the phone. Come down to the office, or let's arrange to meet somewhere so we can talk." He said, "Time is short, I know you are trying to trace this call. No meeting, no double-cross. Just $5,000. You know you can trust me. Uncle Gringo has plenty of money." He hung up again.

He was really presenting a problem. If there were another $500,000 of the counterfeits around, they would give us a fit trying to trace them after they were passed. Yet, the prospect of paying $5,000 to Tiki didn't sit well with me either. He probably wanted to use the money to make a run for it. For some reason, he thought we were going to arrest him. I wished we could, but, up to that moment, we had absolutely nothing on him except a heap of suspicion. It would probably take too long to develop a case against him and, at this point, time was at a premium. The $500,000 was undoubtedly his money and, for reasons best known to himself, he wanted to unload it.

He was on the phone again 20 minutes later. He said that if I wanted the money I'd have to act right away. He reminded me it was going to be moved and he might not know where it would be moved to. He asked me to have the $5,000 in small, used, and unmarked bills and be ready to leave it where he instructed. "For Christ's sake, Tiki," I said, "you're acting like this was a kidnapping case. Stop acting like this is the movies and let's get down to serious business." He came back with, "This isn't serious? You don't want to do business. You're only interested in arresting me. You made me move from my home. I know you are trying to trace the calls. I'm trying to help you with the bad money and you won't trust me."

I said, "Tiki, shut up and listen to me. You are talking about $5,000. That's a lot of money. We have to sit down and talk. We did it before and it worked. You talk about trust, how about you trusting me? Name the time and place and I'll be there. I promise there won't be any arrest." He said, "You talk too much…No $5,000, no deal, no business." He slammed the receiver.

By this time I was losing my cool. Tiki had a way of getting on your nerves. It was time to talk it over with Headquarters and see what they suggested. I talked with a deputy director and was given "carte blanche." He said, "Carmine, you have enough experience; we trust your judgment. You do what you think is right and no one will second-guess you." I was relieved to know that Headquarters wouldn't be a problem. I thought it over, but just couldn't see gambling away $5,000. Perhaps I was more concerned with my own reputation. I had never lost a dime of the government's money and I didn't want the first time to be a whopper. On the other hand, I didn't want my own penurious nature to influence my decision. A half-million dollars was a lot of counterfeit money to let loose on the streets!

The phone rang again. It was Tiki saying, "Are you ready? This is the last time I call." I said, "Listen carefully, Tiki, all I can raise is $2,000. I can't get anyone to authorize a larger amount. If you want to do business, come on down and we can talk." Tiki said, "I will never see you again. You will follow my instructions on the money. This time you must do exactly as I tell you. After I have the money in my hands, I will tell you how to get the counterfeit money. You double-cross me and you lose everything."

I was getting tired of fighting with Tiki and I was sorely tempted to tell him off. But telling him off wasn't a luxury I could afford. My job was to keep counterfeit money off the streets and I couldn't choose the people I had to do business with. If I did, Tiki would most certainly *not* be on my list! At this point, I'd have given a month's pay to wring his neck! I finally told him to make his plans and call me back. He said, "Wait, we didn't agree on the amount yet!" I said, "$2,000 was all I could get." "You liar!" he screamed. I'll come down to $3,000 ...but that's final!" I said I would add $500 of my own money to the $2,000 and if anything went wrong, I would have a personal interest in the matter. I told him I would trail him to the ends of the earth if he beat me out of the money. We had been on the phone for several minutes so he figured it was time to hang up.

According to his modus operandi, I knew he'd call back. I felt we were on the verge of some sort of agreement. He did call back and said that he had made arrangements to get the counterfeit money. He said he would have to add $500 of his own money to complete the deal. I knew he was giving me the business, but I let him continue. He said, "Take your $2,500 in small, used, unmarked bills and have a man — just one man — take it and stay in the midtown area. When he's there, I'll call back and tell you what to do next."

I said "Tell me more. How do I get the rest of the counterfeits and how much is there? He began again, "Trust is the key word. After I have the good money in my hands, I'll have the counterfeits available where you can pick them up. I didn't count the money, but I figure there must be more than a couple of hundred thousand in the box. The important thing for you is that this is the last of them. There ain't no more around and you can close your case. You don't have to worry, I won't double-cross you because I am more honorable than you."

I sent an agent to the midtown area with the $2,500. He was well covered, and the men had orders to see how the money would be picked up, but not to interfere with the payoff. After the men left, I had serious misgivings about turning the money over to him, but I still felt that there was no other choice.

Tiki didn't call back for several hours. When he did, he was terse and to the point. He said, "Have your man go to the Benjamin Hotel, write the name 'Lita' on the envelope and leave it with the desk clerk. After I get it, I'll call you. You trust me now?" I quietly said, "I'll let you know, when it is all over and I have the counterfeit money."

Word was given to the street agent to drop the money at the Benjamin Hotel. It was a small hotel in the dingy section of midtown. It didn't have much of a lobby, so it was difficult to cover. About 15 minutes after the drop-off, a cab pulled up in front of the hotel. An old woman, bent with age, got out and went into the hotel. She was observed picking up the envelope and getting back into the same cab. The agents got the license number and tried to give it a loose tail, but lost it in the vicinity of the bus depot. In keeping with my instructions, they didn't get too close to the scene.

After that, the long wait began. I guess I was expecting a call from Tiki five minutes after the money had been delivered. But, apparently, he wasn't going to let me off the hook that easily. He waited for over two hours and just when I was about convinced that he had fleeced me, the phone rang. It was Tiki.

"Were you worried? You think I ran away? You didn't follow my orders. The money is not old, it is almost new, and you made a record of the serial numbers. Why don't you follow orders?"

"Knock it off, Tiki! Where is the other stuff?"

He said, "You are too impatient. Everything takes time. You don't know if Tiki has outsmarted you and you hate it. That you, the big gringo could be taken in by Tiki, whom you dislike. What will you tell your big boss in Washington if I don't give you the money? But you don't need to worry, Tiki is honorable. Sit by your desk, Tiki will call."

After he hung up, I was really climbing the walls. That SOB was going to make me sweat it out. We knew he had given up his apartment, and it would be extremely difficult to find him now. Elena was supposedly living with a relative, but we didn't know where. We had the airline terminals under surveillance in case they decided to flee to their homeland.

Ten minutes later the phone rang again. I lunged for it. Tiki was jingling a couple of keys together. He said, "You hear that? If you had these keys you would have the funny money. You still worried? You don't have to be. It may take a day or a week, but Tiki will find a way to get you your money." I told him that I wasn't waiting a day or a week. I had kept my part of the bargain and I expected him to keep his. He said, "It's not easy to make all these arrangements. I have a lot of people to deal with, and you only gave me half the money I asked for. You don't appreciate how hard I work for the gringo. You have no choice, you must wait!" He snickered and hung up the phone.

It took a long time to sink in, but for the first time I realized that Tiki really was a "psycho." I could only console myself by remembering that he had given us the plant. This alone would have been worth a sizable reward. It added up that Tiki figured he was reaching the end of his rope and that someone would turn him in before long and he'd be arrested. He probably decided to turn the remainder of the notes, or part of them, over to us, collect what he could get for them, then take Elena, and run for it.

The phone rang for what seemed the millionth time. A very serious Tiki was on the line. He said he had the money in two public lockers, but he couldn't figure a way to get the keys to me. He, of course, didn't want to meet anyone and didn't want to be around when the keys were delivered. "It's simple," I said, "take one of the good $10's I gave you, give it and the keys to a cab driver and tell him to send the keys to our office. I also want you to get the license number of the cab. In the meantime, I want to know what lockers you are using and the box numbers in case the keys don't arrive." He thought a minute and said, "You are a goddamn smart gringo. Good-bye."

Five minutes later he was back on the telephone. He said, "Locker numbers 486 and 487 at the bus terminal. I don't got no more dimes. So long, gringo."

The covering agents were still in the vicinity of the bus terminal, having tailed the old woman close to it. They immediately covered the two lockers. Half an hour later, a cab driver came to the office and delivered keys to lockers 486 and 487. He said an old woman gave him $10 to deliver the keys. He said she hailed him down at the bus terminal. He identified himself, gave a description of the woman, and left. He said the woman acted very strangely. He said he hoped he wasn't getting involved in anything. I assured him that everything he did was fine.

There was every reason to be both relieved and elated, but somehow I felt we still had another chapter to write. The boxes could be empty or filled with garbage. It wasn't hard to believe that Tiki could yet have the last laugh. He was capable of anything.

The agents proceeded to the lockers with the keys and found two cheap suitcases in each. They were locked, but the agents managed to open them. Each contained a large quantity of counterfeit $10's and $20's.

The agent's phone call was most welcome and for the first time in days, I was able to relax. Tiki had been an enigma. No one could really figure him and his motivation out. His hatred for the "gringo" was intense; yet, for reasons only known to himself, he kept his word when it suited him. On the other hand, he exploited his own countrymen with the same zeal as he did the gringo.

There was still a lot of work to be done before we could close this case. We felt that Tiki was on his way somewhere. Officially we still didn't have a solid reason to pursue him. The next best thing was to try to put all the pieces together and perhaps something would fall into place. Elena wasn't a fugitive yet because up to that day she hadn't missed an appearance in court. I assigned several agents to specific tasks to learn all we could about Tiki. When he had been in the office, we surreptitiously took several photos of him. Agents took the photos to the so-called hideout apartment that Tiki had rented in the city. The apartment manager identified Tiki's picture as the man who had rented the apartment several months before. He said he knew Tiki as "Mr. Lopez," and that he rarely used the premises. Since "Mr. Lopez" had always paid his rent on time, there was no reason to be suspicious or inquisitive. Tiki had told the manager that he traveled extensively and would rarely be home. The agents wanted to make a complete search of the apartment and, since the rent was now overdue, the landlord had no objection. There were only a few personal things in the very sparsely furnished apartment — a few winter clothes and some women's clothing. Apparently Tiki had used the apartment for other diversions that Elena wouldn't appreciate.

It was now established that the $25,000 seized in the apartment were, without a doubt, Tiki's. The notes were being processed for fingerprints with our hopes that Tiki's prints would appear on them. We had obtained a copy of his fingerprints from the police as the result of an old arrest for "policy or illegal lottery operation." The agents tried to do as complete a background investigation as possible. He was possibly an alien to the United States, but there was no record of him with Immigration and Naturalization Services. All his relatives were either in Mexico or South America.

The answer to a lot of questions would lie with Elena or Tomaso. She was undoubtedly running away with Tiki, and Tomaso wasn't talking. All passers of this note who had been arrested were re-interviewed, but no one wanted to talk about Tiki. The appearance of the notes tapered off until there was hardly any trace of them showing up in the city.

Tomaso remained in jail because he had several other outstanding warrants. The only thing we could do was to push the case against him and hope he would cooperate before he was sentenced. The case was put on the calendar, called for trial, and Tomaso pled guilty. Two days after the plea, Tomaso sent for me.

I made arrangements to talk privately with him at length because I felt sure Tomaso wanted to cooperate. He definitely was in a position to give a lot of information. His stint in jail was beginning to weigh heavily upon him.

Tomaso was sure he would get a substantial sentence, which he admittedly deserved. What bothered him was that it appeared that he was the only one going to jail. Where were the others? How did the government get the information for the search warrant? I told him I wasn't at liberty to discuss the government's case with him, but I did want to learn who the other conspirators were. I assured him that we would pursue anyone who was involved. Tomaso smiled and said, "Would you pursue Tiki?"

I asked, "Why not?" He replied, "Because he is your number one informer in this case. Without him there wouldn't be a case." I told Tomaso he was fishing. If he had any information about the others involved, I was anxious to get whatever he had. He said he didn't want to be an informer, but he was now convinced Tiki was playing both ends. He said he was ready to tell the whole story.

He began his story with his initial meeting with Tiki about a year earlier at a local dance. He then told about Tiki's visit to his print shop and their subsequent venture into the making of bogus titles, bills of sale, driver's licenses, and commercial checks. He explained how Tiki put him on a salary and eventually propositioned him about making counterfeit money. He stated that in the beginning he gave all the completed notes to Tiki, but later decided to print some for himself. He admitted printing a couple hundred thousand dollars and started to make sales on his own. He named the people he sold them to and the amounts they purchased. He told about the supplies that Tiki purchased. These purchases were later checked out and confirmed, as Tiki was identified in two places as being the person buying the printing supplies.

The interview with Tomaso was very informative and extremely helpful. It gave us several more defendants and, best of all, it gave us a case against Tiki. The interview continued and when it was completed, the matter was scheduled for presentation to the grand jury. Tomaso agreed to be a witness. He told me, however, that he felt we were wasting our time. He cryptically stated, "You'll never get Tiki."

Several weeks later, the case was presented to the grand jury. Tiki and several others were indicted. All we had to do was find Tiki and this case could be wrapped up. We were unsuccessful in locating Tiki and Elena; however, while the search was under way, Tomaso's words of "You'll never get Tiki" were coming true in a crime that was being committed in Tiki's old neighborhood.

Tiki and Elena entered a local supermarket. Tiki walked over to the manager's office, pulled out his .45 and announced, "This is a stickup! Gimme me all your money!" The manager pleaded that a deposit had already been taken to the bank a few hours earlier so the safe was empty. Tiki ordered the manager to open the safe. The manager fumbled, but couldn't open the safe — the pressure of being held at gunpoint was too much for him. Tiki thought the manager was stalling or maybe he had set off a silent alarm. He flew into a rage, striking the manager a savage blow on the head with the pistol, and firing a shot at him before running out of the market. The shot caused a near panic. Customers ran for the doors, hampering Tiki's escape. He fired several more shots in the air to clear the exit. The police arrived on the scene just as Tiki fled the market and ran down the street. Knowing the neighborhood quite well, he decided to try to make it to a local social club where he knew he would be safe. After all, these were his people, and he had done a lot for them. They would hide him from the fat pigs.

Upon entering the club, he ran straight into the men's room and bolted the door. The police were in close pursuit and chased him right into the club and with weapons drawn. The patrons had been playing cards when the activity started. They now remained frozen in place clutching their cards, dumbfounded by the sudden turn of events. No one moved or said a word. Before the police could say anything, one of the card players pointed to the toilet door. The police ordered Tiki to come out with his hands in the air. He replied by firing a shot through the door. The police officers replied by firing back. Then, it was quiet. A pool of blood trickled from under the door. It told the story. It was all over.

Tiki was pronounced dead on arrival at the hospital. Elena was picked up in the neighborhood, and she told the police where they had been and what they had been doing. It just didn't seem as important anymore.

Tomaso's words rang in my ears again, "You'll never get Tiki." But he was wrong — somebody did.

"Cheech"

It's not an earthshaking or original statement to say that informants are the lifeblood of police work. To deprecate the work and value of informants would be foolish. Informants, out of necessity, come in all shapes and forms and the reason that motivate them are many and varied. I guess, in my over sixty years in law enforcement, I handled and worked with more informants than most law enforcement people. The very nature of law enforcement work makes it imperative to use the services of as many informants as we can cultivate. Naturally, informants come from many sources. Some people provide information just because "it is the thing to do" as a good citizen.

There are those who would sell anything, including their friends, for money and there are those who are defendants in cases and feel that informing is the only way they can be given some consideration by the authorities.

They called him "Cheech." There was nothing special about the nickname. In my Italian background, the word simply was Italian for "Frank." He was a contemporary of most of the top syndicate hoodlums of today and he served time with the best of them. He was what is known as a "wiseguy," a "connected person." He was not quite what is known as a "Don" or "Godfather," but he was well respected in the area he came from and the circles he moved in. The word "work," in any of its forms, was not in his vocabulary and he lived by his wits all his life. He ran the gamut of being a truant, petty thief, narcotic peddler, numbers runner, and receiver and fencer of stolen property. The money he earned was used to finance a sizable shylock or loansharking operation. That is, he loaned large amounts of money for short periods of time at exorbitant rates. He was privy to all the crime meetings and at times he was considered a top man in one of the many syndicates that were in operation in New York City.

Since shylocking was giving him such a good income, it was necessary for him to utilize several enforcers to collect payments that were over due. Very often he found himself the owner of a legitimate business that he took over when payments were not forthcoming. As he took over the business he would either bankrupt it out and keep a sizable profit for himself or he would actually continue to operate it as a profitable enterprise. It looked like Cheech would be one of the more successful criminals, and he would be in a position to retire early and live at his leisure. His idyllic existence came to an abrupt end one day when the police came to his house and placed him under arrest.

He learned that he was indicted on an old drug case. It seemed he and a friend became owners of a kilo of heroin at a time when he was very successful in a gambling venture. The person who owned the kilo used it to pay off a sizable debt. It was a year or so later that this person became involved in a homicide. He needed help badly and the only way he could get himself a "deal" was by cooperating with the police. He told of selling the kilo of heroin to Cheech. He not only would testify against Cheech, but he would also get another man to do likewise. The police also had independent information against Cheech and his drug involvement. They put it all together and made a successful case against him. His attorney advised him to plead guilty and take a five-year rap. Cheech knew he was licked but insisted on going to trial. Not that he figured on beating the case, but just to see if the two friends of his would take the stand against him. If they did, there would be no denying that they were informants. They would be under oath, broadcasting it to everyone.

Neither man was afraid of reprisals, as they faced long prison terms and were looking for any kind of reward. The trial was held. The witnesses stood up well and Cheech was convicted. He received a seven-year sentence. He was philosophical about the conviction. It seemed ironic that he was going away on a charge for doing something he inwardly despised. Drugs and narcotics were not his particular schtick. He simply had an opportunity to turn a fast dollar by taking the kilo and it proved to be his undoing. The prison sentence was bad enough, but worse still was the fate of the small empire that he had built. He knew that during his incarceration someone would take over his enterprises and he would eventually lose everything. It wasn't supposed to be that way, but he knew that he had inherited a lot of businesses by the same route. Absentee ownership did not fare well at this level.

The prison years were routine. He met a lot of old friends at the big house and also he made a lot of new friends. He was a pretty affable person and he made friends easily. Long before he was released he made connections with various people in jail who were anxious to do business with him. Cheech had a good bundle stashed away and would be in an excellent position to handle any kind of contraband when he was released. He decided that he would disengage himself from any syndicate and try to operate as inconspicuously as possible.

The years in prison passed uneventfully for Cheech, and it was inevitable that the doors would swing open for him in minimum time. He did not cause any trouble at the institution and was always an eager volunteer. He took part in many medical experiments, some of which were classified as dangerous. His participation helped him get an early release.

While he was awaiting his parole hearing for early release, he decided that his best bet when he was released was to work with four young burglars who were from New Jersey but who were serving time in New York. He liked these young hoods. They had plenty of guts and looked like "stand up guys." He could tell they knew their business and each one had acquired a special type of expertise. One was a good "wheel man," another a "safe" man, another a "lock" man; the last was not only very agile but had worked for an alarm company and could deactivate most of the alarm systems in use at that time. While these men were excellent burglars, they were very poor businessmen. They invariably acquired loot, but never had a good outlet for it. Cheech decided he would handle the distribution for them through his sources. He had connections all over the country and felt he could handle anything as long as there was a good margin of profit.The group promised Cheech they would contact him as soon as they were released.

Cheech made the street and purchased and operated a small luncheonette as his front. It served three purposes; it satisfied the conditions of his parole, it gave him a base from which to operate, and he was dealing in a cash business giving him the freedom to "launder" the profits from his side businesses. He made it a cardinal rule to not keep any loot on the premises as he knew he would be getting plenty of attention from the local police. The luncheonette was actually a profitable proposition and Cheech was quite surprised to learn that he could make a living legitimately.

Several months after his release he married Phyllis, a girl he had known for some time. He set up a comfortable apartment in the city and was doing quite well for a con that had just finished a long stretch. The restaurant was doing nicely, he managed to salvage part of his old lottery operation, a little shylocking, and an occasional bit of local "fencing" gave him a good income.

At about the same time, the "Jersey Four" were released from their prison sentence and soon became more choosy about the types of crime they were going to commit. They were no longer interested in the usual house burglaries. The felt they had graduated to the "big time" and were ready for the major leagues. They knew they were good "safe men" and they decided to burglarize stores, offices, businesses and places where they could possibly obtain checks, bonds, stocks, and any kind of negotiable paper, including currency. They were assured of a ready market for whatever they stole. Cheech had guaranteed he'd take all the "paper" they could get.

Their first "hit" was a small, out of the way, post office. The proceeds of their efforts were several thousand dollars worth of postal money orders and $700 worth of stamps. The Jersey Group immediately got in touch with

Cheech. He purchased all the items for ten cents on the dollar and had no trouble getting rid of the paper at a very good profit.

The visits from the four became quite frequent. As they made their scores, Cheech was always there to turn it into cash for them. The arrangement worked out very well; and Cheech decided he would stick with his new friends, and the relationship proved very lucrative.

It was inevitable that Cheech would have to bring in some of his old cronies. They were asking questions and wanted part of the action. Cheech knew he couldn't play it alone for too long. The amount of paper he was handling was getting bigger all the time and he had to seek out new people to handle the increased volume. Cheech tried to treat everyone honestly and squarely. He rapidly became a "somebody" in the hierarchy of the underworld. He was privy to meetings involving some "respected" people and before too long he found himself as a "Mister Big" in his particular neighborhood. He met with his contemporaries in other cities and found himself sending underlings to handle his business. He was well versed in all criminal activities, and very often he was asked to act as an arbitrator on some "very sticky matters."

Even Cheech should have known that things could not run smoothly forever. He had his ups and downs before and he should have reached a point where he would stop pushing. Money was no longer too important. Lord knows, he had enough of it to last a lifetime. It was the power! This newly found respect and prestige was just what his ego needed. He was engaged in criminal activities all his life. In the early years it was a "dog eat dog" existence, but now things were different. He commanded respect from practically everyone he met and he liked it. He was "Mr. Kingpin," "The Man."

So it was when he arranged a meeting with the Jersey Four. Feeney, the leader, told Cheech quite excitedly that the group had hit a lucky streak and in their last few burglaries they got a large number of U.S. Government Series E Savings Bonds. They figured they had over half a million dollars worth and were anxious to know if Cheech could handle the whole bundle. Cheech was not one to make hasty decisions. He told the group that he wanted a thirty-day option on the deal. He would give the matter a lot of thought and would have an answer within the allotted time. He stressed that he wanted the whole bundle if he decided to go into it and didn't want any local competition.

Cheech gave it a lot of thought. U.S. Government bonds were something he was not familiar with. He knew that by using his existing outlets he could get rid of a good deal of the bonds. He calculated he could buy them for about ten cents on the dollar and unload them for fifteen cents on the dollar. Handling the bonds in large amounts would give him an excellent return on his money. He felt there was still about eighty-five cents on the dollar to be accounted for. Who got the lion's share of that? Cheech made up his mind to learn all he could about the disposition of bonds. He spent hours with people who were familiar with the disposing of stolen bonds and in ten days he learned enough about bonds to decide to handle them his way. He knew bonds were made out in the names of the registered owners. He knew most people did not keep a list of their bonds, and if they were lost or stolen they had to write to the government to get the serial numbers and make a claim. He knew this took a considerable amount of time, and time was a valuable ally for him. Series E Bonds could be cashed only at banks and they had to be endorsed in the name of the registered owner. The bank, of course, would not know the registered owner and naturally would not know if the signature was genuine. Cheech asked why he should sell the bonds at a few points profit. Why not have a group of people to forge and cash the bonds? He would give them a flat fee and pocket the remaining majority share, turning a tremendous profit.

To make sure he understood the procedure, he decided to cash several bonds that he legitimately owned. He entered the bank and was directed to a desk where a bank officer sat. He offered the bonds for cashing out and he was asked if he had an account at the bank. Cheech said he did not. He was then asked for identification. He fumbled through his wallet and produced a driver's license and a social security card. The bank officer wrote the identification numbers on the back of the bonds and after Cheech endorsed the bonds, the bank officer approved them for cashing. Cheech walked out of the bank with a small smile on his lips. He was now satisfied that he could handle the deal.

He anticipated that he could line up enough people to peddle the bonds, and the only thing he would have to supply them with, beside the bonds, were various pieces of identification. That could be a problem. However, he knew a few printers who used to print lottery tickets for him. He felt they could counterfeit almost any piece of identification. He propositioned "Sam the Printer," an old friend and former cell mate who owed him a favor or two. The response was good. Sam had been printing counterfeit checks for a group who also needed some matching identification. He printed some New York and New Jersey driver's licenses, wedding certificates, and some fairly good social security cards. Cheech was delighted. He told Sam he could use several dozen of each and he would send someone around to pick them up. He then contacted the Jersey Four and told them he would exercise his option and take all the bonds off their hands.

He drove a good bargain and got the bonds for nine cents on the dollar. He even convinced them to wait thirty days for the payment. Cheech then began to recruit the people he needed for forging and passing the bonds. He decided to have two two-person teams operating together and he would accompany them on the first trip.

He selected a city in the mid-west as the first target. His two teams consisted of two couples, Andy and Bea, and Benny and Irma. He spent a lot of time teaching and training them the proper procedure for cashing the bonds. He meticulously listed all the bonds, the names of the registered owners, arranging to get sufficient identification in each name from "Sam the Printer." The bonds were registered in the names of both men and women, generally husband and wife, therefore the concept of the two-couple teams.

Andy had a year of college and presented a nice appearance. He was the typical "Joe College" or "all American boy" image. He was 28 years of age, six feet tall, weighed 199 pounds, had dark hair and a quick friendly grin. He had no criminal record.

He was partnered with his live-in roommate, Bea. She had also never been arrested. She had been married but was now separated and living with Andy in a small and cramped apartment in the city. She had aspired to be a showgirl, but now had settled into a domestic routine with Andy. She was attractive at 26 years of age, five-feet two inches, and weighing one hundred thirty pounds. Her hair was a natural blond, matching her blue eyes. To all who saw them, Andy and Bea were a typical young couple.

As wholesome as Andy and Bea were, Benny and Irma were an antithesis. At 42 of age, Benny had a long criminal record but could pass himself off as an average overweight, out of shape, five feet six, 170 lb. businessman. His partner, Irma, was a former prostitute who had been married twice but was now living with Benny. She looked older than her thirty-seven years, with 140 pounds packed onto her short five-feet one inch body. Her black hair had a few strands of silver roots that she tried to cover with a poor dye job. She had been arrested five times for prostitution, which gave her a certain toughness and hard edge to go along with quite a knowledge and education in the ways of the street world.

Cheech supplied the four with enough money for clothes, luggage, airfare and just about everything they needed for the trip. He arranged for hotel rooms and local addresses that could be used when forging the bonds. Cheech had gone to the designated city by car and prepared all the advance arrangements himself.

On the appointed day, they all met in the hotel. Benny was selected to be the first to cash bonds. Cheech gave him $2,500 in bonds and enough identification to stuff his wallet. Irma was assigned to watch the bank from the outside to make sure that all went well with Benny. In the event that Benny was arrested, Irma's job was to call the hotel and advise Andy who in turn would have Bea notify Cheech. They had a rendezvous point selected. All three would meet there and leave town with the remaining bonds. Cheech would then supply Benny, or whoever was arrested, with local counsel and a bondsman.

At noon, Irma drove Benny to the designated bank and parked where she could observe what was going on. Benny went into the bank and asked the nearest teller where he could cash some bonds. He was directed to one of the officers at the desk. He told the officer that he had just come into town and wanted to cash some bonds. He showed the bonds to the officer who inquired about Benny's business. Benny stated that he had just moved into town and was looking around for a business opportunity. He mentioned that he was thinking of opening a bakery. The banker gave Benny the name of a local real estate man who could help him find a location. The officer asked him if he was going to open an account at the bank. Benny replied that yes, he intended to. He was told to sign the bonds and to fill out a new account form. He was then asked how much he wanted to deposit. He told the banker that he would start off with one hundred dollars because he would need most of his cash for business operating costs. The necessary paper work was accomplished in a very short time. The bonds were computed to be worth nineteen hundred-fifty dollars, including interest. One hundred dollars was placed on deposit in Benny's new account, and he walked out of the bank with the rest in cash. He met Irma and they drove away. Benny checked his watch. The whole operation had taken only ten minutes.

When they arrived back at the hotel, they were met by Cheech, Andy and Bea. Benny was excited and very animated as he reported the events to Cheech. Cheech asked Benny, "What identification did you use?' Benny came to a complete stop, surprised. He scratched his head and said, "Holy shit! He never asked for identification! He was so anxious to get me to open an account that he paid no attention to the bonds!" They all laughed with delight at how easy and simple it had been and they had the cash to prove it. Cheech decided that was enough work for one day. He said that they should go out and celebrate. Benny handed the eighteen hundred fifty dollars cash over to Cheech. He kept one thousand and told the group to, "split the rest, go out and have a good time but be ready to go to work early tomorrow."

The next morning they all met in Cheech's room. It was decided to rent another car and have two groups working simultaneously. The plan was the same. One person would enter the bank and redeem the bonds while the other acted as cover or "lookout." They would alternate positions as they moved from bank to bank. If anything went wrong, the covering person would notify Cheech and proceed to the rendezvous point.

Irma was selected to take $3,000 maturity face value worth of bonds to cash. When she went to the bank officer, she told him that she and her husband were new in town,that they were setting up their house and there were a lot of things they needed to buy that required cash. She volunteered that she wished to open a checking account and would deposit more money when she cashed the remaining bonds she had at home. She showed the bank officer a driver's license and a social security card. She signed the bonds and he noted the driver's license and social security card numbers on the back of the bonds. He also gave her a slip okaying the bond transaction and told her to pick up her money at a teller's window, directing her to go to another desk to open her new account. She went to the teller's window first, and presented the bonds and the authorizing form. She was given twenty-six hundred seventy-five dollars in cash. She was so elated that she forgot about opening an account and left the bank.

She met Benny in the parking lot and together they drove to another bank where Benny followed the same procedure that was now becoming the standard routine. He was easily successful in cashing five thousand dollars of the bonds. A young teller, who was apparently a high school or college student working at a part-time job, handled his transaction. He produced a social security card and was attempting to take a driver's license from his wallet when she told him that she could use the social security card number for identifying information, even though the card clearly stated, "For Social Security Purposes - Not for Identification". He put the false driver's license back into his wallet.

At another bank across town, Bea and Andy had started to work. Andy arrived at the bank at lunchtime. An attractive young girl in her mid-twenties was sitting at one of the desks. Andy correctly figured she was filling in for someone else during the lunch hour. He told her he was a nightclub entertainer and he had just completed a "gig" at one of the hotels in town. He said he was going to Europe for a vacation, but when he returned he was going to open up a supper club in town. The girl was easily impressed and taken in by him. She not only cashed nearly thirty-three hundred dollars in bonds for him, but she also agreed to meet him that night for a drink at a nightclub. She never asked for any identification.

Andy met and joined Bea who had $1,500 worth of bonds to cash. She was driven to another bank and was very obviously nervous. This was her first taste of crime and she wasn't sure how she would handle it. She walked into the bank and told the first bank representative she met that she wanted to cash some bonds. She was directed to a bank officer and meekly asked him if he would cash some bonds for her. She showed him the bonds and he asked for identification.

She produced and showed him a driver's license and social security card. The careful banker asked her if she had any other identification. She fumbled through her purse and produced a folded and wrinkled birth certificate in the name of the registered owner. He asked her if she were married. She looked up at him and stumbled a mild "Yes." He then became suspicious that all her identification was in her maiden name. He asked her to wait a minute and left the desk with the bonds firmly held in his hand. As soon as he left, Bea became panicky and fled the bank after grabbing up her identification papers. Andy picked her up in the rented car that he abandoned on a side street near the hotel. He called Cheech and told him what had happened.

They all met at the rendezvous point, since they didn't know if someone at the bank had obtained the license number and description of the "getaway" car. It was decided that they had all better return to New York.

The drive to New York was uneventful. While driving back to the city, Cheech collected the money from Irma, Benny and Andy. It amounted to over seven thousand, two hundred dollars. He kept six thousand and had the group divide up the remaining twelve hundred. He told the group that they had made their first mistake. Bea did not have a good story ready when the bank officer became suspicious. Instead of panicking, she should have told the banker that she was single or that she had been married only for a few days. However, he complimented her on leaving the bank instead of waiting to see what the banker intended to do. He said he didn't care about the loss of the bonds, what was really important was that no one was arrested and they had made a good profit.

The trip back afforded Cheech the opportunity to think about the venture. For a very small amount of effort he was able to clear over seven thousand dollars profit on the work performed by his group in just two days. There was no reason why that could not be doubled or tripled as soon as the group became more experienced. Their share of the bond cashing expedition amounted to approximately five hundred dollars each. They were well satisfied with the results of the trip. Cheech promised himself that he would make sure the identification was proper on the next trip and to be sure to see "Sam the Printer" about getting more identification for the remainder of the bonds.

When they arrived in New York, he told the group to take a few days off and be ready to go out of town the following week when he contacted them. Cheech had other business deals that required his attention.

One of his necessary errands was to stop at Sam's and try to make a deal for more sophisticated identification. Sam tried to beg off by saying he had more work than he could handle. He told Cheech that he was going to try his hand at making counterfeit money. Cheech warned him that making counterfeit money was a risky business that would bring federal heat. "Heat or not," Sam said, "it is one of the best deals I have had in a long time and is well worth the risk. A crew wants me to print a million dollars in counterfeit $100 bills. They've furnished the plates and they are good. All I gotta to do is get the paper and ink." He figured he could print the million in two or three days. Cheech managed to get Sam to agree to make the needed identification for him as soon as he finished printing the "queer."

The following week, Cheech called the group together. He went over the details again several times about how to forge and cash the bonds. He agreed to spend several days with them but after that he expected they would be able to operate on their own. He promised them a flat 25 percent of the proceeds from the bonds plus any expenses they incurred. No one had any objections. Cheech picked out a target city and they left the next morning.

Cheech waited at the hotel as they went about their business. Late in the afternoon of the first day, each reported back to Cheech. Benny had disposed of $5,200 worth of bonds; Irma $4,700; Andy $3,900 and Bea made one successful trip worth $2,700. The sixteen thousand dollar total for the one day pleased Cheech, especially since there had been no bad incidents.

That night Cheech again took them to a local nightclub and they celebrated until the small hours of the morning. The cocktail waitresses, cigarette girls, and the cute skimpily dressed club photographer all paid special attention to Cheech, as he was becoming very generous as the evening wore on. The more he drank, the more generous he became with his tips.

The next day no one was in the mood for work. All slept late and Cheech had found himself with a bad head and a playmate who had managed to share his bed with him. Cheech disposed of her services soon after he awakened, and then took a shower. The "lady" slipped out of the room as quietly and unnoticed as she came in. Later, when he got dressed and was ready to check out of the room, he almost passed out when he realized that his bed mate had not only left with his roll of cash but that she had also taken a sizable amount of bonds. Cheech was furious realizing he had been taken by one of the oldest tricks in the world. Man has a roll of cash, drinks and socializes to excess; meets girl; frolics and falls asleep or takes a shower; girl discovers money; girl and money disappear. He didn't even remember what the girl looked like! He was too embarrassed to tell the others that he had been taken like a young soldier on his first visit to the "big city." He couldn't believe that he, Cheech, had been fleeced by a common whore.

He made an excuse to the group and told them that he had been called back to New York to take care of some important matters. On the return trip the group kidded him about the "friend" he had acquired the night before. The best he could learn in the conversations and ribbing was that he did not pick her up until they left the nightclub. She was apparently hustling on the street, and took up with Cheech and his group while they were walking from the club to the parking lot.

The trip ended up in a total loss for Cheech. He was not in a position to get revenge since he did not want to confide in anyone. He was also concerned that the prostitute had a good bundle of bonds that she or someone else might try to cash. In that event, if anything went wrong, she could lead the authorities to the hotel room where she stole them and she could also provide a good description of Cheech and his friends.

This unfortunate turn of events annoyed Cheech to no end. He was not anxious to accompany his group on another venture. He still had plenty of bonds to dispose of and his other interests demanded his time. Therefore, he decided to make Benny the "group leader" and let the group go out on its own. Benny accepted the offer and decided he could run the whole show for Cheech. While the rest of the group had other thoughts, they decided to accept Benny's leadership, at least temporarily. Benny found another person, named Walt, to add to the group. Benny told Walt all about the operation and he agreed to become part of the group.

Walt was in his middle thirties and at five-feet eight inches tall, weighed about one hundred sixty pounds. He had spent some time in prison with Benny for "paper-hanging" and had more than his share of experience with women. He was very personable and outgoing, and his looks made him attractive to women.

The first night out, Walt made the "grand play" for Bea and she seemed to like the attention she was getting. While this was going on, Andy was doing a slow burn and couldn't wait until he got Bea alone in their hotel room. After arriving in the chosen city, Andy and Bea checked into a hotel room and immediately engaged in a violent argument. Andy lost control of his temper and slapped Bea many times all over the room. The next morning, Bea's face looked like she had walked into a door...over and over again. She told Benny that she was in no shape to go out passing bonds. Benny became furious, strongly and threateningly insisting that she go with Andy as planned.

Bea didn't like the prospect of getting into another argument or possibly worse, so she accepted three thousand dollars in bonds from Benny and left with Andy. He drove her to a bank that had been previously selected and told her to get going and not to foul up. After entering the bank and making inquiries, she was directed to a bank official who specialized in bonds. He invited her to sit down at his desk and he would help her. While handling the transaction he asked her where she lived in town. Bea had many things on her mind and was not paying attention to the bond transaction. She blurted out a non-existent address. He asked her to sign the bonds. While she was signing them he noticed she was writing a different address than the one she had given him. The banker thought he would try again. He asked her why she was cashing the bonds. She said she and her daughter had been in an auto accident and she needed the money for the hospital bills. He asked her what hospital her daughter was in. Bea blew it again and claimed she forgot! The banker was now certain that Bea was lying and was not the owner of the bonds. He signaled the guard on duty near the front door. The guard took Bea into custody and restrained her to await the arrival of the police. Bea was hardly aware of what was going on. She was a bundle of nerves. Her whole body ached from the beating she had received the night before.

Andy waited outside the bank until the police car arrived. He knew something had gone wrong and quickly got into his car and left the area. He then made a telephone call to alert the others. They all met at the pre-selected rendezvous point, checked out of the hotel, made a call to Cheech and quickly left town to return to New York.

When Cheech heard about what had transpired, he became furious with the situation and mad at himself for not going with the group. He told them to give him back the bonds they still had in their possession and to suspend operations until Bea could be taken care of. He told Andy to return to the hotel immediately to see if Bea had tried to contact him. Cheech said he had a bondsman and a lawyer on tap that would get her out on bail as soon as they got the word.

Bea was still in a daze. She remembered being handcuffed very tightly with her hands behind her and being whisked away from the bank and taken to a police station. It was a hot, smelly, creepy place. People were coming in and going out, phones were ringing, radios were blasting, and people were arguing. General bedlam. Not a friendly face to be seen. She finally wound up in the squad room; her hands still immobilized behind her. All the blood was drained from her face. She was placed in a chair opposite a sweaty, fat, old man with greasy, thinning gray hair, behind what looked like a depression era metal desk. He was some kind of detective with a big gun on his belt. His fat stomach pushed against his sweaty shirt that was struggling to hold that bulging mass. He began to ask her all kinds of questions: name? date of birth? address? parents? school? jobs? During this routine another man came into the room. He was a young kid, maybe twenty-two or twenty-three, didn't look bad, said he was a Secret Service agent. "Holly crap! What did they think she was? Some kind of spy…or worse? Secret Service! Now maybe the army will come next and she will be shot. What a relief! They must have the wrong person! Sure she signed and tried to cash some stupid bonds in a bank. So what? They weren't hers, belonged to some woman. They probably were talking to the woman now and knew the bonds were stolen. Where did she get them? Who gave them to her? Who? Who? WHO?"

Christ! She had a splitting headache. Her head was spinning, her lips were swollen, and her body ached. She recalled the beating of the night before. She remembered that Andy said he'd kill her if she ever double-crossed him.

Someone was speaking to her. She could hear him saying, "You don't have to talk…anything you say can be used against you."…Constitution rights–lawyers–public defenders–bond–bail–statements–court–judge: she felt like screaming and those blasted handcuffs were biting into her wrists. She tried to get up but couldn't make it and slumped to the floor. She felt like she was floating around the room. There were no more cops, no bonds, no jails, no Andys, no Cheeches, no nothing, where was mother? A warm feeling of euphoria completely enveloped her. Suddenly, she felt a sharp stinging slap across the face! Andy? Someone with a soft voice was saying, "C'mon, honey, you'll be alight." When she opened her eyes she realized she was on a couch in the prison wing of the county hospital. There was a doctor giving her something to drink and there was that stupid fed who wasn't giving up so easily. At least the handcuffs were off. What did he want? He was going to ask her some questions about the bonds. She felt she had to tell him something. Could she say she got them from Cheech? Then they would want to know who he was and where he lived. The whole story would take hours to tell and then she would have to tell the story again to a judge. Then she would have to worry about the gang catching up to her. She would have to run, run, run. How long could she do it? How long before they caught her? Was it worthwhile to say anything?

The whole mess suddenly became revolting and she thought if she could only turn the clock back, not a whole lifetime, just a few years. Those years which she thought were the unhappiest of her life. Up every morning at seven-thirty, a stupid mother getting her out of bed to attend a stupid school, meeting stupid square kids who talked about dopey things like going to college, getting married, having families, buying a house in the suburbs. No sir, not for her! She was going to get away from this stupid grind. She'd go with the fast crowd, those that knew how to live. Cut school, turn on, sleep around, and do your own thing. It was a million years ago. The break with the family, the running away to New York City, living with a girlfriend, then a boy friend, then anyone who would have her. Up to now she had been lucky. She met Andy and they seemed to get along pretty well. She could not make up her mind if she loved him. Sometimes she felt that she honestly didn't know what love was, but most of the time they were good for each other. He always had enough money and seemed to know what he was doing. When he propositioned her about working for Cheech, she eagerly accepted. The one score that she made netted her a couple of hundred dollars and things were looking up. Then the stupid bank official had to stick his nose in and ask her a lot of stupid questions, and here she was under arrest and not a soul to turn to.

At this point, the fed, who didn't seem to be old enough to vote and didn't know when to quit, was ready to talk to her again. He told her she was going to be arraigned before a United States Commissioner who would read her the charges, set the amount of bail, and schedule a date for a hearing. Nothing of what he said made much sense to her. This being arrested was all new.

She tried to put on a brave front but inwardly she was frightened and would have given anything just to know that her father and mother were near. Her heart sank, why did she think of them now. Both were gone. They died within eight months of each other and she didn't even see fit to attend either funeral. She was too involved in really living and having fun. She wondered what it would be like to have a brother or sister. Someone she could be close to and relate to. Hell, what was the use? Other girls had brothers and sisters and they didn't seem to get along. There was always an age gap, even if it was only a year or so.

The young agent asked her (asked her? What choice did she have? She had those handcuffs on again, didn't she?) to accompany him to a car he had parked outside. She went with him and in ten minutes they arrived at what appeared to be some sort of official building, a post office, or something. They went upstairs to the third floor into a room marked "U.S. Treasury Department – U.S. Secret Service" She was taken into another room and escorted to a table where she was fingerprinted. The ink was messy and her manicure was ruined. Then to another room; they called it the "mug room." Just like on television, her picture would be taken. God! Her hair was a mess and she looked like hell with the bruises, the "shiner" on her eye, and the fat lip. She was sure she would look like a criminal when they got finished. Someone took her whole history. She was then taken to another floor and to the office of a government district attorney. God! He was another young one —cute too. She wouldn't have minded meeting him in a hotel room. He went over the same questions. It seemed like everyone was warning her about talking; yet they were asking her questions. But she wouldn't talk. It was only a matter of time until Andy would come and get her out of there. After all, she didn't hurt anyone and she wasn't too sure they had a case against her. A good lawyer would find a loophole. They always do on television. Isn't that what lawyers are for? Didn't Cheech tell them he would have a lawyer available?

The little government lawyer became exasperated when she refused to talk, and said, "OK, let's arraign her." She was taken to another floor and there, sitting behind a desk as though he were waiting for them, was a kindly looking old man. He was the commissioner. He looked like anyone's grandfather, certainly not an important government big shot. The charges were read: forgery, attempted uttering, US code, and a lot of other words that meant she tried to cash some stolen bonds. The grand-fatherly man asked if she had a lawyer, she simply answered, "No." He asked if she wanted one. She said she thought someone was going to get one for her. He didn't ask any dumb questions. He turned to the cute little government attorney and asked, "What about bail?" The miserable little runt said an awful lot of bad things about her. How did he know anything? He just met her. He said she had no ties, she would run away, and she was part of a group of people who were victimizing banks out of large sums of money. He wanted a bail set at no less than twenty-five thousand dollars. The stupid bastard might just as well have asked for a million. Who did he think she was? "Ma Barker"? Even bank robbers didn't have to put up that much money. She looked at him again in contempt and felt that he would be a waste of time in a hotel room. The kindly old man was no bargain either, he said he would set bail at ten thousand. He advised her to get a lawyer, and set the following Tuesday as a date for the hearing. She didn't get a chance to say anything.

She was unceremoniously led from the office down the hall into a U.S. Marshal's office. Geez did they really still have marshals? She thought they had them in the old days out west or somewhere. This tall, skinny drink of water didn't look like a marshal. He didn't look like a cop. He looked like some sort of preacher, with glasses and all. He wouldn't be much of a playmate, probably had a wife and a dozen kids. He went over the whole business again; fingerprints, personal history, "mug shots." Seemed dopey doing it all again. The Fed who was "Mr. Secret Service Man" said, "Here's where I get off, if you decide you want to help yourself, you get word to me." "Drop dead," she thought. "Who in the hell do you think you are? When Cheech and Andy get me a 'mouthpiece' you'll find out that not everyone talks." The Marshal and a woman deputy then took her back to the county jail. "Geez ! Here we go again — mug shots, fingerprints, personal background, shower (at least that wasn't bad), physical, and searches.

She was taken to a cell in solitary reserved for federal prisoners. The place wasn't fit for a dog to live in. She had been given an opportunity to make a telephone call. She couldn't call Cheech; she didn't even know his real name. Andy's phone didn't answer. He was probably out with some broad, happy that it wasn't him that was caught. She wondered if he cleaned out the hotel room. She had some clothes and personal things there, and hoped Andy took them. It was a long day and she stretched out on the cool metal bunk to relax. Thank God she wasn't in a cell with other women. From what she saw and heard, these bitches wouldn't let her alone. She had heard about the "lizzies" grabbing the cute girls for themselves. She figured she was pretty cute herself (when her face wasn't all bruised and swollen), but no sir! No lizzies for her! She would wait for Andy. The bastard —where the hell was he anyway? Why wasn't he bailing her out? Did everyone forget her? Why didn't they at least send her a lawyer so she would know what to do? She dozed off into a fitful sleep, expecting that she would be sprung at anytime.

Andy smoked dozens of cigarettes. He was mixed up. He knew Bea was trying to get in touch with him. But why him? The Feds would probably listen in on the call and they would be on to him. Why did the dumb broad have to get herself arrested? If she couldn't down the bonds why didn't she admit it and not get involved? She loused up the whole deal and now they all could look forward to nothing but trouble. He would talk to the others in the morning to see what they should do. No matter how he looked at it, Bea's situation spelled bad trouble.

Bea spent a restless and uncomfortable night and was happy to see the dawn. She had some coffee, cereal and bread brought around by a "trustee." It tasted as bad as it looked; however, she managed to finish it and hold it down. It seemed like ages since she had had anything to eat. Still no word from anyone. Would they really desert her? Didn't they know she could open up on them, and they would be sitting in a jail instead of a hotel room? Did they have any idea of what she had been through?

About this time she began to again be aware of the effects of the beating that Andy gave her. Her eyes were still swollen, her nose was sore, her lips were cut and some of her teeth felt like they were loose. She had mixed emotions about what to do. Should she cooperate with the government and blow the whistle on the group, or should she continue to wait for someone to bail her out? She finally made up her mind. She would do absolutely nothing! The first one to contact her would get her cooperation. That was final! If it was a lawyer, then hooray for Andy and Cheech. If it was the young Secret Service man, then hooray for him.

It was about eleven in the morning on the same day when I got a call from Ned, the agent who had Bea under arrest. He said he had something good. He felt that Bea was part of a group from New York and he thought that if someone from New York came up he might be able to relate to her and obtain her cooperation. He knew I had been working on a related case of bond forgeries. I was happy to get any kind of a lead that might help solve some of the multiple forgeries that were plaguing us.

I met Ned and together we made a request to interview Bea. The word was sent up to her and she signed the request form agreeing to the interview. Arrangements were made to talk with her privately. She opened the conversation by saying she was ready to make a deal. She caught us by surprise. We figured she would have to be convinced that cooperation was the best of her options. I said, "What kind of deal are you looking for?" She said, "First of all I want out of this miserable hell hole. I'm not talking in here. Get me out and I'll give you the whole story. If you're satisfied that I'm leveling with you then I want transportation back to my hometown, and perhaps some help in getting a job. For this I'll answer all questions and also testify in court. That is, if I live long enough."

We couldn't have asked for better news. I immediately got in touch with the assistant U.S. attorney who was handling the case and brought him up to date on what was happening. He was fully cooperative. He said he would arrange to have a lawyer appointed for Bea so that all her rights could be protected. We then arranged another appearance before the U.S. commissioner. He went along with us and released her on her own recognizance. After that we took her to the local Secret Service office and, in the presence of her new attorney, we questioned her.

She was more cooperative than we could have asked, and she came through beautifully. She told of originally being propositioned by Andy to pass bonds, of how Cheech put a group together and taught them the finer points of bond passing. She told of the first trip with Cheech, Andy, Benny and Irma. She told of her abortive first attempt to cash bonds. She pinpointed the bank that she ran out of and then told of the subsequent passing expedition where she was a little more successful. She told us all she knew about everyone in the group and then concluded with the incident leading to her arrest. When she finished, there weren't too many questions to ask, as it was obvious she was telling all she knew and at times it appeared she was enjoying it.We still weren't all the way there. We knew it would be necessary to try to corroborate as much of the story as possible. I knew Cheech by reputation, I knew Benny and I felt that Andy, Irma, and Walt could be identified from the information supplied by Bea. The first order of business was to arrange to get Bea out of town and away from the reach of the mob. She felt her hometown was far enough away and she that it was safe enough, as she never told anyone where she was from. Within a few hours, arrangements were complete and Bea was on her way.

Shortly after she was released, a local lawyer came to the county jail and pompously announced that he had been retained to represent Bea. He was quite upset to hear that she was already represented by counsel and that she had been released. The lawyer lost no time in calling New York and informing them of the situation. Cheech had a queasy feeling and just knew th- he would be involved in another police case. He cursed himself for not moving faster. He should have figured that the dumb broad would open up like a can of corn just as soon as someone slammed a cell door on h-

Our real work began just as soon as Bea was on her way. checked the local hotel and obtained the registration cards signed by the oup when they checked into the hotel. We were also able to get a list of e toll calls made from each room. With the help of local police and a s from other field offices, we managed to get pictures of most of the p and further investigation determined their current addresses.

Even though she was miles away, Bea w pful in identifying any pictures and was ready with the answers t related questions we had. She eventually located an aunt who lived outside her hometown. The aunt was a widow and was happy to ha stay with her. It was good for us, too. Bea didn't want any further p and in less than a week found a job.

After all the suspects had been identified, we canvassed all the banks in the cities where the group operated. We were able to get identifications on all the forgers. We knew we had a good case on every one except Cheech, and Lord knows, he was the most important one. The case would not be complete until we had him.

Several weeks later we were still no closer to Cheech. We needed more information to tie up a case against him. I went out to see Bea with the hope she would recall more information that would put Cheech into the picture. She insisted that she had given us all she could remember. She said her story was complete; then recalled that on their most successful day Cheech had taken them out to celebrate and that a nightclub photographer had taken their picture. If what she said could be substantiated, then perhaps we could put Cheech with the group on the day the bonds were passed. This might even be enough to corroborate Bea's story.

The nightclub was located and two or three people recalled Cheech and his group being there. They remembered because he was very generous in his tips and ran up quite a check. The clincher was the photographer. She not only remembered the group but she said she was still black and blue from the pinches she received from Benny. She located the negatives, gave us a couple of prints and was able to document the day the pictures were taken.

While we were in town, we got the one big break that sewed up the case. We were notified by the local police that they had some bond information. We interviewed the lieutenant, and he told us that his men had arrested a prostitute on a narcotic charge. At the time of the arrest, they searched her room and found over sixteen thousand dollars worth of government bonds. He produced the bonds, and it developed that they were the same bonds that Cheech and his group had been passing.

The lieutenant made Sally, the prostitute, available to us. She was no newcomer to the law. She knew her rights and also knew how to make a deal. At the time I spoke to her she was a little sick and she knew she was going to feel worse as the afternoon went on. We had a meeting of the minds (she didn't want to do any federal time for possession of stolen bonds) and she related her story as best that she could remember.

"I remembe had just finished a trick at the hotel and was leaving. I took care of the captain and the elevator operator, and was just going through the parkin it was about three-thirty in the morning and I figured I had had it for the I see this group walking from the parking lot to the hotel; there's three and only two girls. I figure maybe the night ain't ended yet. They are all much plastered. So I give the glad eye to this guy called Chootch or Ch or whatever. He picks me up. So now I know I have me a john for the ni guys and two girls take off to their rooms so I'm left with the guy. By t I figure if I play my cards right I should be able to make a good score. He's got a roll that would choke a horse. We go to his room and I strip down as quickly as possible. I figure this guy ain't going to do any good for himself, but as long as I can make him believe he can, I might get a shot at the roll. Well, we have a couple of shots in his room, he tries playing around but he is too far gone to do any good and he poops out on me. This gives me a good chance to really smell out the room. I go through his pants and find his roll. I grab a couple of hundred just to play it safe in case he wakes up and I don't get a chance to leave in a hurry. I find his suitcase in the closet and go through it. Holy Jesus, take me home! He's got a stack of government stocks or bonds or something. It looks like a fortune to me. He's tossing around in the bed so I decide to creep in with him in case he needs someone to help get into a deep sleep. The next thing I know it's morning and this guy is about ready to get up. He goes to the john for a shower. While he's in there I see my chance. I grab his pants, pocket his roll, grab the bonds, stuff them in my bag, get dressed in a hurry and quietly slip out of the room."

She then tried to account for the disposition of the bonds. Most of them she gave to a narcotic peddler in exchange for some junk. I showed her a group of photos and she was able to identify Cheech and the rest of the group. Sally said she would testify in court if she had to. She didn't know Cheech or his friends and didn't fear them. Sally completed a perfect case against the whole group, and now there were only a few loose ends to pick up before we could proceed against them.

The U.S. Attorney agreed to put the case before the grand jury, seeking indictments and arrest warrants after the indictments. On the appointed day we lined up all our witnesses and completed the grand jury testimony in two days. We then obtained the warrants and placed Irma, Benny, Andy, and Walt under arrest. None of them would cooperate. They were too frightened. They all feared Cheech and did not want to end up on a slab in a morgue. We timed Cheech's arrest for when we knew he would be at home.

The arrest went off without a hitch. He was quite philosophical about the arrest. He submitted meekly and sat quietly while we searched his apartment. He told me we were wasting our time; we wouldn't find anything in his home. I told him I believed him, but I had a job to do and I was going to do it. He was right; there was nothing of a contraband nature in his home. It was as clean as a whistle.

Cheech had no trouble making a seventy-five thousand dollar bail and very shortly was back out on the street. He was able to put all the pieces together, and figured out what had happened when the lawyer he hired for Bea reported she had been released. He presumed she was now on the government's side. He knew she didn't have enough money to swing the deal with a lawyer herself. He made sure that there would be no contraband at his home or his place of business. He knew an arrest was inevitable and he prepared himself accordingly. He quietly put out a "contract" for Bea but no one could locate her. His own attorney suggested that he try to make a deal with the government by pleading guilty to fewer counts. Cheech wouldn't hear of it. He wanted to fight the case, stretch it out as long as possible and then appeal it all the way to the Supreme Court if necessary. Not that he thought he could win the case but he wanted to stay on the street as long as possible. There was no shaking him.

Six months later, he and the group went to trial. Great care was taken to bring the witnesses in only when they were needed and they were as quickly whisked out of town when the court excused them. Bea came into court and looked like she was going to faint. We all held out breath and hoped she wouldn't fall down on us. Shortly after being sworn in, she slowly regained her composure and told the whole story. Her memory was fantastic and, all in all, she made an excellent witness. All efforts by the defense attorneys to shake her story were unsuccessful. The array of witnesses was overwhelming; desk clerks, bank clerks and officers, Sally, the streetwalker, handwriting experts, photos, stolen bonds, stolen bond victims, and police officers. All went into making a near perfect case for the government. The group did not offer any defense. None took the stand. The jury received the case for deliberation at one in the afternoon; by three o'clock they returned with a verdict of guilty on all counts on all defendants.

Two weeks later, all the defendants were before the judge for sentencing. He sentenced them accordingly:

Bea – Suspended sentence; three years probation
Andy – Five years in custody
Irma – Three years in custody
Walt – Two years in custody
Benny – Five years in custody
Cheech – Ten years in custody for the bonds and five years for conspiracy to be served consecutively. This meant a fifteen year stretch for him.

All the defendants were sent to different institutions. Cheech applied for bail pending appeal. It was granted and he was back on the street.

He was very careful to not get involved in any serious crime. He would still keep his loan-sharking business and perhaps some gambling action. He would keep the restaurant as a front. He had a good-sized office in the back of the store. Here he could handle much of his business by telephone. So went the months until finally he received word from his attorney that his appeal was turned down. He would have to surrender to begin serving his term. Cheech insisted that the case be taken to the Supreme Court. Dutifully his lawyer filed the necessary papers and Cheech found himself continued on bail until the Supreme Court either granted or denied certiorari.

He was depressed that night when he went home and for the first time the specter of actually serving fifteen years in prison really struck him. His children, now aged six, five and three would be grown up. He would be past middle age. He didn't know if he would still have a wife when he got out. How many women would wait that long? Was it necessary that he go to jail? Was there any way out? He was trying all the legal ways, but he knew he was only buying time and wasn't going to win in the end. There were ways. He could run away and become a fugitive. Perhaps go to a foreign country. That was not too appealing. He still loved living in this country. He could perhaps make a deal with the government like a lot of other people did. But that was unthinkable and against everything he had always lived. Didn't they stress "omerta" to everyone who joined the syndicate? He tried to go to sleep, but couldn't. He walked the floor half the night and couldn't get the word "cooperation" out of his mind. He knew it was a fancy word; maybe it meant informant, stoolie, rat, traitor, fink, or whatever the current term for providing information against friends and associates was, but to him maybe the word could mean "freedom" and that's what he was looking for. How could he work it? Cooperate with the government? Get a break and not have to serve any time and not have anyone know about what he was doing? It seemed impossible; yet he was sure that there must have been some people who did it and got away with it. Everything seemed to have worked out O.K. for Bea. Funny, he Cheech, thinking of cooperating. This was the very thing that people were killed for. Hadn't he put out a contract on Bea? There were plenty of witnesses against him. No one important enough to do away with. True, he had put a contract out on Bea, but no one could find her; maybe the government did a good job of hiding their friends. That dopey broad who couldn't wait a couple of days in the can. Perhaps if she had been bailed out immediately no one would have been in this predicament. That was it. One person spoiled a good thing and turned a winner into a loser. The milk was spilled and there was no use in even thinking about it. Time was running out. He had to do something and do it quick, and above all, he had to be careful. A wrong move and he would be finished. How to start? You can't just walk into the White House or the Capitol and announce, "Here I am, Cheech. I want to tell everyone about crime in America."

Naturally he could not confide in his lawyer. The lawyer he used knew too many of the "boys" and that would not do. He knew he could supply information to most any city, state, or government agency. He knew they would be happy to get it. But how to start? Which one? Who could you trust? Would they do something for him? Or would he be thrown to the wolves after he served his purpose? After all, he was doing this without a lawyer.

This was one time he would have to be his own advisor. He felt his mind was ninety percent made up. He was determined not to serve the long prison term. He was not going to run away, so there was only one avenue left to navigate...cooperation. As soon as he could work out the details in his own mind, he would make his move. He would try to play it as safe as possible and not to stick his neck out too far. The night passed slowly and dawn, with its new promise, was a welcome sight for Cheech. Sleep was out of the question; that could wait. He had a lot of work to do.

He recalled there was a federal officer who lived in the neighborhood. He was respected by everyone who knew him. This man had a fantastic reputation as a straight shooter. Cheech knew this reputation had to be earned over the years, and he was probably the man he was looking for. Still, there was no sense in taking chances; he had to play it slow and easy. Cheech found out what church the federal agent, Cal, attended, and he made it his business to be at the church the following Sunday. When mass was over he walked alongside Cal and in a low whisper said, "I'd like to talk to you privately. Can you meet me alone tonight at Tare's Restaurant?" Cal knew Cheech by reputation and nodded; he said, "See you at nine tonight" and walked away. No one would have ever dreamed that a word passed between them.

Tare's Restaurant was well off the beaten path and was a good distance away from the neighborhood. Cheech felt safe enough at this location; at least it would do for a preliminary "meet." Cal arrived at the restaurant precisely at nine. Cheech met him in the parking lot and satisfied himself that Cal was alone. He then changed the plans.

He asked Cal to get into his car and they drove off. Cal was told it was a drive to nowhere. Cheech stated he needed a friend and asked Cal if he would help him. He explained his predicament, and asked Cal to be a go-between. Cal told Cheech that he would do all he could, providing he played it straight. Cheech assured him that he already had passed the point of no return and had put his life in Cal's hands. Cal asked Cheech what he could do to show "good faith." Cheech said he would start off by locating two well-known fugitives. He then proceeded to give Cal the addresses of the two fugitives. Cal said he'd check on it. He gave Cheech a code name and a private number where he could locate him. Cheech also provided Cal with a name and telephone number. The two men shook hands in the darkness of the car and drove back to the restaurant parking lot where they parted company.

In just forty-eight hours, Cal was notified that both fugitives were located and arrested. They were at the exact addresses he had been supplied. Cal knew he had a winner on his hands, and made up his mind that he was going to handle Cheech with all the caution and care he could muster. He knew if

Cheech continued to cooperate, he would be worth his weight in gold to law enforcement.

He arranged another clandestine meeting with Cheech, this time many miles away from the neighborhood. A good rapport was established. Cal told Cheech it was time to lay down some ground rules before the game went any further. He told Cheech that the two fugitives were located exactly where he said they would be. Cheech smiled and said, "I knew they were busted and I've already been asked to help them with bail." Cal knew that in order to help Cheech, he would have to get the Secret Service into the picture. After all, they were the good folks who convicted him. He explained this to Cheech who was his usual philosophical self. He was placing himself entirely in Cal's hands and would abide by what he suggested. Cal told him he would contact a guy by the name of Motto in the Secret Service and see what they could work out. Cheech replied, "Yea, I know him, he locked me up."

Call gave me a call and asked me to meet him to discuss an important matter. He was about as outspoken as a fellow officer could be. There was nothing in his voice or what he said that gave me any clue as to why he wanted to meet me. We met and he asked if I would be interested in having Cheech on our side. I told him: "You must be kidding! Cheech is one of the Mr. Bigs, and if he is going to cooperate he'll want the world!" Cal carefully filled me in on what had happened and said that Cheech was willing to cooperate with the government in any way that would not burn him up. He told me that Cheech had already given him two fugitives and other information that was productive. I asked. "What does he want in return?" Cal said as near as he could figure he wanted some sort of reduction in sentence, based on what he was able to produce. It seemed fair enough. I told Cal that I would discuss the situation with the U.S. Attorney's office and then perhaps we could arrange a meeting. Cal agreed.

The U.S. Attorney gave the only answer he could give and it was what I expected. He would bring any cooperation on the part of Cheech to the attention of the sentencing judge, if and when the time came.

The next order of business was to set up a meeting with Cal and Cheech. A city about forty miles away was selected, and a motel was located that was suitable to us all. Cheech and I had met before under much different circumstances. The change in his attitude was unbelievable. I thought the best way to start off was to discuss the bonds for which he was arrested. He unhesitatingly told the story of how he met the Jersey Four and how he eventually became the fence for the bonds they were able to steal. He stated that the Jersey Four had recently been arrested for a post office burglary, and were all in jail in lieu of a very high bail. He said that any action against them as a result of his revelations would have to be held until some later date, because if they were arrested on the bond theft charges, they would know he was talking. It seemed reasonable and we let that part of the conversation drop. The Jersey Four were in jail and it did not look like they were going to make bail. Cheech went on to say that he disposed of the remainder of the bonds after the arrests, and he gave us the names of the people he sold them to. Again he suggested that we not use his name in making a case against them.

The rest of the evening was spent on listening to Cheech's stories on the workings of the different syndicates and combinations in and around his neighborhood. The intelligence was priceless, but all I was interested in was something more tangible that would result in solving some cases. Cheech told me he was very anxious to help and would keep me informed of anything that was in my jurisdiction. I reminded him, just so that he would know, that our jurisdiction included protection of the president and vice president, former presidents, etc. Then I started a litany of the criminal matters the Secret Service was interested in: counterfeiting of obligations of the United States and foreign countries in the forms of currency, coins, stamps, checks, and bonds. That also included the forgery and passing of government checks and Series E bonds. He interrupted, laughing, when he heard the word "bonds" and said he was very familiar with the Series E bonds.

He asked me if I would personally go out of town to purchase counterfeit money. I replied that I most certainly would. He said he might have something for me on our next meeting. We shook hands and left. There was no doubt that this was a very fruitful meeting and I was looking forward to continuing on with Cheech.

Cheech called a second meeting within a very few days. He said he thought he could arrange for me to be introduced to some people in the upstate area who were handling counterfeit money. He said he would introduce me to a local man who had the connection with the upstate people. He said that the local man was going to surrender himself on a burglary charge and wanted to make a big "score" before he went to jail. He stated that this man was not important, and that even if he found out I was an undercover agent, no one would believe him. Besides, the surrender involved serving a seven-year sentence, all appeals were turned down, and it would be sometime before he could talk to anyone involved in this case. I said it sounded good and that anytime he was ready, I was ready. Two days later, I met Cheech and he stated that the local man, named "Duster," would be waiting for a phone call from me at a bar in New York City. He said I should use the name "Tony" and I should mention I was a friend of Cheech. From that point on I would be in a position to get the counterfeits. I did as I was instructed. I called Duster, who said he was expecting my call and suggested I meet him later that night at another downtown bar.

I met him at the appointed hour and we had a conversation at a table near the bar. Duster told me that he had to surrender on a state charge since his appeal was turned down. He thought if he could make some money before surrendering, it might make his stay easier. He tried to pump me on my relationship with Cheech. I made it very obvious that I was not going to discuss Cheech with just anyone. He finally drifted into a conversation about counterfeit money. He said he knew some people out of town who could supply counterfeit money for "only" twenty cents on the dollar. I told him I was interested and intended to buy large amounts but "only twenty cents on the dollar" was way too much. He said, "How much are you interested in?" "If the price is right, I'll take a hundred grand, but for no more than ten cents on the dollar." He though for a minute and said, "I'll make a couple of phone calls and let you know."

He walked out of the bar and returned in about half an hour. Agents on the street followed him to a public street phone, and as soon as he completed his calls, they made arrangements to trace back the call. It was later determined that the call was made to Alex, a smalltime hood who lived upstate but had good underworld connections. Duster told me that the best price he could get was twelve cents on the dollar. Then he also said that he expected to get something he called a "finders fee" from me. I asked him, "Won't your people give you a point or two?" He looked down at the table and replied, "I don't think so." It was all but very obvious that two of the twelve cents was going to him. I didn't call him on it, but seemingly reluctantly okayed the price at twelve cents per dollar. He looked like a car salesman just having sold a used car to a schoolteacher. He tried to look serious while restraining his glee. "I'll put your order in and it should be ready within the next several days. I'll arrange to have my connection bring some samples down and then we can firm up the delivery for the 100 G's'. I'm not sure I'll be here for the delivery because my surrender date is getting close but the delivery should be okay."

The meeting with Duster's friend was arranged and we all met at a local hotel. His friend was Alex, and he was obviously a man who handled many such "deals." After the introductions we spent the next half an hour verbally fencing. He was trying to find out as much as possible about me and I, in turn, was telling him as little as possible. When he had satisfied himself that I was OK, he reached under the bed, pulled up the carpet and withdrew six counterfeit twenty-dollar bills. He held them up but didn't hand them to me, and said, "Before we can move on any deal, I need a sizeable down payment." "I've never fronted any money in the past and it sure ain't my intention to start now." He gave me the samples to look at. They looked good, and I told him I would pay twelve cents for a delivery in New York City, but only eleven if I had to go to his town. Alex wasn't buying my proposition and wasn't going to back down. His mind was made up that he was going to return upstate with part of my money or there was no deal. I was equally adamant and was not going to give him any money in advance, "good faith" or not! I said I wanted "a hand to hand deal," and that's the way it was.

Duster could see things rapidly deteriorating, and he tried desperately to get Alex to change his mind. It was like talking to a stone cold wall and even Duster knew he was waging a losing battle. When it became apparent that neither of us was going to relent, we decided to break up the meeting. I gave Duster a number where he could reach me and he in turn gave me one where I could contact him in the event I changed my mind. We left and Duster was pretty well disgusted (and disappointed) about the way things had turned out. He could see his share of the deal going out the window, and he didn't have much time left to put another deal together before he reported to begin his jail term. I gave Duster some money for his efforts before we parted and wished him well. I told him if Alex and I ever got together on a deal, I'd find a way to cut him in. He thanked me and went on his way.

This turn of events was actually good for our side. I figured that regardless of what happened next, Cheech was in the clear. He never personally introduced me to Duster and he certainly had nothing to do with the introduction to Alex. We knew we could always revive the case anytime we wanted to by simply making a call to Alex. We decided we would wait until Duster had surrendered before doing anything further.

A background check on Alex showed he had been previously arrested for "receiving stolen property, assault, larceny, and burglary." He was considered a big fish in a small pond with some fair out of town connections. The samples he supplied came from the Chicago area. The plant had been captured two years before. We could account for all but about a quarter million dollars that the plant had produced. The notes that Alex had could have been stashed away by one of the principals and, for one reason or another, been recently unearthed.

Nevertheless, if Alex had any counterfeit money we wanted it, plant or no plant! Duster surrendered on the appointed day and was on his way to state prison within twenty-four hours. I decided to let another week go by before calling Alex.

Three days before I was going to call Alex, I received a telephone call at an undercover telephone. I wasn't there to take the call but the message was to call Alex. I figured this was a good break. Alex had apparently changed his mind and was ready to do business. I returned his call, we exchanged pleasantries and he asked me if I could come up to see. He said he might be ready to get me some "tickets." I told him I would come up over the weekend as I had some other business in the vicinity. He suggested that I stop at the Globe Hotel. I told him I would pick my own hotel and didn't appreciate his telling me where to stay. He was annoyed but managed to say, "Okay, Tony, have it your own way. Give me a call Saturday night at seven."

We began to make elaborate plans for the meeting. Cheech had told me he knew Alex by reputation and that he was really money hungry. He figured if we could whet his appetite, Alex would eventually throw caution to the winds and make a delivery without us fronting the money. I decided to take seven or eight hundred dollars with me and make a small purchase from Alex. If it worked I would try to make Alex deliver the big bundle in New York City where he would be away from familiar territory and would be at a distinct disadvantage.

The following Saturday we arrived in Alex's town several hours early. We selected a motel on the outskirts of town. The covering agents obtained rooms in the same wing. It was decided that I was to keep traveling at a minimum and to try to have Alex come to me. Attempting to follow Alex on his home grounds would have been dangerous and foolhardy. We had more to lose than to gain in this particular situation.

At seven o'clock I put in a call to Alex. He answered and asked me where I was. I gave him the name of the motel and the room number. He asked if I could meet him in town. I told him I had brought a package with me and had to drop her off in a nearby town. I suggested he meet me at the motel in about an hour. He agreed.

A little over an hour and a half later at somewhere near eight-thirty, Alex was seen cruising around the parking area of the motel. He was checking out all the parked cars. A young man who had dark hair, a mustache, and was dressed in a light colored suit was driving him. Our agents noted the license number of their car. The driver remained with the car and Alex proceeded directly to my room. He knocked, I opened the door. Without even a greeting, he asked, "Are you alone?" I told him "Yes" as he brushed past me and thoroughly checked out the room. I laughed at him and said, "Anyone as careful as you should be selling bibles." He did not appreciate the humor. Ignoring my comment, he said, "I had you checked out and found out that you are a 'connected' guy." What a liar! I had not given him any information that he could use and Duster knew even less about me. However, I went along with him and said, "I had you checked out too and found that you are pretty good people." He wanted to know if I was ready to do business. I said, "No, I didn't come up to your town with twelve thousand dollars and further I didn't change my mind about a 'hand to hand' delivery." He started to rave. "You bastards from New York are all alike! You don't trust anyone. You think that everyone is like you, 'rob and cheat your friends.'" I reminded him that we wouldn't really have classified our relationship "as being close personal friends and we're not exactly dealing in nationally advertised products." He would not be placated; he said, his voice rising, "Talk, talk, talk, fancy words.

Don't play cute with me. Put up or shut up!" I told him I had enough money with me to buy five thousand dollars worth of counterfeits. "The only way we can do business is by trying a small one. I'll be around until mid-night. If you can produce, I can pay." He muttered something under his breath that sounded something like "...hole." Then he yelled, "Wait!" and turned around on his heel and stormed out.

When his car was safely out of the area, I met with the other agents and told them what had happened. I told them I felt that Alex would return with the counterfeits and since it was agreed that we were going to let this one go though, it would not be necessary to play it tight.

About an hour and a half later, there was a knock on my door. It was Alex and again he looked all around the room, including the bathroom. He threw a small package on my bed and said, "Wait, and I'll call you." And he left. I opened the package and found it contained about five thousand in counterfeit twenties. They looked pretty good and while I was still examining them, the telephone rang. It was Alex. He asked me to join him in the cocktail lounge.

I located him at a dark corner table and when I sat down he said, "See, I trusted you. Why couldn't you do the same?" I took the "buy" money out of my pocket and handed it to him, saying, "I'm keeping my word too; here's your money." He still didn't seem too happy. He pocketed the money without even counting it. I ordered a drink and thereafter the conversation was much easier. He said, "I can deliver as much as two hundred grand worth of the stuff. My people are anxious to get rid of it in one sale. I'll let it go for twenty G's in good money." I replied that I also represented "some people" and if they were satisfied with what I brought back they might buy the whole lot. I said I'd let him know. We engaged in small talk as we finished our drinks, and then he left. We quickly wrapped everything up at the motel and returned to New York City.

Several days later I had a meeting with Cheech and brought him up to date on the developments. He didn't see any problems if we arrested Alex. He told me he had made another case for Cal, and he thought he might have something else for me as soon as we took care of the Alex matter. Before we left, he asked me if I lived in the country. I told him I lived in the suburbs. He then asked me if I had a garden. I said, "Yea, I've got a small plot that grows a lot of weeds." Very seriously he continued, "Don't laugh, but you know, Carmine, I like roses. Years ago I used to wear one in my lapel. Now I don't have any place to grow them and people still give me plants. I have a couple in my car, will you take them and plant them?" I said, "Sure, Cheech, and when they blossom I'll make a beautiful bouquet for your wife." He laughed sheepishly and said, "You're not making fun?" I said, "No, as a matter of fact I would take an awful ribbing at the office if they knew that I liked to grow flowers." He seemed relieved and opened his car trunk and gave me six bushes. I took them home, and my wife was very pleased and she planted them immediately. I just couldn't tell her that they came from a "big syndicate man."

The following Thursday, I received a message to get in touch with Alex. I gave him a call. He wanted to know if I was now ready to do business. I said I was but I had a problem, my people insisted on doing business in New York City. I said that I told them that that would be impossible because my source of the money wouldn't come to New York. Alex asked, "Why do they want it in New York?" I said, "Maybe they don't fully trust me." He said he would try to work something out and get back to me. The following night, he called again and said that if I would get my money together, he would give me another call again and perhaps arrange the delivery in New York City. I said, "Fine, I think I can have the money by morning."

We hurried as quickly as we could to gather the buy money and ready a squad of men to handle the surveillance, raid and arrest. Late in the morning, Alex called again and asked me where I would be at seven that evening. I told him I would register at a local hotel, gave him the name and said I would wait for his call. We rented adjoining rooms at the hotel and were able to install concealed listening devices in my room so the agents covering the deal could hear the conversation and make the arrest at the proper time.

It was nearly seven-thirty when I got a call from Alex. He said he was in the lobby and was on his way up to see me. He came alone, and again carefully checked out the room. When he was convinced that we were alone, he asked me if I was ready to do business. He was starting to sound like a record. I told him I was ready to do business if he were finally serious. He said, "I want see the money." "It's nearby and I can get it in just few minutes," I told him. He insisted on seeing the money and I insisted on seeing the counterfeits first. This did not improve his already nasty and sour disposition. He growled, "Look, I went to great trouble to set this deal up, and if anything goes wrong, someone will get hurt!" I agreed, "If anything does go wrong my people will certainly see that someone does get hurt, possibly permanently!" He told me to get my money ready and wait ten minutes. He left, went out through the side lobby door where his driver was waiting in the car on the street. The driver got out of the car, opened the trunk and removed a suitcase. The driver was the same person who drove Alex around on the day the samples were delivered.

The surveillance agents watched both men as they returned to the hotel and went directly to my room. They knocked on the door. When I answered it, Alex introduced me to his friend, Sal, who was still holding the suitcase. Alex preceded Sal into the room. This time he didn't search it and changed his words, "Okay, we're ready to do business." It was a statement of fact as he took the suitcase from Sal. I asked him, "Where's the stuff?' He patted the suitcase, "Where's yours?" I again told him that it was nearby and that he had nothing to fear about a "rip-off" because they were two against one. I told him to open the suitcase and then I'd get my money. Alex nodded to Sal to open the suitcase on the bed. He did, and it contained a shirt and a pair of slacks. I just looked and said, "What kind of shell game is this?' Both of them started laughing as though they had just suckered a mark. I said, "If that is funny, I don't understand it." Alex said it was just a test to make sure I wasn't "heat" or trying to "rip em" or "set em up." I was thankful that we were prepared for this contingency. It seemed like all the boys wanted to try dry runs before the real delivery. I angrily told him, "I am in no mood for Goddamned games and I'm ready to call the whole thing off." He stopped laughing and told me to sit tight, as Sal was ready to go get the real package.

After Sal left to get the other package, I told Alex that I had put my real money in a hotel safety deposit box in the lobby and as soon as Sal returned and I saw the counterfeit money we would go get it. His little joke seemed to have loosened him up a little or maybe it was the prospect of exchanging all that worthless paper for real money. I figured that it was a safe time to tell him about the safety deposit box in the lobby because we were alone, Sal was going after the counterfeit, and he had reached the point of no return. He said, "Sure, no sweat."

Sal was seen leaving the hotel. He went to his car, opened the trunk and put the suitcase inside. He took out a package and put it into another suitcase and returned to the hotel and up to my room. He rapped on the door with his knuckles. I let him in and he threw the suitcase onto the bed. I opened it and saw that it contained about two hundred thousand dollars in counterfeit twenties. I started to examine the notes. Alex became annoyed again and said, "Hey, do you expect me to sit and wait while you look at every bill? Come on! Let's get your bundle and get going. If there's a shortage or if any of 'em are bad, I'll personally make it up to you. Come on!"

I picked up one of the bills, carelessly looked at it, and said, "This looks like real crap! They are not half as good as the samples!" This was the prearranged signal to our men who were listening in the adjoining room. They now knew I had the delivery and were to make the arrests. I no sooner had the words out of my mouth when several agents came storming through the door and arrested all three of us. The money was strewn all over the bed. Sal had a gun in his pocket but never got a chance to get it out and use it. I was thrown in jail with them and after several hours, a "lawyer" came to my aid and made it appear that I was ready to make bail.

Sal and Alex stayed in jail for ten days before bail could be arranged for them. I discontinued my undercover telephone, thus preventing either one of them from contacting me. Word reached me later that Alex figured I was an informant for the government and set him up for a reward. This was good as it kept Cheech above suspicion. I told Cheech what had happened, and he actually seemed to enjoy the fact that the bad guys were losing.

One day I arranged to meet Cheech in the lobby of a not too distant hospital where he had a relative recuperating from a serious illness. He was in an especially jovial mood. He told me he had a funny experience. He went on to say that the local police had been watching his restaurant for some time because they had received information that he was running a policy bank. They determined that they would raid him on that very day. They watched the restaurant until they thought the time was exactly right. Coincidentally, just before they raided him, an Internal Revenue Service agent carrying a briefcase entered the restaurant. Inasmuch as Cheech had been convicted for handling and receiving the proceeds from many thousands of dollars in forged bonds, Uncle Sam wanted his taxes. The Internal Revenue sent a representative to discuss the matter. After the agent arrived, the police followed right behind to begin their raid. The lieutenant in charge of the raid told Cheech he knew the "policy slips" were there and he intended to find them. Cheech said, "All right you guys finally got me," He pointed to the bespectacled, scholarly looking IRS agent in his suit and bow tie and said, "He has them right there in his briefcase." The police seized the surprised agent and attempted to take his briefcase. The poor man protested and fought to retain control of the case that he insisted contained only official government reports. The bag was opened and it was seen that it did indeed contain official papers. This resulted in a round of apologies and several embarrassed faces. Cheech thought it was very funny, and was laughing about it when telling me. "Cheech," I said, "that is not very funny." "C'mon Carmine, don't you have a sense of humor?" I told him, "Yes, I do, but you are not in a position to be making enemies."

Cheech then became serious and told me that quite a few agencies were trying to get him to cooperate with them. There were some who he was sure he could help and some he couldn't. He asked my advice about what he should do. I said, "You're putting me on the spot. I'll paint a picture for you, and whomever you want to help has to be your choice. The more people you help, the better chance you'll have for a sizable reduction in your sentence. However, this will also expose you to more people and there is always the chance that you will be inadvertently found out." He said he would consider it.

I thought it was about time that we talked about what we could do for him. I asked, "What do you consider a decent break?" "I'll be satisfied with whatever you can do. Chop off a day, a year, how about a suspended sentence?" I told him to forget that. "If you get anything more than a three year reduction, you won't be able to overcome the suspicion it would create." He laughed again and said, "Carmine, that is my problem. I will have to take care of the suspicion. I know my people better than you do and I have to do things my way." I quoted a cliché, "Violence breeds violence."

He looked out the window and a mellow expression came over his face. "Believe it or not, Carmine, I am not a violent man and I know how to handle things without hurting people." I urged him to be careful. I noticed that he was becoming very lackadaisical about where we met. He was not taking the usual precautions. He said we could meet in his restaurant any time. The law was always stopping in and questioning him about something, and he didn't think it would be unusual for federal or state people to stop in to talk to him. He said he decided he would cooperate with some of the other agencies and try to get as big a reduction in his sentence as possible. Again I said, "That's your choice, but it is very risky." I then told him I was going away on an extended investigation and would be gone for some time. He said, "I don't have anything for you right now, but if anything should come up, I'll get in touch with Cal."

Three or four months passed before I had an occasion and opportunity to call Cheech. He again insisted that I come to his restaurant. I refused and said that I stood by my earlier warning that meeting at the restaurant was unsafe. He said his relative was in still in the hospital where we had last met. I agreed to meet him in the coffee shop at the hospital.

Cheech was in an excellent frame of mind. He told me he had been working with several other agencies, and they were all very pleased with the information he was providing. He was happy to report that arrangements were made for him to be re-sentenced and he felt he was going to receive little or no jail time. That afternoon, he went into court and was re-sentenced. He received probation and his whole sentence was suspended. I told him I was filled with mixed emotions. I was happy that he got re-sentenced, but I still felt that a suspended sentence was not a good thing in his case; it was more like a death sentence. I told him, "No matter how you look at it, it spells out that you were helping someone, and for you that is bad!" He said, "Carmine, don't look so sad. You should be happy, you're off the hook, you don't have to do anything for me. All I did for you was for free. The other people had the headache of getting my sentence suspended.

"But don't think I'm a fool. Before the sentence was suspended, I laid the groundwork for my plan. I don't have to go to jail for anyone and I took care of any suspicions. I went to some connected people and asked to borrow $25,000. I told them I had made a "friend" with some feds and for fifty grand, I could buy myself a suspended sentence. I took the 25 Gs, kept it for a while, and then paid it back. In the meantime, the word got around that Cheech had bought himself a "break," and that's just what I wanted. I wanted everyone to know how it happened. You know, quite a few people who were willing to pay to get suspended sentences have come to me for help, but I keep making excuses. I say the heat is on and it's something that can't be pulled too often."

I said, "OK, Cheech, I'm happy for you and I'm not going to spoil your happy frame of mind. I still don't like it and for Christ's sake, be careful! There are a lot of people who might not buy your story. You won a couple of rounds and you beat the jail rap, but the fight is not over yet. Some people have long memories and curiosity. Don't get sloppy!"

I was about to leave when he said, "Carmine, you owe me some money. Remember 'The Duster?' Well, I saw him the night before he surrendered. I gave him a hundred bucks for a little spending money while he was serving his time." I said, "Okay, Cheech, one hundred dollars is cheap enough for the case we made." I handed him the money.

Right at that moment, two nuns walked by. Cheech jumped up and gave the money to the nuns. Before the startled nuns could say anything, Cheech walked away. I said, "Why did you do that?" He smiled and said, as he pointed upward, "That's to buy insurance for upstairs." I kidded him and said, "I think I need it more than they do!" We then got serious and started talking business.

He said he had reason to believe that another counterfeit plant was ready to get into operation. I naturally wanted to get all the information available and started asking him a lot of questions. "Hold it, Carmine," he said, "There's a lot of work to be done. This man is an old friend of mine. He got the taste of easy money once before when he got involved in making counterfeit money. You guys didn't get him then, and he's just gonna press his luck until he does get caught." "For Christ's sake, Cheech, whose side are you on!" I asked. Cheech became indignant and said, "You don't understand, do you, Carmine, I have loyalty too. If I can stop a guy from ruining his life I think I should." He almost floored me with that sentiment. Here he had information on a counterfeit plant that was about to get started, and he decides to act like a reforming social worker. I was not in a position to push him; he certainly did not owe me anything. Yet according to Cheech, this guy got away with it once before. Heavens knew how much trouble he caused us then and now he's gonna do it again. I could see that Cheech was dead serious, and unless we had a quick coming together of the minds, we would be picking up counterfeits one at a time. I said, "Cheech, if your friend gets a plant started and the money gets into circulation, he will face a long sentence when he does get caught. I know you don't want that! If you give him to me now, perhaps we can nip it in the bud and everyone will be better off." He grinned again and said, "Carmine, you are a poor con man. I should get mad at you, but I realize you're just doing your job." I struck out swinging badly and knew it. We had a cup of coffee and parted.

I talked the situation over with Cal. He agreed that we shouldn't try to force the issue with Cheech. He said he would see what he could do with him. He reminded me that Cheech really could be stubborn at times.

In the meantime, Cheech tried to be a good guy. He went to Sam the Printer to see if he had gotten started. Sam told Cheech he had an order to print up to a million dollars in counterfeit tens and twenties. He said he had some trouble with the plates. This time he had to make them himself and he wasn't doing too well. Cheech told Sam that he was making a big mistake, that sooner or later he was going to get caught. Sam laughed and said, If I get caught I'll borrow some money and you can pay off your friend." Cheech, for the first time, felt there was something wrong with the way Sam said it. He made his excuses and left.

He called Cal and me and asked to see us the next day. At the meeting Cheech said he had tried to help his friend but failed. He said he still didn't want to see his friend go to jail and he wasn't going to put a case in our laps. I said, "Cheech, if you're purposely trying to mix me up, you're doing a good job." He looked at me and said, "Okay, hear me out. I know enough about the law to know you can't just bust in on his joint and make a legal arrest. I'm not going to give you an affidavit so you can get a search warrant and I am also not going to introduce an agent to my friend to make a 'buy'. Wait, don't get excited! I'll tell you what I will do. I will give you my friend's name and address and from then on you're on your own. No more help from me." I was relieved and said, "Cheech, it's a deal. Give me the name and address and I'll take it from there." He said, "Remember, no more help." "Okay Cheech," I said, "you got my word." He then gave me Sam's name and address.

Just before I left he asked me how the roses were doing. I told him they were doing real fine. He said, "I have a few more bushes for you." I said "Good." Then he said, "One day, I'd like to see the roses." "Sure, come on up. One of these days pretty soon they'll all be in blossom."

We wasted no time getting a twenty-four hour a-day surveillance on Sam's shop. It was a small shop on the street floor of a two-story building in a run down neighborhood. Close surveillance was very difficult as strangers really stood out. The kids on the block gave every stranger a long hard look and made it impossible for any street surveillance of the shop. We were able to watch the shop from a block away and finally we were fortunate to be able to rent a room near the shop and watch it from a window. Not much information was gained during the first few days. He had the normal amount of traffic going in and out; the usual business for a small print shop. Checking the license numbers of the cars that stopped didn't help much. Sam was working a little late each night, but nothing unusual. He had the windows covered sufficiently so it was impossible to see what was going on. I felt that Sam was working on the notes and was afraid it was getting away from us.

On the eighth day, out of desperation, I had a meeting with Cheech. I told him we had a problem and it looked like we were not going to make a case against Sam anytime soon. Cheech said, "Hooray for Sam. Maybe he found a way to beat you." I asked, "Will you stop clowning around and be serious?" "Carmine, I don't have to be serious. We made a bargain and I expect you to live up to it." This was a new twist! An informant telling me to live up to a bargain! Generally it was the other way around.

I saw it was no use in talking to him anymore about the case. We got involved in small talk. After about ten minutes he said he had to leave. "I have an appointment to meet some people." "What kind of people?" "Your kind." I left, never dreaming that this would be the last time I would see Cheech. There were no two ways about it; Cheech had to be some kind of a different animal. In his own way he had his own special code of honor.

It was about eight o'clock one night, Sam was working a little later than normal. Things were very quiet at the print shop. We were still no closer to making a case against Sam. We had tried all the usual tricks but nothing seemed to work. At about eight-thirty, Sam came out of the shop and put his rubbish on the sidewalk for trash pickup the next day. We waited until he closed the shop and left. At a little after midnight, we stole the rubbish and examined it at the office. Most of his litter was spoiled work and leftovers from the cutting machine. The rubbish we most closely examined revealed that most of the cuttings were portions of counterfeit bills. "We gotcha, Sam! Thank you, Cheech!" Apparently there were a lot of bills that didn't turn out too good and Sam destroyed them by chopping them up on the cutting machine. Needless to say, we were elated! All the days of surveillance had produced nothing. The one act, the one mistake of putting out the trash made the case.

The next day we applied for a search warrant for the print shop based on the evidence we had found in the trash. We had more than sufficient "probable cause" and the judge signed the warrant. Late that afternoon, we raided Sam's place. When we entered Sam collapsed. We had to call an ambulance and for a while it looked like we wouldn't arrest Sam after all. He very nearly died of cardiac arrest. His shop was thoroughly searched. We found and retrieved about one hundred thousand dollars in counterfeit money, a set of plates, negatives, and all the paraphernalia necessary to produce counterfeits. Sam had had plenty of experience with the police. When he was well enough, we talked to him. He was a "stand up guy" and never revealed whom he was printing the money for. The case against him was excellent and I was happy that nothing had happened to compromise Cheech. Sam eventually pleaded guilty and was sentenced to five years in custody.

The pressure of other work both local and out of town took me away from my usual territory. Several months had passed since Sam had been arrested. I had lost contact with Cheech and one day when I got back to normal; I gave him a call at his restaurant. Someone other than Cheech answered the phone and asked, "Who's calling?" I said, "Tell him it's his friend." In a few minutes Cheech was on the phone and said, "Hello, friend." We exchanged some idle chit-chat and I told him I would see him soon. He said, "Fine. Oh, yea, how are the roses?" "They're doing fine, you can see them anytime."

Late that evening a large limousine type of car cruised around Cheech's block like a large black cat biding its time, ready to spring when the chances for success were the greatest. There were no customers in the restaurant. The counterman was busy cleaning up. Cheech was in the back office lazily taking care of a few details before leaving for the night. The car stopped in front of the restaurant. Two tall well-dressed men got out of the car. The driver stayed behind the wheel. The two faceless automatons, bent on a mission of destruction, quickly entered the restaurant. One covered the badly frightened counterman who did not have to be told to put his hands up and keep quiet. As soon as the two men entered the door, with guns in their hands, he knew it was for a dirty business and immediately put his hands in the air and held his breath, praying that he would not be a part of the drama about to unfold. The other kicked open the office door, startling Cheech who looked up and opened his mouth, but there was no time for words. The gun in the man's hand did all the talking. Three quick shots were fired. All found their mark and Cheech slumped to the floor. The assassin, feeling impelled to deliver the "coup de grace," quickly and smoothly closed the distance between himself and Cheech. The final shot was well placed behind Cheech's left ear. Both men, their business finished, left as quickly as they arrived and were carried off by the waiting limousine.

Life went on as usual, and very few people were aware or even cared that gangland had exacted a vengeance in the only manner they knew how. The counterman screamed hysterically for help. The usual crowd appeared outside the restaurant. The police, the ambulance, and coroner arrived. The area was roped off. People were questioned…no one saw anything …no one said anything. The restaurant and body were photographed from every angle. Homicide investigators arrived. More police brass, the press, television reporters. The height of excitement was quickly reached and the curious crowd slowly walked away talking among themselves, the events that had transpired soon forgotten. The coroner's wagon quickly arrived and after the police were finished, Cheech was wrapped in a canvas and rubber body bag, zipped up and unceremoniously slid into the back of the wagon. It sped off with its lifeless cargo. Cheech had held the center stage for a few brief seconds and then became another number and statistic. The local detectives who were "catching" that day, and a couple of men from homicide, were the only people now interested in Cheech. The odds were better than a thousand to one that this would be another unsolved "gang style" murder. It would be news for one edition of the paper and it might make the late night television news. But after that, Cheech would only be a number.

About two hours after the murder, I received a call from Cal who told me he heard about it on the radio. I was a bit shaken, but not surprised. Cheech had been taking too many chances, and the tremendous reduction in sentence had raised suspicions and taken its toll.

The next morning, a lieutenant from homicide came to my office to see me. It did not take him or the press long to figure out a motive. A well known hood gets grabbed by the Feds, he gets a fifteen year bit, and, while still under appeal, gets a suspended sentence. To them, this easily spelled cooperation. While talking with the lieutenant I was besieged by the press, who believed they were on the trail of a big hot story. They practically demanded to know what Cheech had given to the government to warrant the reduction. My stock answer of "No comment" didn't seem to satisfy anyone. The lieutenant asked me to level with him. He explained to me that he had a homicide to solve, and hoped I would give him the whole story. I told him what I knew and brought him up to date on what Cheech had done for us. I also cautioned him about being to hasty in drawing conclusions. I reminded him that I had nothing to do with the reduction in sentence, and for that answer he would have to look elsewhere.

He told me that the assassins had apparently called Cheech on the telephone to make sure he was in. The counterman had told him that a man called on the day of the murder and said he was a friend. When Cheech got on the telephone, he answered by saying, "Hello, my friend." The lieutenant said, "If I knew who that guy was, I'd be well on my way to identifying the killers." I said, "No, lieutenant, that information wouldn't help." He asked, "Why?" "Because," I said, "I made that phone call." The lieutenant shrugged his shoulders in a gesture of futility. He asked if I had anything further that might help. I said, "No, but if I think of anything, I'll call. Can you tell me anything? He said, "No," and was about to leave when he turned and said, "Oh yea, one thing. Next to the body I found a red rose wrapped in a $100 bill." He figured it was a benevolent gesture on the part of the killers. "The $100 was probably for a floral piece of roses."

After he left, I sat alone in my office with just my thoughts. I thought of nothing but Cheech. I apparently dozed off. My mind filled with visions of bonds, Bea, Cheech, Sam, roses, counterfeit money, nuns, and $100 bills. I dreamed that Cheech was standing in a garden surrounded by thousands of roses. They were big and beautiful, deep dark blood red. Cheech was picking them. A big black bird swooped down and pecked Cheech behind the left ear. He kept pecking until the blood flowed. It matched the color of the roses.

Suddenly, the telephone wakened me out of the dopey dream. It was the press again. "No, I don't have any information on Cheech's murder!" I yelled, slamming down the receiver. Damn killing, damn press, damn policework, damn everything! At this point I slipped out of the office and went home.

My wife knew something was wrong. She was relieved when I told her that I was well and nothing was wrong. There were no more questions. No phone calls. No interviews. Just a quiet walk in the garden among the roses.

Retirement

The time comes in every cop's life when the informants, the travel, the reports, the raids, the court appearances, the undercover roles, the press conferences, the schools, the new agents, the excitement of the chase, and the fulfillment of a dream have to all be laid aside to make room for the new generation of agents who come with new ambitions, new ideas, and new energy. The reins of supervision must be turned over to the younger man who is also fulfilling his life's ambition, an opportunity to run things his way, to make his own decisions, recommendations, and, in some cases, to establish policy. If the criminal is becoming more sophisticated, the law enforcement agent must be even more so. The schooling, the training, and equipment has to be such as to give the agent or officer an advantage over his quarry.

As the 33-year mark in the Secret Service approached, I knew I had to make a decision that I didn't entirely want. It was time to step aside from a career that was rewarding, fulfilling, and full of dignity. There were no regrets and there are only pleasant memories — starting from the day that the State Police Quartermaster gave me a badge, a .45-caliber revolver, and a gray uniform — to this moment when I find myself in a downtown restaurant surrounded by friends, family, well-wishers, associates, and fellow agents.

I feel like I am dreaming when the speaker tells of some of my successful exploits. He ends by saying, "In those days, he worked alone and never had a partner." I stand up and have to interrupt, "Charlie, you're wrong. There was never a moment on the job that I didn't have a partner! That partner is sitting next to me tonight — the unsung hero of my career. Gentlemen, my wife, Flora, who has been my partner for over 25 years and hopefully will continue by my side as we enter our 'Golden Years'!"

Epilogue

In the summer of 1970, I was approached by an old friend, Martin Pollner, a former federal prosecutor in the Eastern District of New York. He informed me that he had just been appointed Director of Law Enforcement for the U. S. Treasury Department and asked me if I would be his deputy. He explained that this position controls all the Treasury law enforcement agencies in the Federal government, including the U. S. Secret Service, U. S. Customs Service, the Internal Revenue Service, and the Division of Alcohol, Tobacco, and Firearms. I gave the matter a lot of thought and decided to take the position, providing my post of duty would be in New York City instead of Washington, D.C. I was quite surprised when that was accepted and an office was set up for me in the Customs Court House in New York.

Shortly after settling down in the new offices, I received a telephone call from Marty. He told me that President Nixon had decided that he wanted special "Sky Marshals" on American airplanes and he wanted them in the air within the next 48 hours. We were given the assignment to organize, outfit, and train a group of agents to fly on the planes and prevent or deter terrorist takeover of the planes through what had come to be called "skyjacking."

We immediately arranged for each Treasury law enforcement agency to furnish us with 50 men, in an effort to fulfill the President's order. The men reported to an empty hangar at JFK Airport in New York, and received their photos, passports, and instructions. Then they were placed directly on overseas flights.

Our embassies had to be notified of the plan and they were urged to see that the men were taken care of after landing. Some airlines did not want to extend the courtesy of using their equipment and facilities to take our men from the airports to the hotels.

The problems associated with the Sky Marshal Program were enormous. The men who flew the initial trips were real heroes. They were given the responsibility of safeguarding the plane from "skyjackers" — armed and dangerous terrorists, mentally disturbed people, and other individuals seeking their own course by diverting the plane to foreign destinations. The agent's identity was kept secret so passengers on the planes would not know or be able to identify which passenger was the sky marshal. This increased the deterrent effect, as the skyjacker had no way of knowing which passenger was the Marshal or whether a Sky Marshal was even on that particular flight.

After landing at their destination, no special arrangements for transportation or hotel accommodations had been made for the Marshals. Most of them had to find their own way back to the embassies to await further instructions. In time, the program became a smooth-running operation. We never lost a plane that had a Sky Marshal aboard. We were all proud of the fact that the President's orders were so quickly and successfully discharged. The first men were aboard a plane and in flight within 48 hours, as the President had directed.

In the early days of the program, there were many interesting stories and problems coming out of the ranks. There was the case where two brothers, each working for different treasury agencies, met in a restaurant in London. They had each been selected to participate in the program unbeknownst to each other.

In another case, the treasury agent would not surrender his firearm to the host country after the plane landed. It took diplomats from each country several hours to straighten out the matter. Still another agent could not identify the officer to whom he had surrendered his weapon. A search of all records failed to indicate that the weapon had ever been received. Eventually, all the major and unusual problems were resolved and taken care of and the program was placed under the jurisdiction of the U. S. Customs Service and became a smooth running organization.

After I had been in my assignment as Deputy Director for about four years, the "Watergate" scandal, that would cause a constitutional crisis and topple the President, was starting to take its toll. Many heads of departments left the government to accept positions in private industry. "Marty" returned to private law practice and a number of people that I worked with decided to leave their government positions. I learned that my office was to be closed and I would be transferred to Washington, D.C. I decided to finally wrap it all up and retire again.

I wasn't retired very long when I received a telephone call from former New York Supreme Court Justice Bernard Meyer. He told me he had just been appointed by Governor Hugh Carey to investigate the conduct of the original Attica Prison uprising inquiry. He asked me if I would join his staff. I said "yes" and the next day we had a meeting in his office.

He explained that on September 9, 1971, prisoners in the Attica Correctional Facility in upstate New York, near Buffalo, starting rioting. They took over the prison and seized forty-nine guards and civilian employees as hostages. The prisoners held the facility until September 13, 1971 when, then governor, Nelson Rockefeller ordered the New York State Police, supported by correction officers, to storm and retake the prison. During the fighting, the death toll reached forty-three inmates and hostages.

I told Judge Meyer that I would be happy to work for him, but I thought he should know that I was a former state trooper and since the State Police might be a target of his investigation, I might be a hindrance. He told me he was not concerned because he believed I could be objective. I gave him my assurance.

His staff consisted of some of the finest lawyers in the state: Malachy T. Mahon, Eric A. Seiff, Edward M. Shaw, Judge Eve M. Preminger, Arthur J. Viviani, Irvin Rochman, Bobby C. Lawyer, and Paula Frome. Working with this distinguished panel was a genuine pleasure. My job was to locate anyone the staff wanted to interview. Many of the people I needed to talk to were prisoners, prison officials, doctors, morticians, and others that might have something to add to the investigation.

I was happy to be on the street again. I was always happy when I could sit with people and attempt to put the "jigsaw puzzle" of life together. In the prisons I met many of my former offenders who wasted no time in telling me that they were no part of the riots, and how heroic they were in attempting to free the hostages.

Judge Meyer prepared a final report consisting of five hundred seventy-five pages. The conclusion of the report was that there was no intentional cover-up in the conduct of the original investigation, however there were several serious errors of judgment in the way it was conducted. Many books (and movies) have been written about the Attica Prison Riot. I will not attempt to cover any of its ramifications or phases in this limited forum. Judge Meyer was eventually appointed a Justice of the Court of Appeals and will always be remembered as a hard working and fair judge.

After the Attica investigation, I was offered two positions. I guess I wasn't ready to retire after all. One was to head the staff of investigators from Robert M. Morgenthau's office who was the New York County District Attorney. The other was to be Deputy Commissioner of the White Plains, New York, Department of Public Safety.

Robert Morgenthau was my idea of the perfect man to head the District Attorney's Office in Manhattan. He was the U .S. Attorney during the Kennedy years and had a reputation of being a fearless prosecutor. I had worked many tough cases with his office and the idea of working with him again was exciting.

John M Dolce was Deputy Commissioner of Public Safety in White Plains for over ten years. In 1970 he was appointed Commissioner and asked me to be his deputy. I knew John from our days with the federal government. He had been a supervisor in the Federal Bureau of Narcotics and he and I worked many cases together. Working as his deputy also appealed to me.

There would be no travel and I was pretty well known to the law enforcement officers in Westchester County. I made the choice to work in White Plains and was sworn in as deputy on February 1, 1976. The department had 200 police officers and 189 paid firefighters.

I had been under the impression that I was a pretty good administrator. It wasn't until after I watched John run the department that I realized I had a lot to learn. Pound for pound (and he is getting a little heavier) he is one of the best police administrators in the country. Under John, I learned that good administrators lead with their heads and not with their hearts; but good administration, like justice, is tempered with mercy and consideration. I learned to write ordinances, bring manuals up-to-date, conduct studies of ambulance responses, set up rules and regulations for alarm systems, hold hearings for police and firefighters who were errant in their ways, interviewing and making recommendations for the hiring of new police officers and firefighters, and a host of other details commensurate with the running and administration of a mid-sized public safety department.

I stayed with the department for sixteen years and decided to retire (again). But somehow, retirement did not fit me. Shortly after leaving the White Plains position, I was approached by Mayor Phil Marricini of the town of Harrison, New York. He offered me the position of Police Commissioner of the City of Harrison. Since I lived in Harrison, I accepted the job and tried to modernize the department. Harrison is a fairly large community where there are very few street crimes, and other crimes are at an all-time low. When men are not kept busy they tend to fall into bad habits. For three years I tried to make changes, update manuals, practices, and procedures. I emphasized making the officers as professional as possible. I guess I had some success, but in a town like Harrison, there is always the political factor to be considered. The police, who I believe should be apolitical, were a political force in the city. I found out that hiring "hometown boys" for some positions was, and can be, a mistake. I enjoyed working for the city of Harrison. I hope I was effective. But I was starting to find that the position was becoming more like an ordinary job. The fun, excitement, and challenge were no longer there and the burning desire that began way back in 1932 was now starting to flicker. I could feel that my time on the stage of the drama they call "crime busting" was closing and it was time to move on.

When I approached 60 years in the field, I decided to retire again — this time for good! I don't regret one day I spent doing police work. I came close on a few occasions, but fortunately those days were very few, and those thoughts occurred only with the death of a brother officer or the passing of an associate.

I have been asked if I miss the long hours of tailing suspects, working undercover, preparing reports, working on presidential assignments, long absences from home, and all the other duties that go with spending a lifetime in law enforcement and being *In Crime's Way*. The answer is "Yes," and sometimes I admit to the urge to try it again.

Author's Note: Just as in the movie finale of "Mr. 880," when Burt Lancaster and Dorothy McGuire walk down the steps of the courthouse hand-in-hand and live happily ever after, so it has been with Carmine and Flora Motto. Fade out. The End